D1611729

THE MONEY MACHINES

The Money Machines

The Breakdown and Reform of Governmental and Party Finance in the North, 1860-1920

C. K. Yearley

STATE UNIVERSITY OF NEW YORK PRESS
ALBANY

Published by State University of New York Press,
Thurlow Terrace, Albany, New York 12201

Library of Congress Catalog Card No. 74–112605
International Standard Book No. 0–87395–072–0

PRINTED IN THE UNITED STATES OF AMERICA
by
The Riverside Press, Inc.,
Cambridge, Massachusetts

Designed by Joseph W. Krugh

Permission to quote from the Charles Sumner Papers in the Sumner Estate has been granted by the Yale University Library. Permission to quote from the Thomas McIntyre Cooley Papers and the Henry Carter Adams Papers has been granted by the University of Michigan Library, Ann Arbor.

To the memory of eight men
who died in The Marianas and to
Michael,
Thomas,
&
Scott

Contents

Acknowledgments

Assistance to this study has been generous and sustained. I am particularly grateful for financial aid from the Penrose Fund of the American Philosophical Society, for initial research grants from the Graduate School of the University of Florida, and since 1966 for regular awards from the Committee on Faculty Research of the State University of New York at Buffalo as well as from The Research Foundation of State University of New York.

As scholars will readily appreciate the staffs and facilities of the Boston Public Library, the Chicago Public Library, the Columbia University Libraries, the Duke University Library, the Buffalo and Erie County Public Library, the Johns Hopkins University Library (the Eisenhower Library), Harvard University Library, the Indiana State Library, the Library of Congress, the Library of the State of New York, Albany, the Lockwood Memorial Library of the State University of New York at Buffalo, the Nelson Gay Library (Rome, Italy), the Newberry Library, the New York Public Library, the Ohio Historical Society, the Historical Society of Cincinnati, the Pennsylvania Historical Society, and the libraries of Pennsylvania State University, the University of Florida, The University of Michigan (Ann Arbor), the University of North Carolina, the University of Wisconsin (Madison), and Yale University proved invaluable, reducing the frictions and the tedium of my researches to a minimum.

For an old friendship and the wise counsel attending it I am especially indebted to Professor Francis C. Haber, Chairman of the History Department of the University of Maryland. Friend and colleague, Professor Robert Ganyard carefully read the manuscript driving me to further revisions and the correction of egregious blunders. To my old comrade Professor Robert Sharkey, Chairman of the Department of

History, George Washington University and to members of "The Chapter" of the Johns Hopkins University my personal and intellectual debts are also venerable and large. I incurred a special obligation to Shere Hite of Columbia University Graduate School. Katherine Becker's two years of assistance to me as Director of Graduate Studies in History, rendered with unfailing grace, gentility, and tolerance, has done much to make the continuation of my scholarship possible. The finest professional environment in which I have ever worked is a direct consequence of the superbly creative chairmanship of Robert A. Lively and the good judgment and informed dedication of Lewis Perry, Orville Murphy, and the beloved and respected John Horton. For their many services, clerical and personal, my warm thanks must likewise extend to Margaret Collver, Mary Ann Janiga, Joyce Klein, Dorothy Ward, Esther Munshen, and Fred Henrich of SUNY Buffalo, to Martha Hubbard and Margaret Lough of the Johns Hopkins University Library, to Harriet and Margola Rivkin of Baltimore, and to Margaret Mirabelli of Delmar, New York. Broady Richardson shared my hegira and knows something of the distance we have both come. In return for their confidence and willingness to listen I can only say of my own graduate students—Rosa Lynn B. Pinkus, Arthur Markowitz, Martin Schiesl, and Frank Manuele that I wish all scholars were able to look forward to such fine replacements. Above all for her infinite patience and understanding my most heartfelt thanks must go to my wife, Carlyn.

Williamsville, New York
1969

C. K. YEARLEY

Introduction

In 1860 the fiscal practices of American governments and their extralegal counterparts which had grown up around the financing of political parties were still simple, democratic, and congenial to the peoples of an agricultural society; in 1880 these practices were in decay and under fierce attack; before 1925 they had been brought into closer consonance with the requirements of modern government and the realities of urban industrial life. This book, an historical exercise in the realms of public finance, concerns major aspects of these fiscal revolutions. It is an effort to document the crude initial shifts away from fiscal theories and social assumptions derived from the Physiocrats, from classical economists, and Utilitarians toward the less individualistic assumptions underlying twentieth century economic welfare and its altered balance of public and private authority.

The money machines, as the metaphor is used here, embraced the principal arrangements by which America's most important political establishments—Northern state and local governments and the political parties which created them—raised revenues, spent, and borrowed during the years from the outbreak of the Civil War until the nation's emergence from World War I. They were mechanisms through which political institutions of the increasingly industrial iron rectangle of states extending from Massachusetts and Maryland on the East westward to the North Central Plains financed their existence. Integral to the relationships between interest groups, classes, sections, and localities, they were essential to political and economic evolution. Directly joining the citizen, the parties, and the state, they ranked among the most intimate and fundamental instruments of governing. "Money," wrote the distinguished political economist Henry Carter Adams in 1892, "is the vital principle of the body politic; the public treasury is the heart of the state; control over public supplies means control over public affairs."[1]

The uniqueness of these machines forming "the heart of the state" warrants heavy emphasis, for until the 1920's they had no close duplicates anywhere in the world. The challenges confronting them, to be sure, were very closely related to challenges being experienced simultaneously in Great Britain and in Continental countries, particularly as they were crystallized in the fiscal problems of great conurbations such as London or Paris. "There can be no doubt," noted an American student of public finance in 1896, "that the most pressing reforms of the close of the nineteenth century are tax reforms."[2] Among expert observers from Sweden to the Mediterranean this comment on the urgent necessity for fiscal modernization accurately summed up prevalent opinion. Industrialization, urbanization, wars, depressions, democratization of the masses, changes in public standards and expectations, as well as in styles and tastes, were by then everywhere having their immense impact on fiscal practice and thinking about public finance. Only within the United States, however, did these forces act upon what may usefully be described as two dimensional or dual fiscal systems.

One dimension, the official one, we may assume was familiar to almost everybody. It was amply described by academic or administrative literature, by statutory law, by constitutional provisos, and by daily public discussions and debates over taxing, spending, and borrowing. Viewed in 1870, for example, the official machinery inherited from antebellum days centered its operations around some form of general property tax which, as is always true of taxation, gave public expression to the dominant social values. It assumed specifically, and from critical perspectives naïvely, that all taxation should be democratic; that accordingly all taxable property should bear public burdens equally; that equal taxation was feasible because all property could safely be treated as if it were tangible or corporeal—that is, that it could be discovered readily, valued easily, and taxed fairly. Finally, these rather rudimentary taxes were expected to furnish revenues to fiscal systems whose soundness and virtue depended on government income at the very least matching governmental expenditure. Allowing for its nuances in local polities stretching from Pennsylvania to Iowa, such was the broad picture of the operative revenue machinery. Moreover, despite its distinctions and anachronisms this machinery reflected policies that had been tried and were recognizable to some degree in the fiscal development of most European governments during the nineteenth century, though these European developments were seldom unalloyed successes.

The singularity of American state and local fiscal machinery really lay in a second dimension of its activities. Inseparable from the first, this dimension included party financial functions which were extralegal and very frequently illegal. Public discussions of fiscal affairs, for that matter learned writings on political economy, administration, or public finance, failed to touch upon these functions. Official investigations, reformist attacks and exposés, not to mention political commentaries, of course, often examined sensational aspects of these activities. But invariably they dealt with them separately in a narrow context of partisanship, political irregularities, or party corruption; and such treatment was neither searching nor detached. In sum, they explored the financing of political parties in isolation from the formal financing of government.

Yet in the Northern states, government and party could not realistically be divorced from one another. "Political power," remarked an astute observer in the eighties, "has great affinity for public revenues, and seeks alliance with that organism which can most readily furnish it. It is the pabulum on which it feeds, the instrument through which its functions are most efficiently performed."[3] Long a cliché among political cynics when less politely phrased, the observation was entirely accurate. While the ballot was not always free to ordinary voters due to the prevalence of poll taxes, party membership, a few dues payers aside, was. But access to the advantages of party was one thing; paying regularly, privately, and voluntarily to sustain political organization was another. Thus parties counted on financing themselves primarily by tapping public power and the fiscal resources of government. Public and private revenues, public and private expenditures, public and private *purposes,* consequently interpenetrated the development of each fiscal dimension. Change in one dimension, whether the consequence of mistakes, failures, or reforms, produced change in the other. When the complexities of federalism are added to this unique situation fostered largely by the precocity of professional political organization, the distinctiveness of American public finance begins to suggest itself.

Thus, to summarize briefly, the money machines at the state and local level were composed of two interdependent dimensions, one legal, one extralegal, each engaged in taxing, spending, and borrowing activities, each doing so for the benefit of different elites and each, therefore, doing so for somewhat different reasons. On its legal side, the machinery, as first examined here, operated in conformity with the views of established rural middle classes and their proper, slightly patrician, urban counterparts. By the 1870's and 1880's, however, these controlling views were under pressure from the new strategic elites[4] of the urban middle classes. On its extralegal side, at roughly the same time, the machinery was increasingly bent to the necessities of new political elites, notably those dominating urban political organizations, who were confronted with the rising costs of professional parties whose power not only depended on services rendered to elements of the middle classes but also on service to the new wealth and to some portions at least of the urban masses. In these tensions lay the sources of the machinery's breakdown and change.

The breakdown of the North's dual fiscal systems is the subject of the first main division of this study, their reform and reconstruction the subject of the second. For clarity's sake a few words are in order about the materials and perspectives stressed in each division.

The familiar economic crises and industrial advances which precipitated the dangers to local money machines here figure only as background. Their importance, nonetheless, is undeniable. Civil War financing, unmatched in the scale of the burdens it posed, fell upon existing machinery with enormous force and hastened it on a course to destruction. The depressions of the late nineteenth century battered Northern fiscal machinery anew and the countless problems of expansive cities created relentless friction and fatigue in the fiscal operations of governments and parties alike. But if these and other powerful forces eventually affected nearly everyone, relatively few men were conscious of them or actively aroused about them. Poor men were largely ignorant of fiscal affairs and were indifferent to them, while the rich easily and, in the main, consistently avoided responsible involvement in them.

The fiscal crises of the late nineteenth and early twentieth centuries thus were chiefly crises in the eyes of the urban and rural middle classes. Massive degeneration of local fiscal machinery obviously would have proceeded regardless of who recognized it and, indeed, by the close of the last century, without disturbing most of the populace for long, the machinery's failure was universal in Northern polities. Generally speaking, however, men of the middle ranks, in or out of public life, at least partially grasped the nature and social significance of problems in the legally constituted systems. Usually they alone responded positively to the systems' inadequacies and imbalances. And, as a result, these men were primarily responsible for leaving us the overwhelming bulk of evidence concerning the obsolescence and subsequent rebuilding of local money machinery.

Middle class reactions to the North's spreading fiscal debacles consequently furnish the themes of Part One. In the most obvious sense the great moral indignation inspired among "responsible men" sprang from a natural resistance to what struck them as the sheer magnitude of their public burdens. Unprecedented taxes, expenditures, and indebtedness seemed to weigh entirely upon the investment capacities and the productivity of the sober, competent classes who were a pillar to the community and, according to the accepted constructions of classical economics, the key to economic growth. This seemed especially true in the cities where the frustrations of paying for "progress" came most sharply into focus. Yet in a deeper sense these classes were also reacting to the dynamic realignments of social values everywhere being thrust upon Northern society through incessant local struggles over status, pelf, and power. Notwithstanding conflicts among themselves, the middle classes, therefore, viewed their mounting public burdens as the alarming portents of a new democracy, a democracy mobilized around two predatory constituencies. One constituency was composed of "vulgar" hordes of workingmen and immigrants substantially devoid of a real stake in society; the other comprised the corporate rich and their "unproductive" retinues. Both constituencies were believed to be drawing power from the debasement of traditional morality and from the confiscation of established properties. In respectable quarters, moreover, the aggressive agent in the advancement of this destruction was identified with party organization, usually symbolized by bosses, rings, and machine politics.

Fear generated in the middle classes by these and related estimates of their situation imperiled both dimensions of the dual fiscal systems as a result of the counteractions which they provoked. First, they directly stimulated the flagrant and massive evasion of taxation and inadvertently encouraged its avoidance in more subtle ways. In turn, evasion administered lethal shocks to many of the official machines while gravely weakening others. Inevitably it menaced the parties' vital extralegal revenues. In conjunction with a rising cult of efficiency, civil service reform, and a related cluster of attacks upon political parties, it increasingly threatened their entire financial base. Soon, in fact, the central organizations of political democracy were placed in jeopardy and the dominance of the "political principle and political man" was hotly disputed by self-styled "non-political" economic elites. Suggestions that professional politicians generally surmounted these challenges and, with profound consequences for the modernization of the money machines, remained in control of local political establishments conclude Part One.

How the renovation and reform of the dual fiscal systems proceeded under the auspices of middle class experts, various economic interests, and politicians is the subject of Part Two. Drawn chiefly from the experiences of major cities and the leading industrial states, with little material from other political units, the evidence here is exploratory rather than complete. Thus there is no possibility at present of characterizing these attenuated and detailed processes conclusively. Often they appear to have been crude improvisations which proved inconsistent, ephemeral, and erratic. Rarely were they distinguished by great wisdom, high principle, or imaginative planning. On balance they may be described tentatively as incremental—technical, piecemeal, pragmatic, and yet absolutely essential to the continuation of viable government.

Powerful as its imperatives were, reform confronted serious administrative and ideological obstacles. Ignorance, inertia, limited concepts of citizenship, underdeveloped definitions of public purpose, legislative malapportionment, the resistance of farmers, the restrictive fiscal environment enveloping the cities where reforms were thought to be most urgently needed, and controversies among the reformers themselves, all either warped or for a time blocked change. In so doing they multiplied the complexities, which discouraged popular participation in reform, and thereby virtually assured the initiative of middle class specialists. Accordingly, the backgrounds and proposals of several of these specialists are treated in some detail. Only a few experts, needless to say, enjoyed an overview of their entire problem, although each generally brought competent analysis to particulars. But by the 1890's their individual approaches at the state and local levels formed an ensemble of actions manifested in revived concepts of ability-to-pay, in the taxation of corporations and of incomes, in the segregation of revenues, in administrative centralization, in the controlled sanctioning of novel as well as of large-scale expenditures and borrowings. Such developments occurred, of course, solely within official dimensions of the money machinery which, for one thing, meant that they retained their anti-political bias. Despite this, they still afforded rich opportunities to party financiers. Equally as important as governmental reforms, therefore, were the ways in which professional politicians and their organizations continued to survive, even to prosper, thanks to the fiscal expansiveness of the new systems. A discussion of these party adaptations which offered the country little hope of effective *and* honest political financing but which nevertheless worked—often humanely and flexibly within their ambit—concludes Part Two and leads to summary observations.

The selective approach employed throughout this book has been made more feasible by fresh historical writing touching upon a fair range of economic, political, and social change in American life from the Gilded Age to the 1920's. The interpretive essays of Lee Benson, Thomas Cochran, Sidney Fine, Samuel Hays, John Sproat, James Weinstein, and Robert Wiebe, as well as the valuable controversies involving Edward Kirkland, Gabriel Kolko, Marian Sears, and John Tipple,[5] to mention just a few, have furnished new, if still unfolding, historical settings for the period under consideration here and have allowed concentration on particular strands of change. Valuable in their own right were the now classic theoretical studies in public finance undertaken by Edgeworth, by Sidgwick, and above all by A. C. Pigou in England, by Lindahl, Mazzola, Myrdal, Pantaleoni, Wagner, and Wicksell, among others from the larger European intellectual community, and by E. R. A. Seligman and more recently by Richard Musgrave in the United States.[6] Nonetheless, it is not the concentration which these works have permitted us which lends the money machines their importance; they were *central* historical fixtures, irrespective of the selectivity of the historian. Obviously the revenues which flowed through them did not answer for everything, either for governments or for parties; certainly they did not insure imagination, quality, power, or victories at the polls. Yet before power could become a functional reality, before party government could justify its existence by action, decisions at all levels of political life had to be made about what the public bills would come to and how best they might be paid.

Clearly for men and interests at odds over control of the money machines the stakes involved were enormous. Since money, according to the Reverend Henry Ward Beecher, was not only the "very yeast of enterprise" but was also the "inspiration of morality" and the "moral discriminator,"[7] the stakes for his generation were calculable far beyond the bounds of arithmetic. Whose money morality, for instance, was to prevail? Who was to define the nature, size, equity, and most troublesome of all, the incidence of the public burden? How were public and party moneys to be divided and administered? And so on.

Ineluctably these and dozens of related questions shaded into broad social issues concerning the values and principles around which the society was to be organized and the goals toward which it was to be directed. If these issues were still unresolved in the 1920's, the money machines, nonetheless, were neither constructed nor operated as they earlier had been. The old ones had failed disastrously; the new ones, short on brilliant successes and still heavily freighted with middle class value judgments, were at least a prerequisite to a future with promise.

Part I

BREAKDOWN

If you establish a democracy,
you must in due season
reap the fruits of a democracy . . .
a great impatience of the public burdens,
combined . . . with great increase
of the public expenditure.

BENJAMIN DISRAELI

1

The Menace of the New Democracy

Throughout the North during the generation after 1865 the traditional public mechanisms for taxing, spending, and borrowing were found inadequate for their tasks. The atrophy of this machinery—nearly all of it based on general property taxation—proceeded steadily in town and country alike; but for several reasons the most unrelenting strains upon it were concentrated in municipalities. City governments, for one thing, directly confronted costs attendant upon the rising expectations of nearly every urban group. Demands for greater profits, comfort, and convenience prodded public expenditures upward. Pressures of population alone required expensive social engineering in fields of sanitation, health, transportation, education, and communal protection. The existing tax base, relative to fresh necessities, often visibly eroded under the circumstances, while taxable properties changed form with dismaying frequency and flourished beyond the reach of public obligation just as increased returns from them became most essential. Nor was that all. Municipal tax favors to local mercantilists engaging in intercity commercial competition drained public funds without immediate or even later recompense to the treasury. Familial functions likewise began encumbering municipal finances as industrialization weakened the welfare capacities of many families; and urban extensions of the elaborate paraphenelia of political democracy proved ever more expensive to maintain within the ambit of the law. Disparate in character as they were, all of these factors in conjunction with changing concepts of the role and function of the *communitas* itself contributed to a common deficiency of municipal revenues.

Alarm over this breakdown of urban fiscal machinery spread initially among the urban middle classes. Competent and responsible in their own eyes, they believed—and informed opinion supported them in this view—that public burdens fell upon their properties almost exclusively. Convinced of governmental waste and extravagance, they watched their public obligations continually rising in behalf of people and policies toward which by interest or prejudice they were opposed. State and federal fiscal crises further deepened their concern. Thus, in many cities before the end of the 1860's earlier complaints about exorbitant public bills expanded into staunch resistance against the apparent conversion of fiscal machinery into the confiscatory instruments of a spendthrift democracy.

Boston furnishes us with a microcosm of these events. Nearly a century after the Revolution, for instance, the Adams family again was denouncing unjust taxation. The chief dissenter of 1868, Charles Francis Adams, Jr., acknowledged that many aspects of Boston life were properly reformed and that some redemption for remaining municipal failures inhered in the city's substantial per capita wealth which he reckoned at double New York's. Yet he was not complacent on this account, for basically he found Boston's system of taxation to be "fearfully and wonderfully wrong." The system, he charged, had been framed with "an eye to the encouragement of vice and to the destruction of enterprise." So much the worse if Sin were concealed by a low tax rate. The exactions required of Bostonians were 40% higher at the end of the 1860's than taxes in Chicago and Philadelphia and 17% higher than those in New York, earning Boston dubious eminence as "the most heavily taxed city on earth." Fiscal rectitude, like a state of grace, judged Adams, was still to be attained in New England.[1]

Responsible Bostonians had heard all of this before Adams went to press and they would hear it again and again. Inside City Hall climbing taxes had become vexing before the Civil War; Mayor Bigelow complained publicly in 1849 and in 1850 that "no other city in the world" conducted its civic affairs "at so great an expense as ours."[2] After the war, as we might expect, these complaints mounted astronomically. His fears reinforced by federal census data, Mayor Gaston reported in 1871 that Bostonians were paying higher taxes per head than the citizenry of any large city in the country and each tide of comparative information thereafter made matters seem worse. By 1892 the state of the city's finances had produced a doleful tradition. The shrewd, capable mayor, Nathan Matthews, warned students of the Phillips Academy that while national politics provided more satisfying grist for popular discussions than the "dry details of municipal administration," popular whims missed the sober realities. "The questions that will touch you oftenest and closest in your personal relations," he warned, were those "of municipal rather than of state or national government." Eighty out of every one hundred dollars in direct taxes contributed by individuals to their governments—city, county, state, and national—he reminded his audience, was paid to municipalities. The citizen's urban debt was ten times heavier, according to Matthews, than his state or national debts. "In other words," suggested the mayor, if men gauged their "immediate pecuniary interests" by their taxes, "more than three-fourths of the time and attention" they devoted to public affairs should have gone into a search for an "economical" administration of municipal business.[3] Three years later in a penetrating address to the Boston Council, Matthews noted that during the previous forty years Boston had spent "more money on public account in proportion to population than any other city in the world. . . . The difficulty here," concluded the mayor, "is not Corruption, but Expenditure."[4]

Similar alarms reverberated through Boston's reputable society. Goaded by depression in the mid-seventies, more than a hundred leading citizens petitioned the Common Council against the injustice and immorality of taxes levied on their "over-burdened" real estate. Both the council and the city's chief assessor, Thomas Hills, subsequently were beleaguered by such delegations. By the 1870's also many Mugwumps critical of commonwealth finances continuously assailed "the enormous pressure of reckless public extravagance," the "wanton, wild prodigality" of public spending in Boston, and the general folly of Massachusetts governments in swelling their "evil" debts into a "vast system of delusions" managed by "juggler's tricks," a system enforced by assessors reputedly armed with "every power to extort full information, except the rack."[5]

Other Boston reformers, among them William Minot, Julius Seelye, James Barker, George Crocker, F. W. Bird, and James Whitmore, each of whom possessed some expert appreciation of local fiscal machinery, also attacked the system.[6] Although better known than the rest, Brooks Adams might easily have spoken for them all. From his perspective, as from theirs, the State's fiscal policies at every level of operations had produced an economic blight. Writing in 1878 of the abusive use of taxation,[7] with singular reference to Boston, and of the oppressive taxation of the poor throughout the commonwealth,[8] he further complained that thanks to crushing taxes houses were lying vacant in every street, rents were falling, capital was fleeing, and landowners were on the brink of ruin. Bostonians paid taxes averaging $34 per capita per year—"startling figures," he asserted, "but . . . as nothing [compared] to those which show the burden on property," the property, that is, of the middle classes. More serious still, overwhelming taxes which had settled on these classes were matched by debts which he pronounced "more excessive than any other people ever bore in time of peace . . . Is it wonderful," he concluded, "that we have riots, that we have socialists, that we have repudiationists?"[9] Boston's fiscal career, apparently, could only end in economic suicide.

With similar urgency, outcries against taxation and indebtedness were raised in each of the major cities of the iron rectangle. Thus, Boston's fiscal travail afforded little comfort to New York City, which even before the war had begun grappling with nettlesome fiscal problems of its own. These were an especial source of embarrassment to patrician and bourgeois leaders who were already distressed by New York's reputation as an American Gomorrah. Finding no solace in the reports of the city comptroller, in tracts of the angry Citizens' Association, in publications of the board of aldermen, or in analyses of the proposed tax levy for 1866, local observers warned their fellow citizens that visiting capitalists were certain to detect the city's "ungovernable propensity to vote for spending money" and its politicians' "prompt disgust at any obstacle raised or objection made" about it. Efforts to curb the wild taxing-spending sprees of the ex-butcher boys, barkeepers, and hoodlums allegedly directing local government were disgustedly reported to register on City Hall as "a most gross impertinence."[10] With a population of 200,000 in 1830 New York had been governed at the cost of just half a million dollars a year, noted one critic; but by 1866 with its population approaching one million New York government cost over forty million dollars a year. Over a thirty-five year period the per capita rate of taxation had jumped from $2.50 to $40; the number of inhabitants, that is to say, increased fivefold, while the expenses of governing rose sixteen times.[11]

Despite the growing wealth of the community, about which statistics were generally uncertain, at times silent, the "tendency of running year by year into prodigality" in New York City frightened other respectable commentators. Trade papers like the *Commercial and Financial Chronicle* closely monitored the "evils of uncontrolled local extravagance" after the opening of the 1870's,[12] spurred on partly by the State's pioneering tax investigation conducted by David A. Wells, the noted Liberal Republican economist. Meticulously exposing the weaknesses of New York's state and local revenue systems, the Wells Reports of 1871–72, citing massive increments in taxation commencing in the previous decade, excoriated local taxes in hundreds of instances as "injudicious," "unjust," "ineffective," and "wasteful," thus supplying abundant ammunition to their opponents.[13]

Attacks by non-professional economists like Wells and by journalists were warmly supported in other quarters. Daniel Harris, President of the Connecticut River Railroad and a champion of tax reforms in Massachusetts, sounded the tocsin against New York's fiscal behavior before a Saratoga gathering of the American Social Science Association in 1876. With three grim depression years as a backdrop to his remarks, Harris drew parallels between the nation's toleration of individual excesses and extravagant municipal expenditures. New York officialdom, he felt, had been holding "high carnival." Flashy spending had driven up taxes and expenditures, he reported, until language could add little to the menace of these "ominous figures." By his reckoning New Yorkers shouldered an annual tax equivalent to nearly $35 per capita while simultaneously struggling with a per capita municipal debt of $126, the payment of which Harris predicted would require taxation during the ensuing twelve years "equal to every dollar of their net earnings."[14]

Brief and modest reductions in New York's debt after 1873 failed to dispel fears concerning its fiscal condition; the city, in fact, continued serving for its own as well as many other citizens as the epitomy of prodigal misgovernment. So it seemed, for example, to William Ivins, a local Mugwump. Ivins was thoroughly familiar with city politics and finance thanks in part to his experience as city chamberlain and, then, in 1892, as counsel for the State Senate's Fassett Investigating Committee. Having reviewed the data on New York's financial past, he pointed with alarm at a municipal indebtedness which in 1880 bulked larger than the combined indebtedness of all major Southern cities, larger than the combined indebtedness of all the cities of New England, nearly as large as the debts of all Western cities, and roughly one-third as large as the aggregate debts of all Middle Atlantic cities. Ivins calculated that New York was more deeply mired in debt than even the largest English cities—Liverpool, Manchester, and London—each with serious fiscal problems of its own. Furthermore, where the budgets of all the states for state purposes barely totalled $60 million, the tax budget for New York City alone amounted to half of that sum and its tax rate was substantially higher than those prevalent elsewhere.[15] "Economy in public expenditure" and "a care and conservatism in the creation of new obligations" were, in Ivins' view, essential to a sound society and to "sound morals," but among public officials such views apparently no longer sufficed as guides to action.[16]

However frightening the breakdown of fiscal machinery appeared to the "best New Yorkers," Baltimoreans two hundred miles farther south gravely pondered their own fiscal difficulties. There, too, Mugwumpery and special interests produced the most vigorous protestants. From the 1870's onward they filled the city with speeches, tracts, petitions, and editorials critical of public finance. During the winter of 1884, for example, local spokesmen, after contrasting the tax rates and assessments in twenty of the country's large cities, angrily reported that "New York and Philadelphia with all their enormous debt, including the accumulated plunder of a long series of corrupt rings and machines, do not yearly give up to their local governments so large a proportion of their substance"[17] as did the supine citizens of Baltimore. Typically, a leading Mugwump, William Marbury, hammered on the theme that, comparing their ability to pay, Baltimoreans in 1889 were more heavily taxed than New Yorkers and their future promised them even heavier obligations.[18] Businessman Sebastian Brown told the Landlords' Mutual Protective Association that the local "inactivity of business" and the depreciation of local properties stemmed directly from over-taxation,[19] while Michael Mullin, Vice-President of the Baltimore Taxpayers' Association whose 475 members included the city's chief mercantile leaders, further denounced the two-decade trend which had carried the tax rate and valuations steadily upward and the value of property downward.[20] Mullin, a prominent local builder, decried fiscal practices on the local scenes as "unjust," "unnecessary," even "unmanly."

The "principal holders of medium classes of property," "the bone and sinew" of the city were attentive to what they interpreted as their growing financial plight—without pretending that for economy's sake they would abandon their steam fire engines for the old volunteer companies or that they would revert from Belgian paving flags—the pride of dockside Pratt Street—to cobblestones. Feeling the prick of public spending they questioned if "in this progressive age and . . . progressive community" they could hold their own with their rivals without "large and increasing expenses of government."[21] Theirs was the same dilemma faced by thousands of citizens not only in Boston and New York but, as Michael Frisch[22] has shown, also in Springfield, Massachusetts, indeed, in all the cities of the North. And the moral alarm as well as the economic anxieties which underlay this dilemma passed into the mainstream of twentieth century life.

Of course variations marked the pattern of this discontent—and for fairly obvious reasons. Depressions, particularly the unprecedented one which stretched from 1873 to 1878, but those of the eighties and nineties as well, naturally excited protests unsurpassed by any that erupted earlier in the century and more severe than those, at least prior to the Progressive Era, during years when business was considered good. In addition, taxes, debts, and valuations rose unevenly and with different effects on individuals, neighborhoods, and cities. Estimates of indebtedness help make such variations specific. Taking aggregate indebtedness as it was calculated in leading commercial journals for the years from

1860 to 1866, the average increase in fourteen major Northern cities was 45%. But a closer look indicates that the younger Western communities fared somewhat better—"better" if debt is accepted as then interpreted as an evil—than older Eastern cities. The debts of New York City, Brooklyn, Boston, Baltimore, and Philadelphia shot up steeply. St. Louis, on the contrary, added only a small sum to her indebtedness and Cincinnati actually, if modestly, decreased hers. Or, again, using widely quoted comparisons of municipal population with municipal debt, the Western cities of the iron rectangle were characterized by decreasing ratios, while in the Eastern and Middle Atlantic cities, the increase observed was "very large." These differences were repeated on a smaller scale among the Eastern cities themselves; thus, while the ratio of assessed taxes in Boston stood at $21.98 per capita in 1866, in Philadelphia the same year it stood at $8.17. But none of the news available was good. Hard-nosed taxpayers cast such nuances aside and fed their outrage with the thought that they alone—and in small numbers—were supporting ungrateful and profligate communities.[23]

"Responsible" citizens, it is clear, were presented with the broad picture of a dramatic and sustained upward trend in the burdens of taxation, in the flow of expenditures, and in the accumulation of debts, particularly urban debts. Moreover, on the basis of their experiences it was a picture they accepted. Whether the analysis was invariably a precise one in a literal economic sense, it *was* the one, historically, which they argued from and acted upon.

Nowhere, indeed, did it seem better substantiated than in Massachusetts, by the 1870's the nation's most heavily urbanized state. Massachusetts assessors' figures on the per capita increase in taxes and debts in the commonwealth's cities from 1865 to 1875 illustrate why the middle classes were so full of alarm as they presided over their urban properties. Salem, for instance, experienced a 51% rise in valuations and a 59% increase in taxes in that decade. Equivalent figures for Cambridge were 55% and 74% respectively; for Worcester, 59% and 56%, and for Lynn, 69% and 46%. Other tabulations were even more sensational. Springfield's valuations rose 119%, her per capital taxes, 122%; Fitchburg faced similar increments of 103% and 52% and Somerville of 103% and 115%.[24] While the state's urban population rose from 514,000 to 849,000 between 1865 and 1875, property valuation jumped from $580,000,000 to $1,300,000,000 and urban taxes more than doubled. Providing further fiscal outcry, the funded debt soared from $16,000,000 to over $70,000,000, a per capita leap from $31 to $83. Taxpayers were left to draw what little succor they could from the knowledge that they had plenty of unhappy company in cities outside of Massachusetts.[25]

Fiscal profiles of the largest Northern and Middle Western cities, in truth, were shocking by standards of the time. They nurtured fears that "this immense addition" to middle class burdens would "materially affect the social and political future of the country."[26] How far "the public conscience" had already been "blunted in its moral sensitivities," as some claimed, by the demoralization of the public economies in the largest cities was recorded in a number of Eastern newspapers relying on census compilations on urban population, valuation, taxation, and indebtedness for the years from 1860 to 1875. Chicago in that period increased its population by 261%; but its valuation rose 720%, its taxation 1445%, and its debt 487%. Detroit increased its population 122%, its valuation 147%, taxation 385%, and indebtedness 140%, while the respective percentages for Providence were 99%, 100% 343%, and 529%. Such remarkable increases obviously were not simply functions of demographic growth, for in places such as Newark, New Jersey, population increased only by a relatively modest 63%; valuation, however, rose by 251%, taxation by 559%, and indebtedness by 2658%. Percentages for thirteen of the largest Northern cities were sobering; their aggregate populations rose by 70%, taxable valuations by 157%, taxes by 363%, and debts by 271%.[27]

Yet the largest Northern cities were not always the "most extravagant, immoral, or sorely tried" fiscally. Some of the most burdensome municipal debt, for instance, settled upon the so-called smaller communities where "the people . . . permitted the municipalities to be extravagant to the point of bankruptcy." Four of these cities were in rock-ribbed Maine: Bangor, Bath, Rockland, and Portland; two, Jersey City and Elizabeth, were in New Jersey. Others that found themselves in equally serious financial straits were Brookline, Massachusetts, Memphis, Tennessee, the District of Columbia, and Middletown, Connecticut. The lowest per capita debt among these cities was four times greater than the per capita debt of other cities in their region; the highest per capita debt among them actually ran seven times higher than the regional figures.[28] In one sense, anyway, these communities were truly outstanding.

Small wonder there were social leaders who sought to return men's attention during the latter portion of the century to simple societies of thrifty and solvent people, like those whom the President of Harvard, Charles Eliot, found pursuing "the common mode of American life" on Mt. Desert Island in Maine's Penobscot Bay. In the rural democracy of Mt. Desert Island no one was rich. Few men had not acquired some property and fewer still were not in "condition to bear their share of the public burdens." Methods of taxation were conservative. Valuations were consistently low. Virtually everyone voted taxes and "the tendency of the town-meeting," wrote Eliot approvingly, was "rather to niggardliness than to extravagance." Wants were few. Raising a family cost less than $250 a year—slightly more than the per capita indebtedness of the mainland city of Bath. Eliot concluded that "from thirty to forty million" Americans lived in the same frugal way. Dull, unchanging, and rather joyless, Mt. Desert was nevertheless fiscally sound.[29]

But around this bucolic setting swirled the rising tides of municipal taxes and debts, symbols of extravagance and misgovernment. The isolation of Mt. Desert from the mainstream was highlighted by a regional view of municipal indebtedness. In 1880 each American owed $14 in municipal debt; but the per capita estimate for the Middle Atlantic states approached $30 and for New England it exceeded $31. Comparatively, Southerners owed only $4 and Westerners only $8. Indeed, the industrial North was raising a bumper crop of urban debts; their increase in New England over the previous decade had been almost 70% and in the Middle Atlantic states 203%.[30] The prevalent, and then largely unchallenged, political economy allowed no hope of a bright future under these circumstances.

Speaking for substantial numbers of the North's urban middle classes, Michigan's Thomas Cooley summarized the evils of municipal indebtedness for a Johns Hopkins audience in 1879. Cooley's *Treatise on the Law of Taxation,* published three years earlier had made him the principal American authority in the field. Conceding that the national debt, as some argued, "might . . . have some compensation about it," Cooley quickly noted that urban debts were of far different origins, that they were more intensively concentrated, and produced quite contrary results. Their first fruit, he insisted, was class animosity. Distrust engendered by a city's debts drove its creditors into "doubtful measures" of the last resort, while the classes who were obliged to pay them invariably grew bitter and factious. In addition, he warned, debt sapped the sense of public honor among all classes, leading to the corrupt disposal of valuable franchises and other public properties by city officials, undermining the cities' capacities to continue essential municipal improvements because of the highly speculative nature of the environment they created, and driving capital as well as the "best people" away.[31]

Admonitions like Cooley's, needless to say, had little apparent effect on urban debt structure. Northeastern business and financial circles were far more interested in watching the census returns to see if urban obligations were at last being handled with "due caution and prudence" than they were in academic speeches. And from time to time, as in the Census of 1890, they detected encouraging signs. Municipal debts during the 1880's, it seemed, had been "comparatively much smaller than generally expected." The *Commercial and Financial Chronicle* felt that, in fact, they were finally "on a conservative basis," that "the legacy of the paper money era," along with "the extravagance and prodigality which that era had engendered" were disappearing.[32]

Perhaps. "All this," warned the *Chronicle,* however, did not alter the necessity for "economy in public expenditures and . . . conservatism in the creation of new obligations."[33] The aggregate taxes of New York and Massachusetts alone, after all, totalled more than half the local taxation of Great Britain—where the cry of the ratepayers was already loud and bitter—and both the bonded and floating debts of Northern cities, as well as their taxes, were still rising. Although the rate of ascent of taxes and debts periodically tapered off, prudence rather than joy was the order of the day for self-anointed bands of responsible men who claimed an interest not only in their pocketbooks but also in "good government and sound morals."

Throughout the latter years of the nineteenth century, middle class apprehensions over municipal fiscal problems were compounded by similar problems at the state level. State money machinery after the Civil War was quite obviously growing unsuited to many of the demands placed upon it. Many Northern states emerged from the war almost overwhelmed by their financial difficulties. In five Northern states—Illinois, Maine, Maryland, Massachusetts, and Pennsylvania—the total burden of state taxation tripled between 1860 and 1870; in Iowa it quadrupled; in Michigan it quintupled; and in both Connecticut and New Jersey it increased by six times. In May 1871, *Bankers' Magazine* declared that "in all history there is probably no precedent for so rapid an increase in public burdens within so limited a period." The editors found confirmation of this grim intelligence everywhere. The aggregate of taxation in just one state, they observed, was "greater per capita than that of any other civilized community in existence."[34] Impossible to impugn, given the available data, such observations carried the iron ring of truth.

Massachusetts and New York State provided evidence of why state fiscal affairs were a continuous source of anxiety after 1865. To the disgust of many of its better citizens, Massachusetts, for example, embarked upon the career of a "profligate debtor" in the late 1850's and pursued it briskly until the mid-seventies. The commonwealth's per capita expenditures rose four times over between 1860 and 1868; during the seventies they were more or less stabilized and by 1880 were wrestled down slightly. Soon afterward, however, the trend moved upward again into the twentieth century. Direct state indebtedness, similarly, underwent an elevenfold increase between 1861 and 1868, from $2,300,000 to $21,600,000, and a sixfold increase during the longer period from 1860 to 1906.[35] Someone's property ultimately had to cope with these burdens —and the middle classes were certain that it was theirs.

Across the Hudson in New York State matters took much the same course. Studying the state's fiscal history as it unfolded after the Wells Reports of 1871–72, the Mills Committee of 1916 noted that while New York's population had risen 82% in the preceding generation, state expenditures rose 500%. In the restrained words of the tax commissioner (in 1913), "the State has been no laggard in the enormous increase and extravagance of its expenditures."[36] Rising indebtedness, needless to say, paralleled Albany's rising expenditures with especially sharp increments after 1890.

State fiscal tendencies elsewhere in the North were very similar. "Debt, debt, debt, debt, constantly increasing," complained J. B. Hunt to David Wells in 1873. The postwar decades, as it transpired, proved to be the commencement of a new, exceedingly critical period in state finance. Recalling these decades, the noted New York financial editor, Alexander Noyes, reported that "moral sense seemed . . . to have deteriorated. . . . The [Federal] Government's financial recklessness was readily imitated by the community-at-large; debt was the order of the day in the affairs of both."[37] And so it continued.

The wild breakdown of state fiscal machinery for a time, as Noyes suggested, was aggravated by national fiscal conditions. During the Civil War and the immediate postwar years, the creaking equipment of the federal government appeared headed for disaster. Confidence inherited from a more sanguine, though hardly a wiser, age underwent considerable erosion. Thus, for example, the assurance of men like New England industrialist, Edward Atkinson, that taxation incident to the prosecution of the war would not prove burdensome was difficult to maintain as the fighting continued and costs mounted.[38] Fresh from Harvard in 1863, William Graham Sumner caught the more foreboding possibilities with clarity and prescience. "It seemed to me then," he wrote, ". . . that the war, with paper money and high taxation, must certainly bring about immense social changes and social problems, especially in making the rich richer and the poor poorer, and leaving behind us the old ante-war period as one of primitive simplicity which could never return."[39] However wrong in detail, Sumner's estimate was certainly far better supported by events than was the positivism of men like Atkinson.

Servicing nearly two and a half billion dollars of federal wartime debt unquestionably posed a staggering task to men raised on the lacklustre fiscal diet of pinchpenny governments unaccustomed to taxing massively, spending lavishly, or borrowing feverishly. Inevitably such behavior frightened many of those who watched Washington's attempts to do all three of these things at once. To financiers like Jay Cooke, who was one of its principal midwives, the national debt, to be sure, was a national blessing; but in many other quarters the debt was conceded to be a species of capital "only to those who hold it." To "everybody else" it was "a tax," "an evil," "an incubus," "a source of corruption," and "a calamity." Unsure of precisely how it was to be done, men of this persuasion were eager to pay it off.

Amasa Walker, the Boston merchant, later a professor of political economy at Harvard and Oberlin, was fairly typical of the many spokesmen who voiced middle class fears about the federal debt. He was swift to challenge major "fallacies" which had crept into the debt question shortly after the war: the notion that the debt was a form of wealth—something mid-twentieth century economists would take for granted, that it was also an active, available form of capital, and that it imparted stability to government on the Hamiltonian model. Favoring debt consolidation, he also denounced the exemption of federal obligations from state and local taxation as both "invidious" and "unjust;" among other effects, it purportedly crippled industry by siphoning off great quantities of wealth into the obligations of government and thereby rested unequally on the North. But in Walker's mind, as in many others, federal indebtedness produced specters that lay outside of economics. Removal of "three billion dollars" from the reach of local governments through the federal debt, he argued, would "create a very considerable and influential *class of persons*" enjoying an "influence unfavorable to public welfare." Much like the Progressives who later were to see themselves caught between an upper and a nether social millstone, Walker, in the 1860's, insisted that such exemptions would place laborers and capitalists who held the federal debt in "the same favored position" at the expense of the middle classes.[40]

Before 1870, in effect, the country had been presented with a ragged but sizeable muster of opinion on key aspects of national finance. The careful work of scholars such as Coben, Kindahl, Nugent, Sharkey, Timberlake, and Unger, fortunately, makes it unnecessary to review any of these here. Suffice it to say, that federal monetary and fiscal problems cast a pall over the finances of localities through much of the 1870's, placing local issues in a gloomy context. No doubt men like Ohio's John Sherman, who performed notable service on the Senate Committee on Finance and Taxation, as well as in the direction of the Treasury, were basically optimistic about the successful handling of federal burdens. But among many other reputable men of affairs, the commonest assumptions on this score were pessimistic. They rested on premises like those of Hugh McCulloch—Sherman's predecessor at the head of the Treasury—that Americans had "wandered from old landmarks both in finance and ethics."[41] For just such reasons as McCulloch's, observers were able to record by the early seventies that "one of the most vital questions now before the nation" was the management of federal indebtedness and related problems of revenue and that due to the "exhausting pressure of our fiscal burdens," they were being "discussed with an intelligence and vivacity seldom equalled." The vivacity of discussion gained impetus from the fact that in no branch of political economy (as England's Lord Brougham had written years before) were "errors" and "omissions . . . more conspicuous than in [the branch] pertaining to the increase or decadence of national resources,"[42] resources whose magnitude bore directly on questions of financial burden.

Yet, despite the compounding of municipal problems by those which had unfolded at the state and national levels of government, it is fair to say that by the 1880's the deepest anxieties about fiscal affairs focussed at the local level. Federal indebtedness, to use just one criterion, had reportedly been reduced by 14.5%, while even state debts, albeit temporarily, had been scaled down by 26%, New England states showing a decline of .8% and the Middle Atlantic states a reduction of 44%. But any cheers from the middle classes were generally muted.

In the circumstances, historians must ask why this was so in respect to the middle classes,. What, after all, were their complaints? How legitimate did they believe them to be and how legitimate were they? On the face of it anyway, some evidence would suggest such complaints were either implausible or concocted. Every index, for example, tells us that the nation's wealth was increasing; productivity rose overall by 1⅝% per annum throughout the period under consideration; and there was a steady, long-run increment to the amount, the kind, and the value of many properties. Moreover, the end of each decade left more Americans enriched than the beginning, and the middle classes, particularly the "new middle classes" of the cities (although they remained a distinct minority of the population), added to their numbers decade by decade. What, then, rendered middle class burdens so irksome that many of the leading elements of the middle classes were driven to sustained protest and to reform?

Such questions, obviously, are more easily posed than answered; certainly there is no simple, categorical response to them. But several supportable suggestions are in order.

First, while wealth increased greatly in the North, it was narrowly held. The rich—or the enriched—secured most of it. Since general property taxation theoretically reached nearly all property for public purposes, this, again, theoretically should have broadened the tax base and fattened public receipts. But if the rich as late as the decade of the 1960's have not been required to pay their "fair share" of taxation, the rich between 1860 and 1920 paid almost nothing. Given the then prevalent assumption that investment or growth capital had to come mainly from the rich, this, of course, was often considered justifiable. However, it did not ease public burdens by spreading their incidence.

Second, much of the property added to the North's stock of wealth took intangible forms. A desire to subsidize the production of some of this new wealth often made public officials reluctant to add significant amounts of it to the tax rolls. Where officials were disposed to tax it, the new wealth proved difficult to assess or, more generally, impossible to locate, thanks to evasive tactics. In sum, much of this abundant property lay beyond public purview.

Third, like the rich, the vast majority of American poor paid few taxes of any kind, none really on local property. Furthermore, not much of the local tax burden could be shifted to them. Unlike English landlords who avoided rates on their properties by making tenants and occupiers liable for them, or, again, unlike Continental ruling or middle classes who shifted tax burdens downward through consumption taxes such as the *octroi,* the middle classes of the North in a deflationary period had little chance to shift much of their obligations. Of the notorious exceptions to these suggestions, we must say more later. Meantime, what was left to carry the thrust of rising public costs and expenditures if not the tangible realty, tangible personalty, and subsidized merchandise of the middle classes?

As measured by pre-war experience, therefore, more onerous public burdens, by the late nineteenth century, had become permanent fixtures, admittedly posing opportunities for some, but, as then viewed, posing serious inhibitions for most who confronted them. The deterioration of old fiscal policies and institutions within the cities, moreover, was by the same time well-advanced. Indeed, because local governments were far more intimately involved with men's daily interests than the national government, the primacy of municipal financial problems was a growing fact of life. While the obligations of other governments, for instance, were shrinking somewhat in the late seventies, urban taxes and debts, comprising 10% of the country's total debt in 1870, comprised 23% just a decade later. Time confirmed the trend.[43]

Municipal finances, especially as they affected the middle classes during the late nineteenth century—and into the twentieth—thus were the most powerful force in the breakdown of established fiscal machinery, machinery already severely weakened by the effects of war, depression, and industrialization. In the process, urban financial problems also exposed deep social and political fissures which in themselves help explain the hostile reactions of many of the middle classes to fiscal change. Protests that exploded across the North, clearly, were more than just a reaction against the money costs of government, outrageous as they appeared. At issue were the structure and control of a new society rising on an expansive industrial base and the interpretations to be imparted to the democracy that accompanied it. Resolution of these issues, it was believed, lay with those social elements that manned the creaking money machines.

In respectable quarters the fear was, of course, that these machines were changing hands—or had already done so. "Contractors have captured Olympus," wrote the distinguished Philadelphia geologist, Peter Lesley, to a friend in 1875. Having stormed and vulgarized Chestnut and Broad streets, "the great Dunderhead substratum" had placed its smudgy seal on local government. "I hope the time will come before I die when we shall be under an absolute despotism," added the fifty-six year old Philadelphian who had been raised among the scenes of Independence, "I can imagine no other solution for the country."[44] Hundreds more of "the best men" took up the same refrain over the next quarter century. "What we have accomplished thus far," complained the Boston-born, Harvard-trained, New York lawyer, Albert Stickney in 1889, "is, with some democratic features, a combination of ochlocracy and plutocracy—a rule of mob and money,"[45] the ultimate horror of the middle classes.

To men like Lesley or Stickney who had matured among the solid American bourgeois, in the world of the Commercial Puritans of State Street, or of the Knickerbockers or Quakers in their respective Washington Squares, liberty and democracy represented contradictory traditions. While they were "democrats" all, of course, liberty was more congenial to them than democracy. Liberty was associated with Lockian individualism, with civil and property rights, with a stake-in-society, and with a "responsible" Protestant moral code symbolized by the virtues of thrift, self-reliance, and hard work. Its roots were mercantile and at a commoner level, yeoman rural. Its precepts were embodied in and dominated the Law. As viewed from within established circles, democracy, on the other hand, was identified with ignorant, venal masses. It was preeminently an affair of alternately fickle or highly regimented majorities of propertyless, irresponsible, often Catholic and alien bands bent on public plunder. Its roots were in rural and urban slums where the Law "knew it not." Thus, while rising expenditures, taxation, and indebtedness were treated as symptoms of fiscal crisis within local governments, the new democracy was widely cited as the principal cause.

By the last third of the nineteenth century, the urban middle classes were often haunted by both the apparent illiberalism and the rapidly growing political power of uneducated, unassimilated orders of men.

To be sure, the genius of the century, acknowledged William Sumner, Yale's defender of the middling elements against the social extremes, had been democratic and it was undeniable that "the world" had passed into the hands of new masters. Yet he judged the transfer disastrous. "Where else in history," he queried, "have all adult males in a society . . . possessed political power, honors, and emoluments and at the same time been subject to no responsibilities, risks, charges, expenses, or burdens of any kind—these being all left to the educated and propertied classes?" Where else, he continued, had it "ever been possible for a numerical majority to entail upon a society burdens which a minority must bear?"[46] Precisely because the United States was a *democratic* republic, "the state," he concluded, "should handle as little money as possible;" otherwise the new conglomerate majorities would discover unerringly that "the easiest way ever yet devised to get wealth is to hold a parliament and, by a majority vote, order that the possessors of wealth shall give it to the non-possessors."[47]

With equal directness about the same theme, Brooks Adams declared in 1878 that "the most difficult problem of modern times is unquestionably how to protect property under popular governments." Trouble began when "those . . . untaxed outnumber those who pay taxes;" then, contended Adams, as experience in the great cities demonstrated, it was in the "direct interest" of the "untaxed classes to swell public expenditures to the utmost." By his reckoning, "several hundred million dollars" already had been "confiscated" by these classes in Massachusetts "through state and municipal extravagance and fraud." Fifty to 60% of the commonwealth's rural voters and 80% of Boston's voters, he charged, paid only a negligible poll tax and, as a consequence, the typical "poll" was irresponsible. He cached his meager property in savings banks which were exempt from municipal taxation and "consequently," reported Adams, "he does not suffer from municipal extravagance." The state, in addition, granted him half an exemption from its taxes, making economy "of little moment to him. He may vote one year," continued Adams, "to swamp his town with debt; the next he may move away, after he has pocketed his share of spoil." Devoid of a stake-in-society, eager for spoils, these landless, poll-paying democrats were "already in the majority," warned Adams, "while the rich State, like a ripe prize for plunder, lies temptingly under their hand."[48]

From the 1860's onward, Massachusetts polls were regarded by the established citizenry as a democratic assault wave launched at the nearest treasury,[49] paying nothing to the common lot, but free, as Congressman Amasa Walker then phrased it, to vote heavy expenditures "with entire impunity."[50] The distinguished historian, Francis Parkman, scowled in behalf of respectable men that "if we are to be robbed, we like to be robbed with civility." The robbery alluded to was public, perpetrated from "beneath" by "organized ignorance led by unscrupulous craft . . . marching amid the applause of fools under the flag of equal rights." More ardent for equality than for liberty, wrote Parkman bitterly, the masses realized that thanks to the vote "the prizes held before them [were] enormous." Although familiar with complaints that the rural poor drove up taxes which never touched them, Parkman found "diseases of the body politic gathered to a head" in the cities where "the barbarism that we have armed and organized stands ready to overwhelm us," taxing the industrious to "feed the idle."

Decrying the disappearance from office of "eminent merchants and lawyers," the city's "natural chiefs . . . who had a divine right to govern," many New Yorkers began damning the fiscal proclivities of their own democracy soon after the Civil War. Electoral majorities were accused by respectable men of divorcing taxation from responsible appropriation and cries were revived that "no man should be allowed to vote in any city or state election who [had] not paid a direct tax." Fears were rife that millions would have to be spent "to govern, tame, and teach Manhattan Island these lessons."[51] Probably no one spoke with greater authority on the subject in behalf of substantial elements of the middle classes than E. L. Godkin, redoubtable founder-editor of *The Nation,* one of the country's most influential organs of polite social and political criticism. Conceding that the tides of universal suffrage could not be reversed, Godkin argued nonetheless that the new mass democracy raised "the most serious question which faces the modern world," for it had begun converting taxation into a political weapon aimed against corporations and other types of private property. As a result, he reported, "the ignorance and vice of the City have been organized in an association mainly for the purpose of plundering the municipal treasury and quartering a large body of shiftless people on the public record."[52] Under the circumstances, "our modern experiment in democratic government," he noted, "is really an experiment in the government of rich communities by poor men,"[53] an experiment whose progress was crassly measured by the new democracy's handling of public moneys and its adherence to middle class money morality.

Since New York City more than any of the 32 incorporated cities of New York State strikingly juxtaposed both the virtues and vices of dedicated money-making and expansive democracy, this narrow test was, in fact, widely applied. Such was the line taken by State Senator J. Sloan Fassett of Elmira, one of Boss Platt's chief lieutenants, early in the nineties when he attributed "all local troubles [in New York City] to the temptations offered by our present system of voting" and to its concomitants, "an unscrupulous use of power, patronage, and money." Bad government, declared Fassett, then chairman of the State Senate Committee on Cities, consisted of "the wrong use of money and shows itself in the expense account;" indeed, in his estimate, "the usual motive for faulty administration in city affairs is the plunder of the city's money." The remedy, he added, was a "new form of ballot" reducing the number of voters.[54] "We all admit the necessity of placing some check upon municipal expenditure, of devising some fraud-proof system," wrote one of the city's reform politicians in the early eighties, but the real problem stemmed from local democracy engaged in witless and greedy adventures in municipal finance; the difficulties, accordingly, were social rather than administrative. There was, he claimed, "political work to be pursued, passions to be played upon, cupidity to be provided for," for in the resolution of these financial problems "universal suffrage . . . *does not permit itself to be persuaded by figures, but obeys prejudices.*" The voting masses, he argued, incongruously demanded smaller tax rates along with more munificent spending and "an enlargement of the functions of government," in the process fostering a "lamentable wastefulness of public funds," which, he added, had become "the story of our political methods for the last twenty-five years."[55]

Hostility toward urban democracy inspired a voluminous literature of just this type. Contributors included a cross-section of middle class leadership: college and university presidents, political economists, natural scientists, students of politics, lawyers, statisticians, mayors, ministers, editors, politicians, and businessmen. It solicited regular attention through newspapers, trade papers, and learned journals; it likewise furnished the theme for scores of books. It was a literature that enjoyed currency not only in large Eastern cities but also in smaller, inland communities.

Despite nuances, the picture conveyed remained basically the same regardless of the time or place of its appearance. After the Civil War, it was argued, "the American experiment" had begun operating with a vengeance, for its consequences now clearly involved more than "simply the abolition of property qualifications." It meant, beyond that, "the acceptance of unrestricted suffrage as though fitness to rule came by nature, not by study or experience," with results that were judged "as remarkable in a free government as in a despotism." (Thomas Cooley) "Earthquake shocks" produced by the eruption of this "fiery mass beneath . . . [the] social soil" had thereafter swiftly begun dividing the entire culture. (C. E. Pickard) It could scarcely have been otherwise when "the political influence of a chief justice" was often "annihilated by the vote of a bloated sot," or the convictions of "an illustrious political scholar" were upset by the "momentary caprice of a vacant-headed boor." (Alexander Winchell) Under such pressures, American governments allegedly had not only become "the worst in Christendom," but at the urban level particularly they had also become "the most expensive." (Andrew White) Data were generally adduced at this point to demonstrate the costs of assuaging the fiscal appetites of a "rapidly enlarging and dangerous proletariat," itself "little affected by the vast expenditure of money required." (R. E. Wright) Meantime, with nothing to lose by their actions, "organizations of non-taxpaying voters" swarmed corruptly into public vaults. Unless Northern polities underwent extensive reform or profited from "a drastic dose of the Adams Family," (Samuel Bowles) responsible men were bound to retaliate through "greater centralization in the executive," through "socialism," through some *"force majeure,"* through "a military genius, or . . . a religious reformer"—all forms of the dreaded "one man power." (Charles Reemelin) Respectable men intended to "have protection for their interests—or else." If the new democracy refused to afford that security, "why so much the worse for democracy."[56]

Generally scornful of the irresponsible democracy which, in Cooley's words, was rendering the middle classes "wholly powerless" and provoking "the best men" into open contempt for "republican institutions," respectable elements tended to focus their resentment upon immigrants, especially Irishmen, as symbols of the new order.[57]

The immigrant arrived on a stage already set, in the midst of a drama already familiar to the predominantly Protestant middle classes. Coloring the thought of these "better classes" was a nostalgic vision of the old order from which, culturally, they had sprung: the vision of the New England town of the 1830's and 1840's. Men of letters eulogized it; politicians and historians recorded its seminal influences; popular writing alluded to the homespun, cunning Yankee types raised on simple precepts around the town's rugged hearthsides. Later reified, myths about the New England town left a clear mark across the culture of the Northern tier of states as migrations streamed westward toward the ever-receding American Eden. Once upon a time, at least, Yankees could claim that they had known true communities in which men's virtues loomed larger than life. Otherwise skeptical about the common man, even Francis Parkman believed that the town "would have been safely and well-governed by the vote of every man in it."

Unfortunately, change had proven erosive. Around these idyllic communities, a "tinseled civilization" purportedly had arisen to spread disruption in the form of an "ignorant . . . [and] discontented proletariat."[58] By the end of the seventies, the town with its wholesome traditions, once so integral a part of popular life, had begun yielding physically as well as culturally to cities "with acres of tenements and thousands and tens of thousands of restless workingmen" who failed to conform with nativist images of democracy. Often stereotyped in many middle class minds as inferior foreigners, workers were the more easily dismissed, or abused, as men to whom "liberty means license and politics means plunder," to whom "the public good counted for nothing" against their own "trivial interests," and to whom the love of country depended upon "what they can get out of it." Such men constituted the "imported ignorance and hereditary ineptitude" allegedly fermenting in the cities which, with time, elements of the middle classes found increasingly "insufferable." These attitudes, of course, were often ambivalent and contradictory; democracy to the Stowes or to the Frederick Stimsons undoubtedly meant the theoretical desirability of perfect political equality. But by their own admissions it was a political equality "tempered" by due consideration for distinctions of character or attainment and a "respect for families of proven descent." Their democracy, however well-meaning, was one in which for public purposes there were no poor and no foreigners.[59]

While the town idealized the virtues supposedly underlying native standards of fiscal rectitude, the cities, most notoriously New York City, became symbols of an opposite kind. There, for instance, by the end of the Civil War, the "evil tide" of social flotsam cast up by "seventy-seven thousand foreign voters," reputedly the largest contingent at the polls, grabbed control of the local money machinery from within the chambers of council, the inner sanctum once of respectable power. Who could doubt how these vulgar men, scarcely up to the "management of an oyster stand in the market,"[60] these foreign butcher-boys, hangers-on from the engine houses and billiard parlors would run the money machines?

For many respectable men the question was rhetorical. Charles Nordhoff, for example, a noted editor of German origins himself, declared in 1871 that "without exception" the great cities had become the prey of political jobbers and "it is curious," he added, that "most of these city plunderers work by means of Irishmen,"[61] a prejudice widely supported in newspapers and journals of opinion. "If we take up the hundreds of laments over the degeneracy of our political condition," recorded E. L. Godkin, "we shall find that in nine cases out of ten it is ascribed to the influence on politics of different nationalities," principally the Germans and the Irish. But the field quickly narrowed. The Germans he depicted as a skilled, disciplined, and generally steady breed; but the Irish, among whom this child of English Protestants had been raised, were another matter. "Quick, passionate, impetuous," and "easily influenced," they were marked, Godkin wrote, by "a hereditary disposition to personal loyalty to a leader of some sort," and unlike the

Germans in America, the Irish and their leaders were the worst rather than the better class. Thus, they were segregated from native Americans by habit, tradition, and ideals, while they were constrained at the same time to contend against the "dread of Catholicism" integral to the "mental and moral make-up of all classes of Anglo-Saxon."

In these circumstances, continued Godkin in his famous essay on "Criminal Politics," Irishmen, reverting to type, quickly learned to view the native Americans as they had the "well-to-do class in their own country" as "lawful political prey whom it is not improper to tax . . . without mercy or compunction." Through a mastery of the spoils system, of "pulls" and "boodle," they undertook urban politics in "a predatory state of mind," uninhibited by "any sense of public duty, or of community interest with the rest of the taxpayers." Largely responsible for enmeshing dives, brothels, and liquor dealerships, in which their country men allegedly were heavily invested, the urban Irish placed politics on a "criminal basis."[62]

This was the picture men had in mind when, by the 1880's, they spoke remorsefully of the "Irish conquest" of American cities. "Hibernian oligarchies" became the hallmark of city governments throughout the North. Sixteen major Northern cities, among them New York, Brooklyn, Buffalo, Boston, Jersey City, Pittsburgh, St. Paul, St. Louis, Kansas City, Omaha, and Chicago, were—or so it appeared—under Irish control by 1890. In a score of smaller cities: Troy, Albany, Hoboken, Trenton, Burlington, Oswego, Haverhill, Carbondale, Cincinnati, Dayton, and Duluth, for example, Irishmen controlled key positions in local governments as chiefs of police, directors of public works, or mayors. In Philadelphia, Indianapolis, Baltimore, and Providence, they were powerfully organized but too divided to rule without interruption. Looking over the officialdom of Northern cities in general, a middle class observer of the mid-nineties remarked that a "simple reading of the roll should send a thrill of joy through the bones of Irish kings."[63]

This situation both terrified and embittered many natives. During the great railway strikes of 1877, a native of Ohio wrote President Hayes offering him the lives of her four sons to help check riotous subversions of the Catholic Irish whom she accused of spearheading the outbreaks.[64] No doubt she belonged to the lunatic fringe; but Bishop A. Cleveland Coxe, whose attack on Irish Catholics was pitched in the same hysterical key, did not. With a large religious community behind him, Coxe reacted violently to the foreign invasion of Northern cities in the pages of the *Forum* in 1889. "Shall our children's children see another Centennial Commemoration of Washington and the Constitution?" he asked. Protestant Anglo-Saxons faced the same ruin as ancient peoples inundated by barbarians; though lacking guns and bayonets in America, these hordes, possessing the vote, had been "drilled and magnified into a balance of power" which made them masters of great communities. Thus, the Bishop's New York had been conquered by aliens who "presumed to make it a seat of war," throwing open government to a "religious sect" to be governed by "priests," converting the city to a "New Tipperary" with an alien flag flying over City Hall" as a menace and defiance to the older inhabitants." Ganged up with "servile and sycophant politicians," the Irish, charged the Bishop, had turned communal power upside down, discriminating against native Americans because of their virtues and education "in favor of the vomit" which poured from the immigrant vessels.[65]

Lacking innocence themselves, the "older inhabitants," like the Bishop, fully appreciated the ability of the Irish to confiscate wealth and redistribute it through the use of local fiscal machinery. Moreover, they recognized that the Irish and their allies could proceed directly to this plunder without restraint, for "Irish politics" were believed to be uncluttered with inherited jargon about dedicated public service, about the trusteeship of men in office, about good citizenship or political uplift. Government and party were considered to be synonyms to the Irish as, ostensibly, they never had been to natives. Virtually unknown to the law until the late nineteenth century, party, accordingly, could be treated as just what it was—a *private* organization designed to operate openly on the basis of personal favors and rewards, in the spirit, that is, of Wardman George Washington Plunkitt who "seen his financial opportunities and took 'em."

Two political styles were thus in collision over the employment of fiscal power; or so prejudice, distorted perspectives, and rhetoric made it appear. Reputable people, therefore, sought to run a protective government, the logical projection of their own propertied interests. Their government was a corporation in which the best people comprised the board of directors, contriving decisions or making investments "objectively," profiting themselves and in the process serving the whole community. They acknowledged obligations to the young, to the infirm, the aged, widowed, orphaned, and poor. But their sense of responsibility suffered from certain limitations. One was the belief that in a world of scarcity, available capital could only be allocated safely and wisely to further production, hence it ought to be allocated only to productive people, a category into which few of the unfortunate fitted. Another limitation was more parochial; it was the addiction to an antiquated township approach to the sharing out of social burdens through respectable legislatures whose aid tended to go chiefly to those types of unfortunates with whom they could readily identify. What remained, of course, could be relegated to the grand adjustments of the marketplace, to a trickling down of prosperity, to voluntarism, or to heroic mimesis on the part of the less fortunate—attitudes which were neither unreasonable, unkind, nor expensive in a village context, but which became more and more anachronistic in the face of Northern industrialization.

The growing ineffectuality of these views was obscured, however, by middle class assumptions that irresponsible immigrants and workers bent on jobbery had begun converting urban political machines into self-perpetuating welfare agencies for party members, their families, and their friends. With nothing to invest but their vote, the Irish were widely accused of meeting the exigencies of life with public moneys, supplied not from their own patched pockets, but instead from accumulations of the best men's properties. In Boston, for instance, despite the injunctions of the city charter against councilmen interfering in the executive functions, violations were committed flagrantly in order that taxing, spending, and borrowing could be exercised in behalf of party welfare: hirings, raising salaries, letting contracts, and ordering a variety of goods for the use of party workers and constituents. Politically, the Hub seemed a model of how votes could be swapped for small measures of security drained from the public till. Reputable men counted it a dramatic display of the new fiscal style and, fittingly, the city's last Yankee mayor confirmed their prejudice. Municipal extravagance, he declared, was rooted in the belief that "the community in its corporate capacity owes a liberal living to its individual members.... A gradual change," lamented the mayor, had come over the "spirit of the people." Much of the population, "once the most independent and self-reliant in the world," had begun "clamoring for support as individuals or in classes from the government of the country—federal, state, and city" and party government in Boston, as elsewhere, was thereby faced with "the demand for a systematic distribution of wealth by taxes."[66]

Statistics lent credence to the mayor's remarks. Between 1850 and 1900, for example, Boston doubled its per capita expenditure on health, education, and welfare services; indeed, overall, these expenses accounted for about one-third of the municipal budget toward the close of that half-century period. Similarly, New York City's budget by 1890 revealed that nearly one-half of the $33,500,000 officially earmarked for public spending was spent in the same ways, while of the $50,440,000 spent by the other thirty-two cities of New York State, nearly one-half, again, went to welfare. Nor should it have been forgotten that, as in Boston, public accounts masked the scale of welfarism which was conducted through padded payrolls, through contracts let by the major city departments, through the hiring of unemployables for municipal labor, through various forms of indebtedness, and through bloated municipal salaries, for, as one student of municipal finance noted in the late eighties, all of this too "eventually . . . comes into the tax budget."[67]

But the mayor of Boston, true to form, challenged the theory that "the affairs of a city should be managed like those of an ordinary business corporation," preferring a more personal and clannish view of government. Legally corporate, the city, felt the mayor, still differed radically from a private corporation. It was controlled "by a great number of people," not by a small body of stockholders operating *in camera;* officers were not chosen quietly by other directors, they emerged from the heat of an electoral campaign. Instead of profit, continued the mayor, the city's object was "to provide [for its people's] safety, health, and comfort, their education and pleasure," as well as "to relieve their poor and help their sick." Indeed, "municipal corporations," declared the mayor bluntly, "are organized not to make money, but to spend it."[68]

To the middle classes who were frightened by the new style which the politicized Irish symbolized—and pioneered—in public finance, the issue was not really whether or not to *spend.* Rather, they wanted to be sure about what they were to spend *for* and for whose benefit they were to be taxed in order that the spending might occur. Psychologically theirs was not an age of affluence. They believed that both their properties and their status had been hard won and, as Richard Hofstadter and Eric Goldman have suggested, they lived insecurely with the knowledge that both could be lost easily, perhaps in no way more easily than by having their profits eroded by public taxation spuriously designed to insure the unproductive welfare of relatively unproductive men.

Their action, not just their rhetoric—action organized and sustained year after year—powerfully underscored middle class convictions that the burdens of subsidizing the expectations of a seemingly alien democracy fell squarely upon their properties. Evidence of these convictions, in fact, is overwhelming; but were such convictions firmly founded? Again, did the incidence of taxation really come to rest on the middle classes? Or were local taxes substantially shifted to either richer or poorer groups?

As suggested earlier, an unequivocal—perhaps even a satisfactory—answer is still impossible either from economists or historians. Incidence, barring certain manageable model-building exercises, remains an extremely complex practical question requiring a vast body of empirical materials much of which is not available for the late nineteenth and early twentieth centuries. What is available today, if undeniably useful and interesting, does not encourage sweeping generalization. But, far worse, for anyone who was anxious to discover who was bearing the burden of local taxation in Northern states and cities fifty, seventy, or a hundred years ago, the possibilities of sound generalization were infinitely less great than they are at present. Incidence was a subject that was just beginning to be defined and explored "scientifically" toward the end of the nineteenth century and the experts, unavoidably, were unsure of their conclusions and actively disagreed among themselves.

Although any observations that emerge from inquiries into incidence are likely to be qualified and full of nuances, there are grounds, nevertheless, for reiterating the apparent legitimacy of middle class complaints voiced during the last third of the nineteenth and the first decades of the twentieth centuries. Not only were the rich and the poor effectively out of reach of local taxation, despite the intent of general property taxation in respect to establishing claims against all sorts of property, but the middle classes were also not numerous. Avoiding complex modern efforts at definition of just what *is* middle class, we need only note that even at the end of the last century the United States was not regarded by its own experts as a middle class society. The highest informed estimate near the turn of the century counted only about one-quarter of the nation's families as middle class, while the lowest informed estimate placed the figure at just over 10%. American socialists and conservative Republican congressmen alike were agreed by 1900 that there was little property below the middling elements of the population which general property taxation could tap for revenues. Figures from Spahr and Hunter, among others, as well as from the *Report of the U.S. Industrial Commission, 1900* (Volume I) indicated that from 60% to as many as 88% of the population were classifiable either as "poor" or "very poor." Put differently, census data showed that fewer than one-half of the nation's 8,300,000 families owned their own homes; even among farmers, the national figures indicated that 52% were either propertyless for tax purposes or were only the partial owners of their properties.

Given the fact that at the state and local levels, general property taxation was virtually the sole source of revenues, that there were almost no income, use, or sales taxes, the tax base was narrowly restricted to middle class property holders, really to those of them who were reasonably honest and dutiful. Again, the Twelfth Census suggests just how narrow this restriction was. In Manhattan less than 6% of the population owned their own homes; in Chicago barely 25%; in Philadelphia 22%; and in Boston not quite 19%. Much the same was true of smaller communities such as Fall River, Cincinnati, and Holyoke. If the rich and the dishonest men embraced in these percentages eluded the payment of taxes, the balance were left to cope with the load.

The extent to which the load was shifted is not clear. Doubtless some middle class taxpayers passed their general property taxes onto the shoulders of others through higher prices for goods, services, or rents. But as a general proposition it is difficult to see how many of them managed this. Assuming the economists' friend *ceteris paribus* did *not* apply, a massive shifting would have appeared in rising prices and rents. Yet, excepting the inflation coterminous with the Civil War, Ethel Hoover's Consumer Price Index shows a 7 point decline in rents between 1865 and 1880 and the Warren-Pearson Rent Index covering Boston, Philadelphia, Cincinnati, Louisville, and St. Louis during these identical years shows a 24 point decline. In addition, the most reliable of the cost of living indexes for subsequent years down to 1914 show a steady overall decline, as do prices in this period generally.[69]

In the circumstances, confronted with soaring assessments, expenditures, indebtedness, and taxation at local levels of government, especially in municipalities, there is reason to believe that among many of the middle classes protests against the new fiscal style whether in town or country reflected growing psychological and financial burdens.

Working on the presumption that, in truth, this was the case, William Graham Sumner solemnly cautioned in 1887 that if governments foolishly milked the middle classes for the benefit of the lower classes, the middle classes—the backbone of society, "representing a wide distribution of comfort and well-being"—would die out. Insofar as governments gave "license to robbery and spoilation, or enforced almsgiving," they sanctioned this destruction, in the process causing the "pets" who received public moneys to be "pauperized and proletarianized."[70] Tracing Chicago's misgovernment to its spending on social services—the city's heaviest expense—reformer Frank Crandon warned against "the liability to mistake in connection with our public charities." Supplying relief to the suffering and aid to the needy was commendable, he granted, but almshouses, hospitals, asylums, and infirmaries, unhappily, were "not always managed in the interests either of the inmates or the municipality," their officers and employees frequently landing on the payroll because of their "subserviency to the appointing power." Outdoor relief he found equally politicized by "a class of dependents" who were "imbued with the idea that such support is an inalienable right."[71] Like most immigrants and members of the lower classes, such men, Crandon felt, lived in "a world of favor and not of law;" the police justice, the precinct captain, the roundsman, and most importantly, the district political leader, were all the government known to many of the lower, the working, and the criminal classes.

On the petty scale, party men embodied the classic roles of the state —protection and welfare—and, as many observers were quick to note, the farther one descended in the social order, the more the moralists, the missionaries, and the philanthropists were outrivaled by politicians who, however corruptly, ministered to men's mundane wants through the distribution of party pittances, largesses, pulls, and favors to party workers and camp followers. Scores of commentators and volumes of testimony confirmed the ways in which politicos perniciously diverted public funds drawn from the middle classes in order to become "the principal comforters of the afflicted and the aid of the undeserving unfortunates."[72]

Common biases against this kind of welfare in part stemmed from the fact that nineteenth century reformers often tended, in the words of Herbert Croly, "to conceive of reform as . . . a moral protest and awakening" which, following the ghostly injunctions of the idealized village or town, sought "to restore the American political and economic system to its pristine purity and vigor."[73] As a result, Jacob Cox, William Dudley Foulke, George W. Curtis, Silas Burt, Moorfield Storey, E. L. Godkin, and other devoted reformers conceived of these political services as the vicious consequences of spoils and patronage alone, comparing them unfavorably with middle class, corporative concepts of efficiency. True, not everyone limited his definition of democracy or his humanity to the middle reaches of society.[74] The young Henry Cabot Lodge, Dorman Eaton, Philemon T. Sherman, William Ivins, Sloan Fassett, Alfred Hodder, Sydney Brooks, Herbert Croly, and Theodore Roosevelt, to cite a few experienced men of varied backgrounds, displayed more ambivalence toward the rise of political welfarism, perhaps because they were either close students of political parties or because at one time they were political insiders themselves. They sensed in some measure the anomaly of middle class Puritans trying to govern heterogeneous, pagan, "corruptible," and mercenary masses of voters within the great cities. Often resentful of professional reformers, they bowed pragmatically to the fact that Tammany rule, wherever it occurred, was "really in consonance with the wishes and temperament of the majority of . . . inhabitants;"[75] and, therefore, they preferred their brands of moral realism to impractical, if "uplifting," panaceas. But while their pragmatism carried them somewhat closer to toleration of the new fiscal style than did the fixed and retrospective principles of the "goo goos" and of the dedicated reformers, they were still far from grasping fully or acceding wholeheartedly to the pressures being placed upon parties for the vast extension and formalization of welfare.

It could hardly have been otherwise, for everywhere spokesmen from among the middle classes saw little except evil portents in the fiscal appetites and habits attending the emergence of industrialized democracy. Citing fiscal trends in Italy "as applicable to the United States," Boston's Gamaliel Bradford reported to an audience of political scientists that there, too, "everything ultimately resolves itself into a question of finance." In Italy, "the establishment of a budgetary equilibrium," he added,

> is the constant preoccupation of every Premier who is fit for the post, and the grand obstacle in his way is the Chamber of Deputies. In theory the guardians of the public purse and the vigilant critics of executive expenditure, the representatives of the people have become in practice the stubborn defenders of public extravagance and financial abuses.[76]

So it was also in France. Under the Third Republic, French democracy, wrote the aging economist David A. Wells in 1895, had nearly doubled its taxation in less than a generation while raising its indebtedness by more than one-third, this in excess of reparations paid Germany for the Franco-Prussian War. "Democracy loves spending," concluded Wells gloomily; "give it a firm hold on the reins of government and it is no easy matter as the French Revolution of 1789 and the present fiscal condition of France exemplify, to restrain its excesses." Like many rural and bourgeois Frenchmen, Wells may well have had in mind the struggle of the radicalized post-Commune Paris Municipal Council to wrest control of its budgetary affairs from the central government, the better it was suspected, to spend lavishly, if not corruptly, on the city's indigent masses.[77] Reputedly handicapped by poor soil and "universal poverty," Germany as well as France, it was noted, had likewise plunged heavily into public spending as a concomitant of the extension of the vote; and England, despite paring down its debt during the latter part of the nineteenth century, because of household suffrage, had been forced, regretably, greatly to expand its budgets, hence its taxation. Meantime, social struggles and expectations attending them within the great cities, London in particular, drove up the rates. Of the "reckless" lower class democracy rampant in his homeland, an Englishman announced to Americans that "it would not be frightened tomorrow if a great socialistic experiment were to cost it a hundred million."[78]

However, signs of the new fiscal style in the United States administered great shocks of their own to traditional viewpoints abroad as well as at home. Prior to the end of the Civil War, explained one Englishman, when American democracy was regarded as more ephemeral than it proved to be, experts had predicted that "the one grand evil of democracy would be meanness." Distrust of all official activities likely to enhance the "visible greatness of the state," coupled with an "ignorant impatience of taxation," were expected to keep popular governments on short financial tethers. Instead, with "universal suffrage and the richest of estates," the "extravagance of government" achieved heights undreamed of by a Hamilton or a Gallatin; even Ricardo or

Peel, it was claimed, "could not have been persuaded to believe [it] possible." Expenditures the size of the American pension list, for instance, would have been considered "too absurd for credence."[79] No wonder a dilettante who had the ear of Eastern Democrats in 1896, therefore, could write that "the common people . . . are bitten with heresy," a heresy deeper than Populism or the silver question, constituting a "new revolution" led by the "masses against the classes." The last quarter of the nineteenth century, concluded Richard Ely, the Christian Socialist and Johns Hopkins professorial authority on taxation, was marked by "a deep stirring of the masses—not a local stirring, not merely a national stirring but an international stirring of the masses" seeking changes in "the very foundations of the social order."[80] Change of this order could only come after the satisfaction of new claims against the public revenue and against private properties.

No doubt because they responded more positively to these facts than other Northern institutions, local party organizations suffered as no other institutions did from relentless attacks by the middle classes. Middle class spokesmen scored urban democracy as the major *cause* of fiscal breakdown and pilloried Irish immigrants as its chief *symbol;* but they damned political parties as the *vehicles* through which destruction of the old order was being accomplished. Party spirit, party loyalty, party discipline, and party men were all pronounced anathema. Branded for deficiency of "lawful public spirit," party government was sharply delineated by respectable men from sound government. The "consensus tradition" which Michael Wallace[81] suggests began dying out earlier in the century actually battled against professional politics long after the Jacksonian Era. As mechanisms for a "public will that [had] a right to be enforced," a problem Walter Lippmann and other neo-democratic thinkers grappled with early in the twentieth century, parties, thus, were believed to have been "jostled out of their appropriate functions." Instead, politics had become "the embodiment of perpetual conflicts between the respective selfishnesses," all claiming the right "to war on each other and society for ever."[82] Among the middle classes, obviously, a new explanation of the political process was inching its way to the fore; as a leading political economist summarized it at the turn of the century, "class politics is the essence of taxation,"[83] by which he meant that class politics was the essence of all fiscal conflict.

Linkage of party, spoils, patronage, and soaring public burdens made indictments of party seem easy. The "horde of officeholders, retainers, and party scavengers," or what Cornell's president described as "a crowd of illiterate peasants, freshly raked in from Irish bogs . . . Bohemian mines, or Italian robbers nests," were pictured as an endless human chain passing through the public coffers. Led by "disreputable" professionals, these noisome masses insured the perpetuation of party by plundering the public moneys that made "elections go right" and energized party.[84]

Specific attacks on political parties form a well-catalogued literature generally familiar to historians; but the drift of these attacks deserves emphasis because of the consequences that stemmed from attempts to act on them. Certainly the attacks ought not be treated merely as the tactical ploys of "outs" against "ins," for many were of a much more fundamental nature. Often they sought to abolish party as an effective, that is to say, as a *plural* political instrument that was responsive not only to the respectable but also to social forces above and below them. "Our complaint *is* that there is a party," protested a Baltimore merchant before a taxpayers' association in 1889; he wished that "there was none at all" and was sanguine enough "to indulge the belief that there will be none." Testifying to the New York Senate Committee on Municipal Affairs, a university president similarly concluded that history "without exception" indicated that efforts to curry popularity through partisanship ended in "tyranny, confiscation, and bloodshed." While party and partisanship were synonymous, wrote industrialist A. S. Colgar in 1886, "the day of emotional politics" hopefully was passing and he was prepared to hasten it. Professional politicians, he found, were no better fitted for governing than "pirates would have been for holding religious services;" they were "the natural enemy of every taxpayer." The new politics, he urged, ought to be "economical rather than sentimental. . . . *We will have a politics of dollars and cents.*"[85]

Ironically, it was the Democratic Party of Ohio which harbored the author of the lengthiest and most trenchant commentary on the purported political *mesalliance* between democracy, the "evils of party," and the country's money machinery until Ostrogorski's *Democracy and the Organization of Political Parties* appeared shortly after the turn of the century. The critic was Charles Reemelin, a native of South Germany, who at eighteen emigrated to Hamilton County (Cincinnati), Ohio in 1832. A successful merchant, he retired young, entered the bar in the 1840's and subsequently served in both branches of the state legislature, the State Constitutional Convention of 1850, and in various commission posts over the next thirty years, the last of them being the presidency of the Hamilton County Board of Control. A versatile and learned amateur, Reemelin published his *Critical Review of American Politics* in 1881, virtually summarizing middle class arguments against the new democracy, a democracy which because of its "misunderstanding as to the correlation of taxation and representation," in Reemelin's words, reputedly was embarked on "the most gigantic social spoilation by taxation ever known."

The masses' "insatiability and voraciousness for *voting rights*" and their "dumbness as to *tax-paying* duties," Reemelin argued, encouraged plunder "in the garb of public benefactions." Liberty, as he understood it, therefore had degenerated into having "all rights *per capita* and all duties and burdens *ad valorem*," thus permitting a "false distribution of wealth" to the advantage of "the supposed poor." To him, the real villain was party; "our party governments," he declared, "are sin let loose." Popular parties "domineering over government and spoilating society," he damned as the "most hideous of all tyrannies," turning constitutions "into jests, our administrations into dust, and our reforms . . . [into] nought." Of parties, "the truth is," he recorded:

> they have brutalized the public mind; and envenomed citizen against citizen; so they have rendered nearly impossible the election and appointment of good men; and are . . . a mere convenience for office seekers and jobbers. . . . What sense in talking about reforms of a government and its administration, which has been forced to surrender its most vital normal functions. . . . We have set aside a government that was, by constitutional rule, under considerable responsibility and limited in power, and have substituted for it . . . a government ruled by social elements, whose forces are now being intensified by enjoying political power, which are under no enforceable responsibility nor any tangible restraint.

If drastic, Reemelin's solution to such a condition was no more so than those toyed with by many other anxious men; "we see no remedy . . . except that American society becomes organic and wipes out its standing parties and their evil spirit.[86] . . . There are things," he concluded grimly, ". . . which can only be cured by destruction."[87]

In lieu of popular, professionalized parties, government, insofar as men like Reemelin were concerned, was to be run like a business—by experts and efficiently, efficiency being gauged by tenets of scientific administration and cost accounting. Government, especially municipal government, was to have "no political function;" rather it was to be directed by "business tact, skill, honesty, and a fair share of common sense." Such government, wrote President White of Cornell, was to be managed "as a piece of property by those who have created it, who have a title to it, or a real substantial part in it, and who therefore feel strongly their duty toward it." "It is a joint-stock affair," added Frank Crandon in the mid-'80's, "in which the taxpayers are the stockholders and to them substantially should the management of its business be committed."[88]

Thus, in their alarm over the fiscal manifestations of mass democracy, elements of the middle classes really opted for a "no-party government." What they believed they had was expensive, confiscatory, and dishonest government. An inexpensive, respectable government, honest in the bargain, represented to them an acceptable compromise between the "political idea" of party professionals and their own "corporate idea;" but it was an acceptable compromise *only* on the grounds that democracy learn to handle public moneys in a responsible way. The contradiction in this line of reasoning, of course, was apparent. According to their own definitions and descriptions, no such compromise with any known party seemed conceivable. Expensive party government could not be thrust from power; and any *party* dedicated to "business-like economy" was a paradox. The thinking of many otherwise sober and hard-headed men, as a result, retrospectively seems—as it then seemed to many politicians—academic, ineffectual, unrealistic, and parochial. It even belied an accurate reading by the middle classes of their own situation, for certainly the urban as well as some of the rural middle classes were gaining rather than losing power. Yet in politics as in economics they remained "scarcity-minded;" they had difficulty imagining the expansion of power in any sphere, their own included; instead, they reckoned that none could gain power except at someone else's expense.

Admittedly criticisms of this sort can be too wise after the fact. Middle class alarms were justified. The justification lay in the enormous magnitude of their social task, a task which, basically, consisted of providing incentives in an industrializing society while simultaneously maintaining the public order on which the safety of property, and hence as they understood it, the safety of liberty, rested.

It is necessary to mention only briefly that the fiscal problems generated by mass democracy below them were rendered more ominous for the middle classes by the pressures which they also felt being thrust upon Northern money machinery from above. Decades before the emergence of Progressivism, there was a widespread fear among the middling elements of society of being ground to pieces by the social extremes. They were very conscious in this connection of being a minority, although, they supposed, a dominant one.

Respectable men, therefore, lashed out at party not only because it converted the money machines to welfarism and other uncongenial popular uses, but also because political organizations were considered subservient to special interests and to "robber barons." In this light, Herbert Croly's restrospective remark in his *Progressive Democracy* (1914) that the most serious weakness of middle class reformism, that is, of Mugwumpery, during the late nineteenth century was its "easy acceptance of economic abuses" and its attendant failure to "suspect for one moment that there was anything radically wrong with the American economic system" was greatly overdrawn. On the contrary, from the middle classes came the only protest in the North that consistently—not just when the price of commodities fell or wages declined—exposed economic wrongs and declared forthrightly that, indeed, much *was* seriously wrong with the economic system. That their attempted reforms, as Croly suggested, appeared sterile, timid, or negative was another matter; from present perspectives it is difficult to see how it could have been otherwise, for the problems which they faced had become too complex for anything other than tedious and protracted treatment.

Meanwhile, they were neither indifferent to nor invariably naive about threats to the public fiscal establishment from above. Like many others from his part of society at the close of the 1880's, William Graham Sumner deplored America's swiftly rising plutocracy, not alone for its vulgarity but for the menace which, in his judgment, it posed to the vitality of the middle classes. Democratic political institutions, he feared, were too weak to resist the seductions of wealthy men. "Democracy," he noted, "has a whole set of institutions which are extra-legal" and which, consequently, were easily perverted. Party organization, he found "well adapted to the purposes of plutocracy" since parties had secretly evolved "a large but undefined field of legitimate or quasi-legitimate expenditure for which there is no audit." On these grounds, too, he warned against the expansion of governmental functions which placed "industrial interests" in contiguity to supplies of public money.[89] In the same admonitory vein, Albert Stickney likewise assailed "the rule of money" and the allegedly corrupt influences of rich men upon party to the detriment of the Treasury.[90] And Charles Reemelin whose contempt for the masses was blatant, similarly described "a private interest whose will is law, a standing public danger." Familiar with the corruptions of some private interests through his own pursuit of defalcations in the Ohio Treasury while serving as State Bank Commissioner, he denounced the all-too-frequent combinations of "commercial integrity and mercantile worth to form a socio-political partnership, with brazen partisan impudence." Just as it had supposedly surrendered to popular sovereignty in one quarter, party, felt Reemelin, had abandoned equally vital functions in another quarter to corporations and to the lobbies "of the great pecuniary interests."[91]

Thus, the great "devil theory" of the middle classes had dual application; it figured importantly in the interpretations which they placed on the breakdown of the old money machines and in the actions which they pursued as a consequence. For some of them, as for many of the rich, one set of these actions was evasive, hence destructive.

In this iron age, it is as hard a thing to persuade men to part with money, as to pull out their eyes . . . or cut off their hands.

HENRY SMITH, *Sermons* [17th Century]

A study of taxation is calculated to give one a rather pessimistic view of American law, American institutions, and American character.

RICHARD ELY, 1888

2

The Escape of the "New" and the Old Wealth

Failure of the general property tax as the mainstay of Northern state and local revenues was filled with ironies. Established in times of pervasive economic equality, it became a tax which created and perpetuated inequalities. Trimmed to the requirements of a rural economy and persistently supported by rural-dominated legislatures, it probably wrought as much havoc among the rural middle classes as it did among any other group. Designed to touch equitably upon individual holdings of all types of property, it was already failing by the mid-seventies to reach property in its commonest forms. Expected to fall most heavily on those best able to bear it, it tended to operate in the opposite manner; and yet some of its sharpest critics came from social elements which presumably escaped its heaviest incidence. Considered the tax best suited to a democracy, it was relatively effective in Pennsylvania where political organization was authoritarian by American standards and was relatively ineffective in Massachusetts where party organizations were among the most democratic in the North. In an era when the hallmark of administrative efforts was the trend toward centralization, it strengthened decentralized tendencies; and so on. Indeed, its curious features were legion.

Not only because it was the most central and massive flaw in state and local fiscal systems but also because it was the most obvious evidence of their breakdown, the historian has ample warrant to examine its failures before turning to various inequities it spawned.

Not the least of the ironies attending the tax arose from the disrepute into which it had fallen among the elected officials who were legally bound to assess and collect it. Typically, a New York assessor's report, for instance, blasted the general property tax as "a reproach to the state, an outrage upon the people . . . . a disgrace to civilization in the nineteenth century, and only worthy of an age of mental and moral darkness and degradation, when the only equal rights were those of the equal robber."[1] Consistently deplored by assessors and comptrollers in the Empire State as "unequal, unjust, and partial," it was castigated as "too glaring and . . . too oppressive to be longer tolerated." Drawn from annual reports spanning a full generation after the Civil War, such estimates were but a few of the signs of official disillusionment with it in New York State.[2]

Such disenchantment characterized the official attitude in every Northern state. In Illinois, one high official, precisely like those who came before or after him, described the state's general property tax in 1871 as "without exception . . . the most objectionable law that was ever proposed." Unaware of another act so "justly odious and detestable," he found that its provisions created "a grand inquisitorial and confiscatory office, clothed with powers . . . which if enforced would produce a revolution in Austria or Turkey."[3] By still another midwestern auditor, the tax was depicted as "an imperfect exhibit of antiquated, accidental, unjust, demoralizing, and absurd methods—not worthy of being called a system." Officials in Massachusetts deprecated their own system as without parallel since the Middle Ages; Thomas Hills, Boston's chief assessor, for example, could find "no student of taxation or thoughtful man who can say a word in its behalf." New York City's most learned tax expert, E. R. A. Seligman, recorded that "no institution [had] evoked more angry protest, more earnest dissatisfaction." Maryland tax official and political economist, Richard Ely, similarly rejected the primitive general tax "as not answering the requirements of practical morality,"[4] while in Pennsylvania, generally regarded as a model of equity in the rank jungle of American state and local taxation, a commonwealth official volunteered that "all candid and well-informed persons" conceded "that our present tax system is . . . grossly inequitable."[5] By the eighties, such voices had become a chorus.

Nourished by ill-defined concepts of public purpose and by casual conceptions of citizenship, this contempt for the general property tax, hence for the fiscal systems which it supported, served as an index of its failure; but the technical causes of failure were due largely to evasions of the tax, to the subsequent inelasticity of revenues, and to the inequalities which were so widely produced. Inequities, in turn, encouraged further abuses. There was a tendency for each tax commissioner's office to become the vortex of a vicious cycle of evasion and inequity which frustrated progress.

In the decades following 1865, as a result, states of the iron rectangle experienced a massive flight of capital playing fugitive from the reach of government. "I believe one of the articles of faith of humanity is to beat the tax collector," declared Joseph Weeks, president of the Pennsylvania Tax Conference before the Cincinnati Manufacturers' Association in 1894. Beating the collector, he added, was "the only article of faith they have, and they live up to that with religious zeal."[6] But it was the zeal which chiselers displayed specifically toward the weakest part of the general property tax, namely, the tax on personal property, that Weeks had in mind, and its development merits brief comment.

The taxation of personalty was essentially a rural idea, first inspired in the United States by agrarian democrats of the 1850's seeking to "insure equality and uniformity" in taxation. Legislatures soon reflected the popular theory that in order to accomplish this it was "necessary to subject *all* property to assessment," especially "any form of money capital." Many observers labelled the idea a mistake; but at the time the protests seemed academic. Much of the country's property was still in tangible form and the demands for fresh revenues were relatively modest. Accordingly, the tax caused little trouble; indeed, it was even politic, and it therefore spread universally across the North.

Irrespective of its original intent or merits, personal property taxation was quickly made obsolete by events. Within twenty years after Appomattox, the bulk of Northern property had assumed new shapes: machinery, credits, securities, mortgages, savings, exchange values, "going concerns," and personal possessions. If much of this wealth was tangible, just as the "old wealth" had been, much more of it was intangible, hard to locate, hard to value. Existing fiscal systems embodied neither the experience nor the statutory equipment to handle it properly. As an integral part of the general tax, its unworkability thus created more problems than revenues.

And there were other difficulties. Most intangible wealth was located in cities, and American cities, unlike those of Europe, were creatures of state legislatures which, if not solely dominated by farmers, were dominated conjointly by farmers and the mercantile and legal interests of the rural townships, satirized in their more predatory functions by Thorstein Veblen. No other groups evinced greater affection for personal property taxation and, as might have been expected, no others tried more strenuously to impose their fiscal, hence their social values, upon the cities.

Rural ability to accomplish this was amply demonstrated by New England legislatures late in the last century. In Maine, Vermont, New Hampshire, and Connecticut men who described themselves as "farmers" composed the largest occupational bloc in both branches of the legislatures. Farmers also constituted the largest group in the upper house of the Rhode Island legislature. Only a small percentage of Massachusetts legislators were self-styled farmers, but on closer inspection even there, proportioning representation to population, farmers were over-represented and many of the 87 lawyers and merchants accounting for a third of the assembly were themselves from small agricultural communities.

Legislative apportionment revealed rural legislative power, for throughout the late nineteenth century and into the twentieth century, the countryside, its villages, towns, and small cities, tended to gain relative strength in the legislatures as the larger cities drained population from it. Before 1900 New England, for example, was a network of rotten boroughs. Warren, Connecticut, a town of 412 souls placed one representative in the legislature, while New Haven with 133,605 seated only two representatives. Four of the state's smallest towns with a total population of 1500 enjoyed four representatives against only twice that number to represent the 407,715 inhabitants of the four largest cities. Thus, Tolland County with 3% of the State's population in sparsely settled farming country sent 8.3% of the representatives to the legislature although New Haven, by contrast, with 30% of the population supplied only 16.6% of the representation. Government elsewhere in New England was, in this sense, government by rural towns.

The same was true outside of the Northeast. In New Jersey equal representation at Trenton went to counties having as few as 12,000 and as many as 328,000 people. Within New York State, the political emasculation of Brooklyn and New York City were classic examples of cities governed *in absentia* by malapportioned legislatures. In Wisconsin during the eighties, apportionment favoring underpopulated districts became a commonplace of state politics, while in Michigan neither the reapportionment laws of 1885 nor of 1891 satisfied the United States Supreme Court as being valid, so advantaged was the countryside.[7]

Malapportionment bred coalitions of overrepresented "upstate" interests which inhibited urban development through fiscal policies devised beyond the influence of the great municipal corporations. If the results of these policies eventually distressed the countryman and his legislative allies, as they did, it was not because such policies were of someone else's making. *The Nation* made the point clearly in 1881. Attempts to "tax intangible or invisible property," it noted, lay at the heart of the fiscal breakdown apparent nearly everywhere, but efforts to correct the situation ran "counter to all the fiscal traditions of the farmer, who constituted the great bulk of the constituency of every legislature." A few farmers themselves acknowledged that "it was entirely by their vote that the existing system [was] . . . maintained," thanks to a "political influence vastly out of proportion to their numbers" and a burning "hope of getting at the rich bondholders and goldbugs somehow."[8]

Men of property in Northern cities read the message: the countryside was after their property and it was armed by statute to get it. Farmers, on the other hand, believed that their property was in the grasp of capitalists and financiers. Thus the stage was set for tax evasion on a scale commensurate with Americans' traditional way of doing things.

Taxation of the "new wealth" was dependent upon accurate valuation and assessment for success and throughout the iron rectangle there was plenty to assess and to value. Common sense said so; public officials knew it; censuses confirmed it; and individuals and communities boasted proudly of what they had heaped up so prodigiously.

That is, they boasted until the assessor or tax collector appeared. Then destructive waves of loss, indebtedness, and impoverishment swept even the smallest bastions of capital. Pillars of the community collapsed; capital disappeared or changed form. Responsibility, honesty, integrity, duty, dedication, and good citizenship obeyed the law of the marketplace, rising in desirability as they became scarcer.

Evasion of the general property tax began with perjury. Legal ritual prescribed great oaths for the two principals directly involved in the taxing process: the assessor and the taxpayer. Assessors usually swore to assess at "full market value," "selling value," "fair value," or the like. Where the law made taxpapers their own assessor, they were obliged to swear that their estimates were true.

Throughout the North, notwithstanding the fact that it was illegal and "immoral," it was commonplace for either assessors or taxpayers, or both, to lie. Fiscal honesty where evident was memorable. Baltimoreans in 1888 did empower a chief assessor who lived up to the letter of his oath and Thomas Hills, Chairman of Boston's Board of Assessors from 1866 to 1892, was notorious for his undemocratic rectitude. There were others; but all were remarkable for their rarity.

Before the enactment of Prohibition probably nothing in American life entailed more calculated or premeditated lying than the general property tax. "In some states," wrote an observer in the nineties, "the business of perjury is confined to the assessors who regularly make returns they know to be false, but cannot make true." In Connecticut, Ohio, Vermont, and several midwestern states, perjury was the business of the taxpayer and, as inquiries, commissions, and exposés indicated, their business had boomed after the war. "Their scrupulous consciences," wrote one sardonic reformer, found "a way of escape by omitting . . . to take the oath which they sign;" they were "innocent of everything," he declared, "except lying." Those who were "delicately conscientious" induced others to sign for them, or a "considerate notary" certified the oath before it was taken, "after which it . . . [was] not taken at all." After a thorough survey of tax oaths, one fiscal expert mockingly admitted that "one's faith in American truthfulness" was revived, for where tax blanks were "diligently circulated and oaths insisted upon, the average man will return ten, if not fifteen percent of his property; whereas in the absence of this appeal to piety, he will return nothing at all."[9] Alternatives to the oath, unfortunately, were all unpromising for, among other things, they involved honest law enforcement.

The futility of oaths in the major states was recognized; yet there lingered a fear of abolishing them. A New York State legislative committee in 1862–63 concluded, for example, that a "certain way" of securing taxes was to place every man "under the solemnity of an oath," forcing him to list his property publicly. In deference to "strong objections made to the public inquisition of the listing system," however, the committee conceded that oaths and accompanying examinations should be confined to the assessor and the taxpayer alone, thus stripping the oath of whatever public sanction it might have enjoyed.[10] Admittedly such rituals coaxed forth more revenue than threats of prosecutions or penalties, while maintaining the fiction of American moral superiority to the taxpayers of Imperial Rome, fifteenth century Spain, or pre-Victorian England. But on balance they did not impair evasion.

Perjured assessments and taxpayers' lies produced an endless series of anomalous situations in major Northern cities. In New York City, where there was undoubtedly more personal property as the law defined it than anywhere else on the continent, real estate in 1869 was valued at $684 million, a ratio of two and a half times greater than the valuation of personalty. In Brooklyn, realty was officially valued at $183 million, personalty at a mere $17.5 million, a ratio of one to ten and a half. Rochester's deposits in savings banks in 1870 amounted to twenty-five times the total of the city's assessed personalty, the overall ratio of personalty to realty being one to six and a half. Similar ratios from Buffalo and Albany indicated real estate valuations running from four to four and a half times higher than valuations of personal property. State officials and legislators, of course, never had the slightest doubt about what was happening.[11]

New York City's tax rolls are more informative about the extent of personalty evasion than overall ratios. Dates selected for discussion are almost totally irrelevant for the situation remained substantially the same between 1860 and 1920. With a population of over one million in

1875, for instance, the city had only 8900 names on the rolls admitting liability for "household furniture, money, goods, chattels, debts due from solvent debtors whether on account of contract note, bonds, mortgages, public stocks and stocks in moneyed corporations." Yet city tax commissioners conservatively estimated local personalty to be worth two billion dollars. Again, in 1890 real estate was assessed at $194 million, nine times more than personalty. When the local commissioners opened their books for scrutiny, $1650 million listed in personalty was sworn down to one-eighth of that figure and the number of individuals obligated for personal property taxes was reduced from 24,030 to 13,890.[12] Naturally, with debts deductible, not all personalty was taxable, but reductions of this magnitude were correctly interpreted as signs of gigantic evasion.

The specifics of evasion are easily discovered. In 1889 the New York Surrogate's Office valued the Moses Taylor Estate at $20 million, though not all was liable to taxation. But when a representative of the estate met with Commissioner Donnelly, they decided to negotiate and an estate officially considered taxable on $8 million settled for a liability of half that amount. Similarly when alive, William H. Vanderbilt had paid taxes on $500,000 in personalty; but he was clearly modest. After his death his personal property, "as far as ascertainable," was officially placed at $40 million, again, to be sure, not all taxable. That *any* remained taxable indeed, seems remarkable for the estate's legal representative was the successful railroad attorney and politician, Chauncey Depew. Depew regally offered to pay Tax Commissioners Fieter and Donnelly on one-tenth of Vanderbilt's liabilities. They demurred; but "after consulting for a day or two," they testified, Depew "informed us that if we attempted to press them too hard, he would take proceedings by which most of the securities would be placed beyond our reach." Asked by state officials if Depew's move was "equivalent to a threat to avoid taxation," Tax Commissioner Coleman replied that "it was nothing but what other people are doing all the time." The commissioner might have reflected, however, that "other people" generally operated on a smaller scale.[13]

Evasion was often perpetrated openly and defiantly. Owing New York City $50,000 in personal property taxes, soap manufacturer Babbitt brazenly confronted Tax Commissioner Andrews in the eighties almost daring him to try to collect. Having come to New York with $250,000 in government bonds, Babbitt, in his own words, "went to the bank and borrowed $250,000 on it and then started his business." He frankly admitted that he had done so "for the purpose of avoiding taxation," adding that he "did not intend to pay any personal tax." A conscientious commissioner, Andrews entered litigation to publicize the Babbitt case; unfortunately for the official position, however, the court held for Babbitt and from that time on his victory against tax officials earned him such renown that his business success was "phenomenal."[14]

Certainly men like Babbitt had never been alone. James Bell, former chairman of New York's Legislative Tax Committee of 1862, debating in the State Constitutional Convention of 1867–68, noted that during interrogations of New York's principal men of "intelligence and busiess capacity," he had asked directly if the $80 million in assessed personalty represented as much as one-third of the city's actual personalty holdings. In reply the representative of a major firm stated that "he knew persons owing as much personal property as that within his limited circle of acquaintances." Another legislator, in fact, remarked that he could personally name "*thirty* men whose aggregate wealth is $450,000,000," a sum exceeding by $25 million the state's total valuation of all personal property.[15]

A quarter of a century later with identical laws still in effect little had changed in the city except magnitudes. Roswell Flower, then a New York congressman but shortly afterwards (in 1892) governor, boasted of the staggering wealth of his district, Manhattan's Twelfth, a small area lying between East 40th Street and 68th Street, the East River and 7th Avenue. Flower described the tiny Twelfth as "richer than any state in the Union except New York and Pennsylvania." Nor was this surprising. Residents included several of the Vanderbilts, a handful of Rockefellers, Russell Sage, D. O. Mills, and Jay Gould and family, among others. Even without the Astors, who lived just beyond the pale, their "united possessions" came to more than $4 billion dollars, twice the total valuation of all of the city's realty and personalty under the general property tax, which in that year, 1890, stood at $1696 million.[16]

The well-to-do who paid fully or at all were often simply ignorant rather than honest. Knowing their publics, tax officials tried keeping them that way, of course. Thus when New York Tax Commissioner Andrews insisted on testifying in 1874 before a state committee investigating tax evasion, his colleagues warned that such testimony was tantamount to giving information to the enemy; "I begged him not to expose our methods," declared another commissioner. But, as expected, Andrews' replies to the committee were swiftly collated in a pamphlet destined for the hands of potential tax dodgers. Law firms, for example, snapped up this material and reportedly "made from $50,000 to $75,000 a year getting hold of people who had always paid their taxes in ignorance of what the law really was on the subject."[17] Minting money from a public anxious to cheat itself seemed somehow eminently practical in many quarters.

Men pressed into payment of a sum set arbitrarily by the commissioners did so only once; "that would be the last time that we would be able to catch them," confessed one official. This was true because in New York as elsewhere the "legal" means of escape were so numerous. Early in December each year, for instance, many of the wealthy converted their taxable securities into non-taxable ones, holding them for twenty to thirty days "so they can make affidavits, and change them back again." Officials guessed that the practice involved "hundreds of millions." At assessment time in the spring, there were additional flurries of activity on the exchanges, in banks, investment houses, and law offices as property altered form or disappeared from sight for a brief time.[18]

City tax machinery provided "virtually nothing more than a rough and ready way of catching what you can," as one commissioner explained it. Businessmen who were taxable on miscellaneous goods, on goods owned and manufactured in the city, and on goods bought with U.S. bonds, or capitalists who were taxable on their investments in ships registered at New York, on local mortgages, money in checks, promissory notes, state or city bonds, certificates of corporate indebtedness, certificates of deposit in local banks, or specie in their safes found plenty of "ratholes" for their money in various types of conversion. They shifted taxable capital to such non-taxable forms as imported, consigned, or manufactured goods from New Jersey, to ships registered in other ports, to New Jersey mortgages, to certificates of deposit in the Subtreasury, to specie in the assay office, or to checks on the U.S. Treasury, Treasury notes, U.S. certificates of indebtedness, U.S. bonds, or capital borrowed on U.S. bonds. Or, even more simply, they shifted money from the company safe to their pockets.[19]

Though fraud, perjury, and subterfuge were the rule, the wealthy were not solely culpable for such actions. Of forty leading Democratic politicians in New York City and Brooklyn, I can find only two in 1899 who were prepared to stand assessment or to pay on what they were assessed for their personalty. One was the brilliant and independently wealthy reform mayor of Brooklyn, Seth Low, who paid on an estimate of $167,000; the other was George Clasen who swore down his $75,000 assessment to $10,000 but willingly paid on that sum. Charles Murphy, Ed Lauterbach, Tim Sullivan, and the redoubtable George Washington Plunkitt, politicos all, either escaped assessment entirely or swore off everything they were assessed on personalty. Republican leaders followed suit. Charles Lexow who startled New Yorkers with his famous investigation of the New York Police Department early in the nineties, Frank Moss, the leading counsel of the Mazet Committee investigation of 1899–1900, and Lemuel Quigg, one of Boss Platt's chief lieutenants, all escaped assessment although all were men of substantial means. Another twenty-five of the principal Republicans of the City of New York were either unassessed or swore their assessments away.[20] By comparison, the behavior of J. P. Morgan toward his obligations seemed almost gallant. Morgan's tax affidavit for 1899 showed a one million dollar personalty assessment. Appearing before a local tax commissioner, Morgan "swore to the usual affidavit saying that he was a banker, with no personal property over debts other than untaxable assets;" nevertheless, he volunteered to be assessed at $400,000 and to pay on that sum. Gratified, the commissioner, whose job was cut for realists, consented.[21]

In other municipalities of the North, too, the evasion of personalty taxation became a scandal which, like dives and brothels, thrived on an often respectable clientele. In Cincinnati in 1866, personal property was valued at several hundred thousand dollars more than realty, a very rare situation; but three years later, despite its undoubted increase, personalty declined in value by twelve percent. Information from the annual reports of Ohio auditors and assessors indicated that in 1887 only about one-third as much personalty was on the books as realty, although the proportions certainly should have been reversed in the "city counties."[22] Hamilton County, Reemelin's bailiwick, for instance, yielded a 1 to 3 ratio indicating that its burghers were fully as ingenious as their Eastern counterparts.[23]

But even these statistics obscured the "desolating wave of poverty" that periodically swept over the cities of Ohio. Cincinnati boasted over 13,000 private pleasure carriages in 1882, but taxation rapidly cleared traffic; in 1887 its citizens claimed only 9800 of them. Watches which nestled over the paunches of the comfortable "certainly can and do 'go' with a rapidity not often equalled," declared a disgusted tax reformer. Money on hand vanished even more swiftly; the amount available for assessment in 1882 was cut by half five years later; taxable credits similarly shrank by twelve and one-half percent. Cincinnati's banks proudly listed over $29 million in deposits for advertising purposes but revealed only one twenty-ninth of that sum to the gaze of assessors. Comparable figures from Cleveland indicated that only one sixty-third of its bank deposits had been opened to public officials while in Toledo less than an eighth of local deposits was acknowledged for tax purposes.

Driven to measures then regarded as so novel that they were "unknown or unheard of before . . . in any community under English law or English institutions," Hamilton County, Ohio in 1881 hired professional tax inquisitors to check evasion. Other city counties quickly adopted the same course. But in their desperation public officials proved either less prudent or less self-interested than the avid inquisitors themselves. Each of three statutes (1881, 1885, and 1888) concerning the inquisitorial system, in fact, had been enacted principally through the efforts of two enterprising brothers, C. E. and Henry W. Morgenthaler. Legally limiting themselves to a 20% compensation for the addition of properties to the tax rolls and the collection of secreted sums, they tried to make communal immorality profitable.[24]

Instead, the inquisitors became enmeshed in their own scandals in cities and counties which, ostensibly, they served.[25] They first of all sought only the richest evaders against whom they brought dramatic legal actions for the recovery of large sums; but after the subsidence of such bombast, they usually settled, on the public's behalf, for a mere bagatelle. They were not, of course, responsible officials and their relationship to government was at best quasi-public; yet as we know from the state's own evidence, the vague lines between private and public affairs allowed them inordinate influence over many county auditors and assessors. Moreover, it was an influence they did not hesitate to use. As the Ohio General Assembly discovered in 1896, the inquisitors often entered no bids for their contracts; often they engineered phony settlements with perjurers and frauds. And, though they were beyond legal culpability, the Morgenthalers profiteered from their unmonitored activities. Over a twelve-year period only $840,000 was added by them to Cleveland's tax collections, while the amount they retained for that city's work alone was almost a quarter of a million dollars. Questioned about their profits, the brothers argued that they required high pay in order to operate effectively; it developed that they had secured most of their evidence by systematic bribery.[26]

The real costs of the Ohio inquisitor system soon became manifest however pressing the omnipresent problems of fiscal collapse to which the system was addressed. In 1866 realty composed 60% of the state's total valuation, personalty the balance. Personalty increased steadily, if undramatically, until 1875; it then declined during the depression of the seventies, rose slowly in 1892 and *declined* again by 1895. This deterioration in value affected tangible and intangible properties alike: livestock, merchants' returns, manufacturers' property, and investments in the new wealth. Yet despite linear zigs and zags we know that the main indices of economic growth in which Ohio shared were all upward during the late nineteenth century.[27] Nevertheless under the inquisitors, realty climbed to 70% of the total valuation; credits in Hamilton County dropped by two-thirds; and it was reliably estimated that between 1882 and 1892 $100 million in capital had been driven out of Cleveland alone by the system.

No inquisitors worked in Massachusetts; indeed, the iron dictum of that most democratic of commonwealths might have been expected to crush evasion by sheer weight of official pronouncement. "The individual person," declared the state's commissioners of taxation in 1875, "has no inalienable rights except to his own righteousness. His property, his labor, his liberty, his life, are not inalienably his. The State," continued the commissioners, "may demand everything which belongs to a man, except his manhood and his moral integrity, which he has no right ever to surrender." Unfortunately the doughty capitalists of Massachusetts comported themselves like their brethren elsewhere and evasions ran into hundreds of millions of dollars annually. The state could demand what it pleased; the issue became what could it get.[28]

Seeking "goods, chattels, money, and effects, wherever they are . . . ships and vessels at home or abroad, public stocks and securities, stocks in turnpikes, bridges, and moneyed corporations, within or without the State," the Massachusetts tax commissioners had their hands full; as a consequence, the extent of evasion was daily made apparent. Prior to its annexation to Boston, Dorchester's valuation of personalty under a regime of popularly elected assessors was about $15 million; the post-annexation valuation of 1869 resulted in a 33% increase and led Boston commissioners to remark wryly that the system of taxation "so far as Dorchester was concerned" had been "most imperfectly administered."[29] It was also the Boston Commissioners who designated the City of Nahant "the taxpayers' paradise" because, like a number of other commonwealth cities, it owed its vitality to its function as a tax haven for the comfortable classes of Boston. Officially, estimates were that Boston, in fact, lost $17 million from its assessment rolls between 1869 and 1875 because of "domiciliary changes" by residents who could thereby "evade their just responsibilities." Boston's ruggedly honest chief assessor, Thomas Hills, charged that $13,900,000 in taxable values was carried out of the commonwealth itself between 1869 and 1873 to evade taxation. Nearly $2 million of it represented the assessable estate of people "who established a residence" at Newport and yet who "except for a few weeks in summer . . . could be seen moving about in their accustomed routines" in Boston, whose residents they actually were.[30]

Both the human geography and the economic development of Massachusetts were substantially altered by tax evaders seeking escape from the pall of general property taxation. There were many Nahants and Newports. Early in the eighties more than $9 million "found a lodgment" in eight of the commonwealth's towns, where on what state officers called "the club principle," reputable citizens enjoyed the advantages of rural assessments with city privileges. These towns flourished on public perjury. Assessors lured evaders into them by guaranteeing specially tailored tax rates; and the guarantees were easy to keep inviolable for, of course, the assessors were elected to their jobs.[31]

The state itself revealed specifics of the "club principle." In 1870, for instance, a $2 million dollar piece of personal estate migrated from

Boston to disappear from the ken of the law in a Worcester County town whose total valuation of personalty *after* the addition was only $1,383,915. Another $750,000 block of personalty fled Boston to a Norfolk County town in 1872; yet the town's valuation rose by only a quarter of a million dollars. Attacking the same principle in 1877, William Minot compiled a roster of men whom he personally knew to live and work in Boston whose property aggregated over $260 million, but whose residences for tax purposes were claimed in out-lying communities. As he noted, the millionaire who spent the first of May in Boston for assessment felt he paid a $12,700 penalty for doing so; and he enjoyed alternatives. On an "all or nothing" basis he was quite capable of driving the assessors of other communities into harboring him against Boston taxes. Honest men angrily dismissed such chiselers as incapable of loving their neighbors, but Minot realized that the question was really whether they were prepared "to love their neighbors *sixty percent* better than themselves."[32]

The persistence of these practices was notorious; when the State reexamined its tax laws in 1897, it seemed that time had stood still. Due to "negligent and even culpable administration of the law," personalty kept crowding into favored towns after its flight from the Boston area and rich men continued their collusion with local assessors as to the amount for which they shall be taxed." Flourishing on evasion, Nahant sent Henry Cabot Lodge to the Senate after he had moderated its town meeting for many years; or, as the state's wealthy, Mugwumpish assistant attorney general put it, Nahant continued "to serve up Boston's ideals . . . all cold roasted."[33] Almost a tradition by the nineties, the avoidance of taxation promoted the concentration of personalty into a favored six percent of the commonwealth's towns, giving them one-fourth of the assessed intangibles in the state. Money, hundreds of millions of dollars of it, was as malapportioned as political representation. Indeed, one of the most galling aspects of evasion was that it decreased total valuation and proportionately raised state and county taxes in every community except those thriving on parasitism.

Along with the flight of capital, the evasion of obligations on credits was particularly widespread. The methods employed in these dodges were familiar to public officers. On assessment day a merchant with $100,000 in merchandise reduced his stock to $25,000. The $75,000 representing the balance of the $100,000 and $5000 in profits were then listed among his assets as bills receivable. By law, of course, he should have been assessed for $105,000. But just before May Day, in order to escape such an assessment, he bought $80,000 in non-taxable U.S. bonds, giving the broker his note and leaving his bills receivable as collateral for payment. Then, he prepared his return, offering a tax schedule of $25,000 of stock-in-trade. An honest assessor would promptly remind him that it was commonly understood that he was doing business on $100,000 in capital. That the merchant could readily acknowledge, *except* that $80,000 of it was invested in U.S. bonds. "Have you no bills receivable for merchandise sold?" the assessor would ask. Yes, he would admit that he did, *except* that he had "no money at interest or debts due him for more that he is indebted or pays interest for." The assessor was then obliged to accept the $25,000 valuation and "the rest of the community [was] . . . assessed for the balance." Meantime the merchant returned to his broker, sold the bonds, used the money to discharge his note, and retired from his joust with the commonwealth $1200 richer.[34]

For men of this stamp, federalism was often a blunt instrument. Mortgage holders often found it profitable to employ U.S. bonds as temporary investments to allow the exemption of other properties. The dodge was beautifully flexible. Landowners could cut up property into building lots, selling them to purchasers on special terms: the owners giving bond, for instance, agreeing to the conveyance of the land for a certain price within a certain number of years. Purchasers, of course, were granted possession and building rights since the agreement stipulated that all taxes on the land and interest payments on the principal were to be handled by the buyer until the principal was fully paid. Thereafter, not even the interest paid to the seller was left taxable. Here, again, "indebtedness" screened personalty from public responsibility, and in Massachusetts, as in a majority of Northern states, debts used by "individuals of easy conscience" proved invulnerable to assessors or to tax investigations. Sanford Church made the case with blunt accuracy when he told the New York Constitutional Convention in 1867 that "in the country, and in the towns and cities in the interior of the state, the rule is almost universal for persons to get up an indebtedness of some kind" in hopes of beating the tax collector.[35]

Otherwise useful institutions sometimes became the screens behind which evaders cached their wealth. Massachusetts instructed its officers to exercise "especial care" in watching "institutions . . . which may enable those who have abundant means, combined with leisure, ingenuity, and the disposition, to evade taxation" after the perversion of savings banks came to light. Prior to the end of the Civil War, savings banks had an eleemosynary character, serving chiefly as depositories for poor but thrifty workingmen whose small accumulations were supposedly an investment in a better future. Tax exemption usually followed public recognition of this worthy function, or, as was the case in Massachusetts, such banks were taxed at a very nominal rate. In 1862, for example, their deposits were taxed only a half of one percent; and while the rate rose slightly later, the amount of revenue raised from deposits wes quite small.[36]

During the late sixties, however, the deposits of these favored banks grew so swiftly that it might have been presumed that the poor were rapidly increasing in number or were fast becoming genuinely affluent. A distressing fund of evidence soon forced state officials to draw the obvious conclusion and though bank owners denied that their vaults were a haven for wealthy tax dodgers, Governor Clafin, armed with contrary data, reported to the legislature in 1871 that it was "very evident that a large share" of the increase in deposits was "not the savings of labor," but rather represented "more deposits by capitalists."[37]

Clafin's case won support from two important sources in state government. The Senate Committee on Expenditures agreed on its own evidence that the deposits "belong to people able to take care of their own property" who were mainly eager "to secure high interest rates, and the exemption from taxation." And the newly created Massachusetts Bureau of Labor Statistics supplied additional data in 1872. Conceding to the bankers that the bulk of their depositors were, indeed, wage earners, the bureau nonetheless argued that "the great sums generally credited to . . . [the banks] are not the savings of wage labor;" on the contrary, its investigations showed that they were derived from "profit upon labor in some form." Although the banks rejected such conclusions, the bureau indefatigably gathered more facts and reported with greater directness in 1873 that far from serving mainly as banks of discount, savings banks were serving "manufacturers, traders, and lawyers" as places of "safety and convenience . . . to escape taxation." When savings banks located in rural sections of the state tripled their deposits inside of three years, as one of them did by boldly soliciting business in newspapers and circulars at "seven percent on the money free of taxes," the bureau's contentions were clinched.[38] Coupled with the fact that, overall, between 1861 and 1876, savings bank deposits increased fivefold while, by contrast, the whole of the commonwealth's taxable property had barely doubled itself, grounds were laid for legislation allowing the state to recoup a portion of the properties to which it felt entitled.[39]

The evasion of taxation on personalty in the cities and towns of Massachusetts was typical of the ingenuity that ran riot along this line nearly everywhere in the North. Boston currency *Sixes,* generally considered as safe as U.S. bonds, came into popularity by the mid-seventies because, despite their legal susceptibility to taxation, they were "so easily kept from the sight of the tax gatherers as to be practically . . . untaxable." Their worth as a dodge even brought a swift increase in their price on the market.[40] Or, to illustrate other latent affronts to the good sense of most communities, one need only look at the way assessments of personal estate allowed the rich throughout the century to avoid public obligation. In 1875, for instance, Boston's personalty was assessed at $235 million. The city's Fourth and Fifth Wards together accounted for $89 million of the total, largely because taxes there fell on business capital, merchandise, trade income, and "averages too notoriously known to escape." No one could suppose that the balance of the community's personal estate revenues represented a fair distribution of burdens. The Sixth Ward alone could easily have absorbed the balance several times over. With the "fortunes of a locality where the greater part of Boston's wealthy men live," noted William Minot, a different conclusion would have been ridiculous. Minot himself cited half a dozen households in this neighborhood which were worth $50 million and that still left another 5000 adult males, 3372 of whom admitted residence in the Sixth, to swell the total of personalty there.[41]

Appearances suggest that farmers, and certainly those of the late nineteenth century, were ill-equipped to evade taxation on their personalty, isolated as they often were and exposed to the gaze of assessors, tax collectors, and neighbors. Their capital and livestock were difficult to hide and their commercial relations in their villages or towns were ostensibly an open book. Even among urbanites who were aware of the hostile rural origins of the general property tax, a presumption of innocence favored the farmers' complaints about taxation, and the rural orientation of state legislatures, along with lingering myths of rural virtue, doubtless strengthened the assumption.

But this presumption demands refinement. There were, to begin with, several types of farmers within most agricultural localities and they were not equally affected by taxation. Furthermore, evidence indicates that if livestock and machinery were hard to conceal from the authorities, this was a limitation but by no means and absolute bar to the farmers' ability to evade taxes. Unquestionably some farmers bore a grossly disproportionate share of taxation compared with the rich of New York's Twelfth District or of Boston's Sixth Ward; these numerous cases in most parts of the North are not here at issue. Nevertheless, many farmers simply did not bear any such onerous burdens and shirked those obligations which by law they should have paid. Legally, if not morally, they were no more justified in doing so than the urban property holder or the corporate tax-dodgers whom rural-inspired personalty taxes were primarily designed to catch.

Clearly, the basic administration of taxation often worked in the farmers' behalf. Throughout the iron rectangle, rural assessors were usually farmers themselves. We know this from the testimony of tax commissions from Massachusetts to Iowa, from tax reformers, students of taxation, and the reports of county commissioners. Obviously this did not prevent discrimination between rural townsmen, villagers, or local worthies over their less influential countrymen. But the grand disposition of country assessors was to favor their own people against the citizens of the larger towns and cities. Systematic perjury, compromises, or collusion of this sort may have come from deep convictions about the "plight" of their section, but it was also mixed with crass self-interest. Certainly much of the rural assessors' behavior was determined by the fact that they were elected to office by the people they assessed and by the fact that subsequent to election they enjoyed considerable freedom from supervision. A decentralized administration, along with broad areas of discretion, left assessors in a position to serve the advantage of many individuals in their districts.[42]

Since personalty taxes allegedly bore most heavily upon farmers, the impressive and widespread evidence of the evasion of these taxes in the countryside was not surprising. In fifteen of New York's rural counties in 1870, the state comptroller's report showed a flight of personalty analogous to the ones underway in the cities during years when personal estate was accumulating steadily. A rule-of-thumb comparison indicates that in the major cities of New York State about three times as much realty appeared on assessment rolls as personalty[43] and in all of these cities evasion was extensive; rural assessments against this urban background were so strikingly disproportionate in the last third of the nineteenth century that the state comptroller labelled them both outrageous and ludicrous. Taking Delaware, Cortland, Schoharie, Monroe, Alleghany, St. Lawrence, Schuyler, Essex, and Hamilton counties, he revealed that at the lowest estimate six dollars in realty was assessed for every one dollar in personalty, while at the other extreme sixty-nine dollars in realty was assessed for every one dollar in personal estate. For these nine counties the average assessment of one dollar in personalty for every eighteen in realty was markedly below the state's urban average. Moreover, in counties such as Dutchess, Westchester, Erie, and Monroe where there was no decrease in personalty, as was the case in many other counties during the last third of the century, the increase was so slight that the assumption of rural evasion remained valid. If injustice threatened, a number of assessors and farmers were obviously dancing nimbly aside.[44]

Studies of farm tax trends in relation to other economic factors, as well as in relation to comparative urban data, sustain the impression that many farmers avoided the incidence of the general property tax on personalty, and, although it is not of primary concern at the moment, also escaped the full weight of taxes on real estate.

Reports of the New York State Tax Commission, covering 34 rural townships from the early eighties until 1924, revealed several significant facts. First, from the middle eighties until 1906, the rise in general property taxation was negligible; averaged out, taxes were almost stationary. During the same period, up to 1896, a time of declining farm wholesale prices, the assessed valuation of personalty and realty fell. Except for a dramatic two-year upsurge in personalty assessments from 1896–98, the decrease in assessments was steady and tremendous; one can hardly doubt that in conjunction with the migration of rural populations there was massive evasion through perjury and under-assessment. National census data furnish other clues to this; they indicate that from 1880 to 1924 the value of farm properties rose by 50%. By 1924, to be sure, taxation had increased considerably more than rural property values and farmers were in a serious bind. For the nineteenth century, however, this rise in values juxtaposed to falling assessments accented a common form of evasion. Furthermore, throughout the last quarter of the century, with the exception of New York City, assessed valuations of all types in the 34 townships lagged behind valuations in the 27 major cities of New York State. What then are we to make of nineteenth century arguments that New York farmers suffered from falling prices, rising assessments, and increasing taxation?[45]

At times the farmer's grievance was that his attempts at evasion were less successful than those of city dwellers. "Anyone can see," wrote a friend of the Ohio farmer in the mid-nineties, "that in the counties which include all of the large cities, the assessed valuation of personal property is only about one-fourth of the whole assessment," while in the rural counties he reckoned personalty at "nearly one-third of their whole assessed value." Inadvertently he had based his argument on who was out-evading whom, for Ohio law demanded that all classes of property were to be assessed at their true value in money and at a uniform rate.[46] The same lapses occurred elsewhere. Writing on the taxation of personalty in 1877, Nebraska Tax Commissioner, John Ames, repeatedly demonstrated what he insisted were the disproportionate taxes borne by farmers "whose property is . . . such . . . that it cannot be concealed in vaults and drawers." Yet after documenting his case with reference to Douglas, Lancaster, and Otoe counties, he admitted frankly that "the amount [of personalty] which escapes assessment in the city and country . . . was relatively about the same."[47]

A rich sequence in the Edenic dream, Iowa offered classic examples of rural tax evasion. Political mores which inspired administrative decentralization, of course, set the stage; and after 1858, a year of experimentation with county assessments, the levy, assessments, and equalization were invested officially in men elected by the civil townships of the state. "While the forms of property were daily multiplying and becoming more complex," wrote a critic of the system, ". . . reformers, guided by prejudice rather than reason were . . . perfecting . . . administrative decentralization" which in Iowa, as in most other states, helped "to perpetuate a gross injustice, in fact, a disgrace to democratic institutions." The rural conviction that the general property tax on personalty was a "tax on ignorance and honesty," being paid solely by those "who are not informed of the means of evasion," transformed skillful mendacity into a badge of honor. As one Iowan phrased it, the "fiscal drama" in Iowa proceeded on the principle that "every desire creates its own conscience."[48]

The countryside's attempts to make rich men and city property bear the main weight of public burdens perversely placed "a premium on perjury and a penalty on integrity" within its own bailiwicks. Its property, too, through under-assessment disappeared—for the state as a whole, in fact, rather swiftly. The average assessed valuation of mules, for example, dropped by roughly 70% between 1870 and 1895; valuations of cattle and horses declined about 60% and swine about 55%.[49] Some of the decrease was the consequence of scientific agriculture; but state officials believed that much of it was attributable to evasion.

In this regard, of course, the role of the assessors was central. Iowa's state auditor highlighted their contributions toward the welfare of their own people with statistics on the advance and retreat of local valuations in twenty-five of the state's ninety-nine counties during the eighties and nineties. In Davis County in the southeast of the State abutting on Missouri, cattle were assessed regally at $18.32 a head, while in adjacent Appanoose County they were assessed at $15.47; but in Lyon, the state's northwesternmost county, cattle were officially valued at $6.46 a head and in Winneshiek, northeast on the Minnesota line, they were valued at $6.14. Similarly, Davis and Mills county horses were assessed at more than $42 each, while in O'Brien and Lyon counties they were assessed at about $16. The same differentials applied to mules, sheep, and swine. Allowing for assessors' ignorance or inexperience, such disparities arose mainly from their efforts to screen the property of their constituencies from public obligations.[50]

Evasion and the attitudes that sustained it were constant factors in communal life; thus, when the state auditor again surveyed the scene in 1893 little had changed. "It would be instructive to know," wrote one Iowa tax expert, "what kind of swine was raised . . . in Sioux County, where the assessed value was only fifty-four cents" compared to Webster County "where the assessed value was $4.00." Annual assessment, which might have furnished a mechanism for reform if either township assessors or boards of equalization had undertaken it, altered nothing. As a result, the state's total assessments decreased, at times, as between 1894 and 1896, by the tens of millions of dollars, most of it lost through evasive under-assessment.[51]

Under-assessment did not occur in a social or political vacuum. After the 1850's, Iowa farmers regularly fought to exempt their properties from taxation, an essential step since everthing was taxable until specifically excluded by law, and on the whole they succeeded brilliantly. The *Iowa Code Supplement* was a living testimonial to their efforts. "One is *inclined* to think," wrote John Brindley, a leading student of the state's fiscal system soon after the turn of the century, "that the farmer bears a large part, perhaps an undue share of the fiscal burden . . . at least many authorities so state, and the political opportunists always advance this view." Yet Iowa's vast exempted properties struck him as a contradiction. "Well informed persons have estimated," continued Brindley, "that from one to five thousand dollars worth of property is entirely exempt from taxation on the average Iowa farm—a fact . . . acknowledged by the farmers themselves."

These exemptions represented an indirect victory snatched from a generation-long legislative battle by farm interests to enact a statute permitting farmers to deduct their debts, after the fashion of bankers or money-lenders, from realty values. To be sure, no such statute emerged from the legislature; but, as experts then explained, "in underassessment and in the complete exemption of a large amount of property, the same purpose has been accomplished." What could not be exempted was evaded by connivance with elected township officers. When tax ferrets were authorized by the Legislature of 1900 they discovered a substantial body of properties that had never appeared on the rolls, detailing a picture whose main dimensions had long been apparent.[52]

Measured in dollars the brunt of personalty taxation under the general property tax fell upon the Northern countryside. If no allowances are made for the number of taxpayers involved, if no allowances are made for exemptions or for the redistribution of tax moneys under county unit rules or by rural legislatures to favored counties, there can be little doubt about this. Statistics from Missouri can readily be employed to show that rural areas paid twice as much in personalty taxation as urban areas, that while Missouri farmers paid slightly less taxation on realty than urban property holders, they paid 127% more on personalty taxes; and so on. Nonetheless, because of evasion throughout the countryside, an undifferentiated analysis makes no sense; and, as we shall see later, there were still other factors often mitigating the potentially harsh fiscal circumstances in which farmers sometimes found themselves.[53]

Wherever the general property tax sought out personalty, whether in rural or urban districts the story ran much the same; "assessments were a mere semblance . . . a libel upon the intelligence and honesty of both those who enact and those who administer the laws."

Overall, in 1873, between two and a half and three *billion* dollars of New York City's personalty escaped taxation. A special tax commission sitting that same year in New Jersey estimated that personalty escaping taxation there exceeded half the total value of the state's realty. In Connecticut, experts set the amount of escaping personalty at more than 40% of the well-concealed aggregate and in Massachusetts where the pursuit of personalty was described authoritatively as "more relentless and minute than in any other state in the Union" it was not even officially pretended that assessors in the seventies and eighties were locating more than 75% of it; by 1897, conceding that the tax was "uncertain, irregular, and unsatisfactory," officials acknowledged that they were flushing out less than half of such properties. Conservatively, that meant perhaps $2,750,000,000 was escaping; less conservatively, counsel for the Massachusetts Double Taxation League argued that an *additional* $1,700,000,000 of intangible *foreign* personalty (mainly investments and securities) was also escaping. Thus, the extent of fiscal collapse was shocking even in states presumed to be offering a measure of economic leadership to the rest.[54]

In a nation that specialized in the production of laws, legislative remedies for tax evasion, of course, did not go untried; and sometimes they were partially effective. Doomage laws carrying 50% penalties against evaders in Pennsylvania scared up four times more personalty in 1895 than they had when first instituted a decade earlier. Able to cite only a 16% to 18% increase in the personalty tapped during the eighties, Maryland, Massachusetts, and New York which were without doomage laws seemed relatively backward compared to Pennsylvania, Vermont, and New Hampshire, where threatened with doomage, potential evaders turned in between 200% and 300% more to the state. Estimates were that states with strong doomage laws placed an average of 32% of their personalty under taxation compared with a figure of 17% for those without them. In addition, as a Maine Commission discovered in 1889, doomage laws were fairly popular since "all were served alike." Be that as it may, such remedies were still appallingly ineffectual;[55] they were like corks being used to seal bursting conduits. No improvisations were really adequate to cope with a failing system.

California's experience, by way of emphasis, should have dissipated any remaining confidence in personalty taxation under the general property tax. As far as the proponents of personalty were concerned, the state's programs were launched with all the auguries in their favor. Carried "solely by the farmers' votes," with merchants, bankers, and capitalists almost unanimous in their opposition to it, a new constitution was adopted in 1879. Its tax provisions were comprehensive; farmers had a free hand in drafting policy and they played their roles to the hilt. General deductions for indebtedness were not permitted and all securities and moneys were made liable to public contribution. Corporate stockholders, for example, were treated as special objects of double obligation; their corporate realty was taxed and so too was their capital stock. All in all personalty was supposed to be blanketed.[56]

The farmers' lunge toward the fiscal millenium in California, of course, was suffused with self-interest. While their "fury against the capitalist" took "least count of reason or experience" by including under the term "taxable property" every imaginable possession, they "cunningly provided" for their "own safety by exempting growing crops" and by ordering that assessments fall on the first of March each year, a time when they were "pretty sure to have no produce of any kind, or very little on . . . [their] premises." The farmer, then, was clearly having his day; the critical question was whether he could maintain his sway in California.[57]

While interested parties throughout the North kept tabs on the situation, California's agrarian "rule" was converted into a farcical rout. The State's total assessment for 1880, "even nominally . . . [was] only twenty-one and a half percent larger than in 1879, when the 'money kings' " were allegedly evading their share of taxation. A check of California financial journals, moreover, revealed that the value of securities quoted on the San Francisco Exchange ran over $110 million liable to taxation, while assessment returns listed the total value of securities at only $8,499,329. Again, under the heading of "money" state assessors counted $24,678,330, but the report of the state's bank commissioners reckoned bank deposits in December 1879 at over $82 million, indicating that $57 million here alone was evading taxation. Meantime, despite the primacy of agriculture in California's economy, the $67 million crop yield of 1879, exempted by the farmers' constitutional provisos, paid nothing toward the public burdens. The myopia of such a policy ought to have alerted farmers to what they could expect from their enemies should the power structure alter; and alter it soon did, inspiring in the process some of the bitterest commentaries on capitalist exploitation, ranging from the moral wrath of Henry George to the literary naturalism of Frank Norris.[58]

On balance, this assault on personalty, with all of its "crudities, imperfections, and absurdities," was deemed a "total failure;" dizzy with hopes, wrote Thomas Shearman, later a prominent Single Taxer, the farmers had put their panacea to a disastrous test. In 1861 personalty had composed half of all taxable property in the state; prior to the adoption of the new constitution the proportion had dropped to about 35%. Apparently uninterrupted by the "farmers' constitution," personalty further decreased to 26% in 1880 and to 13% in 1894.[59]

The experiment in California sharpened experts' suspicions that regardless of conditions the tax on personalty produced the same negative results. Writing of such laws as they applied specifically to New England, Robert Luce, Harvard graduate, editor, and tax reformer aptly summarized the obvious lesson. "As the law stands," he wrote in 1890, "it may be a burden on the conscience of the many, but it is a burden on the property of the few, not because there are few who ought to pay it, but because there are few who can be made to pay."[60]

Of the four major ways devised to tax incorporated bodies in the late nineteenth century, that is, taxing their franchises, taxing their capital stock, taxing stock in the hands of their stockholders, or taxing both their real and personal property, this last method, basically a crude general property tax, was the earliest and most significant approach taken by governments to reach corporate wealth. Without question the growing corporate sector reacted toward it exactly as had other segments of society and if the evidence sometimes lagged behind popular speculations, experts and laymen alike could rest assured that evasion was massive. Admittedly the range of corporate properties available for taxation was always greatly diminished by the many exemptions bestowed upon them by local laws, by decisions of the federal courts, or by U.S. statutes; still, exemptions left plenty of incentives to dodge taxation, for though many corporations held more exempted property than most individuals, they likewise possessed more taxable property than did most taxpayers.

Of the many factors that persuaded corporations to try evading their public burdens, the social climate in which they developed—and in which the law took form—undoubtedly made a substantial contribution. It was a popular prejudice that corporations were guilty of extensive evasion, a prejudice all the more bitter to those who entertained it because of the fiscal advantages which they realized governments had extended these businesses. "The ingenuity of corporations evading taxation, even now, is well known," chimed a commentator of the nineties and his conclusion was typical.

Such popular prejudices were a source of anxiety in many business circles. Fear of venal, vindictive, democratic legislators soliciting votes by promising to soak corporations with taxation proved a persistent specter. "More than half the present session," wrote a Chicago editor of the Illinois Legislature in 1877, "has been devoted to a discussion of the problem of whether Capital should not be treated as a pestilence, to be extirpated by all the powers and machinery of government."[61] Analyzing fiscal trends in the mid-eighties, another observer ventured that since taxpayers were the real rulers, taxation had become the art of searching for corporations that could be plucked without "producing a cry liable to strike a chord of sympathy in the popular heart;" large revenues, he noted, were already being drawn from them in several states without a murmur of disapproval from the voters.[62]

Everywhere popular efforts to tax corporations produced a bumper crop of questions marked by what one authority in the eighties described as a "general antipathy toward corporate interests."[63] Where farmers shaped personalty taxation, as was usually the case, corporate wealth was avowedly a major objective and, under the circumstances, corporate lawyers were quick to recognize "antagonisms between Corporate bodies and the Community." A New York expert on corporate taxation, Edward C. Moore, writing for the *American Law Review* in 1882, found it strange that despite their achievements a "widespread feeling" had arisen that corporations were "natural enemies of the people." The origins of this "popular fallacy" he located in "envy," "communistic tendencies," and "popular ignorance." At first too permissive about controlling corporations, public officials, under the prodding of angry voters, had proceeded, he felt, to the other extreme, encouraging the community to "revenge itself on corporations for its own carelessness and omissions . . . extorting from them in the shape of taxes" as much wealth as possible.[64]

Liberal and conservative opinions often concurred on this point. "Demagogues," insisted E. L. Godkin in 1879, "are constantly bringing forward schemes to relieve the whole people from public burdens by taxing corporations." A boon to civilization, corporations, continued Godkin, should have been afforded every "facility and inducement" to enter the state instead of having "excessive and differential taxes" imposed on their capital.[65] New York's influential *Commercial and Financial Chronicle* struck the same theme; state legislative committees in Albany were accused of starting the session of 1880 "with a fresh shot at a new class of corporations each day." Purportedly, the "noblest aim of a legislator" was to "discover a pile of corporate capital on which he can lay another tax." Faced with "an intricate and unattractive" subject, claimed the *Chronicle,* the average lawmaker took this easy way out, especially if he represented rural districts where corporations were few, small, and unlikely to retaliate.[66]

Adding to this social climate the uncertainties and inequities of general property taxes as they affected corporate properties, and a capitalist mentality that judged taxation a waste of investment capital, conditions were ripe for what many businesses considered essential and justifiable tax evasion.

Where evidence exists it may be said that corporations were at least as successful in their evasion as any other taxpayers. Since reliable general estimates are all but impossible to reconstruct, a few specifics are in order. The capital stock of Massachusetts corporations on which taxes should have been paid in 1861, exceeded $225 million; but nearly two-thirds of these private obligations went into hiding without payment. And the liability of this particular corporate property was of a relatively public nature since the state required written registers of corporate stockholders. If this was any index of what was escaping, the situation must have been truly astounding.[67]

Fraud and "official laxity" during the late sixties in New York allowed many corporations to escape. A banker, described as typical by the Wells Commission in 1871, eluded payment so skillfully that he surrendered less than a twenty-fifth part of the valuation of his personalty. Fire and life insurance companies were also early and persistently notorious evaders. Although capitalized at $35 million in 1870, for instance, they were assessed just $9,250,000 on personalty and $3 million on realty. The Hughes insurance investigations of 1905 clearly indicated that tax chiseling in this and many other ways by the leading companies had not stopped. Savings banks also managed evasion by the ingenious manipulation of their deposits and surpluses; such "misuse" was estimated officially to have removed $200 million a year from the bounds of taxation. Bonds, notes, and others securities of the national government, of course, served as a sturdy shield for vast sums of legally taxable wealth, and indebtedness, which few communities were prepared to deny as a source of deductions for corporations, was itself an opening for the fraudulent swearing down of assessments in New York State.[68] This seemed especially the case with railroads which came under fire during the early seventies by taxpayers and reformers who found that because basic tax laws had been enacted when "railroad corporations were unknown to us" the arm of the state was badly palsied when it reached them.[69]

Known and suspected evasion by New York corporations, as was true elsewhere, blended into the broader controversy about the role of corporate organizations in American life. "The most vital issue in the United States today," intoned the *New York Evening Express* in the late seventies, "is whether the State shall be ruled by the people, or ruined by the corporations." Legislatures had been bought like cattle and sheep, though hardly for so little money, found the Reverend Henry Ward Beecher. To be sure, he "did not believe in the sociologists, in the internationals, or in the communists," but when he saw what great enterprises were up to he feared working men would revolt, crying out that they had been "bought and owned by consolidated capital."[70] Exposés such as the Adamses *Chapters of Erie* and the scandals regarding corporate activities during the Grant Era in Albany and New York City lent vitality to such forebodings.

Reformers, professional men, and journalists by the end of the seventies were carefully exploring the subject of corporations and taxation, marshalling public and private records to demonstrate the extent of evasion; if New Yorkers were as active as any others in these explorations, the inquiries which they had undertaken were already underway elsewhere and would continue all across the North.

In New York initial exposures of corporate tax evasion centered on the machinations of the New York Central and Hudson River Railroad, the Lake Shore Railroad, the Erie Receivership, the Hudson and Delaware Canal Company, half a dozen street railways, Western Union Telegraph Company, and several insurance houses. Together these corporations were costing the state millions of dollars a year in revenues before 1880.[71] Earning over 7% a year on reported capital of more than $143 million, while paying taxes on $22 million, Vanderbilt's New York Central (exclusive of leased lines) became a symbolic arch-villain of the piece. Reports from state and local officials, the investigations of merchants, lawyers, and newspapers, plus the sworn statements and publications of the Central's own officers, furnished impressive, if still all-too circumstantial, evidence of evasion.[72]

Escape by the Vanderbilt road was accomplished in part by direct violation of New York judicial decisions aimed against "double deductions" of indebtedness, first by treating debt as diminishing the value of the corporation's capital stock and, then, by deducting it from valuations, the initial computations of which had already included allowances for debts. The Central's leadership was hardly inventive for such ploys had been part of the game in New York for many years; but as a result, by the late seventies, a great gulf developed between the letter of the law and actual assessments. By connivance with officials in other words, the road rated millions in passenger and freight stations, fixtures, engines, car houses, machine shops, and machinery along with more lightly taxed real estate.[73]

That was just the beginning. On its capital in New York City, the real seat of its activities, the Central paid taxes on only $250,000 of capital. This it managed by paying $8000 to local tax commissioners who subsequently decided that the bulk of Central capital was not taxable in Manhattan, although communications to the company were directed to its headquarters in Grand Central Depot. Because the road was not taxed at Albany either, it was charged that collusion between railway and tax officials made it possible to "withhold from the tax-gatherer millions of dollars" between 1867 and 1879.[74]

Critics of New York's street railways vigorously publicized discrepancies between their assessed valuations, which for the seven major roads in 1878 amounted to $4,391,000, and the insignificant burdens borne by them. In one instance, where a company was exposed by the testimony of a former associate of political leader Thurlow Weed, a company director, it was revealed that despite an order by the Court of Appeals not a dollar was paid for the use of the streets which alone annually cost the City Treasury $300,000.[75]

In reports drafted by its own officials as well as by the state, the infamous Broadway and Seventh Avenue Railway indicated many of the methods by which a corporation of its type could evade taxation. And this despite the law, for court decisions were often as much as corporate critics could have hoped for. Late in the seventies, for example, Judge Earl of the Court of Appeals declared that railway corporations held property and exercised their functions *for* the public weal *under* legislative control and that Albany could legally regulate their modes of operation, even their prices.[76] But railway accounting made short work of legal dicta. In 1868, as was customary, charged a well-informed critic, "the cost-price of real estate to be deducted from the value of the stock, is increased, for the purpose of . . . showing that the company has no *taxable* capital," and as a result a street railway bonded for $1,600,000 cost only $522,000, a case of dishonest bonding to shrink the amount of capital exposed to public grasp.[77]

Scores of such specific examples can be adduced for the late nineteenth and early twentieth centuries in New York[78] and what transpired there was duplicated throughout the North; crooked accounts, dishonest bonding, under-assessment, phony indebtedness, the juggling of domiciles, collusion with public officials, or bribing them were all part of the arsenal of corporate tax dodgers. No stone was left unturned if it promised to hide some of the millions at stake from public obligation; where feasible the law was used as a screen, at the very least as a device to weary governments into compromise; where unfeasible it was dropped altogether for fraud, perjury, and other illegalities. Corporate evasion, then, was not only marked by fears of impending popular confiscations and of legislative injustice, but also by a disdain of existing communal rules and institutions, a disdain which at times became criminal instrumentalism.

The methods employed by corporate evaders in New York have been alluded to, but overall what was the extent of corporate evasion in New York State? In 1916 a joint legislative committee on taxation, (the Mills Committee), launched a primary examination of 2500 domestic mercantile, manufacturing, and general business corporations. Insufficient evidence, or their lack of liability, narrowed the working list to 100 concerns whose balance sheets allowed some estimate of what they were liable for, and a further refinement winnowed the list to 24 corporations on which a sound sampling could be based. The total taxable personalty for these corporations was placed at $90,522,000 with an aggregate assessment of $3,300,000; the amount on which payment was made came to 3.46% of the amount for which these corporations were liable, or, as the committee phrased it, "the percentage of taxable personalty legally liable but evaded" came to 96.54%. "Important as these results are in disclosing the failure of the personal property tax of corporations," concluded the state investigators, "they do not disclose the full significance of that failure."[79]

Though saddled with more modest fiscal difficulties than New York, Maryland also grew concerned about the tax evasions of her corporations during the last quarter of the nineteenth century. A Baltimore tax appeal court declared in 1881 that $50 million, mainly corporate funds, were invested in federal securities in hopes of securing them from taxation as personalty.[80] Because of their obvious importance, Maryland railroads came under suspicion from the state's tax commissioners of 1888 after they had armed themselves with county by county statements of the roads' tax status. These revealed a notorious undervaluation of certain railroad properties and rank discrimination in their favor when their obligations were compared with county assessments of other businesses. The Philadelphia, Wilmington, and Baltimore Railroad, for example, although paying 7% on a capital value of $5,300,000, was assessed at less than $1,500,000 for local taxation; in the words of the commissioners, "a fractional proportion of the amount paid by citizens of those counties for local taxes." Its property and franchises, insisted state officials, "can hardly be only fourteen or fifteen hundred thousand." Indeed, taking the Baltimore and Ohio, the North Central, and the Western Maryland railroads together the commissioners accused them of "annually escaping taxation to the extent of about three hundred thousand dollars." Examination of the state's other roads simply added another $100,000 to the estimate. While $400,000 worth of tax dodging by local railroads may seem a modest performance it constituted more than one-third of the entire state tax on property and, relatively, therefore, was a most serious matter.[81]

Railroad corporations, in a sense symbolic of the giant corporations of a newly industralized society, profited from the same situation in many places outside of Maryland. In Indiana fraudulent assessments were again their chief means of escape. There too, of course, the state tax commission was supposed to assess all property at fair cash value and see that corporate assessments were based on "an equality with other property." But amid discussions of revisions in the tax laws in 1892, the true cash value of the state's railways proved pitifully small; in the case of one typical road which was earning about 7% on its capital, its assessments accounted for just 29% of its market value.[82] And so it went.

The urge to evade taxation was by no means limited to railroad corporations and it transcended the particulars of the existing tax systems. Pennsylvania's fiscal methods, by comparison with others, were esteemed by the tax authorities of other states, for the commonwealth itself really had no conventional general property tax to suffer. Moreover, where most Northern states phrased their tax clauses comprehensively, spelling out exemptions very specifically, Pennsylvania reversed the process, constraining officials to demonstrate that the property they were seeking to tax had been contemplated as taxable by the statutes. State and local taxation were in some measure separated, another notable innovation, and corporations were liable only to the state for taxation on tangible and intangible personalty. Notwithstanding such apparent virtues, the extensiveness of one of the commoner forms of evasion, undervaluation, guaranteed by common perjury, furnished a continual source of complaint from segments of the public and, in turn, this led to repeated allegations concerning the state's illicit tax favors to corporations.[83]

Unquestionably, Pennsylvania corporations which were eager to evade their obligations, enjoyed great advantages in their dealings—or lack of them—with Harrisburg even without the use of bribes or lobbies. For while there were popular presumptions, according to the Pennsylvania Tax Conference's private investigations in the nineties, that the commonwealth maintained a complete listing of all taxable corporations, that, therefore, all corporations were exposed to taxation by the state, that the basis of their liability was the valuation of their capital stock, and that some department of government possessed this vital information, not one of these assumptions was true.

Throughout the nineties, in fact, Harrisburg's list of corporations was grossly incomplete and incorrect. Many corporations required to stand taxation escaped by never reporting themselves to officials; names of corporations which did not pay the state thus were unlisted. Many of the names that did appear, as tax investigators noted, were those of defunct organizations. Of the corporations that were paying many were doing so on the basis of their receipts and dividends rather than on the basis of their appraised valuation. Educated guesses about the amount of corporate capital which eluded the state government ran to the hundreds of millions, and if somewhat less serious than analogous situations in Massachusetts and New York, such guesses were sufficiently serious to keep its chief citizens, its leading corporations and private businesses, and its governments deeply preoccupied.[84]

In sum, then, the states' general tax systems were uniformly primitive, while the myriad forms of evasion were quite sophisticated. Geared to tax the vast majority of incorporated bodies by the same means as they would have taxed ordinary individuals, the existing money machinery failed either to locate or to convert the new wealth into government revenues; a failure of this magnitude, obviously, could only prove fatal.

Men evading taxation on personalty under one part of the general property tax displayed no compunction about trying to evade taxation on their real estate under another. Evasion was almost a commercial way of life. A Wisconsin "gentleman of prominence" confessed to Richard Ely in the eighties, "You see in me a monument of the iniquity of our present system of taxation." When young and poor, he claimed that he "had paid on all that I had;" but corruption had engulfed him. "Now that I really have something," he told Ely, "I keep still and pay taxes on only part of my property. Indeed, when I think about taxation in our States and cities, I feel like turning anarchist and blowing things up with dynamite." Charles Bonaparte, a leading Baltimore lawyer, later Attorney-General of the United States, a reformer and founder of the National Municipal League, remarked with equal candor to Baltimore businessmen in 1889: "I hope . . . that I have not wholly lost my character as a man of business if I admit that I once, when a young man, told the truth to a taxgatherer."[85] No doubt the audience forgave him.

Realty supplied the mainstay revenues in most municipalities, counties, and states until well into this century, although in four states it was always limited chiefly to local taxation. The situation in New York in the early eighties was typical of the rest of the North; in twenty-four of the state's cities realty carried anywhere from 64% of the total tax burden (in Kingston) to nearly 99% (in Long Island City), the average being 88% of the total revenue. Undoubtedly, evasion was more difficult where tangible properties were involved than was the case with personalty, hence the frequent exhortations from reformers and tax critics "to seek for taxation those objects which are fixed and tangible."[86] Nevertheless, such evasion was widespread and commonplace.

The nature and extent of this defiance is readily exemplified in Manhattan and Chicago, their vast concentrations of realty plus commercial guile rendering them peculiarly susceptible to this form of illegality.

Requiring assessment at "full and true market value" but leaving definitions of "full and true" to elected assessors, New York's law opened a vastly exploitable gap between taxable and nominal values; and the exploitable was exploited. Caustically discussing the absurdities of general taxation, the *Commercial and Financial Chronicle* declared that, "We could occupy a page in recounting instances of inequalities and evasions." Reform was pressed but, noted the *Chronicle*, "it is idle to imagine that men will ever be persuaded, out of a sense of fairness and duty, to stand and meet taxation cheerfully;" property simply would "run and hide" from authority.[87] And so it did.

Realty fled so effectively in New York City and valuations were manipulated so extensively that tax experts regularly described them throughout the late nineteenth and early twentieth centuries as utterly chaotic. Solemnly warned by statute that if they swore falsely they would be guilty of "willful and corrupt perjury," New York City's assessors perjured themselves almost as a matter of routine. Addressing the State Constitutional Convention of 1867–68, a Manhattan Delegate-at-Large announced that "I am well aware that our system of taxation is a gigantic fraud in the great commercial city of New York;" the city's largest property holders fully realized, he declared, that "every year, in the strict eye of the law, they are actually in complicity with fraud on the part of assessors and collectors." Other delegates charged that assessors had taken up their books "with perfect consciousness that their neighbors who owned land were to be robbed." Small wonder the result was described as a "general demoralization," the inevitable consequence, as David Wells saw it, "where assessors are dependent for their tenure of office on political favoritism."[88]

Collusion arose from mixed motives both on the part of officials and taxpayers. Governed from Albany, property owners in Manhattan felt they bore a strikingly disproportionate share of the state's burdens; as late as 1890, for example, 161,000 pieces of taxable property, roughly one-fourth of all the lots in Manhattan, paid 43% of all state taxes. At the same time, Manhattan lacked a single representative on the State Board of Assessors. Thus, one city official frankly advocated educating local taxpayers in evasive tactics to counteract plots against their realty hatched in Albany, although the record suggests the superfluousness of such education. Responding to state investigators in 1891 about what authority he had to assess city realty a penny less than full value, and pressed to state if he was "more interested in protecting the interests of New York City" than honoring the law, Tax Commissioner Coleman retorted that he ignored the letter of the law because "we are paying more than our share." But, asked the state, "have you a right to do that?" If so, under what provisions of the law? Under "a higher law perhaps?" "We must act, be damned, and governed by justice and equity," argued Coleman. "We are not putting the screws that way on the good people of New York," added one of his colleagues.[89] The state felt there was slight danger of that.

Forbearance by local officials registered statistically; after the mid-seventies Manhattan realty assessments ran about 60% of value despite notable exceptions; the average clearly reflected substantial evasion. During the eighties when we know that many property values rose substantially in Manhattan, increased valuations for taxpayers were very modest. Total assessments for 1880 came to $942 million; by 1890 they had risen to $1398 million. Twenty percent of the rise was attributed to the refusal in 1888–89 of the Rhinelanders, the Goelets, the Astors, Lorillards, and Hoffmans to sell their profitable downtown properties, though the full reasons for the rise were never ascertained. As Manhattan assessments rose, the tax rate declined slightly; in fact, the apogee in the tax rate was reached in 1866. The low rate itself evidenced official chiseling; to insure the low rates of 1889–90, for example, rising valuations were juxtaposed to apparent decreases in expenditures; these were managed politically by the administration's $2 million raid on the sinking fund and by its refusal to include a portion of state taxes in the budget. Thus, was under-assessment disguised throughout Manhattan's 24 wards.[90]

Specifics are easily cited. Second to the Tenderloin in taxable wealth, the Twelfth Ward was so strikingly under-assessed that its realty valuations were raised comfortably by $20 million in one year, by $42 million inside of two years. The closest runner-up, the Twenty-second Ward, showed only a $7 million jump in one year. Official attempts to avoid culpability for this were invariably weak, if amiable. The Thirteenth Ward, for instance, showed a $1,805,000 rise in valuation in 1889. According to the assessor the increase was due to $600,000 worth of improvements in the ward. But what of the remaining $1,200,000? "Well," testified the assessor under state interrogation, "when a man . . . puts in an application to the building department . . . he puts in a little below what the property will cost . . . for the purpose of evading taxation;" as a consequence, the amount on the application was officially doubled just to raise the assessment to about 60% of value. Both operations, private and public, were illegal; but as a city tax commissioner confessed, "so many things take place every day that I am not surprised at anything."[91]

Evasion, whether to save the city's quota on state taxes or to minimize risks unforeseen except by wary officials, tossed together a number of strange bedfellows, the Astors and their ilk mingling with reformers. Indeed Astor property was assessed almost affectionately at one-fourth to one-half the rate applicable even in other parts of Manhattan. Yet they were not alone. One of the show pieces of Manhattan's late nineteenth century realty was 233 Fifth Avenue, a superb house belonging to Amos Enos who sold it to the New York Reform Club for $200,000, the price being in the public domain. Nonetheless, the valuation placed on the building by the assessors was $85,000 and there was no subsequent record of the club's reformist energies being channeled to correct it. Few comparable properties ranging from Samuel Sloane's fine house and stables to the richly endowed Trinity Church holdings, the City Hotel, or the Hoffman House, were assessed for more than half of their marketable value; when pressed by investigators during the late eighties, in fact, the president of the City Tax Commission was unable to specify a single piece of property then being assessed according to law.[92]

Because assessors displayed "remarkable athletic performances in their minds," Manhattan became a crazy-quilt of values. Banks, trust companies, and breweries located side by side were frequently assessed at ten to thirty percent differentials. Astor House block where large additions to assessments might have been expected in rare years of re-evaluation would thus rise 25%, whereas in Vesey Street off Broadway where rates might have been expected to have remained low, valuations in the same reassessments jumped from 33% to 50%; one block of Broad Street, reflecting this situation, showed assessments ranging from 17% of real value to 126%. Tammany saw to it, moreover, that people who were not politically influential or collectively important, suffered increments from 70% to 80% higher than those who counted.

Serving the well-to-do and the influential, evasive assessing was also a service—one for which they paid in other ways—to some of Manhattan's extensive underworld. The notorious Bowery concert saloons, theaters, and dives—Atalia's, Paresis Hall, McGurk's, the Haymarket, and John Daly's—or equally "disreputable" spots elsewhere in town like Gombossy's and French Kate's, all benefited from favorable assessments, creating the "suspicion in the minds of the people at large," according to a city official, "that capitalists and roughs were favored by the tax department and that a man of moderate means" was overassessed because "the commissioners are open to influences from moneyed men."[93] And so it went.

Chicago's property owners and city officials behaved in much the same way as their fellows in Manhattan during the late nineteenth and early twentieth centuries. "Inequality of assessment is carried to such an enormous extent in Chicago," wrote a revenue reformer, "as to leave no . . . doubt that it is largely due to actual bribery." An assessor's job in a small ward filled with great office buildings, for instance, was reportedly worth $75,000 a year, another indication that the wages of sin sometimes pioneered for many others.[94] With such inspiration at hand it was small wonder that the incentive to dodge taxation was calculated to have been seven times greater in the city than in adjacent rural areas.

Again, as in Manhattan, one excuse for evasion was the fiscal warfare between country and city. Illinois' rural counties competed so successfully in under-assessment that the state's realty in 1894 was still valued at only 14.7% of market value, compared, say, with a comparable 50% prevalent in Pennsylvania. And this desire to escape filled rural officialdom with a compensatory urge to tax Chicagoans. The natural objective, of course, was personalty. But while the city's 23,000 acres was packed with it, most of it systematically escaped. Thus, a rural legislature sought redress through the imposition of relatively steep tax rates on real estate. However just as rural assaults on realty increased in vigor with each failure to reach Chicago's personalty, so high rates applied to realty stimulated evasive undervaluations which they were designed, hopefully, to counteract. The disease of Chicago's fiscal situation, remarked John Commons, was cumulative; and that continued to be the case while Illinois assessors were elected officials.[95] Rural spokesmen, of course, complained that general property taxation as applied to the city had become "a scheme by which the rich may escape their share of public burdens and a greater load may be indirectly added to the oppressions of the poor;" an attitude that belied a grasp of the consequences of rural-dominated legislation.[96] But reason and fiscal policy were rarely mated. Meantime, the city could only hope to attract or retain the capital on which it thrived in the teeth of unconscionably high tax rates by electing assessors who, in Commons' words, would "grossly violate the law."[97]

Chicago's incentive to avoid the thrust of these rural taxes was amply attested by the enormous wealth located there. By 1878, for example, when values were still relatively low because of the mid-decade depression, 23,000 acres of city real estate were valued at fourteen times more than the 1,100,000 acres of Bureau County in north central Illinois. That picture did not change during the next generation. In 1893, Bureau's acreage was still worth only 1/14th of the 45th part of the realty concentrated in Chicago. Proceeding county by county through Illinois, the differentials in values were similar, if not always as dramatic.

Whatever the justifications offered for the massive flight of Chicago properties from public obligation, the scandals attending it produced a continuous surge of discontent. Surveying state taxation during the two decades prior to the nineties, the aggressive reformer, George Schilling, Governor Altgeld's appointee as Secretary to the Illinois Bureau of Labor Statistics, published an unprecedented statistical exposé of state taxation. "As a source of convenient material," wrote one reader, "it will be to tax reformers what a dictionary is to rhetoricians—a storehouse of facts with infinite possibilities, a magazine of economic dynamite."[98] Schilling tied his materials to the assumption that "taxation has always been the chief instrument of tyrannical power" and was therefore responsible for the "lamentable condition of the industrial class."[99] In Illinois he sought to prove that this tyranny rested on evasion of fiscal burdens by the propertied classes, symbolized by the realty holders of Chicago.

Schilling's inquiry pivoted around the rhetorical question: "How can the fraudulent character of these valuations [in Chicago] be doubted?" And his evidence of evasion conducted on grand scale by assessors and taxpayers alike was impressive. Large tracts of valuable land such as Judge Lambert Tree's Garfield Race Track, bought for $50,000 in 1870, which appreciated hundreds of times over during the subsequent quarter of a century, ended up assessed at less than a tenth of their full value, paying hundreds of dollars less than they had originally.[100] High-toned residences along Lake Shore Drive were typical, claimed the bureau, of the way assessors "systematically" ignored rising land values. Potter Palmer, for example, bought a strip from the Catholic Bishop of Chicago in 1882 for $90,000; breaking it into lots, he sold it in 1885 after it had already appreciated 118%. At the time of original sale, the assessor's valuation on the twenty-two lots involved was close to 20% of real value, but by 1885 the valuation had actually shriveled to 5.09%. The situation did not improve with time. Chicago realtors conceded in 1893 that even without improvements the Palmer lands were worth $595,000, representative of a 556% leap in value since the original sale. Nonetheless, the assessment fell below 6% of this value, or, as the books showed, an assessed value of $34,780. By comparison, homes costing less than $4000, illegally assessed to be sure, were assessed at more than double those on Lake Shore and 6% more on the average than the assessments of seventy of Chicago's tallest buildings, including its famed skyscrapers.[101]

Again, the "costly and magnificent residences" owned by some of Chicago's most notable reformers, members of the Civic Federation, "an organization," observed an admirer of the Schilling Report, "which has posed for some time past as the great municipal reform agent of Chicago," profited from under-assessment. For thirty mansions valued at from $20,000 to $1,300,000, the highest assessment for any was 12% of true value, the average valuation totaling just 7.78% of the true value.[102] The Bureau of Labor Statistics was correct in labelling such valuations as "fradulent." Why, asked the Report, were the owners' standards of "honor and honesty so radically different when the issue is with the people instead of with a merchant over a question of shirking taxes instead of over purloining goods?"[103] If the question was a sound one, the answers generally were unsatisfactory.

With nuances of scale, Chicago and Manhattan exemplified what was occurring as the old money machines collapsed inside the cities of the

North; but evidence from rural areas after the Civil War indicates that realty was being hidden there too. In New York State, as in most others, evasion of realty taxes flourished because the state's own creatures, the counties, were thrust into fiscal competition with one another. The state set quotas for county taxes on the basis of the county's own assessments, thus in effect encouraging elected assessors to vie in undervaluation.

Before the end of the sixties, the results were sufficiently sobering to preoccupy the state constitutional convention. One delegate described the system of rival jurisdictions as the greatest "manufactory of perjury on the fact of the earth;" towns and counties were depressing their assessments to the lowest possible point and no efforts were being made "to get at the honest, actual value of the property of the country."[104] Valuations everywhere mirrored the losses. Rural realty assessments sank to a fifth of their worth in some places, to one-third or one-half in others. Real estate in Oneida County (735,000 acres and almost entirely rural) showed increases in assessments over a twenty-year period of little more than $4½ million; between 1865 and 1869, in fact, the assessed value of both farms and livestock showed a decline and the average assessment for *all* realty in the county, inclusive of valuations in Rome and Utica, remained at less than $20 per acre for many years.[105] Such developments were the rule and analogous figures for all 62 counties indicate, now as then, that most low assessments were evidence of evasion.[106]

Once again complaints that farmers bore far heavier burdens under general taxation of their realty than city dwellers, if commonly accurate, were inaccurate in many instances. Official findings in New York State during the early seventies reflect what was true in many other times and places, namely, that "in a majority of cases in the country," valuation on real estate varied from 25% to 35% of true value, while rising to highs of 50–60% in the cities.[107] Over the last third of the century, Illinois realty admittedly bore over 70% of the aggregate assessed valuation of all property, but its distribution between rural and urban areas was one index of rural successes in fiscal competition. Board of Equalization statistics showed that beginning in 1867 city lots comprised two-sevenths of the total assessments on real estate and excepting the general rise in assessments under the revenue law of 1872 in which urban realty advanced a little less than rural property, the assessments of urban properties rose both "absolutely and in comparison" with rural assessments. Moreover, rural valuations were "steadily reduced" until 1890 when they were barely half the figures of 1873. Meantime, there was a "stupendous increase in the actual valuation of city property." In short, the lowest percentages of real property assessments were in rural counties,[108] the highest in large urban or suburban populations,[109] indicating that some countrymen were more than holding their own in the internecine fiscal struggle.[110] Similarly, in Ohio, despite the fact that farm property tended from the seventies through the nineties to be taxed on the average closer to full value than any other realty in the state, assessors, elected from their respective senatorial districts, tried "to reduce the . . . valuation of the part of the State which [they] represented, all oaths to the contrary nothwithstanding."[111]

Limited rural successes were also familiar elsewhere. County commissioners from Maryland's rural Caroline County testified in the mid-eighties that the real injustice in the operation of the money machines, despite farmers' complaints about oppressive taxation, was visited upon country merchants. "It is a well known fact," explained the commissioners, "that a majority of county merchants finding they are not paying expenses, sell out, wind up or go to the wall, bankrupts" due mainly to "onerous and burdensome" taxation. Meanwhile, the "progressive and successful farmer" was "always busy studying to improve his property" over the decades, "increasing the value of his real esate ten, twenty, or thirty dollars per acre, with no increase of taxes, except for buildings, and they are oftener not assessed than assessed," observed the commissioners.[112]

Farmers in Iowa likewise battened on evasions throughout the last century, driving the state, in desperation, to "ferret" laws. Governor Jackson informed the assembly in 1894 that for years it had been "a notorious fact" that under Iowa's "peculiar" tax laws millions of dollars in rural realty had evaded assessment; and a number of newspapers such as the influential *Iowa State Register* joined the call for reform early in the nineties. But local pressures soon altered the editorial tone. The *Register,* for instance, still acknowledged in the mid-nineties that farms—and half the population of the state still lived on farms—were assessed at just a fourth to a third of their cash value; yet by its reckoning two-thirds of all state taxation was falling on farmers and the railroads, hence any increase in assessments threatened to "breed extravagance" in government expenditure and stimulate the "corrupt tax-eating" underway in the cities. The solution offered by the *Register* was to locate the wealth of personalty in the cities and leave the countryside to itself. What was "placidly" being alluded to, as one expert phrased it, was state tolerance of evasions, which by 1888 had cost it an estimated $1,300,000,000. Thus, as the century closed, assessments in some rural counties stood at 17% of full value and in others, while the market value of realty appreciated, they actually declined to as little as one-sixth of real value.[113]

Even Pennsylvania's "advanced" fiscal system failed to forestall the evasion of realty in the countryside. Statistical evidence on total taxable property in the commonwealth prior to the nineties is unreliable, but during that decade the Pennsylvania Tax Conference, staffed by representatives from the major elements in the state's economy, reported that the law on realty assessment was regularly being violated, often "under the positive direction of certain county commissioners," often by local assessors, and often by outright fraud on the part of the owners of realty.[114] The conference concluded in 1892 that the assessed valuation of all Pennsylvania real estate was just over 2/3 of its actual value. Of this, 37% was assessed to rural areas, 14% to boroughs, and about 49% to the cities. Each of the 67 counties yielded evidence of extensive undervaluation. Realty in Luzerne County in the heart of the anthracite district, for instance, was assessed at barely 17% of its true value; slightly higher but outrageously low evaluations applied to 14 rural counties and nowhere did rural realty rise above assessments of one-third of true value.[115]

The Pennsylvania Revenue Commission of 1889 gave short shrift to rural charges that farmers were bearing the bulk of the public burden while capitalists and corporations profited from hidden caches of hard-to-tax personalty. Granting that farmers were suffering "short run decreases" in profits and land values, the commission accused them of living beyond their means, so much so that as prices and land values returned to normal after a temporary season of inflation, they were unaware of it. "Are rates of taxation on farming property excessive?" asked the commissioners. Drawing on evidence supplied them by the Secretary of the State Board of Agriculture, they gave a categorical no to the question. Boroughs and cities, they noted, paid up without complaint on valuations from 30% to 50% higher than the farmer paid. The real impetus behind rural protests about unequal taxation, they charged, came from "a small minority who are interested as capitalists in farms" and who, disappointed over their profits, hoped for financial aid diverted from the pockets of their fellow citizens by changes in general property taxation.[116]

Having scanned the masking of property in both country and city, so disastrous for existing fiscal machinery, one might agree in spirit with Charles Reemelin's judgment that "America's serious mistake, now its chronic disease has been that it has made the desires and interests of its individuals the standard of public conduct." At least it might be conceded that Northern fiscal systems suffered the vices of their virtues. Unhappily for some, the vices proved fatal.

. . . only through evasion can the corporations avoid much injustice in matters of taxation.

Had a general property tax been rigidly enforced . . . and had the corporations been unable to evade the law according to some of the well-known methods in this State, some . . . might have been forced to the wall.

Report of the Joint Legislative Committee on Taxation,
State of New York, 1916.

The State of Kentucky received more revenue for the year 1912 from its dogs than it did from all the bonds, monies, and stocks in the State.

Report of the Kentucky Special Tax Commission, 1912.

3

Inequity and Inequality

Failure of the money machines was due to evasion and to the revenues that consequently never materialized for needy governments; but it was not caused by evasion alone. Often the flight from public obligation sprang from the seeming justifications furnished the perjurer, the wayward official, and the fraud by inequities in the operational system, and, just as inequities stimulated evasion, so evasion in turn was responsible for further and more serious inequities.

The monumental unfairness of Northern revenue systems contrasted sharply with the pretentious theories on which the money machinery of state and local governments rested. Such theories were proudly and primly considered different from those accepted in other countries because they were ostensibly democratic. Borrowing from Ferdinand Lassalle, Charles Spahr, a noted American socialist, argued in 1886 that Europe had experienced only two systems of taxation: a system of landed aristocrats whose cardinal tenet was non-taxation of the land; and a system of capitalist plutocracies whose fiscal philosophy centered around the non-taxation of capital. Spahr regarded the assumptions of the American system as distinctive for American communities, he noted, had "instinctively" accepted the principle of "the equal taxation of all property, the non-taxation of labor."[1]

Despite variations to the effect that taxes should be proportioned, reasonable, non-discriminatory, uniform, and for a public purpose, such "democratic" principles suffused the mores and the mores had long since become law. By the mid-seventies, they were solidly incorporated into the taxing philosophies of the post-Civil War generation. Since the state, it was explained, "protects a man in his person and property" while affording him conveniences and enjoyments, "that man should pay the state his proportional equivalent." Indeed, it was argued, governments related to their citizens in the same way that an insurance company did to its policy holders: "Pay me so much money, and I guarantee you so much protection." Everywhere there was insistence on "equality before the laws," extending to industries as well as to men. To the Supreme Court of Maine all "useful laborers" irrespective of their fields served the state by increasing its aggregate wealth, hence nothing of a public nature entitled the "manufacturer to [greater] public gifts than the sailor, the mechanic, the lumberman, or the farmer." In nearby New Hampshire, the state's chief justice declared that even a selection or classification of subjects for taxation invariably resulted in some men paying their neighbors' share and divided the community into "inferiors and superiors." Government, created for the common good, would under these circumstances have been prostituted to the interests of "the privileged class;" in New Hampshire, no doubt, the railroads.[2]

These sentiments were commonplace. In Pennsylvania, the distinguished jurist, Judge Sharswood, observed that when government used the property of one portion of its citizenry to the advantage of "favored individuals" or private enterprises, it was "none the less robbery" because it was perpetrated "under the forms of law and taxation." A number of Pennsylvania governors spoke to the same point. In each of his two inaugurals Governor Pattison attacked unjust discrimination in taxation as "working an untold evil to our people . . . oppressing the poor . . . exempting the rich . . . compounding unfortunate social distinctions" alien to American principles of government, destructive of happiness and energy, and fatal to the hope of the country "becoming the home of a contented people."[3]

By 1875 Massachusetts had gone farther than any other commonwealth in elaborating "a true theory of taxation." Citizens of the state, it was proclaimed, were taxed neither to pay the state for protecting them nor as "a recompense . . . for any service" in their behalf; rather, they were taxed officially because their "original relations to society require it." Property and wealth were described as a "wholly social creation;" it was therefore deemed both "wise and right," in the state's view, for individuals to accede to the payment of whatever contributions the "true interests of society" demanded of them. A man paid taxes because "the law of his own well-being summoned him to do so" and because the state expected "the righteous surrender or subjection of the individual to the will of the community."[4] Rousseau's general will could hardly have been embraced more concisely.

Yankee cunning, of course, was not utterly abandoned to theory; until love dominated the general run of men, the tax commissioners recognized that selfishness and greed would continually be exerted to pervert any scheme of taxation. Hence, they acknowledged that "the most important point" in the success of a fiscal system was the basic "honesty, purity, and unselfishness of its subjects;"[5] and unfortunately, on this score, there was little in the American experience conducive to optimism.

Thus, the gulf between fair-minded and democratic public theories codified as law and the realities of late nineteenth century social and economic life was enormous. In that fact lay one of the greatest failures of general property taxation; it would be hard to imagine a system more prolific of inefficiency and injustice.

Inequities of the system were so numerous and extensive that they lend themselves to classification. Summarizing Northern experience with such injustices, an Ohio tax commission cited five types of inequality created between individuals by existing money machinery. They included inequities between the owners of realty and the owners of personalty; among owners of realty and owners of realty; between the owners of real or personal property on the one hand and the owners of corporate properties on the other; and among corporations. It was these inequities and their numerous ramifications that led a state comptroller in the late eighties to remark typically that "the present result [of general property taxation] is a travesty upon our taxing system, which aims to be equal and just."[6] Everywhere the tax lacked uniformity as manifested in the general disparities in assessments; everywhere it lacked universality, particularly in its failure to reach intangible property; everywhere it encouraged dishonesty; everywhere it was believed to burden the already overburdened; and everywhere it provoked serious problems of double taxation.[7] Each defect hastened the breakup of the inherited money machinery and raised a host of vexing problems for revenue reformers.

Perversely, the desire for fairness led to unfairness; inequalities in assessments, for example, stemmed from the fact that the property tax was apportioned, theoretically in deference to varied abilities to pay. Instead of levying a fixed rate on all property, the state determined total revenues required and allocated shares of the burden to lesser units of government in terms of their local assessments. The rate of taxation, it was hoped, would "therefore vary only with local needs;" but in practice "it is a notorious fact," declared a reformer in the eighties, "that in scarcely any two contiguous counties is the property, even the real estate, appraised in the same manner or at the same rate."[8]

For more than half a century evidence of this rose mountain high throughout the North. In Pennsylvania even after reforms had been initiated in 1893, the range of assessed to true values ran from 16% to 121% in Armstrong County, from 15% to 88% in Beaver County, on farm lands from 15% to 110%. In Ohio, as late as 1907, assessments for the entire state averaged 46% of full value, but the range through the counties was from 27% to 70%; in Indiana the variations ran from 40% to 80%; in Maryland, averaging 65% of full value, valuations ran from 45% to 70%; in Minnesota where the average was only 38%, county assessments ran from 27% to 55%; and in Pennsylvania counties varied as widely as 57% from one another.[9] Small wonder that critics and reformers cried out that "inequalities in assessments in the various counties" thrust "an undue proportion" of state taxes on the cities.[10]

The wildest inequalities occurred, as might have been expected, where personalty was actually assessed. In Ohio in the eighties personalty valuations ran from 3% to 300% of true value, a situation unmatched even in the grossest misassessments of realty. Although "not ten percent, perhaps not five percent" of the state's personal estate was listed—in fact, assessed personalty included only 3% of the intangible properties believed to have been located in Cincinnati (Hamilton County) and only 4½% in Cleveland (Cuyahoga County)—the rates charged once it was discovered were tantamount to levies of from 25% to 45%. Unequal burdens accordingly fell all the more unequally on realty holders in town and country as personalty payments declined in the face of threatening confiscation from $17½ million in 1868 to $7 million in 1895.[11] State by state, the best available testimony revealed the same patterns.

Corporate properties, precisely like the property of more ordinary taxpayers, were frequently victimized or faced with victimization by inequities in the operations of the general property tax. Advantages won by particular corporations from governments, or awarded to them by governments, were sometimes heavily counterbalanced by inequities. Exactness in such matters on any appreciable scale is almost an impossibility, but it would appear that this was especially true of various manufacturing, railroad, and financial corporations in every state of the North. Injustices between such enterprises, again, were sufficiently numerous to tempt investigators to classify them. New York State's Mills Committee in 1916 cited inequalities as between unincorporated businesses and corporations, between various corporations of different character, among corporations of the same character, and between domestic and foreign corporations, injustices which all were further complicated by inequities between corporations located in the same place and between corporations located in competing towns. While none of these types requires extensive comment here, a few examples of discriminations which vexed corporations under the general property tax might suggest nuances in the usual picture of corporate offenders against society, or might at least provide another explanation of why some were driven to offenses.

One continuous source of frustration both for corporations and governments was the unequal taxation of stocks, inevitable as this was in some measure. The problem even existed in Massachusetts where by the end of the seventies impressive steps had been taken toward rectifying corporate taxation. Thus, shares of the Hamilton Manufacturing Company were officially rated at $1000 each in Belmont and in Carlisle but at only $83 in Pepperell. Similar disparities appeared in valuations in the shares of the Appleton Company which were $900 apiece in Medford and $40 each in Brookline, while stock of the Lawrence Manufacturing Corporation was assessed at $800 each in Groton and just $75 in Quincy.[12] It was a brand of frustration and injustice brought on by assessors throughout the North.

Inefficient political administration, one consequence of the decentralization and localism still cherished in many places, produced a "multitude of varied and discriminating exactions" among New England industries; and these were correctly described as "real and discriminating deductions from profits." Some of these inequities were caused by the vagaries of interstate taxation, but most were due to the vagaries of local politics. In Maine, where corporations were taxed under provisions of the general property tax until the opening of this century, the pulp wood industry, an important one in the state's economy, was assessed in almost as many ways as there were towns and assessors. In Maine—in fact, in New England townships generally—communities were often "saddled" with costs which elsewhere were assumed directly by property holders; therefore, official obligations were incurred at times with a weather eye cocked on promising sources of revenue and the pulp corporations were frequently voted the chief benefactors of local governments in town meetings. The unequal taxation of these enterprises was thus traceable to fluctuating needs for local revenues rather than to principled policy. Where population was sparse and investments were scanty, public expenditures derived from inequity; Maine's public corporations evidenced just as powerful survival instincts as its private corporations.[13]

Because of its vital importance in the economy, its relative novelty, and its massive size and sprawl, the railroad industry, whatever the advantages vouchsafed it by public authorities, suffered from most forms of fiscal inequity and discrimination; in that sense it can be treated as symbolic of many of the types of injustice confronted by many other corporate bodies. Again, politicized assessors were responsible for blatant discrepancies in railway valuations, already notorious at the opening of the seventies. In 1871 and 1872, the Wells Commission denounced the taxation of railroads in New York as "imperfect and objectionable as it well can be." Road beds and line realty were assessed in the towns through which tracks passed "according to no uniform standard, but at the discretion, or rather the caprice, of local assessors." In several communities the state found that the rate of railway taxation depended on the amounts locally required to defray highway expenses; in one town cited by the commissioners, the erection of an "expensive bridge" for the railroad over a navigable river "was regarded . . . as a sufficient warrant for the erection of a new school house" paid for eventually with money taxed from the railroad. In still another town where the railroad had replaced an unsatisfactory stationhouse for the town's benefit, the town promptly reciprocated by increasing the corporation's taxes. Similar railway property located in two adjoining counties of New York was assessed with a $24,000 per mile difference between them; while in other counties the variations ran as high as $20,000 a mile. Valued at "an immense sum per mile" in one county, railway property, remarked the state, would be treated like "a piece of grazing land" in another.[14]

It was situations of this kind which led Charles Francis Adams, Jr., and two fellow commissioners on railroad taxation to report in 1879 that railroads were paying as much as one-third of all the taxes in a number of towns in New York while the assessed valuation of their properties varied from $100 a rod to $400 a rod. "In certain states," observed the commissioners, railroads were viewed by officials as a species of windfall "from which everything which can be extracted in the way of taxation is so much pure gain."[15] To be sure, some roads readily forgot to mention their public blessings and there was no doubt much spurious wailing in the market place, but clearly predacious urges flowed *from* as well as *toward* public authorities in late nineteenth century America.

However advanced Pennsylvania's fiscal system was considered to be, it was, as a close student of the state's industries and government observed early in the nineties, "an impossibility for its system of taxing railroads" to function "equitably as between roads." On railway realty the informed opinion was that the roads were paying taxes "fully equal to the average taxes paid on real estate by other taxpayers" which only made the taxation of personalty under the other half of general property taxation all the more vexing to highly competitive railroad men.[16] Indeed, the inequities complained of among the railroads lying entirely inside the boundaries of the state were apparent during the last quarter of the nineteenth century. The bonded indebtedness, to begin with, formed a substantial, in some instances, a major part of their capital, much being held in other states. Consequently, the company stock on these roads were virtually untaxed. One road holding $230,000 in bonds outside of Pennsylvania showed a taxable capital of $384 on which $1.92 was due the government of the commonwealth. Compared to a competitive sister road which held all of its $200,000 in bonds, plus $80,000 in stock, inside of Pennsylvania, the tax advantages—and inequities—were obvious.[17]

Inevitably the intricacies of determining a railroad's taxable value, a matter quite apart from the motives of officials, also produced unequal taxes and unequal burdens. By the early 1890's investigatory and reform organizations across the North had begun elaborating sophisticated criteria for estimating the fair valuation of a road's taxable property. The advice of the Pennsylvania Tax Conference along this line, for instance, was to add to the actual value of the share capital the market value of the funded debt, that is whether the bonds were above or below par, and when deductions from the aggregate share capital essential to avoid double taxation had been made, "fair value" remained.

During previous years, however, legislators or men familiar with railroad construction and finance were reluctant to admit, perhaps in some cases as a result of understandable ignorance, that the par value of a railroad's stocks and bonds did not necessarily reflect the road's actual value. Objectively there were several reasons why this was so, a major one being that stocks and bonds frequently were issued for much less than their face value; sometimes, in fact, stocks were given away free to bondholders. When chances for profit seemed unattractive, both stocks and bonds might periodically be sold at reductions to cover risks. Moreover, after a road had been constructed, overbonding and overcapitalization, or such common factors as poor choice of location, heavy grades, tunneling, or shoddy contracting often adversely affected the corporation's earning power, driving its value below cost. Often too, roads which cost the most per mile, and hence seemed to be those enjoying strongest financial backing, because of cuts and fillings, bridges or tunnels, proved the least profitable and the least valuable. As the Pennsylvania Tax Conference argued, a railroad costing $100,000 a mile was sometimes less valuable than one costing $30,000 a mile; the higher priced road might even have sold for less than the less expensive one. Unfortunately for the principle of equal taxation of corporations, assessors, required to determine actual values, rarely equalized the impact of inequitable taxes on railroad corporations.[18]

Complex inequities in the taxation of railroads were far from singular; banking institutions also fought strenuously against what they regarded as unfair taxation throughout the last quarter of the nineteenth century. By 1866 Congress had made New York bankers sensitive to their burdens; at that point the solons were already being blamed for levying upon them "every tax it could devise." In this context concurrent state and local taxes which bankers believed were the handiwork of avaricious and demagogic politicians proved particularly galling. More galling still in the teeth of such "injustice" was the low estimation bankers believed the man in the street had of them. Pro-banking editorials sometimes reflected the contempt of the unenlightened and unsympathetic public beyond the teller's window. People who talked "glibly about banks shirking taxation," declaimed the *Commercial and Financial Chronicle* in 1881, were simply baring "their entire ignorance of the whole subject," for there was "no species of capital in the United States, contributing today in equal proportion to the support of the government." Often the point had merit, though not necessarily because of the intrinsic virtue of the banking fraternity.[19]

The most persistent fears of the New York bankers were of local rather than of national origin and it was easy to understand why. The culprit again was the inequitable general property tax. In 1881 the total assessed value of personalty for New York State was reckoned at $332 million, almost $100 million of which was for national bank shares alone. State assessors' reports in 1880 indicated that banks were heavily discriminated against by personalty assessments; Albany banks, for instance, paid 58% of all the taxes collected on personalty in that city, while the banks of Manhattan paid 36% of the personalty taxes there. Or, to put the matter in a slightly different light, state taxes on the entire City of New York in 1878 were only three-quarters of a million dollars more than city banks paid to the federal and state government on one and a quarter billion dollars less capital. National banks in the city paid more taxes "than all the State taxes collected in the whole State," outside of four very rich counties. On a capital of more than $10 million the Bank of Commerce alone paid $264,000 to the state and city, considerably more than was paid to those governments by all the insurance companies of the city except the life companies.[20]

New York bankers thus decided that their capital was being "selected out" by assessors because it was relatively easy to reach; and assessors admitted that by 1881 bank capital was being assessed at 85% of true value while other property was often assessed at less than 10% of true value. This was the situation to which banks referred when they denounced "the inveterate disposition" of legislators to subject their class of corporations to "statutory discrimination."

Some discriminations, of course, worked in favor of banks, their laments to the contrary. Bank buildings and realty in Manhattan were assessed on a higher portion of their true value than other real estate so that bankers could avail themselves of larger deductions from assessments on their shares of capital. They also found it feasible to convert or threaten to convert capital into nontaxable federal securities. Notwithstanding this, or the many other privileges which they enjoyed, banks claimed that an honest response to the high rates of personalty taxation would have meant a serious curtailment of their profits, impairment of their competitive positions,[21] outright confiscation, and sometimes liquidation.

Disadvantaged locally in many instances, Manhattan banks also felt at a loss in the face of outside competition. With "oppressive and illegal" taxes resting on them, they argued through the 1870's that vis-à-vis banks in Chicago, Milwaukee, Boston, or Philadelphia paying 3% against their 5%, they were the most heavily taxed banks in America.[22] The Bankers' Association, as at Saratoga in 1878 for instance, decried the vulnerability of New York banks to local taxation and pointed with alarm to the flight of bank capital from the state. Between 1875 and 1881, informed estimates were that Manhattan bank capital declined by over $24 million, allegedly because of unjust burdens. Bank authorities reported that by 1879 another $70 million had gone out of the banking business despite the vast increase in the volume of commerce. With the possibility of making 20% on capital invested in a textile mill or an iron foundry contrasted with the barest possibility of making 6% to 8% in banking—and making that only with the benefit of large surpluses and valuable connections—an investor's choice was manifest.[23]

From Nebraska to New York, from Iowa to Illiois to Maine, state documents year after year were filled with "complaints and open confessions," like those of the banks and railroads, that corporate taxation under the general property tax was grossly unjust. Boards of equalization, gradually introduced in some states in the last decades of the century to cope with the lack of uniformity and other inequities, even disappointed the men who urged their creation as "a clumsy and cumbersome attempt to accomplish the impossible." Under the circumstances the courses left open to corporations were clear; what is more, most officials recognized that many enterprises were caught between paying confiscatory or highly inequitable rates and evading their obligations. "In the final instance, it is the opinion of this Committee," concluded New York's Mills Committee in 1916 speaking the mind of many such bodies, "after a careful investigation through consultation with a large number of the principal manufacturers in the State, that the manufacturing industry as a group is thoroughly willing to bear its just share of the tax burden." But, added the committee, "the widespread evasion which has resulted to date is a direct result of the attempt to enforce a most inequitable tax."[24]

Practically speaking, this meant that the more corporate personalty increased, the less of it, proportionately, was likely to be paid into public coffers. Nearly every state and federal census between 1870 and 1910 confirmed this. The statistics compiled county by county in New York State in 1914, 1915, and 1916 were indicative of the trends which state comptrollers, assessors, and treasurers were reporting everywhere. For example, of the 51 domestic corporations assessed in the town of Esopus, Ulster County, corporations whose capital had risen to over $33 million, less than one-fifth of one percent ($60,700) was paid in taxes for personalty under the general property tax; in the town of Washington, Dutchess County, a corporation with $16 million of capital stock ended with an assessment of $50,000 on which only a few hundred dollars in taxes were actually paid, a dutiful performance—six others with nearly $20 million in capital stock outstanding, one-fifth of it taxable, paid nothing. And there were hundreds of corporations whose profiles were scrutinized, like a manufacturing concern with a capital stock of $1,600,000 and total assets of twice that amount, which while admitting to $1 million of taxable personalty paid not a penny to the state.[25]

It was corporate evasions of this sort that produced some of the ridiculous evidence in official reports of the fiscal system—and the distribution of property which it affected. In 1877, for instance, one New York town returned only $5000 in personalty taxes, but an adjoining one, a manufacturing town of roughly equal prosperity and size, returned over $700,000; in 1888, again, a New Jersey township dependent on manufactures acknowledged possession of just $591 in assessable corporate personalty; and still another manufacturing town which had returned more than $2¼ million in corporate realty mustered less than $50,000 in personalty payments. Yet these absurdities were a national phenomenon.[26] As one authority noted, whole classes had been exempted from taxation by express provisions of the law in parts of Europe during the Middle Ages; but in the United States during the late nineteenth and early twentieth centuries whole classes were inadvertently exempted from taxation "by the ineviable working of the law."[27]

These inequities associated with collapsing fiscal machinery naturally became an enormous hotbed for white collar crime—and this was fully recognized. In 1886 the Illinois Tax Commission described general property taxation as "debauching to the conscience and subversive of the public morals—a school for perjury, promoted by law." Connecticut officials in 1887 denounced the "demoralization of the public conscience" which had arisen from general taxes as "an evil of the greatest magnitude." Stirred by the loss of moral appearances, New Hampshire commissioners declared in the midst of the depression of 1876 that the "mere failure to enforce the tax" was insignificant compared to the mischief caused by "the corrupting and demoralizing influences" of the system itself. Law to the contrary, West Virginians were reported through the last years of the century to be treating their public obligations precisely like the donations they made in church or Sunday school;[28] general taxation, in short, had become a tax on ignorance and honesty.

The courts, which might have brought some clarity to matters, though their roles were neither easy nor uncomplicated, simply added to the confusion and demoralization in many cases. Seeking honorably to defend some broad interest or principle, they at times perversely sustained frauds and evasions perpetrated against existing revenue laws.[29] In February 1870, for example, the day before Kansas personalty was to be listed for taxation, a citizen wrote a check payable to himself in tax exempt U.S. notes against his bank balance of nearly $20,000 in current funds. Paid over to him, these were deposited in a sealed envelope in the bank's vault. Two days after listing, he placed his money on deposit again. Learning of the dodge, tax officers jumped his assessment $9000 for moneys on deposit. Unable to have himself stricken from the rolls, the evader then asked the courts to have the tax enjoined; this, the courts refused, noting that his remedy was at law. Yet while the transaction was undeniably conducted in order to evade taxation, the court salvaged him by deciding that his notes were tax exempt, precluding further action by anyone.[30] Similar cases arose elsewhere. In 1877 Indiana's Supreme Court determined that the very device employed in Kansas was "an effectual means" by which individuals could legally place their credit beyond the state's taxing authority, and a New York Court of Appeals, to cite just one other instance out of many, argued that assessors were legally bound by certain transactions even though the court itself recognized them as bald devices to escape taxation.[31]

Confusion and demoralization, though sometimes compounded by the courts, were hardly caused by them; rather, it was the confiscatory nature of certain general property taxes when they were actually applied that provided a major incentive to evasion, especially by corporations. Notwithstanding their "model" fiscal system, Massachusetts taxpayers were reminded by their Tax Commission of 1897 how deeply the state was capable of biting into the property of security holders; "the rates now common with us," explained the commissioners, placed the taxation of securities in the commonwealth "higher than has ever been contemplated in a civilized country." Prevailing interest rates rarely exceeded 4½%, while the tax rate averaged 1½%, a third of the income likely to be derived from securities. "Can we expect . . . to collect honestly, equally, and effectively" a tax amounting to 33⅓% "levied upon the most elusive type of property?"[32]

A number of revenue reformers began many years before the end of the last century to denounce the confiscatory effects of general taxation. Writing on the strength of experience as both a manufacturer in Pennsylvania and Ohio and as a tax reformer, John Winslow Cabot vigorously attacked Ohio's confiscatory rates of the eighties. Convinced that the brunt of taxation fell directly on "the great middle class of property holders," Cabot illustrated the inequities of a high tax rate by reference to his own investment in Chicago, Burlington, and Quincy 7% bonds on which his payment to the state was equivalent to a 47% tax on gross income. Not surprisingly, he labelled such taxation "a monstrous injustice" which was "almost universally evaded" in Ohio; perjury was cheaper than 47%.[33]

Before the century was out, it was clear that neither corporate nor individual taxpayers were moral heroes; nor for that matter were the men who collected. When in 1888 a Baltimore tax collector tried enforcing levies on personalty, property holders who had grown smug with extended evasion signalled acute distress and forced the momentary abandonment of official good intentions. They were mollified with the news that those who voluntarily returned personalty would be fairly treated, that officials to put it more bluntly, would willingly violate the law to pacify them with partial taxation. Explained Richard Ely in 1888, that "was the best a practical man could do" under the Free State's laws. Money at interest or money invested in taxable bonds brought only 4% or less, thus a tax rate of $1.78¾ was equivalent to what Ely described as a "truly exorbitant" tax of 45%.[34]

Confiscatory rates, added to the common knowledge that taxes were being evaded, confirmed many taxpayers in the belief that the price of civic honesty was the assumption of other people's bills. "The honest taxpayer," wrote a reformer in the nineties, "would willingly bear his fair share of the burden, but he cannot concede his obligation to pay other men's taxes."[35] Businessmen grew sensitive to the costs of an honorable relationship with the state because of the blows that might be dealt their capacities to compete with firms that were evading personalty taxation. A conscientious Baltimorean cited by a state commission illustrated the plight into which some of his kind could fall. Requesting that the value of his personalty be raised from $5000 to $20,000, he was informed by tax officials that now the valuation of his book accounts were liable. Shocked, he declared that his competition with untaxed firms was too severe to allow further payments and the compassionate tax officers assured him in hearings before the Court of Appeals that his book accounts would be ignored. Any other course, suggested Maryland's commissioners, "would have been mean as well as disadvantageous to the city [of Baltimore]." Yet, as their report correctly observed, "it was not the law."[36]

Threats of confiscatory burdens were compounded by menacing forms of double taxation, again a product of general property taxation as applied to an increasingly complex society, and a source of great distress to both individuals and corporations. Of these forms, there were two broad types which were especially prolific of anxieties and inequities. The first type included debt exemptions; the second and closely related type embraced complications of double taxation which arose from the profusion of American political units and from interstate rivalries or misunderstandings.

Debt exemption policies revealed what one authority accurately described during the late nineteenth century as "the greatest weakness in the general property tax." That was probably allowing too much, considering the claims of its other weaknesses. But there is no question that debt exemptions roused interminable controversies over state and local taxation. Across the North, as a result, there were vocal groups demanding that they be taxed solely for what they owned rather than for what they owed. In short, it was the taxation of both borrowers and lenders, coupled with the reluctance of various states to offset many forms of indebtedness, that lay at the heart of the dissidence.[37]

Debates over the taxation of mortgages crystallized the chief arguments in behalf of debt exemption. Attacking Massachusetts' policy of taxing mortgages at full rate, Brooks Adams defined the problem in 1878. Charging that the commonwealth's "preposterous" handling of mortgage debts resulted in oppressive burdens on the poor and in the disillusionment of the "most reliable and conservative portion of society," the small landowner and thrifty self-reliant workingmen, Adams argued that double taxation was extracting $1½ million a year from them. Indeed, it was "crushing them." If a man purchased a two-thousand-dollar farm on which he paid half and borrowed the rest, it seemed to Adams irrational to tax the purchaser on two thousand dollars of property and simultaneously to tax the lender on one thousand dollars as well. On this view, of course, the issue was drawn, for where he saw two thousand dollars of property, irrespective of how it might be divided between borrower and lender, the commonwealth saw three thousand dollars of value, assuming—as Adams did not—that the debt actually increased the amount of property in existence. Drawing statistics from the state's Bureau of Statistics of Labor in 1876, Adams also examined the interest rate in Massachusetts, the better to dramatize the effects of double taxation on the poor. Since untaxed government bonds paid 4%, men were paying 7⁴⁄₁₀% on their mortgage loans, Adams concluded that 3½% of this figure represented the inroads of double taxation. That is to say, if personalty taxation on mortgages had been abolished, workers and small landowners might have borrowed on their property for substantially less interest than they were actually required to pay.[38]

Adams felt the commonwealth could hardly have done more to discourage property holding among the middle and lower classes. And yet the inequity had emerged from the democratic hope that every citizen would be taxed according to his individual ability to pay; since a mortgage composed a portion of a man's property, it followed that he ought to pay on it. But Adams believed that it was *property* that ought to bear taxes, not *men*. The "supposed ability" of citizens to pay he considered irrelevant; only the intrinsic worth of property constituted wealth. Notes, bonds, and mortgages, on the contrary, were nothing more than evidence that money had been loaned on the assumption that the property involved possessed inherent value. A tax on the mere evidence of a debt was a double tax, he felt, since taxing the property itself and then taxing the money raised on the strength of it was to tax twice. Thus, when Adams labelled this "absurd in theory" and "iniquitous in practice," a source of inflationary pressures on the interest rate, a crimp on industry, an accentuation of injustice, and a spur to discontent, he was speaking for thousands of others in the North.[39]

Hoping to abolish taxes on intangible properties and to end double taxation, William Endicott, Jr., carried the argument against double burdens levied upon book debts, municipal bonds, and railroad bonds. His criticisms of efforts to tax railway bonds were, in fact, typical of his objections to most duplicate taxation. The Fitchburg Railroad served as one of his examples. To secure funds for laying a second track early in the seventies, the road had to issue mortgage bonds and pay 7% to borrow the money. Of necessity the railroad subsequently had to draw from the communities which it serviced sufficient earnings to cover its expenses, interest payments, and profits. Supposedly, the interest rate on the bonds included the tax, but Endicott questioned "if one-quarter . . . of such bonds pay tax anywhere." The result, he insisted, was that the public paid the tax to the road when it used its facilities; the road paid it to the bondholders; one-fourth of the bondholders paid the tax to the commonwealth; and the remainder of the bondholders kept the money for themselves. "Why should the bonds be taxed?" wondered Endicott. If they were not, the railroad could have borrowed money for 5½% to 6% and might thereafter have operated at lower rates. From his perspective, once the corporation was taxed, all the property it owned had been taxed. Why tax it a second time, he asked, simply because it owed money?[40]

Equally pertinent questions were raised about the taxation of investments outside of a state and about the taxation of shares in foreign corporations, for in these instances also the tax on the lender was considered a tax on the borrower. Boston's William Minot, reviewing Massachusetts money machinery in 1876, argued the unfortunate consequences which ensued when the state taxed bonds held by its citizens and thereby taxed the foreign corporations (railroads in this case) which sold them. First, by interfering with industry elsewhere, Massachusetts was imposing penalties on its own people who were seeking profits in other states. In addition, honest taxpayers were being forced to pay levies on the same property twice—once in Massachusetts and again in the foreign state. Worse yet, declared Minot, they shouldered taxes which the dishonest escaped as well as the higher prices chargeable by businessmen who were free from a measure of competition thanks to their evasion.[41]

By the mid-eighties, arguments by such men as Adams, Endicott, and Minot had gained some success, particularly in respect to the double taxation of personalty, corporate properties, or the properties of men who were interested in them. Some states even tried to remove the problem by legislation. Legislative elements in Maryland and Connecticut, for example, sought to reshape policy by conceding that the capital stock of a corporation constituted its "whole property." And, naturally, the practical advantages of a lower interest rate, greater attractions for floating capital, and boons to the community at large were expected to result from such proposals, although in fact they never did in any demonstrable way.

In other states, however, these proposals were viewed with alarm; certainly this was the case in the vast majority of Northern legislatures. Without denying the assertions made by opponents of double taxation, the greater number of tax authorities and revenue reformers, insisted that once any allowances were made for further deductions of indebtedness, injustice and evasion would totally debilitate already tottering state and local fiscal machinery. Given the embryonic state of civic virtue, the ranges of opportunities and temptations, the limitations on administrative capacities, and the differentials in local tax rates, everything in Northern experience supported this dubiety. New Jersey, for instance, allowed deductions from the value of both real and personal estate for debts due persons in the state; that policy stood from 1851 to 1868. Afterward, however, following the arguments of Chancellor Ogden before the legislature in 1867, deductions, except in counties adjacent to New York, were substantially disallowed, a change provoked by a series of evils and inequities. Massachusetts had similarly run afoul of innumerable difficulties in the seventies when allowances were made for incumbrances or mortgages; the commonwealth not only experienced the anticipated frauds but also endless controversy between towns as to whose tax rates should apply.[42]

Thus, as one expert explained in 1884, despite the recurrence of petitions, mainly of rural origin, urging legislatures to exempt property from double taxation, it was neither expunged from the statute books nor vitiated by judicial fiat. Occasionally certain exceptions were enacted in behalf of special classes of corporations; in other cases, as in

Kansas and Iowa, the states' legal attitudes were indeterminate. But generally the risks of abandoning double taxation were judged too great. The Massachusetts Tax Commission in 1875 admitted that despite the letter of the constitution, the people of the state could exempt certain categories of property, such as mortgages, from double taxes; however, the more vital question, they felt, was whether such taxation comported with the state's true theory of taxation—and they found that it did not.[43]

Identical decisions were made elsewhere; the Illinois Constitution empowered the legislature to tax corporations as it saw fit and enabling legislation permitted taxation of all property within the state, inclusive of corporate capital stock over and above tangible corporate properties. When challenges were brought to these provisos before the state supreme court it ruled that since tangible corporate property and capital stock were distinct kinds of property the taxation of both was neither double taxation nor unconstitutional. Acting under similar presumptions of unlimited power, the Pennsylvania Legislature consistently enacted laws calling for the double taxation of corporate wealth. Moreover, in *Pittsburgh Railroad v. The Commonwealth,* the state judiciary unequivocally sanctioned double taxation as always having been lawful in the state. In the eyes of the court, Harrisburg possessed as much power "to tax twice as to tax once;" indeed, as the court further explained, the state constitution did not require equality of taxation. The conflict, therefore, between legal mores and "sound economics" as then widely understood could hardly have been sharper; fiscal inequality was legally justifiable; but economically it flung wide the gates to injustice and confusion, nowhere more dramatically than in the relations of corporations and the state.[44]

Double taxation of corporations assumed five important forms: the double taxation of property and debts, or of income and interest on debts; double taxation of property and income, or of property and stock; double taxation due to interpolitical complications; and double taxation of the corporation and of its holders of stocks and bonds. Theoretically, none of these forms was inherently pernicious insofar as either the public or corporations were concerned. However, in operation they all displayed pernicious qualities.[45]

How fiscal and legal problems attending double taxation helped cripple the money machines can be illustrated by examples of interstate corporate taxation and by the taxation of corporations and their stock and bondholders. Migrations of intangible wealth, of course, as we saw in the last chapter, were contemptuous of political boundaries; what, then, was the taxable *situs* for this wealth? The question repeatedly perplexed legislatures and courts, creating chaos in state laws. Generally, a man's personal estate was taxed where it was located in a state, but the legal fiction that personalty followed its owner was elaborated because of the remarkable mobility characteristic of the new wealth. Therefore, if the owner of a bundle of stock was not a resident of Massachusetts, his personalty was taxed once in that commonwealth and once again in his state of residence. Avoiding this trap required devious special legislation. Yet precisely the same situation confronted the corporation, for its personalty was usually assessed at its place of business. An apparent solution seemed to lie in exempting portions of corporate property taxed elsewhere, but without federal compulsion to create uniformity or interstate comity in the face of "local mercantilism," the conscience of the states never developed very vigorous roots.

Special difficulties arose because of the simultaneous taxation of the same corporate stocks or bonds by two or more states. A spate of legislation, like that passed in New York and Pennsylvania during the late seventies and the mid-eighties, strove to tax only so much of the capital stock as was employed in the state and at times this approach made sense. With railroad corporations, specifically, it proved feasible merely to assess capital stock in some proportion to the road's mileage lying inside the state. But for other types of corporation, the guiding phrase "capital employed within the state" clarified nothing. What, after all, constituted corporate capital—stocks alone, bonds alone, or both together, taxable as corporate capital? What corporation doing business on an interstate scale, moreover, could then have determined accurately how much of its capital was located outside of a particular state? And even if such estimates had been possible, how was evasion practiced beyond the jurisdiction of the taxing state preventable? Many assaults were launched against these problems, but no solution was forthcoming.[46]

State revenue laws often treated the property of foreign corporations as if it were the property of domestic concerns. Though admitting the injustice of double taxation resting on their own corporations, few states were prepared to tolerate the exemption of foreign corporations upon which full taxation had already been visited elsewhere. This was more than an issue of fees and licenses exacted from out-of-state businesses wishing to operate in another state; those tolls were regarded as legitimate payments for the privileges extended. But the assessment of corporations without legally determining whether they were foreign or domestic and taxing them frequently in each of several states on the basis of the whole amount of their business or their capital stock, was a constant cause of anxious complaint. It undoubtedly disposed many concerns to view the general property tax as a blanket under which they might suffocate.

Other difficulties centered about the issue of whether a state could or should also tax individuals who owned corporate stocks or bonds if a corporation's property was taxed. Certainly the law was without uniformity on this subject. In some states individually owned corporate stock was exempt when the corporation's other property was taxed; Michigan, Maryland, New York, Ohio, and West Virginia, for example, all followed this policy, Its exact reverse, however, applied in Illinois, Indiana, Iowa, Maine, Massachusetts, New Jersey, and Pennsylvania. Positing that shares of stock drew their value from the corporate franchise and corporate property, these states distinguished between the property of shareholders or bondholders and property of the corporation, and the courts often sustained this view. Policies in many states, though, were simply ambivalent. Certain types of corporation were taxed directly and their shareholders were then taxed also; other classes of corporation were effectually exempted from all duplicate taxation; while in other instances, corporations were taxed and shareholders were exempted. In sum, contradictions piled high upon contradictions.

It was too much to have expected the judiciary to have brought instant lucidity to such complex, novel, and dynamic situations; and on the whole the judiciary managed not to do so. United States Supreme Court decisions were oracular or conflicting; or so they seemed to men waiting for enlightenment about the perversities of their money machinery. In the *Van Allen* case and the *Delaware Railroad Tax Case* (1873), the High Court initially upheld double taxation of the corporation and its shareholders, but not for long. It subsequently handed down several decisions which presumed against the legitimacy of double taxation without denying the states' legal right to levy such taxes if the legislatures willed it.[47]

The same legal chaos, reflecting the *ad hoc* twists and turns of legislatures, characterized policies for the taxation of corporate mortgage bonds, although the disagreements were less pronounced than those over the taxing of stocks until the last decades of the nineteenth century. Up to that point, corporate loans were infrequently assessed by most states. Connecticut, an exception, did simultaneously tax both the corporation and its bondholders. Nonetheless, where such taxation occurred, the Connecticut approach usually was not adopted. Thus, Maryland and Pennsylvania each in fact, exempted its individual bondholders. And so it went. After the *State Tax Case* on foreign bonds was decided by the Supreme Court in 1872, the judicial tendency was to find that a tax on bonds was a tax on bondholders, not on corporations. Therefore, as the taxation of corporate loans became more general, the double taxation already familiar in the case of stocks likewise grew commoner. As astute observers recognized, beneath the chaos lay a fundamental question which the nineteenth century simply could not resolve conclusively: namely, what was the incidence of taxes levied on corporations?[48]

Both the opponents and advocates of double taxation were partially correct, although neither group had the evidence to clinch its case. Some experts conceded the injustice of taxing borrowers and lenders on the same property; others stoutly emphasized that only property and not men should be taxed. Governments frequently took the position that property should have been taxed only because it served as an index of the individual's ability to pay and that ability obviously was diminished by indebtedness, "true taxable property" consisting of a man's surplus after the subtraction of his debts. Yet this posture, too, had its difficulties and those who like E. R. A. Seligman reasoned their way to it, also argued that when the law sanctioned offsets for debt, the opportunities for fraud had been and always would be so great that they would prove a grant of immunity to those best able to pay.[49] Thus policies of no-debt-exemption, which almost invariably caused double taxation, and policies of debt-exemption alike came to be viewed as equally unendurable. "The states shift from one policy to the other in equal despair," wrote Seligman in 1890, "we are therefore forced to the conclusion that the whole system is unsound."[50]

Injustice and inequity, then, in this area as in so many others came from the general property tax. Wherever levied, its rates tended to increase as the property being taxed decreased in value. It landed squarely on certain private and corporate holders of realty, notably on those who were honest, scared, ignorant, or devoid of political pull. For these people and corporations, the tax was truly general and, thanks to the evasion everywhere underway, it was also burdensome and in many instances, as charged, grossly unfair.

The collapsing fiscal machinery of Northern polities, therefore, was left all the more vulnerable by the social attitudes which developed around—and partly as a result of—the inequities it spawned. In America, as in Europe, many decades had been required to create a responsible taxpaying public accustomed to identify itself with the support of government. The model taxpayer, like the model industrial worker, was the product of time and a substantial measure of social discipline. The willingness to share in the handling of public burdens, both in the impersonal atmosphere of urban-industrialism and in the increasingly decadent quarters of the countryside, presupposed a highly developed sense of civic obligation. To arouse this social spirit among propertied elements, governments, lacking clear guides to what constituted "public purpose,"[51] were forced to bend and trim in order to justify their policies and fend off continuous criticism. Even so, Northern money machines were run grudgingly and ineptly, amid continual disgruntlement, while corporations, men, or communities which adjusted to inequities and still cheerfully and honestly contributed to the common burden were exceedingly rare.

What we call machine politics springs from the cost of elections.

HENRY GEORGE

"Money in Elections," *North American Review,* March 1883.

That great and growing volume of political work to be done in managing primaries, conventions, and elections for the city, State, and National governments . . . and which the advance of democratic sentiments and the needs of party warfare evolved . . . needed men who should give to it constant and undivided attention. These men the plan of rotation in office provided. Persons who had nothing to gain for themselves would soon have tired of the work.

Politics has been turned into the art of distributing salaries so as to secure the maximum support from friends with the minimum offence to opponents.

JAMES BRYCE

The American Commonwealth, 1888.

If then we are to have parties and if we really desire their presence, if they are an essential part of the great task of democracy, how shall they be financed? Under the spoils system they were financed by government itself. . . . The party machine was furnished with fuel and lubricant at public expense.

ANDREW MC LAUGHLIN

"The Significance of Political Parties," *Atlantic Monthly,* CI [1908].

4

The Cult of Efficiency and Party Finance

To this point we have examined only the formal, legal dimension of the North's dual fiscal systems; it is to the informal, to the extralegal, and to aspects of the illegal dimension of these systems that we must now turn.

Like the feeding of Siamese twins, the financing of political parties and of governments were inseparable acts; the starvation of one meant the starvation of the other. Faced with the collapse of local fiscal systems, a collapse caused chiefly by the stresses of the new urban-industrial democracy, the effects of massive evasion, and great inequities, politicians everywhere in the North became acutely conscious of the fact, as one of them phrased it, "that so long as the present system of taxation is maintained, the raising of revenue will be resisted and rendered impracticable."[1] They were entirely correct and the threat to their party revenues and party structure was obvious and genuine. Smarting from the incidence of general property taxation, the middle classes sought to pare down their obligations, not only by chiseling, but also—and for the greater part—by treating government, most particularly municipal government, as they would have treated any business corporation. Thus, as Boston's mayor noted in 1895, "the theory that the affairs of a city should be managed like those of an ordinary business corporation is attractive and widespread." Unpersuaded by the popularity of the proposition, the mayor argued forcefully that "bodies politic" differed "distinctively and widely from private and moneyed corporations both in organization, government, and action. . . . their object is government, not profit."[2] But among respectable voters, the mayor's views won little support. On the contrary, even politicians who doubtless agreed with him soon took refuge behind a facade of platitudes aimed at deflecting taxpayers' sallies against the sins of extravagance. Arguments in behalf of heavier public burdens paved the way to political retirement and excellence in government came to be equated with overall economies and semblances of efficiency which were often more apparent than real—but which were nonetheless necessary politically.

In short, the criteria for judging governmental performance, especially as battles over civil service reform mounted in intensity during the eighties, fell under the influence of a middle class "cult of efficiency."

Throughout government a censoriousness about taxing, spending, and borrowing—with a regularity and to a degree never before experienced—began haunting officialdom. "Ninety-nine per cent of all questions" which confronted city councils, legislatures, or executive departments, reported one seasoned politician, were fundamentally questions of expenditure; "the contest in almost every case," he noted, was "between extravagance and economy, between expenditure and retrenchment,"[3] rather than between the parties. As a consequence, during the last third of the nineteenth century, a fiscal "starving time" continually menaced government and party alike. The breakdown of the money machines and the resistance of the middle classes to "unjust" and "extravagant" policies, tended to constrict the vital resources of the state. The tax base grew less expansive than the many demands placed upon it by militant agricultural lobbies, heavy industries, a host of smaller special interests, and a variety of bustling political corporations, most notably the great cities.

As immediate fiscal pressures upon governments multiplied geometrically, so too did the financial obligations of the political parties which made all of these governments possible; indeed, it is these pressures and the vital responses to them which have so frequently been ignored in interpreting the years from the start of Reconstruction through the early nineties. These years have generally been depicted as a slough of despond lying between the dramatic eminences of the Civil War on the one hand and the Populist and Progressive crusades on the other hand.[4] Until recent reëvaluations,[5] the period was an historical wasteland populated by spoilsmen and nonentities, stigmatized by a lack of divisive "issues," by the prostitution of public trust to the service of private greed, by alternate cycles of corruption and prating mediocrity, and by the maladjustment of the political establishments to rapid changes in other areas of American life.

Yet these benchmarks of moral history, however useful in their day, leave many questions unasked and unexplained. Particularly was this true for the indistinct but enormously important realms of party finance upon which the extension and ramification of a democratic society hinged, if only because they so deeply determined the vitality and viability of political parties. In politics, of course, money was not everything; as veteran politicians such as Platt, Quay, or Roosevelt observed, the power of cash incentives in political life, especially in the upper echelons of party, could be and often was overrated. Still, neither party victory nor party survival was conceivable in any significant sense without the money to pay for it.

Well-begun in the generation before the Civil War, spoils had sufficed, at least in substantial measure, to pay for party operations. Party workers fed like leechs on the revenues flowing to and from public treasuries, mostly, to be sure, in the form of salaries or fees legitimately drawn for their jobs. Others recouped campaign losses or reimbursed themselves by securing bounties, subsidies, contracts, or concessions dispensable by the authority of party from the public till, this despite the fact that until late in the last century, political parties were fully private institutions, unrecognized by public law and unprovided for by direct public appropriations.

The extralegal fiscal systems of the parties were subjected to a powerful squeeze after the late sixties. The depredations of Tweed in Manhattan and of the Black Horse Cavalry in Albany, the scandals of the Grant Administration and of Reconstruction regimes in the South, provoked such great disaffection with party—even among partisans—that flagrant theft became not only reprehensible but dangerous. The brilliant reform mayor of Brooklyn, Seth Low, observed in the eighties that there was only one Tweed and that his techniques were "so hazardous as to have fewer and fewer followers." If many segments of the public were indifferent to allegations of venality in government, other segments continually threatened political death to anyone caught raiding the till or to anyone heavily tainted by corruption. Prosecutions for corruption certainly failed to swamp the jails, yet strong suspicions of corrupt activity became a political handicap, as some of the most popular politicians in the country, Blaine, for example, sadly came to appreciate. The very lustiness of outcries against public malfeasance and peculation, in fact, indicated rising public sensibilities against unauthorized or irresponsible fiscal operations,[6] these ultimately being determined by the rules of commercial cost accounting.

In short, the abstract standards of political behavior in America, as James Bryce remarked in the eighties, were exceedingly high—perhaps impossibly so if one subscribed to the dictum of a noted Kansas politician that the hope of purity in politics was an iridescent dream. The lofty uplift of middle class political morality, in part an outgrowth of respectable men's resistance to new rural and urban interpretations of democracy, thus generated demands that the spoils system itself, which they identified with Tweedism and gross political buccaneering, be destroyed.

This challenge to party organization was in every sense fundamental. Granted that a spoils system had posted "robbers, muddlers, bastards, and bankrupts"—as Sir Lewis Namier depicted members of eighteenth century Parliaments—to jobs in government, the fact remains that this procedure fulfilled several vital functions which permit much to be said in its favor.[7] To many Americans whose immigrant origins, low status, or depressed conditions left them uninstructed in select Anglo-Saxon concepts of citizenship, the system, though often tainted, was flexible, personal, and in its own way, democratic. These attributes were hardly imaginable of a nineteenth century civil service system whose operations were formed by middle class biases and whose personnel were chosen for middle class skills. Although officeseekers and hosts of the importunate were at times a trial to incumbent politicians and although reputable men often ridiculed this "degrading" process, it was, nonetheless, as one observer in the eighties remarked, "a legitimate fruit of our democratic institutions."[8] The vulgar swarmings and petty jockeyings associated with spoils politics were, in truth, earthy reactions to the increasingly irrelevant governments conceived under quite different auspices by patrician Fathers and their subsequent descendants of the townships and villages. Fearing "the impulses of the people," wrote Arthur Richmond in 1886 for the *North American Review,* the Founders abandoned as little as possible to the discretion of the governed; seeking to "make the government solid, they made it immovable;" it became "cast iron from end to end." Government by parties, and by spoils, overriding in Richmond's sardonic words "the wise saws of the framers," furnished "brute numbers" the chance to gain possession of the state[9] and to do so without first having to undergo some sort of social or moral elevation.

Consequently, while Mugwumpish reformers fought for the passage and then for enforcement of civil service legislation, the political power of the masses rendered such a course utopian to men who had to deal with other realities; to them the differing standards of competence entertained by the middle classes and by the less fortunate men and women below them in the social scale were not reflections of right and wrong, virtue or the lack of it; rather these standards reflected disparate social skills and different competitive positions. If to the powerful elements of the middle classes party seemed first designed to service their special interests and in the bargain to service society, the lower orders saw party as an agency to satisfy myriad wants associated with the trials and tragedies of daily life. Numbers, as Bryce and others observed, made the latter viewpoint more general than the former and politicians and the public service registered a substantial measure of this reality, too large a measure for the middle classes and not enough for the less fortunate. Spoils were rooted, therefore, not only in party but also in the nature of the society. "Not until we have a radical and at present . . . unexpected change in the attitude of the average voter," wrote the noted political scientist, Chester Jones in 1916, "can we hope for a cutting down of pressure for spoils."[10]

Meantime, it must be noted that spoils-built bureaucracies of the late nineteenth century were more effective, stable, and honest than we once believed. The Mugwumps were, for better or worse, incompetent to speak for the society-at-large, though it was their perspective that we once embraced, their denunciations that we once accepted. Even the New York Customs House, the perennial target of allegations after the Civil War, failed to conform fully to reformers' descriptions of it as a vast agency for plunder, commercial blackmail, and the distribution of boodle. Five-sixths of the country's levies on imports were collected there, so there was doubtless ample opportunity for corruption. The collector's duties, however, which were arduous and responsible, were quietly and ably performed. The assistant collector, who by the mid-eighties had served for a generation on a "miserable" income, brought talents to the job which *Harper's* ventured "would have made him one of the most eminent and successful of our leading business men." Both of these key figures oversaw the evaluations of thousands of imports as called for by exceedingly complex tariff laws, a task patently impossible to undertake without good sense and continual guesswork. That neither was totally corrupt, let alone that both were substantially above suspicion, is surprising. But they were not exceptional. The chief of the auditor's department and the surveyor, to whom the management of two hundred ship inspectors was intrusted, each had long records of impressive public service on the waterfront.[11] These aspects of the customs house had their analogues throughout government establishments at all levels. Regardless of the partisan criteria for the selection of officeholders, there is abundant evidence that many of them were competent and reasonably dedicated. James Bryce, who had few illusions about the weaknesses of American governments, did not find them inferior to their European counterparts.

The case propounded by the opponents of spoils, understandable and admirable as it was in many ways, was nevertheless overstated, as were most political criticisms of the nineteenth century. For small pay, uncertain tenure, and with more modest facilities than many private concerns doing equal volumes of business would have tolerated, many so-called spoilsmen labored with good effect even by middle class standards. And they often did so with integrity. It was for this reason that one of the original chroniclers of Tweed's byzantine career, Matthew Breen, cautioned against the facile presumption that the scandals of spoils politics implied "kindred corruption throughout the whole fabric, state and federal." Breen found it "illogical and unfair" to draw "sweeping conclusions from narrow and restricted premises" established by the "hysterical charges of emotional moralists."[12] In much the same vein, New York's reform politician, William Ivins, laid the unprofitability of discussions about municipal reform to the "incapacity of the critics" to grasp what cities were. Far from scorning urban administrations for their addiction to spoils and political corruption, Ivins argued that "the cities of this country are generally well governed." Even New York City, he believed, was as capably administered as might have been expected "under existing laws and political conditions." It was indeed "better governed" than might have been anticipated "if . . . the difficulties of good government under a representative democratic form" such as necessarily prevailed in a city of a million and a half inhabitants were properly understood.[13]

Appraising the worth of party-created bureaucracies dominated by spoils-men in the eighties, James Bryce, usually a negative critic, commended them for "enlisting more ingenuity and skill in their service" than was the case, he judged, anywhere else in the world. Nowhere else did he discover "so much order" issuing from "so much complexity." American governments at all levels were manned by "a fair proportion of upright and disinterested men" whom he reckoned were as honorable as their British counterparts.[14] Bryce was fully aware that municipal governments in particular suffered at times from spoils politics, but he also recognized that urban problems had roots quite apart from politics. Urban administrations faced tasks so staggering that he declared it impossible either to define or measure the corruption supposedly connected with their operations or to determine what standards ought to guide estimates of their performance. Favoritism and honest graft were obviously basic components of spoils politics and yet he guessed that aside from New York and Pennsylvania blatant venality was rare. Thus, assaying the whole system which derived its basic form from spoils, Bryce recorded approvingly that:

> The American masses have been obliged, both by democratic theory and by the structure of their government to proceed upon the assumption of their own competence. They have succeeded better than could have been expected. No people except the choicest children of England long trained in the practice of self-government could have succeeded half as well.[15]

Recent studies tracing a slow, spotty, but decided improvement in governmental administration from the federal level to municipalities during the last third of the nineteenth century support Bryce's evaluation.

At stake, then, when the spoils system was challenged, was a viable method of tying party coalitions together, of creating party governments, and of financing them, a method of doing all these things, in fact, on a grander scale and as effectively or more so than they were done anywhere in the world. The costs of spoils can only be measured against what might have prevailed without them. Certainly men who under a more aristocratic or more bourgeois system would have been excluded from public life because of ethnic, educational, economic, or social disqualifications were introduced into government under cover of the public payroll and to this extent spoils facilitated the sharing and transference of power among disparate groups. Between the first Jackson Administration and the Civil War, this arrangement smoothed the shift of authority at many levels from patricians to professional politicos who were more representative of business and commerce as well as of the expanding cities and their multiple interests. Over the subsequent generation the system broadened, eventually embracing on either side of the numerous middle class the Hannas, the Lodges, and the Roosevelts, on the one hand, and the less respectable Kellys, McLaughlins, and Crokers, on the other. Governments, as a consequence, were manned by an increasingly motley crew; but the crewmen socially as well as politically were heralds of the twentieth century's diverse and contradictory governing coalitions; they assuredly were not, as has sometimes been suggested, hangovers from bygone ages becalmed in a political Sargasso.

Today few would dispute the efficacy of employing public servants on a merit and career basis. But if the skills marshalled in such career bureaucracies are of a higher order than those plied by spoilsmen, the new bureaucrats have yet to demonstrate that they are more effective in their context than spoilsmen were in theirs. Moreover, where bureaucracies of the new style have been relatively powerful in the modern world, evidence suggests that congresses, legislatures, councils, and parliaments have been relatively weak.[16] Efforts to reform spoils politics consequently were not an unmixed blessing. More than that, considering the profound confusion about and contempt for party itself which underlay this brand of reformism, it posed a great danger to democracy without offering real alternatives.

To be sure, had parties been financed voluntarily or through the legal assignment of tax moneys, spoils might have been localized and restricted earlier and more rapidly. However, conditions which might have allowed this did not exist in the United States nor could anyone reasonably foresee them. The threats to parties produced by civil service reformers and by public resistance to the adequate expansion of the fiscal basis of each level of government, therefore, struck at the stoutest underpinnings of the American party system. Middle class viewpoints sanctioned political penury as well as governmental economy, an attitude which inherently aggravated and prolonged what this class often most despised. "The extension of Civil Service Reform," remarked Richard Henry Dana, "by cutting off the supply of offices, must tend to increase the demand for and the direct use of money for the support of the politicians."[17] And that was to say the very least of the matter.

Professional political establishments were menaced, in short, by an official financial drought commencing in the last quarter of the nineteenth century and it proved all the more serious because of the rising costs accompanying the increase in the number of voters, the number and frequency of elections, the geographical extension of party facilities across the continent, the attempts to expand party machinery in Northern cities as well as in the South, and the growing appetites of politicians and special interests.

The latter part of the nineteenth century was an age of organizational revolution, but political organizations in particular had grown on a scale without precedent elsewhere in the society; they were accordingly intricate and expensive. With a population of more than 100,000 in the mid-eighties, for instance, New Haven boasted a Republican organization which ranked among the largest bodies of any kind in the community; twelve hundred men constantly "guarding the common interests" and their vigil was not cheap. Tom Platt's state Republican machine in New York from the eighties to the turn of the century, counted between ten and thirteen thousand regulars whose "maintenance" cost nearly $20 million a year, from $1500 to $2000 per man. Matt Quay's Pennsylvania Republican machine, probably the most tightly disciplined in the land, was even more impressive and costly. While affiliated with Philadelphia's Reform Committee of 100, John Wanamaker reckoned that Quay controlled at least 20,000 regulars, more people than were employed by the Reading Railroad, the Baltimore and Ohio, the New Jersey Central, or the Lehigh Valley, and two-thirds of the number employed by the Pennsylvania Railroad, then purportedly the largest corporation in the world. Into the pockets of these party professionals, Quay poured an estimated $24 million annually during the late seventies and the eighties, a sum equal to two-thirds of the commonwealth's official annual expenditure as of 1888.[18]

Party obligations and expense were fully illustrated in New York City. Tammany's 60,000 reliable votes—those on which it could count even in a clean election—represented a very heavy financial commitment. In the eighties, for example, the city had 812 election districts, over 1000 by 1900. On election day, four inspectors and two clerks were assigned to each district by law, in 1887 a total of 4872 election officers, half Democrat, half Republican. The three men furnished by each party to the districts were paid $7.50 a day for five days, a total cost of about $183,000 for both major parties. But in a general election, nearly 45,000 additional men labored at the polling places, more than four-fifths of them being paid directly by the parties and, not surprisingly, by 1887 expenses for these contests were running over $700,000.[19]

Following the City Consolidation Act of 1882, the Board of Estimates and Apportionment assumed certain election costs in the name of the public, a very advanced step for the time, and by 1886 costs were up to $290,000, or about a third of the anticipated expenses in the legal machinery of local elections. This helped but did not end the financial plight faced by parties.[20]

National elections which required the services of U.S. marshals and their aides added thousands of dollars to political bills. Appointed for ten days at election time, aides to marshals, for instance, were paid $5 a day; federal law stipulated, in addition, that two election supervisors be appointed also at $5 a day for up to ten days of work in each district. Since some of this money came out of the public till, what the parties were able to give they were also in some measure able to take away again; but they had need of taking much more.[21]

By the eighties presidential elections cost more than half a million, all of which had to be paid directly by party organizations. The Cleveland contest of 1884 alone was reliably reported to have cost the New York Democracy one million dollars. Some of the costs were itemized: a single parade held in the Tenth District, for example, in which 1500 men, 600 of them in uniforms, turned out cost $1300. For the transportation of twenty-five men from each assembly district in company with their delegates to Chicago—in all 650 men at $22 each—the aspiring Warwicks of the County Democracy paid $14,300. Bed and board for this lusty phalanx at $20 apiece for seven days cost another $45,500, while so-called parlor expenses, principally wines and liquor, ran to another $10,000. This sum hardly quenched a drought and an additional $2200 was spent on "booze" at the famed Hoffman House to further heighten the campaigners' morale.[22]

Elections established heavy short-run demands, but the drainage of party moneys was perpetual. In each of the 812 districts, Tammany was obliged to retain four full-time workers in the field tending the potential vote and conducting daily party business, much of it connected with "welfare." Of greater expense and thus of greater importance were the assembly district leaders who even above the aldermen were the chief "comforters of the afflicted" and the "undeserving unfortunates" within their bailiwicks. There were seventy-two of these leaders representing all parties in 1887 and about $330,000 was spent annually, or $4750 on each man. Tammany's share of this expense for eighteen of its twenty-four assembly leaders was about $119,000. For the remainder of the parties' thousands of political captains and their followers, the best guesses were that expenses exceeded $1 million a year.[23] Even in slack years, Tammany and the County Democracy were reported to have spent between $75 and $100 at each polling place; Irving Hall expenses were put at between $40 and $50 and workers for independent candidates spent about $15 per polling place. Many figures exceeded these as was the case in the mid-eighties in the Fifteenth Assembly District where the County Democracy expended over $100 in the polling places and up to $85 in each of the polling places in the Tenth Assembly District.[24]

If the minimum spent in every polling place came to $220, then as one expert observer estimated, forty-four men in every one of them was receiving party funds, but other experts felt this guess was too low and added an additional ten men on party stipends at each polling place. In other words, since 219,992 votes were cast in the heated mayoralty contest of 1886, over 20% of the vote was paid for partisan labors. By 1900 this percentage had increased, although by precisely how much no one can say; George William Curtis, one of the ablest of the civil service reformers, observed, however, that over $30 million was being spent by the parties each year on the municipal elections of New York City.[25]

Similar situations on varying scales were prevalent throughout the iron rectangle; in New Hampshire, Connecticut, or Indiana political spending went to partisans bought by the head and marched to the polls;[26] in many states and cities it went to the boarding house gangs packed in for election thrusts. In Pennsylvania by the nineties, with over one million voters, the spending of party professionals had persuaded over 200,000 of the electorate to think of themselves as party functionaries bound to heed their leaders' calls.[27] Politics meant machinery to produce votes and that machinery ran full time; its lubricant was money.

Parallels between political and economic developments, of course, seems apparent; vast political organization and the modern corporation each enjoyed remarkable growth during the late nineteenth century; each rested upon complex financial arrangements and on the money machinery for sustaining and extending them; each emerged as dominant national institutions almost side by side. Yet without obscuring demonstrable interactions between them, the vote as a commodity invited organization before extensive horizontal and vertical integration of corporate structures. Sharp observers were noting by the early twentieth century that political organizations, far from being manufactured by captains of industry to serve their economic needs politically, had emerged first and possessed entirely independent reasons for their existence. "To consider the specialized organization of our local politics as the direct result of specialized organization of American business," wrote Herbert Croly perceptively, "is wholly to misunderstand its significance." Of the boss, the symbol of the great political organizations, Croly added, "he put in an embryonic appearance long before the large corporations had obtained anything like their existing power."[28] Thus, for example, at the heart of industrial America, Pennsylvania's Cameron Dynasty, and the political armies which it marshalled, preceded formation of the commonwealth's great railroad and mining enterprises, as well as the state's general laws of incorporation. The urgent mandates of universal suffrage anticipated the mandates of industrialism with profound consequences for the adjustments between liberal governments, the middle classes on which they substantially rested, and the polyglot democracy thrusting to the surface in the cities. Parties had learned to finance themselves effectively before the great corporate entities arose either to aid or to threaten them—and that was to make all the difference.

The existence of local governments was totally dependent upon political organizations tapping the funds to continue making, operating, and unmaking them; and tap them they did, deftly expanding their earlier practices and systematically elaborating and enforcing new techniques. To reformers and to the informed middle classes, therefore, while the public money machinery was unjust and ineffectual, the private machinery of the parties was considered pernicious and corrupt. Curiously, although the two sets of machinery dovetailed, their relationships were seldom understood among the middle classes.[29] Nonetheless, both sets of fiscal machinery occupied adjacent portions of a political and economic continuum thereby allowing an unexpected versatility. For one thing, the resources from which the extralegal machinery drew power differed from those available to the legal machines; also the character of their expenditures and services, if complementary to the public sector on occasion, differed widely from it.

There is considerable evidence, especially from Northern cities, of whom the major parties taxed extralegally, of how they did so and often for what purposes. To begin with, while many believed that property was the proper object of taxation, professional politicians, regardless of their rhetoric, often behaved as if the object of taxation was people and the people they had chiefly in mind were officeholders, political candidates, and party workers, who together provided parties with their primary tax base and with bread and butter revenues. "The capital of the machine," wrote William Ivins about Tammany in 1887, ". . . consists of nine thousand nine hundred and fifty-six subordinate places on the pay rolls." His estimate was modest for it excluded at least eighty department or bureau chiefs in Manhattan, as well as senators, congressmen, assemblymen, and aldermen along with their immediate retainers who would have swelled the figure beyond ten thousand. Still another thirty thousand profited from the party's professional activities and while much less reliable were nonetheless taxable.[30]

Payment of political assessments by those who constituted "the capital of the machine" was technically mandatory. A Philadelphia Republican "mandate" of 1880 threatened the party faithful that "at the close of the campaign we shall place a list of those who have not paid in the hands of the head of the department you are in,"[31] and everyone must have been familiar with the hackneyed dictum, "Your money or your place." Rumor had it—and politicians did not refute it—that over 1600 removals had occurred in the New York Customs House between 1865 and 1871 for refusals to pay party taxes. In the seventies and eighties, however, there is little evidence that assessments were either unexpected or that there were many ousters when they went uncollected. To be sure, the Republican National leadership insisted that payment of the "tax," as it was then called, determined "the fate of the Republican Party" and, therefore, "the prosperity of the nation," but we also know that while the Republican National Congressional Committee of 1878, the first so-called "extortion committee," sent out 100,000 demands, only 11,500 apparently responded, or, as one observer reported, the people whom "the committee insulted, met insult with defiance or silent contempt,"[32] reactions already familiar in the public sector. A tax was a tax. Nonetheless, parties strove to collect with a vigor uncommon to governments.

Resistance to political assessments repeated the cries of plunder and corruption already familiar to public revenue officers. "Could the curtain of secrecy be lifted," wrote a critic of party taxes, "we should see a vast dragnet of extortion . . . thrown out . . . over the whole land . . . with every humble official and laborer . . . entangled in its meshes; and busy among them, for their prey," he added, were a host of "tax extortioners." Books in hand, they haunted public corridors, "moused" around bureaus for names and salaries, waylaid "clerks going to their meals," obtruded their "impertinent faces" upon teachers, navy yard workmen, scrub women, "poor office boys," and men "enfeebled on the battlefield." Reputedly, no one in any way connected with party escaped this "merciless, mercenary, indecent conscription,"[33] a point somewhat dramatically driven home when a New York judge was sued by his party on the basis of his promise to pay his obligations to the machine.[34] In sum, critics of party were fully prepared to indict it for the grand inefficiencies of spoils while ironically paying high tribute to the extraordinary efficiency of party taxation, a major constituent of this extralegal fiscal system.

In effect, political assessments, the party counterpart of the general property tax as a chief revenue producer, constituted an extralegal income tax and, despite attacks upon it from some party members and from most respectable circles, evidence argues that it was well-administered, equitable, and no more tainted by corruption than the general property tax.

There were six regular levels of extralegal taxation: national, state, county, mayoralty, ward, and district. Bosses and their lieutenants, of course, sometimes added emergency levies to these normal ones. It did not follow that those who were assessed were expected to pay at all levels, however, and the system was more merciful, therefore, than it was depicted. Thus, we know of a Philadelphia post office worker who in 1881–82 paid his party's national political tax of $16, a state assessment of $20, and a ward assessment of $5; on a salary of $800 a year, that is, he was taxed $41 or 5% of his income. Similarly, we hear of a New York letter carrier whose thousand dollar salary was taxed 3% by the National Republican Committee and another 3% by the party's New York State Committee.

Typical of party critics everywhere, New York reformers recognized that the "abolition of assessments would be a deadly blow to the machines," insisting that political expenses be handled by the "application of strict business principles" to the essential operations of parties. Yet political assessments were very businesslike. Even the moneys which the candidates paid "voluntarily" toward the furtherance of their campaigns were separated, as sound taxation demanded, from the more regularized and more general assessments. A New York State Committee of Republicans in 1880, for instance, performed in a far more businesslike way than many public tax authorities did when in October it not only demanded $800 "due from employees" in one state office, but subsequently branded those who had not paid as "delinquents."[35] Reformers, of course, often refused to concede that a populace which supported its schools and its charities both publicly and privately "more liberally than any other", would fail to contribute "anything needful to maintain in healthy life those great parties" which made liberal government possible; but politicians, preferring regular streams of cash to occasional floods of rhetoric, continued levying upon the faithful with a consistency that encouraged the equation of death and taxes.

From the mid-seventies through the early nineties, an informed guess would be that total annual assessments by the major parties on New York's combined public payrolls varied between two and six percent of the jobholders' salaries. Since public payrolls annually ran between $14 and $15 million dollars, they were a major resource for party financiers to draw upon. Notwithstanding this, such levies were still considered utterly inadequate in party circles, so much so that bosses like Tammany's John Kelly in the nineties called openly for higher salaries for public employees in order to broaden the party fiscal base and to allow the imposition of heavier political assessments.[36]

For political candidates assessments were certain and heavy. Joseph Bishop informed the New York Commonwealth Club in 1887 that candidates for the mayoralty were taxed from $25,000 to $30,000 for the backing of the machines. The support of two of the city's political organizations cost candidates for superior court and for common pleas judgeships between $10,000 and $15,000 apiece, while taxation on the supreme court judgeships often rose to $20,000. Because of the sensitive nature of his post, the City Register, for example, paid from $15,000 to $40,000 for his assessment. Luckily not all positions were as highly sensitized; candidates for comptroller, sheriff, or county clerk were "soaked" less heavily. Their assessments were a flat $10,000, while mere district attorneys on-the-make paid only half of that amount.[37]

Assessments were usually tied directly to the calculable costs of waging campaigns in each of the city's eight hundred districts. Both Tammany and the County Democracy taxed their contestants for alderman from $15 to $25 per district; assemblymen whose offices were less remunerative and whose campaign costs were accordingly less burdensome paid a toll of $5 to $15 per district. Their considerable influence and their two-year terms of office made state senatorships a real prize and elections were correspondingly hot and expensive. Senatorial candidates were taxed from $20 to $30 a district normally; but there were years when these assessments assumed sobering dimensions. In one hard campaign of the eighties two opposing candidates each paid party taxes in excess of $50,000 for a crack at the Albany senatorship; in another senatorial contest which succeeded this one, the hopefuls also paid heavily. Candidate Morrissey was required to pay $10 per district plus an extra $2500 to each of twenty-four assembly district leaders on the eve of election. Less fortunate, Morrissey's opponent, Augustus Schell, was not only taxed five times more per district than Morrissey had been, but was further obliged to muster an additional $60,000 for his party's assembly district leaders as an emergency tax designed to "guarantee the result." Guarantees notwithstanding, Schell lost and like many taxpayers discovered that while levies were certain, their agreeable or successful employment subsequently was very uncertain.[38]

Few reformers were prepared to leave the subject of political assessments alone and many of the parties' own workers resisted and evaded this form of taxation as no doubt they would have resisted any other. One of the reform-minded men on whom the mantle of New York's senatorial leadership had fallen in 1881 declared publicly that political assessments had made "the conflict between the system of patronage and that of merit as irrepressible as the old conflict between liberty and slavery."[39] Embarked on his own anti-machine crusade, Alderman Philemon T. Sherman lashed out at the extravagance characteristic of the estimates and budgets of New York City during the late nineties, extravagance which he linked directly to Tammany's bleeding the city to pay ever-rising public salaries which, as he noted in a public letter, were "the mainstay of the Tammany organization."[40]

Yet until election expenses were charged legally to the public's account, professionals had little choice but to finance their operations in this manner. Testifying before New York's Mazet Committee in 1900, Rastus Ransom, who a few years earlier had served as New York county surrogate, voiced a very common party position. As a candidate in the mid-eighties, Ransom had paid the Tammany treasurer the equivalent of one year's salary, $12,000 to cover his assessment; half went to the County Democracy which had endorsed him, and half went to Tammany. No one had instructed Ransom as to his obligations; there were unwritten laws which his iron-fisted boss, Richard Croker, himself a former tax collector, did not have to explain to him. "It was understood by men in some way," testified Ransom, "I don't know how, that it was . . . proper . . . to pay the money . . . Every political organization, Democrat and Republican had to provide by its own means . . . for the entire expense of the canvas."[41] In the same vein, New York's comptroller, Bird Coler, explained that a few weeks after his nomination at the turn of the century, he also "wanted to contribute" because he was not a poor man and . . . was willing to give whatever was fair." Exclusive of the several thousand dollars he had already spent in his own behalf, Coler suggested $15,000 as a fair sum, but the county treasurer declared this amount extravagant and set the more reasonable figure of $10,000, half of which Coler then paid to him and the other half of which he paid to the treasurer of Kings County. Although his testimony before state investigators had a casual ring, Coler realized, of course, that his payments were required. There were compensatory requirements, too, for as a party "wiskinkie," or tax collector, he in turn levied a four percent tax on the salaries of his subordinates and had proceeded to tap businessmen for contributions irrespective of their party affiliation.[42]

All in all, there was probably as high a sense of responsibility, and certainly as much fear of the consequences of failure, within the "disreputable" confines of the party about paying taxes as there was in the public sector. No one speaking to the record argued that political taxation was suited to the best of all possible worlds, but the alternatives once seriously explored seemed unfeasible.

Thus, when New York newspapers, the City Club, the Central Committee of the New York Citizens Union, and the Chamber of Commerce supported a state bill in 1900 which sought to prohibit the assessment of judicial candidates and to bar candidates' contributions toward their own campaigns, the judges gave little assistance to the reform. Of the twenty-eight judges representative of the major courts who responded directly and six additional ones whose views were incorporated into a state investigation, only two, Levintritt and Ingraham of the state supreme court flatly condemned what they called "political taxation." For his part, however, Levintritt admitted voluntarily paying $5000 toward party expenses in one election, defending such *free* acts as neither "unproper" nor "immoral." On the contrary, despite popular opinions on the subject of assessments, he argued that "in making the contribution," he was not "doing anything more than discharging an obligation" and doing so quite without impairing his "judicial character." Judge Ingraham took the position that demanding a man pay "any sum of money for judicial nomination" was "outrageous and most subvertive;" but by the same token, he found it incomprehensible that any candidate should refuse to pay his *campaign* expenses. Allowing anyone else to assume these burdens, he declared, was like "asking them to pay his butcher bill."[43]

Other justices even more positively doubted the advisability of banning assessments and contributions. "I know of no especial reason from my experience," remarked a judge who had been elected to Common Pleas in 1893, "why a judicial nominee should be relieved from payment of the proper expenses of the campaign, or of his portion, than any other candidate on the ticket." The whole electoral process, the judge agreed, fell short of the ideal and yet as one of his colleagues pointed out, "this very thing you speak of is the direct product of universal suffrage and if you can tell me of any other way it could be done better, I will be happy to agree with you." There were plenty of Americans more than ready to shake the judges' convictions, but the common sense of the bench appealed to men with a grasp of the realities of party finance.[44]

It remained for Justice Charles Van Brunt of New York's appellate Division to try and enlighten his fellow citizens on the inseparability of party and government finances. "Organization," declared Van Brunt, existed "in order that political parties may be effectual; and it seems to me that political parties are necessary to our system of government." But there were legitimate expenses which it was "absolutely necessary that organizations should incur" to maintain their existence. For this reason he opposed the pending legislation; far from producing reform, he explained, it would tend "to create concealments" and stimulate the nomination of unsavory candidates who were prepared to be dishonest about their campaign contributions. Worse yet, striking at this segment of party finance would eventually lower the caliber of judicial nominations.[45]

The sources of party revenues, of course, were hardly exhausted by the assessment of jobholders and of candidates, by the solicitation of voluntary contributions, or by the use of legally appropriated public funds. Administered under the auspices of commissioners of public works and city comptrollers and collected by a variety of city officials, employees, or wiskinkies, party taxes reached deeply into several quarters of every community, including those poorer sections where the assumption seems to have been that the financing of local governments fell directly on the middle classes and the rich, upon employers and owners, and represented the price which these classes paid for their social advantages. Yet while legal and extralegal fiscal matters were only dimly appreciated among the enlightened portions of the community and, aside from visceral slogans and raw opinions, were scarcely understood at all among the impoverished peoples of Bulfinch Street or Mulberry Row, assumptions that they were being passed over entirely were often false. The government's general property taxation fell upon the middle classes leaving them little chance to shift the incidence, but political taxation in one form or another not only reached many of the rich but also extended beneath the classes into the masses.

The lowest ramifications of party money machinery were sometimes barely discernible due to their quasi-legal or downright criminal character. Official as well as reform-sponsored investigations, the usual committees of seventy or one hundred, furnished a substantial body of evidence across the North on the fiscal resources of the major political organizations, especially in the great cities. Again, Manhattan, thanks to committees of fourteen and fifteen, and a number of state investigations stretching from the seventies until 1911—among them the Lexow, Fassett, and Mazet Committees—supplied details of operations which had their analogues elsewhere.

Aside from its reputation as one of the world's great police departments, the New York police force, for example, was also a great tax assessing and tax gathering arm of the Democratic Party; an "army of policemen," reported a New York reformer in the eighties, "contribute to the election expenses of the several Machines."[46] And those contributions began in their own ranks. Throughout the last half of the nineteenth century into the early years of the twentieth, a sizeable minority of police applicants customarily added from $250 to $500 in cash to their qualifications in seeking to join the force. Once on the rolls, moreover, they were frequently taxed heavily, in some cases for as much as $10,000, for significant promotions. These moneys, we are told, augmented the incomes of top police officials who were invariably party wheelhorses, while unspecified amounts culled from the "take" at all levels of the department found their way into party coffers on a regular basis.[47]

A resource themselves, the police, in turn, had resources of their own to draw upon. Their fiscal power was inherent in their power to decide which of the vast corpus of middle-class laws should be enforced in the disparate neighborhoods of a polyglot society. For a price they determined which fruit stands or business displays were permitted to sprawl onto sidewalks or into the streets, which pushcarts did business at particular locations, which saloons cracked their doors to dispense schooners of beer to workingmen on Sundays, which pool parlors or policy shops were allowed to operate, which theaters could offer "spicy" entertainment, which bail bondsmen could operate before police magistrates or in criminal courts, which establishments could sponsor boxing matches and cock fights, and which clip joints, opium dens, flop houses, and houses of prostitution were permitted to flourish. They likewise selected the polling places, a choice often profitable to small businesses, and thereby profitable to the party, and they monitored the voting as well, a service of considerable financial value in some quarters of town.[48]

Still another significant and lucrative source which the police farmed for party financial managers was the saloon keeper and liquor dealers of the city, all of whom were required to be licensed. Technically, licensing was the duty of the City Excise Department, but the nature of the Excise Department's job by the eighties had rendered excise laws, as one official report observed, "a dead letter" and their "execution a formal humbug." By 1885 applications for licenses ran between eleven and twelve thousand a year, each ostensibly necessitating an official examination, while the scrutiny of licensed establishments numbering just under 9,000, the issuance of nearly 900 new licenses a year, the revocation of hundreds more and a backlog in the courts of nearly 5000 untried excise cases, stretched the capacities of the city's 56 excise inspectors beyond their breaking point. Consequently, it became "a matter of general notoriety," testified Excise Commissioner William S. Andrews, that the underpaid, overworked inspectors received a payment of $25 each time liquor dealers came to make their applications. But the inspectors' take was relatively inconsequential,[49] too inconsequential really for party leaders to allow.

The lion's share of levies and collections fell to elements of New York's 7000 policemen. Information and recommendations requisite to licensing came chiefly from them and as a rule were acted upon automatically by the Excise Department. The police, in effect, drew revenues from decisions about when, where, how much, and how long a hard-drinking urban populace could drink; in so doing they determined the limits of one of the most extensive and commonplace businesses catering to the masses—saloonkeeping. Their political tax was levied on estimates of an establishment's income, $5 to $25 a month from ordinary liquor dealers, plus a receipt for subscription to the party's subsidized news organs, but $100 to $250 a month was not exceptional for flashy places like Gombossy's, Billy McGlory's, the Alhambra, Gridiron, Harry Hills', French Madam's, or San Souci, whose notorious reputations meant that higher taxes were needed to cover their protection.[50]

Although it is true that the division of this Police Protective Tariff among various echelons of politicians was obscure, the division—like the levies—was systematic and constituted an integral party of party fiscal machinery. John Goff, Chief Counsel for a New York State Investigating Committee in 1895 disclosed details of these specific and *ad valorem* taxes and again his findings were corroborated in other quarters. The initiation fee for disorderly houses, for instance, was $500 and their monthly payments, depending upon the assessment of their income, ran from $50 to $100. Unlicensed concert saloons paid from $50 to $250, unlicensed cafes from $15 to $25, and unlicensed liquor saloons from $5 to $10 a month. "Green goods" men whose occupation was conning victims into accepting bad money for good, depending on the number of "turning joints" they operated, paid no less than $1000 a month. Legitimate enterprises, of course, paid along with the illegitimate; milk-shade peddlers were taxed $25 a month; merchants were entitled to use of the sidewalks for from $2 to $10 monthly. By the week, bootblacks were assessed $.75, peanut vendors, $5, and pushcart vendors, $15. Larger businesses likewise paid along with the smaller ones. Steamship lines, for example, paid monthly from $15 to $25 for the preemption of street space across from the wharves and for minor police services in connection with the traffic of their operations. These taxes were regular and predictable, hence many of them, especially those borne by the several thousand houses of prostitution and related places of assignation, probably passed on to the consumer.[51]

How much slippage or administrative inefficiency there was in the Police Department's tax collections is unknown; a number of officers —the unfortunate Captains Schmittberger and Devery among them— clearly increased protection taxes in order to pay for their own promotions. Generally, however, a skimpy record suggests that the taxes levied were set by custom in the neighborhood or particular business location irrespective of the roundsman or precinct captain so that changes were not often sudden or out of line with what the traffic could bear. Few of the police or department officials who were examined on charges of corruption, moreover, seem to have cached significant sums of money. The "take" as well as the "cut" were regularized; chiseling by the collectors was easily detectable, partly because their "taxpayers" when pinched complained individually, as was the case with a few independent madams, or through the "syndicates" or associations which had already developed in segments of the underworld by the late nineteenth century. Thus, there is reason to presume that despite aberrations most such political taxation moved up through the hierarchy of party into the hands of Tammany treasurers like McQuade or chairmen of vital finance committees like Croker.

And improvements in efficiency were always being sought. Dissatisfaction in Tammany's upper levels, for example, caused Richard Croker to draw the collected tax moneys largely and directly from the Liquor Dealers Association rather than from police officials alone, as district treasurers had been doing previous to the nineties. No doubt Croker knew what he was about, for he had risen to power not only because of his celebrated physical toughness but more particularly because he was an expert in party finance; one of his earliest public posts had been collector of taxes, subsequent to which he served as marshal for the City of New York collecting arrears of personal taxes. And his fiscal responsibilities were impressive; the best estimates were that the liquor interests alone paid Tammany between $2½ million and $10 million a year at the turn of the century.[52]

Additional sources of party revenues were sometimes more sensational, chiefly because they were subject to perennial accusations and exposé. At one level these revenues came from voluntary gifts of rich individuals and of corporations: the Metropolitan Railway or the Street Railway Association, the Sugar Trust, the Beet Sugar Industry, the Jockey Club and other race track interests, the Milk Dealers' Association, fire insurance companies and life insurance companies. On a broader scale, hundreds of smaller enterprises were systematically tapped by the wiskinkies. The most likely and therefore the most sizeable contingent of these concerns were those whose business was naturally with the city, hence with the political machines; examples were asphalt firms, contractors, construction and paving companies, draymen and liverymen, building supplies, architectural firms, hose, hydrant, valve and fire equipment outfits, gas and water companies, dredging and garbage disposal companies, brokerage and realty houses, insurance, mortgage, and underwriting firms, newspapers and printing offices, brewers, auctioneers, rapid transit companies, banks and investment institutions, to name only a few.[53]

The extralegal side of New York's money machinery had its parallels, not necessarily in scale but in kind, throughout the polities, rural as well as urban, of the North. Philadelphia reformers consistently assailed corrupt Republican organizations from their own city to Pittsburgh, along with their "servile allies in the rural sections of the State" for the consummate skill with which they financed party operations during the years from 1872 to 1912. Republican supply lines spread into all areas of Pennsylvania life, and Mugwumps like Wayne MacVeagh, himself a successful politician and a former attorney-general, had no difficulty discovering them; party finance to MacVeagh and his colleagues was tantamount to "looting the treasuries of Philadelphia and Pennsylvania," and out of this loot political machines allegedly raised their "gigantic corruption funds," most of which came from the pockets of officeholders "upon the payrolls" who were required "to pay into the treasuries of their masters a considerable percentage of their salaries." In this regard, "almost every mayor was their tool, and every man hired to run an elevator in a public building was their tool," argued MacVeagh. Party critics realized that "the chief duty of policemen for many years" in the commonwealth's cities had been to protect "the most loathsome vice and crime" in order that "politicians of higher or lower degree might receive an infamous revenue from them;" and the critics might just as accurately have indicted most other major departments of local governments.[54]

Despite all this, Pennsylvania's party treasuries were bottomless pits, just as the official treasuries of twentieth-century governments have proven to be; inevitably, therefore, there were additional supplies of money. A fund "exceeding ten million dollars," for instance, had been distributed "for many years at each session of the legislature among the charities of the state;" and these moneys, too, were channeled so as to turn the wheels of party. "Vast deposits" of public money in "favored banks and banking institutions" likewise paid off and contributed to "debauching the electorate." The ties between "the larger business corporations" and city bosses, if not always specifically detectable, also caused expectant business leaders "to pour golden streams annually into the all devouring maw of the 'organization.'" Public service corporations were obliged to respond not only with cash but also with places for those who, though deserving, could not be accommodated on the public payroll.[55]

The political repugnances, if not the torpor, of the citizenry at large, which led reformers to try to banish from politics "the peril of being conscripted into the working gangs of any party or of being plundered for paying its expenses," thus forced professional politicians into these extralegal, indeed, often illegal, fiscal maneuvers. Many of the politicians' critics were prepared to acknowledge that parties were perhaps inevitable and that they required money for legitimate purposes; but the operative reservation was the word "legitimate," for in the last analysis it reduced their acknowledgments to mere rhetoric. They wanted discipline removed from political organization, a step intolerable in any organizations of their own, and they hoped to divorce the most effective party machinery from party financial operations. They sought an early retirement for men "who had no other business in the world than politics," and their implicit distaste for a democracy of the masses was calculated to remove all but their own kind from the political arena.

The contemptuous tones of respectable men were unmistakable; "this year we have twelve liquor dealers," wrote Joseph Bishop of New York's Board of Aldermen in 1887, "eight political workers" in "various degrees of badness" and "four honest men," all told, the assembly was composed of "five liquor dealers, no less than seventeen professional politicians, and two useful men."[56] Yet Bishop's attitude, if technically accurate, was premised on assumptions which threatened a devitalization of broad areas of American life, by steadily restricting its range of tolerance and understanding. Attacks on governmental extravagance and public finance menaced vital social institutions and instruments of social mobility as well threatening "the loss of . . . splendid human qualities," even if corrupt ones, in favor of what one social worker termed "the stupid, comfortable, self-satisfied unsocial respectability of the city middle classes."[57] Many spokesmen of these classes intended to have their cake and eat it too, for they eagerly sought the benefits of sophisticated political machinery and expanding public services while eviscerating both fiscally in the name of cost-accounting efficiency and middle class morality. In the meantime, it was the breadth and depth of the parties' own fiscal devices, of the *dual* money machinery, which permitted organizations of plural constitution to survive capture or domination by any single bloc of interests.

I apprehend that many corporations, which are now called upon before every election to contribute large sums of money to campaign funds, would find in an absolute prohibition . . . a reason why they should not make such contributions. I think it will be a protection to corporations . . . against demands upon them . . .

ELIHU ROOT

"The Political Use of Money," *An Address*, September 3, 1894.

There is a . . . satisfaction to me . . . perceiving that the business men of New York are at last taking an interest in their own public affairs; that you are at last taking an interest. . . . before it is too late, in the law and administration which create opportunity or hamper enterprise.

The business man of America has been at a heavy discount of recent years. . . . The business man alone has seemed to be paralyzed [politically] . . .

ELIHU ROOT

"The Business Men and the Constitutional Convention," *An Address*, March 25, 1915.

The ruler of the state during the greater part of the forty years of my acquaintance with the state government has not been any man authorized by the constitution or by the law. . . . The party leader is elected by no one, accountable to no one, removable by no one . . .

ELIHU ROOT

"Invisible Government," *Speech*, August 30, 1915.

The truth is that the boss is the one conspicuous man who has made a success in American government; he is the discoverer of governmental efficiency . . .

A. B. HART

American Political Science Review, VII [1913].

5

The Dominance of the Politician

The functioning of party money machinery, from the assessment of public salaries and the taxation of candidates to the tax-gathering activities of policemen and wiskinkies, ran afoul of middle class mores and reinforced respectable men's prejudices against political parties as a governing force. Among businessmen particularly this was manifested by a deep and sustained distrust of the "profligacy and ineptitude" of legislatures as well as of other representative bodies and a deep repugnance toward politicians as a breed, this notwithstanding the involvement of party professionals in business or businesslike "honest graft" and despite the politicians' frequently amiable response to the wishes of business interests whose money and votes they courted.

Yet in the period considered here such hostilities present the historian with an apparent contradiction. If thousands of economic interests, large and small, profited from symbiotic relationships with politicians, why was there so profound a mistrust, even a fear of politics among them? If a few tycoons like Andrew Carnegie felt that the general political situation during the last quarter of the century was conducive to a genial *status quo,* why did so many others seem to feel so differently? Why, indeed, did conceptions of the politicians of this era which saw them as just another set of businessmen or as the paid lackeys of business interests prove so remarkably unacceptable to businessmen who might have expected to recognize it first and appreciate it most? Why, in short, if businessmen were "top dogs" in the power structure of the North did they speak and behave as if convinced they were not?

Hypothetical responses to such questions, obviously, are legion. In addition, the baffling range, variety, and vagary of evidence frequently sustain several seemingly viable interpretations, preclude conclusive findings, and encourage informed conjecture.

Notwithstanding this, historians discussing American elites between 1870 and 1920 have tended to commit a basic error which, fortunately, sociologists, the original source of the error, have recently begun to correct. That is, historians have generally confused the *recruitment* of political elites with their *function*. They have assumed, for instance, that because growing numbers of businessmen were entering politics from Northern economic elites, they were continuing to function for the same social purposes as they had in business.[1] Without presuming to argue more than can be proved at present, I contend that regardless of their recruitment, businessmen who remained in politics for more than a term or two were constrained to adapt to and function within the context of a different strategic elite than the one from which they had sprung. Politics was not a mere continuation of business; it was not an adjunct to it.

What is suggested here is that the root of the businessman's fears and hostilities lay in the realization of the stubborn dominance of politicians, irrespective of their origins, over the dual fiscal systems of Northern polities. On this fiscal bedrock which included the politicos' control over the economy of spoils and patronage, over official taxing, spending, and borrowing, and over the elaborate extralegal machinery engaged in shaking down businesses whether legal or criminal, the parties raised their superstructures and ramified their "invisible governments."

To the extent that this suggestion is sustainable, we must reexamine several major interpretations of the late nineteenth and early twentieth centuries. Until recently the leading interpretations of the Gilded Age and the "chromo-civilization" which supposedly succeeded it, have insisted that under the aegis of Robber Barons and their venal political flunkeys, a "politics of acquisition" emerged after the Civil War which permitted special interests, mostly composed of new industrial and financial corporations, to convert governments to their own purposes. It has been claimed, in effect, that economic man triumphed over political man. Writing for the most part contemptuously of the "sovereignty of the business empire" during a political "age of negation," a series of brilliantly provocative observers from Moisei Ostrogorski and Charles Beard to Matthew Josephson and Richard Hofstadter, taking their themes from the reformist spirit and reform literature of the period, have given this viewpoint its most persuasive statement; and while the economic evidence underpinning their analysis of men, institutions, and events has undergone very significant modification, their political characterizations have survived largely intact. "There is no drearier chapter in American political history," scholars of their persuasion have concluded, "than . . . the period from the end of Reconstruction to the Populist Revolt of the 1890's." In this era masterful financial and industrial chieftains "whose grip was firm, whose experience was cumulative, and whose goal was clear," purportedly guided the destinies of the country. Politics, they argued, "was largely a Punch and Judy show. Business ran politics and politics was a branch of business." If politicians were sometimes conceded "important historic missions," the scale of their operations was Lilliputian; their annals were suffused with "greed and meanness" ending always in "mimic disaster."[2]

Unfortunately, these perspectives cannot adequately account for the financial relationships, or the attitudes which colored them, between highly differentiated and deeply divided business interests and Northern politicians. Only a revised evaluation of the competence and effectiveness of politicians, in fact, helps explain their persistent ability to bend fiscal machinery primarily to party purposes.

It is precisely this high level of general political competence which renders unviable the thesis that business profited from and ran politics. Without comprehension of these political abilities, neither fiscal developments, nor their consequences, can properly be understood. This was especially true because post-Civil War governments frequently were without clearly definable mandates and they were usually contrasted invidiously with their highly idealized predecessors as having been "instituted for the purpose of dispensing with . . . heroic virtues."[3] Neither dramatic circumstances nor popular attitudes conspired to leave them well-remembered. But then change is often a matter of undramatic increments.

Many factors beside high political capacities worked against, if they did not invariably prevent, the dominance of business elements in society generally and for any significant length of time in politics. Economic historians, for example, have produced impressive evidence of the deep divisions and disagreements characteristic of late nineteenth and early twentieth century enterprise.[4] Capitalists were enfeebled by their own parochialism and pluralism. Harrisburg, Trenton, or Springfield rarely hosted one phalanx of businessmen which was not simultaneously opposed by others. Of course, there were exceptions; "one-company towns" or single-industry districts heavily influenced politically by the overweening power of mining, textile, or railroad corporations were harsh local realities. Yet there were many sectors to the economy and their number was growing. Thus, notwithstanding local monopolies, most forms of economic power were diffuse and others, to use a Galbraithian idiom, were variously counterbalanced. For example, controversies over the flexibility of the money supply between rural and urban, Eastern and Western, large and small bankers, battles between hard and soft money men concerning currency issues as well as over related conflicts about tariffs, struggles between mercantile interests and railroads, and rivalries among the great cities themselves over everything from taxes and trade routes to transport facilities, all ironically lent the economy an anarchic quality which historians once ascribed solely to the country's political establishments during these years.

This measure of anarchy in their midst was not conducive to businessmen directing political affairs even where they had the will to do so; moreover, it furnished politicians the opportunity to extract their pound of flesh from every enterprise expecting service from party organizations, while extending their own political lives. Without pretensions either to conventional honesty or to principle, professionals exploited this leverage so brilliantly, in fact, that they soured much of their generation on what Henry Adams dubbed "political morality."

Questions of political competence, integrity, and independence must, of course, focus on political bosses and their machines; had it not been for these men and their organizations anarchy in the commercial and industrial world would have been more closely matched in the political arena. For some men, to be sure, bosses were the epitome of all that was rotten in Denmark, the linchpins between what E. L. Godkin called "commercial immorality and political corruption."[5] For others they were the accepted brokers of special privilege, the source of less tangible favors, of welfare, or of a meal ticket. No one has doubted that they were the hub of relationships between business and government, nor that, practically speaking, they were overseers of the most vital portions of state and local money machinery whether in their own or others' interest.

As acute, often scholarly, observers testified during the late nineteenth century, the boss was usually an impressively able figure in his political context. "His ethics aside," wrote a leading student of bossism early in this century, the boss "is by all odds the most 'efficient' figure that the American municipal system has produced." James Bryce in the *American Commonwealth* shared this estimate; cautioning readers against drawing "too dark a picture of the Boss," he credited him with "high abilities" as well as with tact, understanding, decency, and courage. A hostile witness, Ostrogorski, the Russian liberal to whom permanent political parties were anathema, grudgingly acknowledged that bosses were generally men of superior intelligence with "a very delicate appreciation of particular situations," while Theodore Roosevelt, in his style of strident masculinity, proclaimed his acquaintance with several bosses "who are ten times over better fellows than are the mild-mannered scholars of timorous virtue who criticize them." Roosevelt conceded that some bosses were apt to be immoral, but for his own boss, Tom Platt, he often voiced a patronizing admiration which became unqualified when it touched directly on Platt's consummate mastery of his machine.[6] Vulnerable when held to middle class standards of cost-accounting efficiency, bosses were disturbing elements in respectable quarters precisely because they were invulnerable to charges of incompetence in their political environments.

In confronting what some historians have called "triumphant enterprise" with their competence, the bosses were party professionals who knew their craft well, profited from it, and liked it. By the 1880's increasing numbers of politicians possessed business backgrounds or business affiliations compared to the political figures of the agricultural era, but the styles of the politicos were not primarily bourgeois. They were professionals who worked full time to win elections and to retain power. Just this kind of man in New York, New Jersey, Pennsylvania, Ohio, and Illinois, for instance, occupied at least half of the seats in state legislatures. In municipal governments, as in Congress itself, they held key positions and even the substantial numbers of inexperienced men in city councils, boards of aldermen, or in assemblies were party novitiates. Such was the case in all quarters of the political arena.

Of the rank and file of hard core party men one thing at least is clear. Like their leaders they were denigrated by the articulate opinions of their day. Brilliantly and without a shade of humor, Ostrogorski caught these views exactly when he wrote that "to the low types which the human race has produced from Cain to Tartuffe, the age of democracy has added a new one—the politician. And it is not the least despicable. There is a somber grandeur in the crime of Cain and its expiation," he continued, but ". . . nothing of the kind is to be found in the motley soul of the politician; it is made up of innumerable pettinesses, with but one trait to give them unity—cowardice."[7]

Other views of machine politicians, however, were more charitable, although not necessarily more congenial toward corruption and disregard for what passed as the public interest. Scanning the ranks of the political armies within his range, Theodore Roosevelt denied that "these men are all actuated merely by mercenary motives." On the contrary, he insisted that "the great majority entertain . . . a real feeling of allegiance towards the party to which they belong, or toward the political chief whose fortunes they follow; and many," he remarked, "work entirely without pay and purely for what they believe to be right."[8] Such men were integral parts of what Simon Newcomb, the noted mathematician, astronomer, and political economist, defined as "the great development of the art of political management, of which we are all witnesses, but of which no one can see the ultimate result."[9] The calculations of this organizational art, as well as the bases on which it rested, namely, the manipulation of votes and symbols, was distinct from the businessman's commercial calculations, and members of the political fraternity were set quite apart by this.[10]

Privately proud of their "game," professionals even displayed a contemptuous amusement at times about their wealthy, influential, and powerful clients. Politicos, after all, were specialists in their own right and they were secure in that knowledge. While still active in New York State politics, Roosevelt, always eager to divorce himself from the values of the bourgeois, expressed such opinions openly and with spirit—and so, too, did men who were less self-righteous or didactic. Although he always possessed several business interests, Tom Platt, the listless, phlegmatic, and virtually inarticulate boss of New York's Republicans at the turn of the century, impressed all who knew him by his disinterest in balance sheets except as they related to party needs or the necessary hedge against political losses.[11] And it was the boss of Pennsylvania's "highly industrialized" politics, Matthew Quay, who observed regretfully to a political friend, an ex-governor of the state, this his son, Dick Quay, was "nothing of a politician" but "only a maker of money."[12]

At the root of this professional snobbery and sense of superiority lay the long and often ignoble apprenticeships which the somewhat patriarchal organization of the political machine entailed. Except for occasions when political tickets required hasty "window dressing" or the unusual lustre of some amateur's reputation or funds, bosses seldom permitted significant positions to come to men with less than a decade of party experience. There was little room for greenhorns from the business world and the pickings for them were slim unless they were broken to party operations and the specialization that it required. District leaders, captains, and the holders of high elective of appointive office were ordinarily men with fifteen to twenty years of service. Fifty-seven of Chicago's political leaders whose careers began in the years preceding 1886 averaged just over fourteen years of party service, and random samplings in Philadelphia, New York, Baltimore, Philadelphia, and Boston during the last quarter of the nineteenth century indicate about the same thing. Thus the boss sought associates "whose hearts are in their work and upon whose unbribed devotion he can rely."[13] Out of this winnowing process came the peculiar skill, the discipline, and the loyalties which left many businessmen feeling much beyond their depth in political matters and provoked the bitter denunciations heard from reformers.

The "rebuffs, insults, calumny, ridicule, defeat, and disaster," which had to be endured by professionals, made service in political legions seem pointless and grim to reputable outsiders. Sustained and serious campaigning required "patient labor, self-denial," and some measure of sacrifice in the abandonment of "comfort, pleasure, luxuries, [and] necessities" by the more comfortable men from the middle or upper classes; but among professionals, such sacrifices produced a sense of solidarity and a boisterous élan. Consequently, "with all his faults, his follies, his amusing characteristics," wrote a governor of Massachusetts in 1896 about his fellow professionals, "the 'practical politician' is a *constant force*. He never lets anything go by default. He is, indeed," continued the governor, "a machine, tireless, fearless, conscienceless, and remorseless—at least in his own sphere of action."[14]

Regardless of whether the professional was, in Croker's words, "working for his own pocket," continuing a family tradition, venting personal frustrations, satisfying "a need for achievement," seeking the money or status denied him by his origins and education, or expressing what Louis Brownlow called his "passion for politics," he was rarely a business puppet. Often the hostilities of businessmen toward the "ignoble" and "earthy" concerns of politics, to "things of the pocket, of the sewer, of the gutter," and to "its disagreeable people . . . [and] disagreeable places" must have been a reaction against having to filter their requests through Philadelphia's Betz Building or New York's 49 Broadway—or the equivalent political headquarters elsewhere.

Hoping for swift achievement of their goals, businessmen discovered competent professional political armies camped on the heights commanding privilege and profit. Their power and weaponry were impressive. They could form up battalions of great variety—foreigners, mobs, hirelings, reformers, and silk-stockings, and deploy them according to the dispositions of the enemy and the terrain. Their reënforcements were always formidable because of their hidden possibilities; who knew how numerous "the farmers," "workingmen," "all patriotic voters," "friends of good government," let alone "the people," would prove to be?

Although the picture is a cloudy one and generalization would be foolish, the power of the machine when facing business interests was certainly very great in states and localities of dense population and widely varied local economies. For example, this seems true in Pennsylvania, the most highly industrialized state of the latter nineteenth century as well as a leader in the development of the modern corporation. Accordingly it was also a state in which the dominant Republican Party was sufficiently powerful, even in the opinion of its critics, "to meet the business corporations of the State at least upon equal terms." The organizations of the Camerons, of Quay, and of Penrose were regularly charged with favoring "corporate interests at the expense of the Commonwealth," yet these favors came from organizational power which functioned, in the judgment of these same critics, as a two-edged sword, for the machines remained "capable of being used to restrain and control corporate power."[15]

The politicians' ability to call the shots in relations with representatives of private enterprise was evident on many occasions. Driven from active participation in government by the professionalization of local politics, Philadelphia's business and social elites had ceased to govern by the close of the Civil War. Far from being dominant, their companionate marriage with the machines was an important instrument of their survival. Moreover, the initiative in forming the alliance lay with the bosses, most notably, with the Cameron and Quay dynasties. Referring to the business élite of the city in the nineties, Philadelphia publicist, reformer, and artist, Herbert Welsh, explained that such men did not "defend the course pursued by the bosses; but at the same time they will not quarrel with them, or in any way weaken their hold on power." The reason was simple, claimed Welsh; bosses were "the necessary though unsavory means of maintaining party supremacy, and so of preserving the business interests of the community." The alliance neither weakened politicians in any demonstrable way nor converted them into errand boys, for as Welsh correctly observed, they "derived power from both these classes of men"—that is, from both the social elite and the city's "financial geniuses" by finding "a leverage tenfold stronger in joint action with them."[16]

The superiority of the politician in politics clearly distressed many Philadelphians irrespective of the arrangements which some of their number had effected with City Hall or with Harrisburg; no political organization was either kept or bought except on the most narrow and temporary issues. One consequence of this slippery independence was the organization of local reform committees during the seventies and eighties by respectable, often upper-middle class taxpayers. Their own properties, of course, were relatively modest compared with those of the commonwealth's great railroad corporations, but they were sufficiently large to offer them the hope gaining fresh power and influence. They unquestionably resented their own subordinate roles in the local power structure, a subordination which exposed them to threats and plunder by state and local politicians.

As a result, what reformers depicted as the "degradation of Pennsylvania politics" was actually an oblique tribute to the triumph, for better or worse, of the political professional over the bourgeois. Of the half dozen factors held responsible for the lamentable condition of the commonwealth's political establishments—including poor administration, the spoils system, machine politics, and the evils of partisanship—none suggested the politicians' vassalage to the power of businessmen. Indeed, an entirely opposite presumption prevailed, for every act of government, as one group of reformers phrased it, was determined by "an organized band of robbers" calling itself the Republican Party before whom entrepreneurs seeking privileges came hat in hand.

Reformers, nevertheless, were often accurate about the venal connections which existed in specific instances between businessmen and politicians; the distinction perhaps best borne in mind in this instance is between symbiosis and parasitism. In Manhattan, as in many other places across the North, the Committee of Seventy and Good Government Clubs, or their equivalents, revealed a series of scandals from the sixties to the 1920's, ranging from the depredations of Tweed, at which some of the "best" men in the city had winked, to revelations of the Erie fights, the exposure of Gould's pliable justices, the unraveling of the Ramapo water steal, Jake Sharp's franchise grab, and the Hazen Hyde insurance investigations. In not one of these instances, and there were others like them, was party organization plundered or weakened. Quite the contrary, these were all to the immediate advantage of party, the real cost being imposed elsewhere. It was for this reason that the state's inquiry into the government of its cities in 1877 registered such outrage at the "introduction of State and national politics into municipal affairs," at the "capture" of the cities by the major parties and their conversion of the money machinery to their own ends with the resultant "volume of debt and excessive rate of taxation." The detailed observations of the Evarts Commission left absolutely no doubt that throughout the communities examined professional politicians were firmly in the saddle.

From reformers' perspectives generally, the City and the State of New York were run in no uncertain terms by political bosses for the benefit, principally, of their own machines. *Business* government was what reform elements consistently wanted and their complaints repeatedly made it evident that they did not believe they had it. Certainly they should have been excellent judges, for a great number of them were affiliated with the business communities. Typical of opinions frequently printed were those where reformers credited Richard Croker with having established in New York City "a government unknown to the Constitution, but just as effective as if it had been discussed in convention and voted on by the people." It was a government, according to the reformers, which flourished on "the levy of money on the corporations of this city," a statement indicating little doubt about who exercised the political initiative.[17] When reformers glanced toward Albany, they likewise failed to find enterprise triumphant. Instead, they saw Boss Platt's government "as strong as if he held the State with a victorious armed force." Platt was considered sovereign against all comers and he reputedly felt toward the chamber of commerce, the

Committee of Seventy (among whose members were some of the leading businessmen of the state), and all other such bodies, "as Louis Napoleon might have felt toward Paris after 1851."[18]

Whatever Platt and his organization did to satisfy special interests—and there is evidence that they did a great deal—there were no implications that they were servile appendages to business. If some reformers were disgusted by businessmen's failure to learn the difference between bribing legislators and "feeing waiters," many others were of a different mind. From within New York's chamber of commerce in the mid-eighties, for instance, came the complaint that politicians were unmoving and unmovable—anything but lackeys: "They sit there at Albany and simply laugh at us," ran the protest. "They treat us with contempt and ignore our reasonable requests. Our liberties are fast being taken away from us by those politicians at Albany."[19]

Businessmen were much less secure in their relationships with the state during the period of this study than they were during the twenties; thus, the "dictatorial" temper of politicians was a source of real concern. Writing in 1894, a commentator in *Century* sarcastically observed that governments had fallen so completely under the sway of politicians that the only way to break their stranglehold was to "make something out of being governed" instead of intrusting government to rings and "[putting] up its offices, the . . . management of its affairs to the highest bidder."[20] Such attitudes were widespread among businessmen and it was widely assumed that bosses, almost invulnerable with their vote-getting machinery, retained their power by "collecting blackmail from corporations and individuals as the price of immunity from hostile legislation." To many business leaders and the middle classes from which the bulk of them sprang, political bosses seemed to be saying: "you are our servants, not we yours . . . We possess the government and we intend to run it to suit ourselves,"[21] a remark reminiscent of that made by George Baer on the position of the rich in America. Strike bills, sandbagging, the manipulation of assessments, and the deployment of scores of other political weapons by political organizations naturally encouraged such opinions among the business classes.

Reputable businessmen feared that politicians were bent on the harassment and "discouragement of business." Echoing other elements in the fourth estate, *The Nation* denounced New York's legislature in 1892 for having "fulfilled every ideal opposite to those which should have distinguished it as a deliberative body." The flood of legislation released at the close of the session of 1892—715 statutes spread over 2500 pages—threw the law (a chief bulwark of the middle classes and of business stability) into doubt, as indeed it purportedly did at the close of each session. Lawyers themselves, argued *The Nation* would be a long time is discovering how best to advise their business clients, while "only after extensive and protracted litigation" could it be determined "how the ordinary transactions of business are to be carried on." A bad situation was further compounded by one new statute which repealed all or parts of nearly 3000 earlier enactments and reinforced much business opinion of the politician's brazen commercial ignorance and hostility. Gall was added to wormwood when these seemingly cavalier legal maneuvers were identified as the work of Governor Hill's lieutenants whom businessmen described as "much better known for their connection with his political activity than from their professional distinction." Hill's henchmen failed to include businessmen, lawyers, political economists, and statesmen; hence, proceedings at Albany seemed an "act of outrageous recklessness" certain to foster a "long heritage of mischief" for the state's private enterprises.[22]

The legislator's mischief had long been of immediate concern. One instance of its form was a corporation law relative to the use of proxies, a law whose "exasperating and senseless features" evoked "universal complaint." For thousands of the state's corporations, business critics of the legislature charged, it made management "complicated and difficult." In addition, politicians who were obliged to implement the law, were accused of viewing "every act of a corporation . . . with suspicion, and every stockholder as presumptively activated by iniquitous motives." Albany, it was claimed, had spiked the measure with "vexatious provisions" and "needless and arbitrary requirements," this despite pleas from business interests and their spokesmen that the corporations of New York were "no more dishonestly managed than ordinary business partnerships." The entire performance was simply attributed, as was so often to be the case, to the "malign influences" of professional politicians who seemed determined to drive enterprise from the state.[23]

The size of the enterprise (in the relatively few instances of which we have knowledge) did little to alter the anti-political bias of its leadership. The chief authority on nineteenth-century railroad leaders, Professor Cochran, tells us that railway executives "had a deep distrust of legislatures and government officials. With virtual unanimity," Cochran reports, "they doubted the wisdom, honesty, and efficiency of politicians." There is even evidence that lobbying, though undertaken as an essential defensive measure, was uncongenial to a number of these leaders. Any engagement in the political process, in fact, was considered dabbling in pitch. A top official of the Illinois Central complained typically in 1885 that railway property appeared to be a species of wealth which "demagogues, politicians, and communists" preferred to attack and many other railway executives shared the prejudice that their lines were prime targets of vote-currying politicians. One of these leaders, John Murray Forbes of Boston, urged his fellow railroaders to eschew entanglement in politics, while the president of a prominent mid-Western road advised other officials that attempts by their lines "to enter politics . . . so as to control legislatures or politics" was "unwise" and would "certainly lead to disaster."[24]

Advantages which accrued to many railroads as a result of their excursions into politics, it must be said, hardly smacked of disaster; there were abundant rewards in legislative manipulations whether in Albany or Harrisburg, Springfield, Burlington, or Sacramento, not to mention in the halls of Congress from the 1850's through the 1870's especially. Instances of buccaneering, however, underscored the common repugnance toward politics manifested by railroad chieftains who set the tone and shaped the values of their youthful industry. Men like the Pennsylvania's Franklin Gowen were exceptions, albeit in his case a brilliant one, soon rejected even by their colleagues and successors. Moreover, these biases were endemic among financiers, bankers, and brokers in company with intellectuals and reformers like the Adamses, who, while deploring injustice and inefficiency in the political economy, echoed this basic distaste for political affairs and the men enmeshed in them.

These attitudes were limited neither by time nor place. Like so many organizations of its kind, for example, a gathering of taxpayers' associations composed of businessmen in the remote, forest-locked towns and counties of Michigan, mobilized in 1894 to preserve themselves from unjust taxes levied by "petty local political bosses and machines" purportedly working for their own ends. Local investors, capitalists, and landholders argued that they exercised little control over these political banditti and their township treasurers who each year seemed "to be chosen from a more ignorant class of people." In another northwestern state during 1894–95, the businessmen of twenty-six counties were advised by their leaders to refuse to pay over 40% of their taxes as a protest against incumbent politicians. Antagonisms engendered by political plundering were so sharp that in one of these rebellious counties circulars called for rejection of "everything in this county—State, county, town, highway, school, and other taxes in every township and city."[25]

Businessmen discovered that conditions in New York were similar to those in the mid-West. New York's aldermen in the eighties and nineties still symbolized much that was unwholesome even to the most broad-minded spokesmen for the propertied classes. Enterprisers dismissed public officials as "illiterate and poor men drawn from the lowest walks of life." No such political body, charged business interests through the chamber of commerce, dared gather "as representatives of a commerical community in any other country of the western world." They were a standing menace; "any man in business," wrote James Canfield for the New York Society for Political Education in 1883, "knows that he has enough against which to contend without his success or failure hinging on a popular election and the mutations of a legislature" like the board of aldermen.[26] To responsible businessmen "no such spectacle as the New York City government" had been witnessed anywhere outside of the Reconstruction South since the "fall of the Roman Empire." So it went among "practical men of affairs" up and down the coast.[27]

Undoubtedly businessmen everywhere did have plenty to worry them, but their reactions to politicians are interesting chiefly because they were swollen, or so it would appear, all out of proportion to their immediate problems. Eager to assert power, they were reacting to a political establishment from which in the main they derived very tangible benefits, but over which they exerted far less authority than they believed they needed to secure their positions.

Had politicians lost control generally of the money machines, business antagonism almost certainly would have proven less acute. Without this control, parties could not command privilege and professionals could not exact a price from entrepreneurs; they could have threatened neither to interdict business operations nor could they have called businessmen back from the green pastures of these operations.

In the best of all possible worlds, professional politicians might not have been chosen to protect an aspiring mass democracy from the political triumph of new economic élites, but these professionals, however unwitting, were nevertheless one of the few blocking forces available. It was neither their inherent strength of character nor their ethics which checked business interests; rather, it was the inner logic of their organizations, their style of winning and holding power, which was basically the control they retained over the money machinery of state and local governments and their successful operation of the "invisible governments." Of this, businessmen were much aware.

And well they might have been. There is now good reason to accept that even the official operations of state and local governments, their aid to enterprise, investments in public services and internal improvements, extensions of credit, and regulatory powers were as extensive as those of any other economically advanced nation.[28] But when state and municipal political machines raised and spent sums of money which at times approached what governments formally collected and spent, the full range of their operations becomes clearer.

The separation of official from unofficial fiscal activities was in this sense deceptive because it obscured the intimacy lent them by political parties; yet official budgets were fully understandable only when considered as interrelated with party finances. Writing in the late nineties, Edward Dana Durand, New York's former legislative librarian, later Professor of Administration and Economics at Stanford, touched on this matter indirectly. "The outer form and the practical working of the financial system [of New York City]," he noted, "have been intimately dependent upon the conditions of the general municipal administration [run by political machines] and of state and national politics,"[29] an insight gained from the most exhaustive investigation of any city's finances undertaken before the turn of the century.

Fear of the party's central role in fiscal processes made businessmen reluctant to invest resources in taxation or public spending, for to do so was to pump money through the sluicegates of the political machines "economy and frugality did not necessarily mean smaller expenditures which so many of them detested. Many business interests clearly were not frightened of expanding governments *per se;* like one articulate Kansas Republican and free trader, some were prepared to admit that or lower taxes."[30] On the contrary, they often agreed that taxation might be as costly as any other form of investment and still be "a matter of profit" to individuals and their communities. But this was a type of investment which they failed to control and on which, therefore, politicians were believed to be waxing fat. Party meant plunder and the plunder was their money. To queries about what it was that had caused the coalescence of political machines in the first place, many respectable men would have replied that it was "simply the wealth of the Republican Party and its enormous campaign funds made up of the assessments upon officeholders and levies upon the great protected manufacturers."[31] They saw the beefy hands of politicos everywhere; "our city pay rate . . . has already attained the enormous size of over two and a half million dollars per annum," groaned a Baltimore businessman, ". . . Is there any reasonable expectation of its being reduced to any extent so long as our present system of patronage continues?"[32] For his part, he accurately envisioned only rising tax bills and growing public payrolls, and, in fact, it is hard to imagine the survival of the two-party system in a plural society without both.

In the meantime, with the old money machines a demonstrable failure and with the assault on party finances underway neither the survival of the dual money machinery nor its future form was predetermined either on an official or an unofficial level. Yet it was in this unhappy environment that the renovation and reform of the North's fiscal machinery began, a reformation constrained from the outset to take account somehow of both the efficiency professionalized parties demanded and the different type efficiency demanded by the middle class.

Part II

RENOVATION AND REFORM

There is no one act
which can be performed by a community
which brings in so large a return
to the credit of civilization and general happiness
as the judicious expenditure,
for public purposes,
of a fair percentage of the general wealth
raised by an equitable system of taxation.

DAVID A. WELLS, 1896.

Plan or no plan is no choice at all; the pertinent questions turn on particular techniques: Who shall plan, for what purposes, in what conditions, and by what devices?

Incrementalism is a method of social action that takes existing reality as one alternative and compares the probable gains and losses of closely related alternatives by making relatively small adjustments in existing reality, or making larger adjustments about whose consequences approximately as much is known as about the consequences of existing reality, or both.

Incrementalism is an aid to the rationality of the electorate and therefore to polyarchy.

ROBERT DAHL AND CHARLES LINDBLOM
Politics, Economics, and Welfare.

6

Obstacles to Reform

The obstacles to fiscal reform were both numerous and serious, but broadly speaking they sprang from four major constellations of factors, none of which was really separate from the others. Since all four factors may be viewed from several perspectives, no attempt is made here to assign them degrees of relative importance; reform had to grapple with them all.

The first factor arose from the peculiar interrelationships and structure of American governments. In one dimension, therefore, it posed administrative and jurisdictional problems. In another dimension it involved the decentralization, proliferation, and dispersal of official authority; in another, the parochial competition and restrictiveness natural to the relations between political units; and in still another, it embraced the inevitable complications of trying to finance government *and* party in the face of a growing cult of efficiency. The second factor was rooted in the sometimes contradictory and ambivalent courses of action undertaken by special interests which were seeking changes in fiscal machinery, most notably in taxing and spending operations. A third factor, or constellation of factors, was the widespread ignorance of fiscal subjects among specialists as well as among the public at large. Finally, divisions among the revenue reformers and special interests they had in specific fiscal issues constituted a fourth factor. Because some of these obstacles are implicit in earlier discussions, they require less extensive comment than others, but none of the discussions below can do more than briefly suggest the context within which reforms occurred.

An illustration of the first factor might well begin with Washington, for the federal government, especially during the twenty years immediately after the Civil War, had a provocative effect upon local fiscal developments and attitudes toward them throughout the North. In part this was due to the continuing uncertainties about federal responsibilities with respect to the states and, conversely, with the states' obligations toward Washington, some of which were unresolved by the war. It was also due partially to the pressure of the burdens which localities had assumed to save the central government from destruction and partly to the threats directed at local fiscal machinery by federal fiscal activities. Debt exemptions furnished to local wealth by United States securities, for example, enormously stimulated the evasion of local taxation without dramatically lessening the burdens of the national government and it was a source of grave concern, if not of outright hostility, among local officials. Federal excise and wartime income taxation, criticism of which had been stifled during the conflict, afterward became centers of sharp local struggles. This was true not only because of their underlying controversial social assumptions, but also because they excited local industries—banks in New York City and distilleries in Indiana—into attacks on local money machines, the better to decrease their obligations. In many quarters federal income taxation, with its seven-year record of disaster, served as a blunt instrument against the creation of state income taxes well into the twentieth century. Fiscal issues relevant to the extended battles over specie resumption and the greenback question likewise raised acute anxieties about the impact of national policies on the localities. In Ohio, for instance, Charles Reemelin, wondered if "excessive" employment of greenbacks and back notes had not dried the wellsprings of the state's private credit by producing immense losses which, he felt, were disingenuously concealed. Their circulation, he argued, led the public, which was really paying the bills through heavy taxation, to believe, as federal officials suggested, that taxes paid by banks and the interest saved by greenbacks covered all losses and left the country stronger than ever. And so it went.[1]

Massachusetts experienced many of these vexatious relations with Washington which substantially altered the local fiscal environment. One of the ablest students of the commonwealth's finances, Charles Bullock, succinctly concluded that "whatever might have come, otherwise, of the attempt to dispense with the state tax, the Civil War brought such dreams to an abrupt end." The state reaped a fiscal whirlwind in the form of internal dissensions about how to handle its burdens. It had cost $3,500,000 to equip its troops, nearly $9,500,000 to aid families of the volunteers, and over $16,300,000 in bounties—and these were just the costs to the state. Townships spent an additional $13,000,000 in the war and immediate post-war years. Who, then, was to pay? Reports of state treasurers and attorneys general between 1867 and 1872 amply illustrate how these national problems turned the local marketplace into an arena as savings banks, fire and marine insurance companies, railroads, foreign corporations, and town fathers tried to shift the burdens imposed on them. Although the scale may have differed, analogous situations prevailed elsewhere. Insofar as such dissensions highlighted interdependence and the desirability for cooperation between various levels of government, they were not utterly lacking in utility, but, unfortunately, they generally had the reverse effect. In the public sector the competition for scarce resources was exceedingly keen.[2]

Whatever their merits, and they were great, the decentralizations, proliferation, and dispersal of authority further troubled relations between governments by evoking novel problems within a welter of hazy jurisdictions. Reformers found themselves in a beehive; breaking through one cell merely meant they were enclosed in another. Although cities, for instance, faced the greatest crises in the breakdown of money machinery, it was hard to know where to begin reform, for governments lay around them in rings. Municipalities, to be sure, were creatures of the state, but the states had many other creatures as well—counties, towns, villages, sanitary districts, school districts, health districts, and other special districts—which, in turn, dealt with, through, and for urban governments. During the latter third of the nineteenth century, for example, counties frequently assessed properties and determined the tax levies for many cities. Tax levies were often certified to county officials, clerks or auditors, and county authorities actually collected taxes. Pennsylvania, Wisconsin, Michigan, and the counties of Northern Illinois were exceptions, but cities sometimes received from a county officer the taxes which they themselves had levied.

Characteristic of American government, of course, matters got much more complicated. A great city often arose within the bounds of some county; Philadelphia and St. Louis, for instance, became coterminous with counties and county officials disappeared, their *jobs* being assumed by city officials but their *functions* continuing. Similarly, New York County became the Bronx and Manhattan, and Kings became Brooklyn, each county ceasing to have its own treasury, their respective funds going to the city comptroller. Boston also absorbed county fiscal machinery, held former county property, and paid county expenses through its own treasurer and auditor. In every case, this atrophy of county government inspired political infighting which hindered reforms. Midwestern cities of moderate size like Fort Wayne or Indianapolis, Indiana, or Akron, Ohio tried unsuccessfully to avoid such difficulties by employing county treasurers at extra pay to handle city funds. In New England, the towns traditionally ran the tax machinery, including the machinery of their counties and commonwealths. When some of the towns grew into cities, they possessed entirely independent money machinery linked directly to the state. In Pennsylvania, Wisconsin, Michigan, New York, and Illinois, where town systems of government prevailed, taxes were the business of town collectors.[3] But, again, other localities deviated from this approach. In the case of New Haven, instead of a town growing into a city, the city superimposed itself, fiscally and otherwise, upon the township; while in Chicago a number of towns superimposed themselves upon the city; indeed, the assessment and collection of taxes in Chicago was a town function until the spring of 1901. Finally, whatever the dictates of common sense, the North's myriad school districts did not necessarily dovetail fiscally with their related units of government. School boards, furthermore, frequently constructed their own budgets, certified tax levies to county officers, retained and spent their own funds, borrowed money, and held title to various properties. In some states they enjoyed the rank of municipal corporations, with the result that their accounts did not appear in city budgets. Much the same was true of other special districts; Chicago's three park districts and one of its sanitary districts, each with elected boards and each independent of city government, operated as municipal corporations complete with "all the financial powers of a city." The many advantages of these arrangements for parts of the public did not prevent them from becoming obstructions to the reforms of others.[4]

If for no other reason they were obstructive because they infused the relations between political units with parochial mistrust, sharp competition, and narrow restrictions. The entire hierarchy of local political subdivisions was locked in continuous mutually destructive battle, the purpose of which was to funnel as few resources as possible into the money machines, while shaking as much as possible out of them. This warfare assumed many forms. One, as we saw earlier was characterized by the jamming of intangible property into eighteen Massachusetts communities serving as tax havens for Boston's rich. The cost to the rest of the community was high. That phase of the struggle represented the refusal of private wealth to commit itself to public responsibility; the second and equally typical phase consisted of the withdrawal of public funds for further private benefit, accomplished in this instance by the right of these taxhaven communities to receive disproportionate shares of tax moneys drawn from the personalty revenues which the commonwealth plowed back locally on the basis of their resident shareholders. Familiar elsewhere, these combats varied only as to the classes or interests involved. In Iowa, to illustrate farther, the "railroad counties" seized and retained advantages against their out-of-the-way neighbors by means of the state's redistribution of railroad taxes to localities. In Pennsylvania, the City of Philadelphia, in much the same fashion, obtained disproportionate sums from personalty taxes paid to Harrisburg, nearly half of the amount dispersed in fact. In New York, conflicts between Albany and Manhattan resulted in Manhattan bearing a heavy share of public obligations—half the cost of the state's educational expenses, for example—while the state repaid to its farming counties (forty of its sixty counties, that is) more than these counties paid in total taxes to the state.[5]

These competitions might be called intramural; others were intermural. Cities and states fought one another across their respective boundaries with fiscal weapons. On occasion this competition was designed to save political wear and tear locally; often it was pure economic conflict which grew sharper as business activities reached regional, then national dimensions. New York's sensitive financial communities thus were periodically aroused in the seventies and eighties by charges that with malice aforethought Albany was trying to stampede capital out of the state and raise the interest rate. Businessmen were alerted that tens of millions of dollars, fearing confiscation, had gone underground and tens of millions more had either refused to enter the state or had departed it. Seeking an end to personalty taxation in 1888 and speaking again on the same theme a decade later, New York's Mayor Hewitt reminded the community of the necessity of luring capital from outside with fiscal dispensations. Pennsylvanians were similarly instructed about the adverse effects of taxation on the competition of local polities with those beyond the state line. When personalty taxation was advocated before the Philadelphia Common Council in 1871, the council's Law Committee declined to prepare such a bill, arguing that it "would injure the business of the city, and stop or retard the growth of our industrial establishment." That, felt the council, was the kind of policy which had driven capital out of Massachusetts and Connecticut to Pennsylvania's initial advantage; clearly it would be folly to reverse it. In Baltimore, a city considerably poorer than many her size, city council meetings covered the same ground during the last quarter of the nineteenth century, especially concerning the city's fiscal posture vis-à-vis competition with Philadelphia capital.[6]

Nearly everywhere, fiscal machinery was crudely linked with the creation of prosperity and the guidelines to succesful competition between political units soon described practical strategies. In his widely-cited tract of 1873, Enoch Ensley of Nashville enjoined governments to "never tax anything that would be of value to your State, that could or would run away, or that would come to you." Had Memphis' taxes been levied on New York's wealth but not on her competitors, argued Ensley, he could guarantee "to transfer in a short time, hundreds of millions of the trade, money, etc., of New York to those cities," depopulating her more efficiently than a plague.[7] In this light it becomes increasingly apparent why fiscal experiments roused fear change would redound to the advantage of the nearby polities, not to local parties or local capital.

Suspicions and competition between governments usually developed into the imposition of fiscal restrictions by one level of government or one branch of government on another. Though not confined to them, these restrictions were most notorious when imposed by state governments on their own municipalities, where they were further complicated by traditional separation of powers and the fights of local political organizations.

Chicago's municipal history richly illustrates this type of combative restrictivenes. The Illinois Constitution of 1870 imposed a number of limitations on local political subdivisions. Basically they were expressions of predominantly rural legislators, abetted by certain corporations, who almost invariably represented either a different party or faction than municipal leadership in Cook County. Between the Civil War and 1900, to be sure, Chicago's city council, the new state constitution notwithstanding, appeared to continue the pre-war pattern of conciliar dominance within local government. It seemed to enjoy real power in levying taxes, voting bonds, creating municipal debts, and making provisions for the expenditure of public moneys; but the functional realities were otherwise. State restrictions constrained the council to forego the possibility of raising adequate revenues for the city in an equitable manner; by generating or enlarging internal divisions they further hamstrung city financial operations. It goes without saying that Chicago's government reacted to this; a defensive fiscal initiative was seized by the mayor and his comptroller, "the discretionary head" of municipal finances, and the elected treasurers were elbowed aside. But the cost of the maneuver continued to be a divided government. Therefore, while concentration of authority in the executive branch superficially opened the way for more flexible action, the imposed checks and balances produced situations which often stultified it. In the words of the chief student of local government, Chicago was "a strange anomaly of a number of competing responsible organs in a so-called system of concentration."[8]

In theory, reformers might have expected assistance from the State Board of Equalization which might have bridged Chicago's administrative morass with a measure of fiscal sanity and equity. But theoretical aid was all anyone ever received. A "curious mixture of the primitive and the modern," the board proved to be the "grand inquisitorial and confiscatory office" which polemicists and some officials feared could provoke revolution in Illinois. Created in the late sixties, then remodeled in 1872, it was composed of officers elected singly for four-year terms from each of the state's congressional districts. True, the board possessed the competence to do even more than its title implied by touching upon all types of property in the state. Just one reservation affected its potential; unfortunately, however, it was a fatal one. It could neither raise nor lower the state's total assessed valuation by more than 1%, making substantial equalization in the circumstances nearly impossible. As a result, the board spent its time evaluating the fiscal reports of county boards of equalization, a boondoggling review rather than a significant fiscal operation.

The board thus served the narrow political role intended for it to the detriment of reform. Given rural-urban antipathies and the jockeying for favorable assessments among local units of government, the rural membership stood fast, the better to aid standpat business interests profiting from a paralysis of the state's fiscal machinery and, at the same time, thrust the burden of taxation toward Chicago's beckoning wealth. In so doing, it drove Chicagoans to further evasion. Otherwise the board remained "an absolute farce," "a perfect burlesque." As a careful student of Illinois' revenue system reported in 1914, after the board had undergone some modification, "No one seems to find anything worthy of praise in the state board, except its direct beneficiaries, the members of the board themselves; and even they are often far from unanimous in their estimate of the value of the machinery of which they form a part."[9] Worse yet, it perpetuated the very abuses which ostensibly it was designed to correct.

Of itself insignificant, the Illinois state board characterized the chaos produced by the restrictive rivalries of hostile or overlapping political jurisdiction. Cook County also contributed to complications thwarting reforms. Like other counties, Cook had its own board of equalization which, in microcosm, dealt with competitions between the county's own rural and urban elements. The board's work, of course, was based on the original estimates of town assessors and, technically, its decisions should have carried weight locally because by the nineties Cook County consisted of 33 towns, slightly more than a third of which lay partially or entirely within Chicago. Added to this, were the park, school, and drainage districts with fiscal powers of their own. Again the anarchy of local government overwhelmed it. "The complications arising from these superimposed tax areas are obvious," exclaimed a local official at the end of the nineties, "while the problem is made still more intricate by the absence of system or standard valuation employed by the town assessors." Faced with this mélange, the Cook County board had little option save to attempt central administrative control over the process of local assessment, but its efforts merely "induced and encouraged a pernicious rivalry on the part of the various town assessors." Assessors, after all, realized that the major qualification for their job was the exercise of "an active and watchful care in the return of low assessment values." Cook's equalization board, consequently, ended up administratively sterile, maintaining practices which did violence to prospects for rational change in local money machinery, while the towns over which it presided were considered to have "long forfeited their rights of existence by a failure to perform the essential work for which they are retained."[10] Thus, despite the "moral effect" which furnished "the most vital argument for its reorganization," the "American anarchy of local autonomy," as Sidney Webb once called it, triumphed.

Special as to details, Chicago's case, from the 1870's until the present century, was actually typical. Major cities, all with wornout fiscal machinery, faced the imperatives of their new social problems under the restrictive hand of competitive or hostile political authorities above or around them in the administrative hierarchy. At the turn of the century, it was still accurate to declare, as did one member of the American Economic Association, that cities had been given "no authority . . . to do anything and everything."[11] Powers delegated to them by the states were surrendered cautiously and enumerated specifically. Legislative malapportionment kept the restrictions intact and when doubts arose officially over the existence or interpretation of a municipal power, the courts were disposed to decide against the claims of municipal corporations. Few clear lines were drawn between fiscal activities which were *permitted* by the state and those which were *required* by it and this penumbra became a no-man's land for chicane by one set of authorities and aggressions by another. On the opposite extreme, however, the minuteness of some regulations applied to cities seems remarkable. From the sixties to the eighties, even the disposition of New York City's local tax levies was determined by Albany. Of $18 million collected by the city in taxes in 1868, for example, the state allowed only $4 million to be returned for expenditure by the city council. New York's Consolidation Act of 1882, also drafted in Albany, specified what offices the city police force should consist of and the pay allowable to each grade; indeed, the city's general salary list prescribing the number, kind, and pay of civil servants was Albany's tool. State legislatures, likewise, tried compelling cities to pay interest on their bonded indebtedness and to establish sinking funds which allowed some payment on the principal. "The Legislature once went so far," wrote Mayor William Gracie in 1883, "as to make one municipal budget upon the reports of its own committees."[12]

State legislative restrictions over municipal finance assumed many forms. The Tennessee legislature abolished the government of Memphis entirely in 1879 in order to repudiate the city's embarrassing indebtedness. The community was then resurrected from the legal ashes as a "taxing district," upon which the legislature imposed the essential taxes directly. After compromise by its creditors, taxing power was restored to a reconstituted urban government.[13] Although by the end of the nineteenth century, several states, following the lead of California, enacted legislation reducing limits placed on local fiscal operations, most legislatures, including some of those which had undergone this reform, still allowed legislators to prescribe whatever items they wished to appear in municipal budgets. Everywhere the grip of the statehouse relaxed very slowly. Cities generally suffered fewer restrictions in borrowing than in other regards, it is true, but the leeway enjoyed was modest; fears of skyrocketing municipal debts never left state authorities after the experiences of the late nineteenth century. Courts, too, usually sustained the principle congenial to state circles that cities possessed "no incidental or inherent right to borrow," that, in fact, borrowing power had to be granted expressly by the state. Generally, therefore, state constitutions limited municipal indebtedness to a stated percentage of their assessed valuation, a procedure, naturally, on which there were legal variations. In Massachusetts where the commonwealth's constitution was silent on the subject, restrictions on borrowing were set statutorily at 2½% of the assessed valuation of each of the state's thirty-odd cities. Elsewhere in the iron rectangle, the prevailing limit by the eighties was closer to 5% of assessed value, although for comparison outside of this area, Richmond, Virginia was allowed 18%.[14]

Legislatures also tightened cinctures around city finances by restricting the rate of taxation. In the cities of Massachusetts, excluding Boston, the rate was set at $12 per $1000 for current expenses; no such limits applied to state or county taxes. Variations included limitations of a blanket nature, or, as in Minneapolis, limits were set on specific rates applicable to taxation for streets, permanent municipal improvements, parks, schools, and the like. Substantially this meant setting the upper limit for major items in the budget as was done in Syracuse and Detroit. Of the 68 large Northern cities examined at the turn of the century, over 40 were controlled by charters fixing the maximum tax rates. Considering the narrowness of their tax base and the demands which they confronted locally it was a rather grim prospect.[15]

Rarely thought of in this sense, the epitome of purposeful restrictiveness was the budget itself, the impact of which was first noticeable in municipalities. Defined in the last quarter of the nineteenth century as "a valuation of receipts and expenditures or a public balance sheet, and as a legislative act establishing and authorizing certain kinds and amounts of expenditures and taxation,"[16] it had been developing since the Jacksonian Era, most significantly from the Civil War onward. Clearly, then, it had practical features commending it as a tool of government. Nevertheless, its extension after the sixties represented a major effort by the middle classes to block the socio-political forces which they feared were fingering the levers of the money machines and trying the door of local treasuries. Budgets were a type of control imposed by the rural middle class and their allies through state legislatures, and independently underwritten by respectable elements in the cities. For many urbanites, budgets promised to bring government closer to their conception of it as a business. Like civil service reform, budgeting was a blow aimed at "private" and "irresponsible government," at bosses, logrolling, pork barrels, spoils, patronage, and party rule. "Above and beyond its relation to economy and efficiency in public affairs," wrote A. E. Buck, reviewing budgetary developments from the perspective of the early twenties, "it may be made one of the most potent instruments of democracy,"[17] and there is no doubt that he meant middle-class democracy. It was, as he explained, "something more than a method of checking or reducing the tax rate, more than any scheme of accountants and efficiency experts;" it was, in fact, a set of criteria for determining the right kind of democracy. "Given at least manhood suffrage," Buck noted:

> any government so organized as to produce and carry out a scientific budget system will be susceptible of extensive and intelligent popular control. On the contrary, those governments, whatever their other virtues, which fail to provide adequate budget methods will neither reach the maximum of efficiency nor prove to be altogether responsible to the people . . . It was the uncontrolled and uncontrollable increase in the cost of government that finally jostled the public into an attitude of hostility to a system . . . so fondly called the 'American system.' This growing hostility to doing business in the dark, to 'boss rule,' 'invisible government,' became the soil in which the 'budget idea' finally took root and grew. . . . More than any other principle of control, it is commanding the confidence . . . of those persons in the nation whose influence is being felt in legislatures and constitutional conventions, and other assemblies charged with the responsibility of redrafting our public laws.[18]

The "public" behind the budget and the private municipal research bureaus which did so much to spur its refinement were property owners, most notably, urban property owners whose viewpoints were spoken for by local tax reform associations, chambers of commerce, public and academic experts, and private corporations. Demanding higher quality public service, and more of it, while urging lower taxes, such taxpayers were in a quandary. In effect, therefore, they tried passing the squeeze on to public officials, asking them to do more *for* less and *with* less by cutting party revenues, a step which, as we have seen, politicians persistently and successfully resisted. Thwarted by politicians, the commercial opponents of high taxes looked upon the budget as a means of securing information on public expenses the better to argue for their reduction. Finding it difficult to pay dividends in times when taxes took larger portions of their revenues, railroads, for example, mobilized their stockholders against the costs of government and by raising their own rates on this pretext caused their shippers to insist on an accounting from public authorities. It was men and interests of this stamp who lauded the appearance of the English Budget of 1909 (little understanding its implications, ironically enough) as the "most vital event in the whole history of taxation;" indeed, as "the most important event of the last fifty years."[19]

Underlying the enthusiasm for the budget was the growing "cult of efficiency" noted earlier, the tendency not only to think of government as a business but to view efficiencies of time and cost a virtue in the factory, the department store, the study, the classroom, and the kitchen as well.[20] Highly touted as a reform, the cult, where it impinged on public affairs, often proved a major obstacle to governmental efficiency. This was true because its proponents were hostile to party as an instrument of a democracy more plural than they preferred and because they attacked party revenues as well as the boodle and welfare expenditures on which the retention of party cadres depended.

If nothing else, the cultists were zealous. If during the seventies governments of Illinois cities, under pressure from their leading citizens, abandoned operation of public burial grounds for the poor because of "their small importance as sources of revenue," costly patronage establishments could not be expected to be spared. Nor were they. Typical of thousands of party revenue and welfare redoubts hard hit by the efficiency crusades was the Boston Sewer Department early in this century. Thanks to party machinery, department payrolls had been heavily padded with party men who because of age found other employment difficult. Consequently, when the reformist Boston Finance Commission, composed of substantial middle-class organizations such as the Associated Board of Trade, the Chamber of Commerce, the Clearing House Committee, the Boston Merchants' Association, the Real Estate Exchange, the Central Labor Union, and several local improvement societies, convened in 1908 the fiscal guillotine was raised to the ready by the pull of cost-calculated efficiency. One-third of the department's 140 men were labelled "superfluous." Three-fourths of them were over

40 years of age; nine were over 70; and twenty-one were over 65. By commission standards such jobholders were obsolete and disposable parts and while it was true that day labor accounted for an important share of city expenses, what the commission refused to tolerate was the extralegal political welfare involved in their hiring.[21]

For the Boston Commission, as for its counterparts across the North, the attack on a single department was only a small part of the full investigation of every major governmental operation. Typically, therefore, the commission discovered that local political establishments were in "a state of demoralization." Intelligent administration was wholly lacking. Boston, for instance, employed two and a half times more clerks than any other city in the commonwealth and paid them three times as much; even invalids with political pull were retained in well-paying jobs, the commission learned. Notwithstanding reforms, departments had proliferated outrageously with the result that "politics [was] taking the place of business methods," a neat turn of phrase, for those business methods had never prevailed in American government. Convinced that men of their own sort were already saddled with city burdens, that only 16½% of Boston's voters were assessed for property taxes, and that their number had been declining since the 1880's, the commissioners sought to hold back departmental revenues on which political battalions fed. "To discover new funds or to invent new schemes of taxation merely to increase the volume of municipal expenditures," they argued, would simply tend "to provoke extravagance in administration." It was a foregone conclusion that they would also find "no need of increased taxes or additional income from any source to meet *legitimate* expenditures of the city."[22]

Professional politicians reacted instantly; the lone professional on the Boston Commission, John F. Kennedy, charged that his colleagues owed their selection not to personal merit but to the chief commercial interests of the city whose opinions they mirrored, a neat counterpoint to the commissioner's allegations about the merits of patronage jobholders. Kennedy, in fact, brought a confrontation between the party viewpoint of the necessity for its welfare and revenue arrangements and the cult of efficiency. Chopping payrolls and cutting public expenditures, he charged, deeply injured labor. Moreover, the commission report impugned the former administration of Mayor Fitzgerald which Kennedy frankly credited with humanely spreading work and with discouraging the cut-throat competition in city business operations that had thrown so many old employees out of their jobs. The way in which the mechanisms of party government were assailed by the commission he likewise declared unfortunate since it rendered distinctions between taxation and forms of the police power very hazy.

Anxious to enforce it own morality through the use of public fiscal machinery, the commission, he felt, was purveying opinions which revealed "an entire misconception of the principles of a free government" and were "certain to entail evils greater than the abuses which . . . [they were] designed to remedy."[23]

Similar confrontations occurred across the North. Under attack at the end of the eighties from a taxpayers' association for padded payrolls and "exorbitant" wages in the street-cleaning department, Baltimore's Mayor Latrobe reminded his critics that goverment not only was *not* a business but that the city's hiring policies were a way of helping these men and their families.[24] Three major investigations in Manhattan before 1902 produced the same kind of testimony.[25] This costly "charity in Tammany politics," as the political leadership of all the great cities realized, was an essential ingredient of their power. In the cities, it was the poorer, ignorant classes, as the first generation of professional political scientists explained, who by "reason of their solidarity and numerical voting strength, hold the balance of power." Thus, regardless of complaints of the public expense, it was "to this class that the ward boss minister[ed] in a very direct way . . . continually." Bosses were all the government that these people knew and, as a few observers were then prepared to confess, "in thus realizing this ideal of democratic government, the ward or district boss has . . . been vastly more successful than the ordinary reformer." So it was everywhere—and not alone in the cities. Reform on significant scale could only come through the political establishment, but professionals could only allow it if and when viable substitutes were found to replace their extralegal money machinery and the welfare it supported. Meanwhile, the politicos resisted reformers by trying to expand the official side of the money machinery and the official budgets instead of cutting them. In turn, this stimulated even more frequent and more vigorous attacks from devotees of the cult of efficiency. In this clash of social perspectives, governments were often too divided to satisfy any of the forces which were eager for change.

Contradiction and ambivalence in the courses pursued or in the policies advocated by important interest groups, themselves sometimes anxious to effect changes in fiscal operations, also made reform harder to achieve.

Massachusetts farmers in the mid-nineties perversely demonstrated ways in which groups favoring expansion of governmental activities, including economic regulation, perpetuated situations with which they and other middle-class elements were dissatisfied. Though agriculture in Massachusetts was supposedly "on the decline," the Census of 1890 showed 34,000 farmers in the state, the average one working 87 acres on an investment in land and buildings of $4000, a far cry from the near peonage of many Southern farmers. Feeling themselves grossly overburdened with taxes costing them, by their reckoning, the per capita equivalent of 43 days of annual labor, they were described as "fully aroused to the importance of taxation." They were capable, moreover, of acting vigorously in their own behalf, for they were probably more thoroughly organized than farmers anywhere else in the land. In 1895, they boasted 260 associations of their own, few of them ephemeral and several of them very large. The State Grange, for example, claimed 12,000 members, while 35 other incorporated farm groups claimed thousands of members each. A minority of the commonwealth's population, farmers nevertheless enjoyed a disproportionate share of power on state boards and a disproportionate number of sympathetic legislators in Boston.[26]

Naturally, farmers tended to be ambitious for themselves at public expense. "They have not failed to secure for themselves as many advantages as possible out of the expenditure of public money," admiringly wrote C. S. Walker of the Massachusetts Agricultural College in 1897 and abundant evidence sustained him. From most legislatures of the eighties and early nineties, farmers had won generous appropriations for education. Their votes had built Walker's distinctive, modern, and well-endowed agricultural college; they had secured liberal expenditures for their public schools and their teachers; they had won state tuitions for rural students who were forced to attend schools outside of their native townships and state subsidies for holding teachers' institutes in small rural towns. To supply country towns with teachers, thereby providing farmers' children with a better education at public cost, the number and endowment of normal schools had been increased steadily. State moneys also furnished free textbooks, and rural communities were granted funds for building and maintaining public libraries. Each of these services resulted from the husbandmen's political action. A proud figure, the Massachusetts agrarian was perhaps justly described as "the best educated farmer in the world," which helps explain his organizational abilities and "his potent influence" in "molding public opinion" to attain his goals.[27]

Not surprisingly, farmers also garnered millions of dollars from the state for the direct promotion of agriculture. According to state estimates in 1896, spending for farmers included funds for the advertisement of abandoned farms, bounties to agricultural societies, payments to the Board of Agriculture, to the Dairy Bureau, and to agricultural institutes. Large appropriations went for the destruction of the gypsy moth, for the suppression of tuberculosis and other contagious diseases among livestock, as well as for the construction and repair of country highways.

For these items one year's bill totalled $1,067,800. Added to it were the considerable costs entailed by state inspection of fertilizers and the prevention of the sale of margarine as butter, each enforced at the behest of agricultural interests.[28]

Farmers had no quarrel with these expenditures; they cavilled only at the thought that they were bearing the principal burden of paying for them. Their problem was how to shift the tax burden onto the backs of those whom they presumed were best able to pay, namely, the individual and corporate holders of personalty. Their formula for tapping this resource was the general property tax on personalty. Long after such taxes "no longer had a friend" among experts, they were still held in "superstitious reverence" in rural districts. This was the trap laid by the commonwealth's farmers—and unhappily they mainly sprung it on themselves.[29]

Reformers early warned the countryside of the almost insuperable administrative problems involved in reaching the new wealth by this method. But a combination of habit and bad experiences probably determined farmers to stick to their course. In 1881, for example, farmers had acceded to the proposition of urban reformers that the passage of a mortgage-exemption law would relieve them from taxation on this important form of rural indebtedness. But despite stipulations that the mortgage holders pay such taxation as was involved, mortgagees simply inserted a clause in their documents that the mortgagor was obligated for all taxes. In retrospect it is hard to see why this obvious ploy was not envisaged at the time; in any event, the reform effort, insofar as farmers were concerned, was defeated and the situation was left, if anything, worse than before, for the new statute had lured large sums of money from the tax rolls into mortgages in order to escape taxation. Farmers quite unwittingly had provided a tax sanctuary at their own expense for the very interests they sought to tax. Blame for the fiasco came to rest on the Anti-Double Taxation League, which represented, in the idiom of the disheartened farmers, "wealthy, learned, and influential men," much of the press, mortgage holders, and capitalists, all eager to subvert the structure of personalty taxation. Thereafter, the countryside opposed any further proposals aimed at the exemption of personalty.[30]

Reformation of the commonwealth's fiscal system, as a result, was seriously impaired, first, by the retention of antiquated methods for reaching personal estate and, second, by divisions within the ranks of potential reform votes. The upshot was a series of legislative stalemates which did not literally stop change but slowed it and gave it a patchwork character. To be specific, farmers continued pressing their legislative campaigns to convert the traditional machinery to their advantage against the well-financed and intelligent programs of corporations and reformers. They secured a favorable report in 1893 from a special state legislative committee studying revisions in the commonwealth's fiscal operations; the sweep of the report was extensive, but its theme was the necessity of the state channeling the "new wealth" to public uses through broadening the scope of personalty taxation.[31] This was to be achieved by ending the exemptions on mortgages, shares of foreign corporations, and municipal bonds. It also envisioned legislation forcing foreign corporations to divulge the names of their shareholders in Massachusetts and the enactment of more stringent doomage laws. Failure occurred, however, when the legislature convened and the farmer's bills, which had evolved from the committee's recommendations, died one by one on the floor.

The rural offensive subsequently collapsed. But the rural defense succeeded—one might almost say disastrously. For while the bills of the opponents of personalty taxation were defeated *seriatim,* a long impasse ensued. In this static condition, farmers were left with the old ineffectual money machinery and the opposition prevented its becoming effective by ambushing supplementary enabling legislation. In short, an uncongenial environment was created in which the groups most desirous of change in the direction of more state services blocked any general gains for one another.

Had substantial agreement about the actual operations of fiscal machinery existed throughout the business communities of the North, reform certainly would have come earlier and on a more generous scale than it did. As it was, business revealed mixed sentiment, just as farmers had, about many aspects of fiscal policy. Above and beyond the innumerable discrete conflicts between individuals and interests over the specifics of taxing, spending, and borrowing, the choices and situations faced by many businesses produced serious ambivalence within their ranks.

Following the Civil War, for example, a number of businesses actually became "strenuous advocates for continued and rapidly increasing taxation," recorded David A. Wells. Counting taxes as constituents of their costs, producers and speculators in distilling, railroads, ironmaking, and matchmaking industries discovered windfall profits in tax hikes. Between 1864 and 1867, for instance, distillers, according to official estimates, had $128 million legislated into their pockets in this manner by the federal government alone.[32] This was frequently true as well of the illegal industries such as brothels, gambling casinos, opium dens, policy shops, concert saloons, and the like which often profited from increases in their political taxes by raising the price of sin to the consumer.[33]

There were also mixed feelings through the business world about what types or levels of fiscal authority were most desirable; it was hard to know. Some railroads, for instance, found personalty taxation a sword of Damocles and roused whatever opposition they could to it; but they, like the Maryland railroads discussed earlier, also found the momentary protection behind its unenforceability profitable. Furthermore, they were not clear about what was an acceptable substitute. Similarly, business did not necessarily prefer taxation by local governments on the assumption that they were the most amenable to their interests. Some did prefer official decentralization, but many others wanted centralized authority. Railroads discovered themselves over this barrel. Everyone agreed, after the 1880 report on the taxation of railroads and railroad securities directed by Charles Francis Adams, Jr., that there was "no method of taxation possible to be devised which is not . . . applied to railroad property." Testimony before the U.S. Industrial Commission of 1902 indicated that, though changed, the situation was far from satisfactory. In one place railroads were taxed just like other property; in another they were taxed on gross receipts; elsewhere they were taxed on net receipts, and so on. "Scarcely any two states have the same system," complained a nineteenth-century railroad leader. In some localities, corporate taxes were divided between state and local governments; in others they were consolidated at the state level. Methods of assessment varied enormously. Thus, on the one hand, railroads faced a chaos of localism illustrated by the 1,900 separate tax bills one New York line paid and by the disagreeable necessity for many roads to retain local attorneys and lobbyists. On the other hand, they faced the courts.[34]

It was natural for railroads and other increasingly complex businesses to anticipate clarification of their public roles from the judiciary, but the courts neither always clarified the position of the railroads nor favored their cases or those of other corporations. State courts in major industrial states often sustained the disparate levies of local governments, as Cooley's well-footnoted *Taxation* indicated, against the interests of railway corporations. This included juridical support of mutually competitive government tax jurisdictions, double taxation, personalty taxation, and "unfair" systems of assessment. Cities like Burlington and Dubuque seemed aggressively eager to tax railway properties within their bounds and the lines were well aware of it. Disagreeing with many other urbanites, embittered by their lack of "home rule" and local fiscal power, commercial spokesmen from Boston, Baltimore, Philadelphia, New York, and Chicago often protested state bestowal of "unlimited and imperial power of taxation" on city governments, a power which purportedly menaced "the use and control of the entire property of the citizens." One authority on American commerce claimed, in fact, that "no such plunder was ever sanctioned or practiced before in the history of civilized governments." Delegation of extensive fiscal decision to municipalities, he thought, constituted the gravest defect in the national political system, requiring a check of the "most absolute kind from state legislatures." Unwatched, the "evils resulting from this extraordinary surrender of their supreme jurisdiction" to "complicated, ill-organized, and irresponsible cities" motivated by "extravagance and cupidity" could lead to commercial disaster. It was really "no apology," added a Bostonian, "that city governments [were] chosen by popular vote;" personal rights stood above "the voting power." Under circumstances like these, many businesses toyed with or surrendered to the logic of centralizing fiscal power at the highest level of government.[35]

But even that seemed risky. Guarded by the courts, state legislatures presented threats of their own to express companies, telegraph companies, and other interstate corporations as some had occasion to learn during the 1880's and 1890's. An instance of this occurred in 1894–95 when in search of fresh revenues, the Ohio Board tried uncovering them in the extra-territorial taxation of telegraph, telephone, and express companies. Without pretending that its move was premised on the discovery of untaxed company property within Ohio, the board simply added half a million dollars to the assessment of an express company's obligations. The addition was based on company holdings in other states which, ostensibly, of course, were under federal protection afforded by the commerce clause. But the litigation in Ohio courts, the U.S. Circuit Court, and the Supreme Court proved disquieting, for the Supreme Court sustained the state's extraterritorial aggression, a shock that led one national fiscal expert to suggest that such a principle "would antagonize all formerly accepted theories and legal decisions" on the subject and "ultimately destroy all interstate commerce." That no such consequences followed does not belittle one reason for consternation in the business world about the safest and most profitable fiscal course to pursue with the multitude of surrounding governmental authorities.[36]

Reform in existing fiscal machinery depended upon knowledge, but while the complexities of fiscal problems increased enormously after the Civil War, the acquisition of fresh understanding and the dissemination of information needed to cope with them proceeded more slowly. Insofar as the many publics were concerned, their need to know and the perceptions they actually entertained about fiscal affairs may never again have been in such near harmony as they were throughout the Middle Period of American history. These publics had not generally thought either persistently or seriously about local fiscal problems because they had none which required it, except very briefly, after the Revolutionary Era. As Charles Reemelin explained it, his Strasbourg professor in 1840 had praised the American tax systems as among the best in the world, whereas in 1870, he found them to be among the worst. With greater academic authority, Charles Dunbar, whom President Eliot had installed at Harvard in 1871 to sustain the traditional political economy, confirmed the observation. Until the Civil War, Americans had learned nothing about taxation, noted Dunbar, and in subsequent decades evidenced only a slight advancement. The hallmark of their tinkering with the inefficient and inequitable fiscal machinery was their utter incapacity to master their practical problems, he felt. Yet in the postwar collapse of local money machinery, even experts were quick to confess their deficiencies, or at least the mysteries of their subject. "There are no natural laws of taxation, that is, there is no science of taxation," wrote William Graham Sumner in 1874, a statement updated twenty years later by the influential economist, Arthur Latham Perry, in his declaration that "there *can* be no science of taxation." Much reform activity, as a consequence, was made all the more crude by reduction to rules of thumb. This is not to derogate from the achievements of American fiscal specialists; on the contrary, it made their work all the more impressive. But it did mean that they could count on little popular understanding or interest of the sort required to intensify their efforts.[37]

Certainly, "that class of the community to whom questions of morality and religion are especially entrusted," wrote a political economist in the mid-nineties, "rarely if ever give the subject of taxation any thought."[38] Except perhaps for church tax exemptions which freethinkers occasionally trotted into the arena, the remark actually applied to all fiscal questions. Although the clergy performed impressively as a popular educational force in American life, few thought about fiscal issues enough to rise above comforting moralisms. Those of their brethren who proclaimed the Social Gospel or who, like R. Heber Newton, joined Henry George's Single Tax Crusade, tended to be interested in broad social reconstruction rather than in the specifics of renovating the money machines.

Despite notable exceptions like Thomas Cooley, lawyers and judges were considered by their own professional leadership to be ill-equipped to handle significant questions of public finance. One of the more distinguished members of the American Bar told David Wells in 1895 that notwithstanding the importance imputed to economics by a rising generation of political economists, then brilliantly assembled in the American Economic Association, economic principles or even an interest in them had "no place in the legal profession." A prominent academician explained that the age just recently past had been "one of constitutional reform" in which lawyers had played a salient role, but the present age, he depicted as "one of administrative reform" in which lawyers were unprepared for participation. Some observations were more astringent. An Ohio reformer wrote in 1881 that "another hindrance to a successful administration of . . . finances and to consultations with men that had technical experiences . . . was the strong tendency to intrust public positions to . . . men who were mere lawyers."[39]

As professions went, of course, lawyers were probably less parochial than most others and their neglect of political economy, let alone of public finance, was understandable. But this situation still had adverse effects on reform by aggravating what revenue reformers described as the "incongruity between economic conditions and legal facts." E. R. A. Seligman, who was, by the nineties, the country's leading tax authority, observed that "legally we still have the system of taxation which grew up when each community was isolated from its fellow community," a situation he declared "no longer in conformity with economic facts."[40] Besides lawyers, a great many legislators, the drafters of state constitutions, accountants, and public school teachers contributed nothing to closing this gap.

Hostility toward existing fiscal practices was often based on inadequate knowledge of public finances. Farmers were a case in point, for few groups were more deeply persuaded of their unjust treatment. Yet according to their friends and spokesmen, countrymen were vastly ignorant about taxation and related fiscal machinery and until well into the present century were wary of most proposals for change. Since farming interests wielded a major share of political power in the Northern states, any systematic or knowledgeable attention which they might have paid to the fundamentals of public economy unquestionably would have speeded change.

By the opening of this century, however, a few farmers' organizations took an informed interest in the renovation of public finances. The State Farmers' Institute at Springfield, Illinois worked systematically to educate its followers along such lines. In Iowa, several hundred farmers gathered in Des Moines to form a statewide order whose principal function was to spread the gospel of tax reform and check the growing centralization and costliness of fiscal operations. In most states of the iron rectangle, university extension divisions, like those in Minnesota, Michigan, and Wisconsin, as well as state granges tried to furnish similar services on a modest scale to their members. New York State sought to enlighten farmers on fiscal questions by issuing state bulletins and by means of regular conferences with the state's 2,000 assessors. In New Hampshire, where most of the state's 700 assessors were farmers, information on taxation was circulated in each district, a process facilitated by small but very active granges.[41]

Regardless of these educational measures, though, farmers displayed more passion than understanding. Convinced that they were being bilked and bled by the cities, their rich men, and their corporations, the farmer was contemptuous of the new generation of "experts" and rejected ideas unsupported by their own experience. "Farmers of the state," declared an Arkansas tax commissioner, "are generally suspicious of anyone who discusses the subject of taxation—they think he wants to raise taxes." On the education of farmers, added the commissioner, no work had been done. Despite the formation of a few tax leagues, Kansas farmers, according to experts of the day, had no grasp of the principles of taxation. They received no advice from the state and were not prone to accept advice from private sources. In Iowa it was farmer opposition, reported state tax authorities, which killed recommendations raised before the general assembly for a permanent tax commission. Nebraska farmers, or at least the Single Taxers among them, without any systematic knowledge of taxation, defeated a constitutional amendment designed to lift the general property tax from their backs. Even where fiscal questions were thrust to the fore, as in Nebraska, they were likely to be pursued in a "desultory and fragmentary" manner and confined to "purely local issues without regard to the fundamental and underlying principles of taxation."[42]

Farmers were typical of much of the population; little information outside of official reports and investigations of fiscal affairs, especially on taxation, came from the experts until the last decade of the nineteenth century. According to one political economist of the nineties, the place of taxation in extant literature was "insignificant." David Wells noted that the respected *Scienza delle Finanza* by Italy's Luigi Cossa, first published in 1882 and translated in 1888 by Horace White, failed to cite a single title on taxation in English. As in 1895, added Wells, no English language publication was "entitled to be considered . . . a full and complete treatise" on the subject.[43] The estimate no doubt was gloomily overdrawn; it ignored Richard Ely's *Taxation of American States and Cities* and E. R. A. Seligman's *Progressive Taxation,* along with work by Thomas S. Adams, Henry Carter Adams, and Arthur Perry, by speaking in terms of an ideal complete study, which in fact was not many years away. And Wells' remark minimized work, notably on local taxation, by England's Edwin Cannan or Lord Goschen, not to mention extensive studies by royal commissions. Nevertheless, it called attention to the dearth of scholarly materials which interested parties or public officials could use to guide them as they moved their debates into the public arena. All that was readily available, tracts like Edward Canfield's or Enoch Ensley's aside, was Adam Smith's chapter on taxation (Chapter II, Book V, of the *Wealth of Nations*) and it, along with Ricardo and other classical economists, was nearly a century or so behind events. Placed in a slightly broader perspective the American situation was hardly unique. Thorstein Veblen's translation of Gustav Cohn's *Science of Finance* observed that "during the period from Adam Smith to the close of John Stuart Mill's activity [1873]—that is, for fully one hundred years—English political economy treated the science of finance," which pivoted on questions of taxation, "as nothing better than a scanty appendage."[44] While Americans could not fairly be ranked behind other people in such matters, (indeed Americans probably assumed that in actuality they were much ahead of everyone) the task of renovating outworn fiscal machines was made no easier by the lack of useful analysis and guidance.

The forces for change composed of specialists, men with vested interests, public officials, and revenue reformers broadly agreed that "something had to be done" about the inadequate and unjust money machinery, but they were deeply divided about precisely how to do it. Partly a result of misunderstanding and indecision arising from the complexities of specific issues and the question of who was to pay, these divisions, in conjunction with the other factors discussed above, greatly slowed change.

Two illustrations of this, one concerning proposed franchise taxation in New York State and the other concerning railroad taxation in Iowa, must suffice.

Commencing in 1899, a sharp battle erupted in Albany over the taxation of one type of utility franchise which had implications for individuals and interests across the state. The issue crystalized in two rival bills before the legislature, the so-called Rodenbeck Bill and the Ford Bill, both of which were privately inspired and each of which incorporated provisions for altering existing franchise taxation. At the heart of the ensuing controversy lay two fundamentals: first, the manner in which the new corporate wealth in the state was to be defined and earmarked for social purposes, and, second, the way administrative power was to be distributed between state and municipal governments in order to achieve these public goals.[45] Governor Roosevelt, who had styled himself a "true reformer" in the affair, wrote the state's former civil service commissioner at the time of the fight: "I do not know—and if you do you are the first man I have met who does—exactly the best form in which to tax these corporations."[46] In search of advice, the governor had consulted with a number of experts and critics of the existing arrangements from George Gunton, Richard Ely, and Seth Low to E. R. A. Seligman without arriving at an unequivocal determination of his own, thanks to differences among these men over which bill was superior.[47] No one dissented from Roosevelt's statement to the legislature in March 1899 that "a corporation should pay to the state [a] just percentage of its earnings as a return for the privileges which it enjoys;" but once espoused, this principle still left the practical problems of deciding what was *just,* what constituted "earnings," and what prices could be levied by governments for the extension of "privileges." Roosevelt was later to write a Philadelphia reformer that while governor he had "made the first great advance in the proper taxation of special franchises enjoyed by the enormously wealthy individuals and corporations."[48] The advance referred to was the Ford Bill, later designated the Franchise Tax Law, which the governor eventually signed into law. But when Roosevelt wrote to the New York Speaker in the spring of 1899, he was still confused enough to back the passage of "either the Ford or the Rodenbeck Bill," although they had opposite inspiration and were far apart in principle.[49]

Urban support for the Rodenbeck Bill came from New York utilities and steam railway companies, which Roosevelt charged had come to Albany to browbeat him at one point. The bill likewise had the backing of a number of Republican legislative leaders. Support for the Ford Bill came chiefly from New York City real estate associations, the city's leading newspapers, and rural reformers. The prospect of relief for "overburdened" realty offered by the bill temporarily joined some normally hostile elements of the city and countryside, for the bill's objective was to make "municipal monopolies" pay more taxes on either their capital stock or on their real estate at the local level for local purposes. This was a difficult feat to accomplish, however, since street railways and utilities did not own the streets over which, on, or below which their investments ran—and, therefore, they possessed only modest amounts of tangible property assessable by local authorities. Thus, the Ford Bill reached for the implicit franchise inherent in the utilities' *use* of just this space above, on, or below the public highways. To accomplish this, it was designed to isolate and then tap the difference between the value of a utility's tangible assets, its realty, and its visible properties, on the one hand, and—insofar as it could be determined—the total value of the corporation, on the other.

After a hot fight, Roosevelt, at the close of the session at Albany, described the Ford Bill as "one of the most important measures (I am tempted to say *the* most important measure) that has been before the legislature,"[50] ostensibly because it was a reform measure. But the fact was that reformers and their enemies drew comfort from aspects of both bills. Although its opponents claimed, for instance, that the Rodenbeck Bill was susceptible to evasion, both bills were; only the types of evasion differed. Moreover, New York City utilities had legitimate cause for concern about the malfunctions of the existing tax system and had every reason to hope for state control over all types of corporate taxation, a trend then underway throughout the North. The Ford Bill, however, left the crucial task of assessing city utility property to local assessors and the importance of this registered heavily on corporate leadership, for New York City assessors were Tammany troops and the power which the bill thus accorded the Hall was enormous. Republican Boss Platt argued that the political advantages delivered over to Tammany were sufficient to throw the city into Democratic hands again in 1900, and in his correspondence, Roosevelt for these reasons later acknowledged the need to amend the tax law.

Beyond political considerations, and they were doubtless of preëminent importance, there were sound reasons to anticipate that even if the Ford Bill became law, the ultimate costs of its reform would be borne by the working people who rode the cars. No one seriously expected the incidence would settle on the utilities; nor, apparently, did it.

Thus, while all articulate groups wanted change, the objectives of the Ford Bill were obscured by the division and complexities marking the contest at Albany. The law which emerged caused as many problems as it solved, except in a very temporary sense; it created no new precedents, failed to shift the burdens where many felt they ought to have been, won no political advantages for either reformers or for corporations, and, overall, assumed an unsatisfactory *ad hoc* character.

Similar incidents occurred across the North during the latter part of the nineteenth century and continued into the early part of the present century. Basically, urban interests such as tax and realty associations, municipal leagues, public officers, corporations, and various experts labored for redefinition of corporate properties in the quest for fresh sources of revenue.[51] Usually these efforts took shape as franchise taxes, taxes on capital stock, taxes based on mileage, or on gross receipts. The subjects normally were railroad, sleeping car, street railway, telegraph, or telephone companies. Of necessity they implied the revamping of state and local taxing authority, especially with an eye to the extension of local power over either taxation itself or over the distribution of its proceeds. The results rarely represented great breakthroughs in the restructuring of old fiscal machines and because of the complexity and novelty of the circumstances surrounding them, they were seldom satisfactory to anyone concerned.

A classic alignment of urban and rural reformers, nearly all anxious to make railroad properties bear a heavy share of the public burdens, occurred in Iowa with just such consequences. To begin with, the Civil

War increased the public burdens borne by almost all major interests and to meet this fiscal challenge a review of corporate contributions was undertaken not by grangers but by realty holders and commercial elements in the "river cities," such as Burlington, Dubuque, and Davenport, as well as Keokuk, Ottumwa, and Des Moines, who stoutly maintained that the time had come for railroad properties to be taxed like the property of other individuals.[52] Railroad properties, of course, were not so taxed. From the mid-fifties until 1862, the honeymoon period between Iowans and the railroads then beginning to lace the state, railroads were taxed only through the shares owned by resident and nonresident shareholders, an exceedingly crude system. Taxes collected by the counties were transferred to the state without subsequent provisions for their distribution.

Wartime changes in taxation drastically altered this procedure and sowed the seeds from which sprang urban demands for still further reforms. Under the law of 1862, railroads were taxed on their gross receipts. The state treasurer, not county officials, collected the tax and, after deductions, distributed the proceeds to the counties in proportion to the mileage of main track located in each of them. These moneys went directly to the counties, it should be stressed, not to the cities. Regardless of the merit of the gross-receipts law over earlier arrangements, it deprived the cities of a "right" to tax corporate properties locally, a right they were reluctant to abandon to higher political authority.

The issue was a vexatious one on several counts. Urban interests, exercising what they construed as their inherent right of local taxation, first of all, wanted the railways passing through them taxed as if they were resident individuals and they also demanded a better distribution of moneys collected by the state from the gross receipts tax. For cities such as Burlington or Council Bluffs, the argument seemed only reasonable, since they were sites of terminals, depots, offices, and expensive bridges, yards, and repair facilities, all enjoying the protection and service afforded by city government, yet they were removed from the ambit of local taxation. As it was, a number of rural townships with only railroad tracks to show for tax purposes received larger sums of distributed railway taxes for their schools and highways than they paid to the state under the general property tax. Less than a fourth of Iowa's rural townships, in fact, were favored recipients of the vast bulk of the state's distributed railroad taxes. Municipalities, meantime were obliged to pay for the privilege of having railroad properties located within their bounds, a privilege which in the fifties they might have acknowledged but which seemed an intolerable presumption in the post-war years. Finally, the heavy indebtedness which these communities had incurred as a result of generous subsidies to the railroads years before stimulated the desires of city editors and commercial interests for heavier taxation and more stringent regulation of railroads.

After a decade of battling constantly for changes in the gross receipts law, urban reformers and disgruntled rural elements secured a modest compromise in their favor in the General Assembly session of 1870. But that was little enough; the main stumbling block to effective corporate taxation still remained the divided urban-rural proposals for reform fully as much as the opposition, strong as it was, of the lines themselves.

This division was demonstrated several times during the assembly debates of 1870 when two substitutes for the law of 1862, the so-called Hopkirk Bill and the Russell Bill, were being considered. The Hopkirk Bill was essentially an urban measure. Its approach was familiar: since the railroads had been so handsomely underwritten by the propertied citizenry, they should pay for government just as individuals did under the general property tax. By its modifications in the distribution of railroad taxation to the counties and its a progressive principle applied to the receipts of the lines, the Russell Bill, on the contrary, found favor among counties benefitting from redistribution and, naturally, among the railroads themselves. Supporters of each bill, however, accepted the general proposition that railway corporations should carry a more impressive part of the public burden than they had done in the past. More specifically, even the advocates of the Russell Bill, which a majority of the Ways and Means Committee defended against city reformers, claimed to be seeking higher taxation of the railroads, but the methods proposed by the opposing Hopkirk Bill, really a variation of the general property tax, left them cold. Featuring a "buckshot" approach to corporate taxation, the Hopkirk Bill insisted that if the gross-receipts system were truly sound is ought to be applicable equally to all corporate enterprises, an oversimplification that precluded intelligent discrimination between various kinds of railroads and railroad problems, let alone among corporations in general. Since some of Iowa's lines were then running at a loss and were sustained chiefly by governmental assistance, their sensitivity to the urban viewpoint was understandable. They preferred change to come through modifications of the old gross-receipts law which embodied a tolerably uniform mode of assessment by state rather than by local assessors. It was also very simple to evade.

But the reformers of Dubuque, Muscatine, Davenport, Des Moines, and Burlington who had earlier petitioned the legislature to abolish the gross-receipts law as "unconstitutional and unjust," (to which they later added allegations of railway fraud) rejected this as well as rural proposals for the distribution of railway taxes. They did not reject the proposals entirely; rather they offered suggestions which seemed blatantly self-interested. Furthermore, although even rural spokesmen agreed that all Iowans bore debts incurred by the railroads, urban reformers failed to devise any plan to win over those counties which lay beyond the rail lines but which nonetheless had helped pay for their construction and had received little benefit from subsequent reallocation of tax moneys.

The Russell Bill which the railroads and many rural interests supported, had much to commend it to the countryside beyond the lines, and it took on added glamor from the careful arguments of a rural legislator handpicked for his role. Should the Hopkirk Bill pass, he argued, with a subsequent rise in the municipal taxation of railroads, the roads would simply shift these onto farmers and merchants who were dependent on railway transport. "Let me repeat," declared B. F. Keables, the Marion County legislator, "that the cities at the termini do not pay the freight on railroads, but it is paid, nine-tenths of it along the line, and it is the essence of injustice to make my neighbor in Marion County pay a part of the expenses incurred by Lee County in securing some local measure."[53]

Arguments over both bills were filled with additional absurdities which did little to clarify understanding. Valuation figures were determined by an emphasis on cost rather than on earnings; one senator suggested that roads without earnings, beyond their running expenses, be made to bear their ordinary share of taxation anyway; constitutional provisions requiring uniformity of taxation were interpreted to mean uniformity of assessment; assessment was often confused with taxation; and reformers insisted that when they won local taxation they must also have local assessment, though actually state assessment was entirely compatible with local taxation. Consequently, while the rural-railroad alliance carried the Russell Bill through the assembly, it proved nothing more than a fuzzy compromise which failed utterly to end demands for changes in the state's fiscal structure.

Reformism was stronger than ever in 1872, especially in the river cities along the Mississippi, which were embittered over the railroad rates that diverted the farm trade of the interior from their commercial houses and entrepôts to Chicago. In fact, the tides of change seemed irresistible; both major parties spoke for the uniform taxation of corporate properties as if they were the properties of any other individuals; the outgoing and incoming governors each openly backed reform legislation to banish dissidence over railroad taxation for once and for all; and there were indications that railroad men, in the face of popular reproaches and mounting legislative pressures, were prepared to face and facilitate changes in the existing machinery. After a decade of tinkering, in short, it appeared that something impressive might be done.

A spate of bills, "some grossly oppressive to the roads," according to an editor with reform sympathies, "others intended to fix a cushion more downy than the common taxpayer enjoys," were introduced in the assembly, but the session soon centered on the Gear Bill, whose Burlington author vowed to secure greater corporate tax revenues for Iowa's angry cities. Debate over the bill, despite heady rhetoric, was swiftly reduced to the earthy question of distribution. Under compromises in the Russell Bill, one-fifth of the railway taxes were paid to the state, the balance to the counties on the basis of railroad mileage within their bounds, a formula distasteful to everyone. Critics argued that the Gear Bill's supposedly equal distribution of railway valuations among counties in which railway properties lay would actually operate very unequally by taking taxes raised in one county and dividing them among counties where there were no such properties. Since Burlington in Des Moines County was the site of heavy railroad investments in terminal facilities, the critics claimed this meant taxes would be levied on the people of Des Moines County for the benefit of rural Jefferson County. A more discriminating system, the critics believed, could be devised if assessments were placed in the hands of local assessors. Attacks along these lines eventually destroyed the bill amongst its likeliest friends, the urban reformers, for none could stomach the redistribution scheme which had been thrown in purposely to win needed rural support for the measure.

By this time the Gear Bill had died and the ironies of Iowa tax reform were strikingly manifest. Spokesmen for the railroad interests who had clung tenaciously to a modified gross-receipts plan suddenly dropped it for the position defined in the Gear Bill. The urban reformers meantime shifted their ground so as to resist any attempts to centralize powers of taxation or assessment in the state government, pleading that such moves would impugn Iowans' capacity for local self-rule. As these issues dragged on, all strategic sense disappeared, and amid the noisy infighting between the urban and rural spokesmen, the railroad men on the floor of the assembly recovered first and, exploiting the situation, "quietly march[ed] to an easy success." Contriving a scheme for taxing railroad properties as a whole and thereafter distributing the proceeds according to mileage, they propitiated rural cupidity while escaping the onus of locally assessed urban taxes. "Thus," wrote the most capable of Iowa's tax authorities reviewing the developments of 1872, "the *ad valorem* system of railway taxation with unitary valuation, State assessment, and pro rata mileage distribution was finally established in Iowa as the result of a strange . . . compromise between the farmers and the railroads." A generation later, Iowa cities were still struggling to recover what their earlier sallies at reform had cost them—the right to tax railroad properties locally and effectively.[54]

Similar obstacles, rich in nuances and variety, confronted the straggling, divided, and querulous forces of change everywhere in the North; and yet the failures of the old machinery and the demands of "new governments" and parties were so massive that these forces persisted.

But in the Great Society instinctive action on a great scale is impossible. A hundred thousand men cannot surge passionately into Hyde Park. However completely they may be under the sway of Instinct, they will not get through the gates unless some one with a map and a list of marshals before him has worked out a route and a time-table.

GRAHAM WALLAS, *The Great Society* [1920].

7

The Experts and the Instruments of Reform

A study of fiscal reform reveals the extent to which it depended on the activities of a small minority of men who had become expert in the field. Since the most massive collapse of the old machinery occurred in the cities and since it was the urban middle classes who had reacted most vigorously and consistently to the breakdown, it is not surprising that this reformist minority sprang from the established elites of these same urban middle classes.

Along with most leaders and critics of late nineteenth and early twentieth century life, they shared a native-born, white, Anglo-Saxon, Protestant background. This was just as true of those who lived in New York as of those living in Illinois or Iowa. A selection of 110 prominent advocates of change in state and local fiscal systems between 1867 and 1925 indicates only a handful of exceptions to this. A few like Bolton Hall, J. Whidden Graham, or Charles Reemelin were immigrants, but barring their foreign origin (Iceland, Nova Scotia, and Germany respectively) they fitted the mold. The most notable exception was E. R. A. Seligman, a New York Jew of assured wealth and social position. Otherwise the pattern was unvarying. Reform ranks were studded with names such as Adams, Ames, Atkinson, Bradford, Brindley, Bullock, Cabot, Canfield, Cowles, Dunn, Eastman, Fairlie, Foote, Haig, Howe, Kinsman, Lea, Minot, Noble, Perry, Purdy, Whitmore, and Winn. Their main occupations confirmed their place within the respectable and responsible classes. Among them were businessmen, including an industrialist and a financier, public officials, politicians, corporate lobbyists, writers, journalists, editors, and a few inveterate full-time reformers. But their largest contingent was composed of political economists, most of them professors, who accounted for nearly one-third of the sample. While several reformers had worked at a number of jobs, very few had any experience out of their class, in the shop, the mill, or in manual labor on the land. Only Enoch Ensley described himself as a farmer and he was one of the wealthiest producers of his region. As sharply as any other factor, education marked most of these men off from their fellow countrymen and from most of their own social stratum as well. Half of them were college graduates, just under half of whom held one or more advanced degrees from institutions such as Harvard, Yale, Princeton, M.I.T., Columbia, Johns Hopkins, Oberlin, Cornell, and the University of Michigan.[1]

In brief, by the tenets of their day, they were moderate and reasonable men, well-trained, anxious to be scientific, devoted to financial and administrative efficiency. Inclined to measure efficiency in the light of cost-accounting and inclined to treat government as a business, they did not hold to these prejudices as narrowly or dogmatically as many in their class. They were frequently "non-partisan," or more frankly, anti-political, with the result that their conception of the fiscal system was one-dimensional. Occasionally they attacked party, that is to say, and they clearly reflected common middle-class attitudes towards spoils, patronage, party welfare, and bossism, but basically they ignored the problems of financing a sophisticated and highly organized political democracy. The vast majority of them, nevertheless, accepted an expanding range of services on the part of all governments and they firmly grasped the necessity of thoroughly revamping the old fiscal system to make this possible. A small number of them equated the advance of civilization with higher taxes and larger budgets and almost to the man they were eager to broaden the tax base both above and below the middle stratum. Seeking to untangle disparate problems and make their handling more flexible, most of them favored greater fiscal independence for the cities through the administrative separation and centralization of other fiscal authority at the state level, although in company with several others Henry Carter Adams wanted both more government and more decentralization in order to preserve traditions of local self-government. With notable exceptions the majority of these men were gradualists of great patience and persistence.

Excluding Henry George,[2] it was no part of the strategy of these men to appeal to the masses. Partly, this was a matter of style; but it was scarcely that alone. They realized that they could rarely count on much from the general public except indifference—or a measure of what Henry Adams harshly described as "the mental inertia of sixty or eighty million people." Yet while often vexed by it, they accepted indifference as a natural recoil from the nature of fiscal reform. "These problems," wrote a tax reformer early in this century, "are beyond the ken of average citizens, for they require so much detailed and technical knowledge that the citizen with a private business cannot afford to undertake their mastery." Therefore, reformers concentrated upon what they conceived to be the decision-making centers of state and local government and upon sensitive positions in the hierarchies of the major parties.[3]

If the causes of their discontent were rooted in middle-class feelings about the cost of the new democracy and the menaces of the new wealth, a variety of specific events or situations provoked them into action. Thus, Henry Charles Lea launched Philadelphia's modern municipal reform in the late summer of 1870, the provocation being Harrisburg's appointment of a building board empowered to tax and spend in the city without formal accountability to anyone. A scholarly publisher and long-time public critic, later a historian, Lea seized upon this local tax question to organize and direct the Citizen's Municipal Reform Association, a fiscal watchdog later restyled as the famous Committee of One Hundred. Milwaukee businessmen turned to reform of their fiscal machinery when, in the depression of the mid-seventies, they pitted themselves against the Wisconsin legislature's "arbitrary" increase in the local tax levy. Under the banner of their own Committee of One Hundred, they spent the next five years fighting to have the levy reduced and the city's charter reorganized to forestall subsequent threats to their properties. In New York, it was Tweed's enormous additions to the tax burdens carried by 5% of the city's population which inspired the upsurge of reform. Revenue reformers rose to battle in Baltimore after they detected a deterioration in the city's financial condition following the Democrats' capture of City Hall in 1867; thereafter, they sustained the fight because of their conviction they were paying the taxes of steam and street railways, rich monopolies, liquor dealers, the holders of large blocks of unassessed personalty, and welfare-minded politicians. In the "critical and belittling atmosphere" of Boston, Adams, Whitmore, Minot, and others began their protests soon after the depression of 1873 magnified the burden of rising taxes and debts, and brought to a head "the wrongs, the abuse and persecution" they claimed local capitalists had suffered over the preceding forty years. Long before the start of Henry George's great moral crusade, practical reforms of this sort had emerged nearly everywhere in the North, although their subsequent development differed.[4]

Fiscal questions inevitably furnished pretexts in local elections for viewing incumbent administrations with alarm or for pointing to their records with pride. There were few post-war elections in states like Michigan or cities like Buffalo, for example, in which fiscal issues were not salient; similarly, as we saw in Iowa, fiscal battles tended to preoccupy most regular legislative sessions and were a major cause of special sessions. As a result, reformers were not readily distinguishable from men or interests which were jockeying for momentary advantage; indeed, they were not always above this themselves nor in reality could they have been. What set them apart from the narrow politics of these engagements, however, was their somewhat broader and more sustained vision of the overall danger to middle-class values inherent in the breakdown and "misuse" of the existing money machinery. Compared to special interests, they showed a clearer perception of the opportunities afforded their conception of society by fiscal machinery designed to reach all elements of the community. Consequently, while reform efforts ultimately found expression on the hustings and in the legislatures—and while some of them both began and ended there—their major development unfolded in the more congenial environments above these battles, behind the scenes, and inside of the bureaucratic structures of government and party.

Reform of the official money machinery proceeded simultaneously through four important channels: first, through the work of officially appointed commissions; second, through the activities of certain public officials; third, through the ideas and analyses supplied by academic experts or intellectuals; and, fourth, through the actions of groups organized specifically to achieve fiscal reform.

Probably the main contribution of state and local revenue commissions lay in taking careful stock of the machinery which they were appointed to survey and in defining in generous statistical detail the nature of the problems confronting their governments. Usually without much legislative result in the short run, they proved a very great influence among public officials and political economists over the long run, particularly through their collection and synthesis of the raw data requisite to serious deliberations about policy.

A handful of public officials, notably treasurers, comptrollers, city chamberlains, or chief assessors contributed substantially to a practical administrative grasp of fiscal problems from inside the operative machinery. Many of the initial warnings about the deficiencies of the general property tax came from them and, as changes in policy were engineered, they were among the first to have to relate these alterations to specific situations.

The principal contribution of the ideas developed among experts and intellectuals, thanks to the outspoken generosity of the men who embraced them, consisted, as Thomas Cooley once explained to Henry Carter Adams, in "laying down certain general propositions and principles of taxation toward which legislation might work."[5]

Finally, although a number of organized fiscal reform groups were combative in nature, their principal achievements really lay in the dissemination of ideas and techniques among the relatively modest number of interested men in each community who wanted to dedicate themselves to effecting change but were too ill-equipped to undertake it alone. In addition, these organizations supplied much of the strategic leverage required, over the long run, to move governments into action.

With these general remarks in mind, it would be useful to examine each channel of reform in greater detail.

Between 1867 and the mid-twenties, nearly fifty commissions investigated extensively the conditions of state fiscal machinery, in the process often examining urban machinery as well, while a score of major cities conducted additional investigations through commissions of their own. Before 1900, this type of commission, always excepting some, constituted a major instrument of reform, and, by 1910, the experts agreed they had set fiscal reform "fully in train."

Two pioneering commissions particularly, each of which owed the excellence of its work to a single outstanding commissioner, reached conclusions and laid down guidelines which subsequent commissions discovered to be singularly valid and useful. New York State's Commission of 1871–1872, led by its chairman, David A. Wells, was the first of these; Maryland's Commission of 1888, whose chief member was Richard Ely, was the other.

Creation of the New York commission was a response to public pressures and urgent fiscal problems, most notably the need for more state revenues. The rising indebtedness of state and local governments as well as the maldistribution of public burdens and benefits had driven some of the state's leading interests into angry dissent. Businessmen suspected a lethal drainage of capital into the rickety political institutions with which the Constitution of 1821 had saddled them. Industry, they feared, was being discouraged, while neighboring New Jersey and Pennsylvania were growing lustily at their expense. And for this alleged exodus of capital both the state's fiscal and political machinery were held responsible. Caught by these forces, the politicians acted swiftly to cope with them; they formed the commission and found the best man they could to lead it.

To the task of commission chairman, Wells brought impressive credentials. His fiscal expertise was appended to a solid New England background, an excellent education, broad early experience in the journalistic and scientific worlds and, as his extensive correspondence shows, active political convictions. His reputation and the contacts on which it depended had been shaped in wartime Washington. Greatly influenced by the noted Pennsylvania protectionist and laissez-faire economist, Henry Carey, Wells tells us himself he had followed in Carey's footsteps and involved himself primarily in national financial problems: the tariff, currency and revenue questions, and other matters affecting national solvency, all of which had assumed unprecedented importance during the Civil War. Scornful of the federal revenue system's exemptions, duplications, inequalities, and generally debilitating effects upon production, consumption, and foreign trade, he persuaded the Lincoln Administration to create a commission to review the effectiveness of federal revenue operations and, soon after the war ended Wells was appointed Special Commissioner of the Revenue. Acting, among other things, to advise the Secretary of the Treasury on modifications in taxation and the methods of collecting national revenues, he worked at the heart of national fiscal machinery as it was being subjected to some of its worst stresses. When he quit his Washington post in the summer of 1870, he was one of the most practiced fiscal specialists in the country; and he was anxious to assume leadership in the scientific examination and practical application of fresh canons of taxation at the local as well as the national level.[6]

Despite two colleagues, Wells literally was the commission. Aside from what the report indirectly owed to New York City's Isaac Sherman whom Wells considered the greatest authority on taxation in the land,[7] its strategy and substance were entirely his. Aware that Albany had acted primarily to choke off criticism and that it was unlikely to accept sweeping reforms of the fiscal system, he took a long view and coverted the report into a vehicle for enlightening the state's intelligent public.

The report was simple, logical, and direct. Wells began by reciting the fiscal evils of New York State statistically, continuously making further statistical comparisons with conditions prevalent in nearby states. While he willingly admitted that heavy taxes were a hallmark of all higher civilizations, he also found that the unprecedented increases in New York had been accompanied by gross inequities in the distribution of public obligations. In locating the cause of this, he discovered neither the usual monopolistic devils nor corrupt capitalist plots; he ascribed them, rather, to haphazard growth and too little official calculation. The real culprit was the general property tax, particularly its provisions for the taxation of personalty. It was, in Wells' words, "a relic of medievalism" and he repudiated any reliance upon it. Even modestly successful attempts to ferret out personalty under the existing system, he reported, would require exceedingly stringent laws and inquisitorial powers granted to assessors. Still more powerful authority, in turn, would have to be invested in a state tax commission to keep the assessors reasonably honest. Taxes levied on indebtedness, one of the commonest forms of personalty taxation, he believed, were especially indefensible both economically and morally. In his judgment, furthermore, the oaths extracted from taxpayers and assessors alike simply accelerated the decay already begun by inequities; New York's system, in short, was philosophically and practically bankrupt.

To the question of what could be done about it, Wells responded with a three-part plan. First, corporations created in New York enjoying a monopoly status—utilities, state, national, and private banks, railroads, bridges, marine, fire, and life insurance companies—were to be thrust into the arms of the tax collector and forced to pay their share of public burdens, although not all of them were to pay in precisely the same way. Railroad property received special attention since it was to be taxed by the state rather than by local governments on an aggregate valuation adduced from the market value of their stocks and their funded and floating debts. No additional taxes, however, were to be imposed upon them. Collections from the railways, Wells either wanted distributed to New York's towns in proportion to their property valuations, a refinement of what came to be the Iowa system, or retained by the state entirely for defraying its own expenses.[8]

Wells' second and third recommendations were to tax the land itself on 50% of its fair marketable value and then to tax the buildings apart from the land. This, he thought, would represent "the owner's personal property on a full valuation as indicated by the rent actually paid for it or its estimated rental value." Uniformity was the virtue here most sought after. Rural lands would have paid the lowest taxes and rural buildings would have been valued at less than the land on which they stood. Taxation would then have risen automatically as one moved from the sparsely settled countryside to urban Wall Streets or Fifth Avenues where the value of the buildings eclipsed the value of the land on which they were built. Properties not embraced by these three proposals were to be tax exempt.

Equity and uniformity were the principles pursued throughout the report; honesty, the reliability of revenue producing machinery, and the enlistment of a public interest in fiscal matters Wells considered as important as any immediate rise in the state's revenues. The assumption was that if these objectives were achieved the necessary revenues would be forthcoming. In pursuit of these ends nearly every relevant and available form of documentation, public and private, local and comparative, was deployed, so impressively, as far as many readers were concerned, that there was no other fiscal report in the country equally specific and complete.

The reaction of the New York legislature, nonetheless, was as negative as Wells had anticipated. "Generally," he wrote years later, the report was regarded "as antagonistic to the theory of taxation as accepted and taught by most economists, and incorporated into statutes by lawmakers."[9] Still, within the narrow circles from which tax critics or reformers emerged, it was in wide demand, both in the United States and in Europe. That his work on the commission had been a local failure Wells readily granted, but the "result has been," he wrote twenty years later with his eyes on the national scene, "that while as yet little . . . reform in local taxation has been effected through . . . State Legislatures, a progress rapid, continuous, and complete to an extent which neither the bar nor the public seem to have . . . comprehended, has been made . . . through decisions of the U. S. Supreme Court." Shaped by findings such as his own, the Court, felt Wells, had resolved "vast intricate questions" over which it would have been "hopeless to have expected early and concurrent agreement" among the states; if nothing else, these decisions had destroyed the assumption that to tax equitably, state and local taxation had to fall upon every type of property.[10]

In time more reflective observations on the report came from other experts. A generation after publication, one of the country's chief tax reformers, A. C. Pleydell, a leader of the pioneering New York Tax Reform Association, cited it as "a landmark in the history of tax reform. That report," continued Pleydell, "recommended substantially the system which has since been adopted to a large degree: the raising of state revenue by specific taxes, and the exemption of personal property from direct assessment to the individual."[11] E. R. A. Seligman, labelled the report "the starting point in the discussion of modern American problems."[12] Without hesitating to reject certain of Wells' ideas, Seligman praised the report's mass of hard-won information, its useful account of prevalent legal conditions, and the then-novel attack on the taxation of personalty and indebtedness. No subsequent state report of this nature was to have quite the same positive impact.

The Maryland Tax Commission Report of 1888 in terms of the attention it received, however, was a close runner-up. Like the New York Report of 1871, its influential part was the work of a single individual, in this case political economist Richard Ely. It mattered little that Ely was neither chairman of the commission nor that his views publicly ran counter to those of his three colleagues. "Whereas the Chairman and two additional members sought to adopt methods [of tax reform] suited to effect the honest and diligent enforcement of our existing constitution," Ely, according to the commission majority, sought to "abolish" Maryland's constitutional provisos on the subject, "abandon our entire system of taxation and venture the experiment of wholly new methods, with the hope of producing better results." These hopes were embodied in a 105-page *Supplementary*

Report on Taxation published between the same covers with the 91-page majority report.[13]

But the majority were unknown and Ely was not. Spendidly trained in American and European universities, a leader of the "new school" of American economists and a founder of the American Economic Association, well-placed academically at Johns Hopkins, Ely had contact with the most advanced economic thought of his day; in addition, he had several years of practical experience as a Maryland tax official.

Without denying virtues to Maryland's fiscal machinery, Ely minimized them by assailing the mainstay of the system, the general property tax. The malfunctions and injustices associated with it he ascribed to an "impractical theory," permitting property which was best able to bear "the burdens of government"—the property of the urban rich and corporations—to escape taxation, defects greatly aggravated by the lack of periodic reassessments.[14] Urging the exemption of all Maryland personalty from taxation, Ely called for a separation of state and local revenues. Realty, he recommended, should be withdrawn from state taxation. In its place the state was to shift to corporate taxes and to an income tax. Local revenues, in turn, were to be drawn from realty, from taxes levied on the rental value of business establishments, and from the taxation of natural monopolies. He recognized that a proposal for an income tax would shock many people, but maintained the critical question was not the introduction of such a tax but whether it should be administered by the states or locally and whether it was to be a direct tax on incomes. Failing to register shock, Annapolis also proved unmoving. But as with the Wells Report, the recommendations of the *Supplementary Report* became common fare for revenue reformers and much of what Ely had learned from his commission experience was summarized in his *Taxation in American Cities and States,* published a few months later as the only private scholarly survey then available on the subject.

Between them the commission reports identified with Wells and with Ely drew conclusions and laid down guidelines with which subsequent commissions agreed despite pertinent reservations, variations, and innovations. The reports first showed officially the utter inadequacy and inequity of the general property tax, especially as it related to the assessment of personalty in all of its guises. Secondly, they made the point that administrative centralization of important fiscal activities and the creation of permanent tax commissions to control the corrupt and chaotic weaknesses of local assessment was essential. Their third contribution consisted of demonstrating the necessity for a separation of state and local revenues and their fourth suggested new and viable ways of taxing corporations and incomes. Best of all, in a subtle sense, to the kind of men engaged in fiscal reform, these commissions manifested an "anxiety to deal correctly and yet conservatively with the problem."

In the field of fiscal reform it was patently false to charge, as often was done, that public officials were "so deeply impressed with the importance of their positions and so anxious to magnify the worth of their labors" that they were prone, "to take the rosiest view of any part of the great clanking machinery intrusted to their care."[15] In state after state, city after city, public officers warned of the breakdown of machinery with which they had to work daily and, though numerically a small group, they greatly advanced what the middle classes regarded as reform. Thomas Hills, Boston's long-time chief assessor during the late nineteenth century, ranked high in this group as did his fellow townsmen, Charles Andrews and Nathan Matthews. George Schilling of the Illinois Bureau of Labor was another of these officials, as were Governor Carpenter of Iowa, Governors Foraker and McKinley of Ohio, Charles Reemelin and John Tracy of Ohio, and John Hunter, Richard Pattison, Abram Hewitt, John Gaynor, George Andrews, William Ivins, Frank Moss, Henry Winn, Andrew Green, and Lawson Purdy, all of whom held public posts in Eastern cities.

One exemplar of the cult of efficiency serving in public office was James A. Roberts, Comptroller of the State of New York from 1894 to 1899. An intelligent, "hard-headed business man," Roberts apparently arrived at his conviction that things were fearfully wrong with the fiscal structure of the state simply because of his obligation to supervise its finances and his desire to do so capably. "This country," he wrote in 1897 just after the Bryan campaign, "has just passed through the most threatening political campaign in its history. The portents of 1896," he continued, "were vastly more dangerous than those of 1860." If some of the issues involved had actually earned support among a majority of the electorate, he declared, they "would have undermined the very foundations of American institutions." These menacing issues sprang from the discontent of "the farmer, as a class, the work people, and the small trade folk" with "existing conditions in this State."[16]

Yet rather than taking the more usual course and assailing disaffected elements as deluded, communistic, or criminal, he noted in 1898 that his "four years of close official study of the State's finances" had compelled him to concede that there was "serious ground for complaint" in the enormous increases of public expenditures and public burdens. "While the contests against unjust and oppressive taxation," he confided in his State Report of 1899, "have been the contests of freedom and civil and religious liberty in the world, it must not be forgotten that unjust . . . taxation has been . . . the most prolific cause of national decadence as well." At the close of the century, European states seemed to him to be "dying of dry-rot because, to meet their immense expenses and to pay interest on their great bonded debts, taxation has been increased beyond the safe limit;" indeed, the sources of national prosperity, he believed, had been taxed "so that they ran dry." Both the exodus of farming people to the cities and the spreading degradation of urban slums were in his opinion, products of this fiscal process which was rapidly eliminating the narrow margin between independence and dependence. Hatred of the rich, denunciations of capital, contempt for the church, bloody "insurrections" of labor, general rancor, as well as the "tyranny of trades unions and government regulations," he attributed to fiscal problems spawned by wars and politics.

A self-styled advocate of laissez-faire which, he felt, had been the "rallying cry of democracy and free government at the beginning of the century," Roberts denounced the expansion of government, the spread of regulation, and the increase of revenues to sustain them. The swelling budgets attending these evils he blamed directly on the imperatives of party, "the greed of politicians and the delusion of social reformers." With unerring middle-class instincts, he struck through the medium of his state reports at party money machinery inside the formal framework of government. To fill the "insatiable maw of politicians," thirty-six new offices and commissions had been created in the state since 1880, he observed. Formed in 1886, for example, the State Board of Arbitration and Mediation, by his reckoning, had cost nearly $32 million, adding $1 million a year to the budget, while serving as one of the state's "asylums for decayed politicians," as a stepping stone for young and ambitious ones, and as a center of political intrigues.[17]

If Roberts discovered boards and commissions were the politicians' bait with which to lure public moneys into party coffers, so, too, he thought, were the "vicious tendencies of legislation." Designed, he argued, for the "robbery of one class . . . for the benefit of another," the bounty law for the destruction of fishing nets, for example, allowed the manufacture of cheap nets which were then illegally planted in state waters, seized by prearrangement, and made the basis of fraudulent claims on the treasury. Equally immoral to Roberts was the law allaying the clamor of bicyclists and bicycle producers by providing that one-fourth of the cost of good roads be paid by state. Since cities and villages, Roberts explained, were exempt from its provisions and since all taxpayers paid for the roads, it actually constituted "a gratuity to the towns for the benefit of country roads." He likewise condemned the Raines Liquor Law, originally a lovechild of reformers, as a blatant attempt to shift taxation from the country to the cities. All of these legislative devices lubricated party machinery, the comptroller felt, at great cost to everyone.[18]

But the most serious bite into the reserves of the taxpayer for party purposes had been made under "the pretense of charity," he charged. To sustain fourteen charitable institutions in 1897, he explained, had cost the state nearly $7 million. Furthermore, nearly every locality containing a state charity, declared Roberts, had solicited the charity to subsidize local political managers along with local wholesale and retail dealers who depended on the moneys siphoned out of the treasury through his office. As he shrewdly grasped, the costs of state welfare had become contingent not upon the realities of expenses but upon what Albany could be expected to appropriate. For supporting the politicians in their extravagance, he blasted the "new reformers" who furnished them with the pretexts for jacking up the costs of the state's houses of refuge, reformatories, industrial schools, and institutions for the deaf, blind, and insane.

True to his cult, Roberts employed his annual reports as exposés of the items that raised New York's taxes and expenditures. Salaries, expenditures for the State Capitol and the State Library buildings, costs of the forest preserves and of the racing laws, expenses for members of state investigating committees, the bills for purchases of stationery and printing, borrowings to cover shortages caused by insufficient appropriations, excessive allowances for attorneys, uncertified payments by county treasurers, and defalcations, all came under his scrutiny. Waste and fiscal deterioration, he reported, were everywhere in evidence in New York State. Tax evasion, which hardly needed further sanction from officialdom, he described as the only recourse open to those who were unwilling to "succumb to the pitiless law of the survival of the fittest." Far from being "exhibitions of hopeless depravity," it represented" a natural desire for self-preservation" which the state, he urged, should heed and study.[19]

Not loath to attack his fellow officials, Roberts acknowledged that fiscal injustice often came from the legislators' honest desire "to still the voice of discontent and complaint" in observance of "the principles of humanity." But the consequences were a series of confused and conflicting "legislative makeshifts' 'and "blunders." Screened by these, were the most serious evasions and inequities: unsound assessment of realty, wholesale escape of personalty, watering of corporate stock and use of corporate debts to avoid obligation, the trick of incorporating in nearby states in order to operate without being taxed in New York, and so on. Thus, Roberts knew precisely what it was that he wanted reformed. He urged the levying of both new and heavier corporate and franchise taxes and demanded a graded inheritance tax on the grounds that "special privileges conferred by governments, such as tariffs, corporation or franchise laws, public franchises" and the like, formed the "foundation of most of the great fortunes of the country." Centralization of corporate taxation in state hands and the implied separation of revenues among governments that accompanied it, he believed to be essential, along with state rather than local control over the inspection of the court and trust funds handled by county treasurers. Finally, for those positions requiring skill and knowledge, he hoped that the state would enlist "a corps of enthusiastic scientists . . . who have more than a pecuniary interest in their work."[20]

The New York Comptroller was typical of a number of middle-class officials, honest and basically anxious to conserve the values of a "responsible" society. Their rhetoric suggests that they would gladly have done this with the old machinery had it been possible, for the past and its institutions were mostly quite agreeable to them; but they had learned at first hand this simply was not possible. Staggering on with the old system threatened a destructive disorder provoked by rich corporations in one quarter and corrupt circuses associated with party welfarism in another. To a considerable extent these menaces, they believed, were already realities which little could be done to change. But they could be *controlled;* first, by fashioning fiscal machinery that was centralized, efficient, and run by depoliticized experts; and, second, by using this machinery to make those forces which menaced them and their values pay their own way.

Far beyond the amateur's competence, fiscal problems were made to order for intellectuals and academic experts. As a result, in few other areas of reform were they able to make such a quietly effective contribution. Their performance was a modest precursor of their eventual role as "action intellectuals" in twentieth-century American life. Within scores of governmental establishments before the turn of the century, "brain trusts," often from nearby universities, emerged to lay the educational foundations and the theoretical guidelines according to which officials might eventually move.

"I am free to say," wrote Professor Henry Carter Adams in 1887 to Columbia's E. R. A. Seligman, "that I have not thought out clearly the exact limits which should be placed to the conceptions, Society, State, Government." Like many of the "new" political economists who turned their minds to fiscal affairs, the open-endedness of their general opinions was reflected in particulars, in this case in Adams' views on taxation. Iowa-born, Hopkins-trained, with a career at Hopkins, Cornell, and then the University of Michigan, Adams, whom Joseph Dorfman judged "one of the most creative figures in American economics," was a major prophet of the economic liberalism identified late in the nineteenth century with one wing of the American Economic Association. His broad views were expounded in his *Relation of the State to Industrial Action,* an essay against the economics of free competition in favor of expanding government, especially at the state and local levels and a lucid explanation of the intimacy between private enterprise and government.[21]

As his papers show, Adams was acutely aware of the obsolescence of existing fiscal machinery and of its pernicious results. "When one considers the laws for raising revenue in the state, in the minor civil divisions, and in the cities," he recorded, "one is at a loss for words sufficiently strong to express the criticisms which justly may be urged." At fault, of course, was the general property tax which having ceased to fit the requirements of modern life, he associated with two widespread evils. The first was the theory that all property should be taxed, for, in practice this meant the virtual exemption of the possessors of the new wealth from further obligation. The second evil, Adams noted, lay in efforts to sustain the general tax by means of equalization boards which were themselves symptomatic of failures to assess fairly, to choose assessors wisely, or to end fiscal competition between communities which should have been bearing the common burden.[22]

The better to overcome "the peculiar difficulties encountered in the administration of . . . [the] existing financial system," Adams presented his "Suggestions for A System of Taxation" to the Michigan Political Science Association in 1894. It was, hopefully, a "plan of taxation" which would "fit the political adjustments and industrial customs of the American people" and consisted of three general principles. Adams first insisted that the sources of public income should be "segregated" according to the needs of the various levels of government. His second principle repudiated taxation of "the original fund created by industry." And he urged finally that legislators abandon the idea that equality of taxation required taxing every species of property.

There were "four grades of government whose financial existence" he had to reckon with, but he dealt seriously with only three since federal problems were, in his judgment, less important than those of local governments. At the level of the states, the minor civil divisions, as he called them, and the cities where he focused his attention, Adams realized that the abandonment of the general property tax could only come after decisions about how revenues were to be segregated and what would replace the tax. In his view, the criteria on which such decisions should be based were strictly functional. Commencing with the counties, townships, and school districts, Adams observed that their chief duties were to provide education, roads, police protection, and local justice. Since agriculture was their major industry, the major investments were in land. He concluded, therefore, that a general land tax should be applied to those polities exclusively. The arrangement had the dual advantage, as he saw it, of effectively abolishing boards of equalization while simultaneously decentralizing power and strengthening local self-government. The desire to revitalize local government, Adams felt, in no way contradicted his hope of centralizing government and making it more powerful at other levels, the better, as he phrased it, "to correlate public and private activity so as to preserve harmony and proportion between the various parts of organic society."

In answer to natural queries as to what sources of revenue were left to the state if the land tax was placed exclusively in the hands of localities, Adams proposed a corporation tax. "The state creates corporations," he wrote, and it was therefore "the duty of the state to regulate their action." Taxation was one of the most excellent means of potential regulation. If state authorities derived their funds from the net gains of corporations, then, felt Adams, the worst objections to the general tax could be overcome, for no longer would it be necessary to attempt the taxation of individual personalty. In addition to these corporate revenues he wanted to assign states the right to levy inheritance taxes as well as special taxes upon certain monopolies.

From his viewpoint, however, the most important task lay in finding solutions to the problems of municipal, rather than of state, revenues. Like most critics and reformers, he was keenly sensitive to the financial pressures generated by the swift development of enormous cities and by the accompanying need for flexible schemes of taxation which provided "frequent adjustments as between citizens." Accordingly urban tax reform to him meant the taxation of natural monopolies, especially street railways and utilities. Prospectively these constituted an expansive reservoir of wealth available for public purposes. But alone they were insufficient. To augment them, he further called for a real estate tax which by being based on rental values, he believed, would prove far more equitable and resilient than the levies arbitrarily imposed by local assessors. But that was not all. He strongly recommended that municipal authorities determine what portion of city expenses should be met directly by its professional men, that is, by doctors and lawyers, as well as by those in the insurance and various mercantile businesses. For tax purposes, he proposed the division of each professional group into distinct classes, the members of each class being permitted subsequently "to apportion the payment between themselves as they see fit." Critics and reformers though some of these men were, Adams realized that they were also "one class of citizens" from whom contributions proportionate to their ability to pay "were not demanded" and by bringing them under obligation in this manner, he obliquely approached the radical question of a progressive municipal income tax of a type being discussed in the nineteen-sixties for many major cities.[23]

On balance, the quality of Adams's work typified that of the middle-class intellectuals and academic experts. His efforts, first of all, were derived thoughtfully from explicity general principles not only respecting fiscal affairs but also in regard to society at large; as a result, he avoided the confusing, reflexive, stop-gap improvisations which characterized much of the criticism of the old machinery and many of the attempts to keep it operative. Similarly, while he redefined problems that most critics were more or less familiar with, he did so as a preface to the presentation of positive alternatives. Almost imperceptibly and in very low key, he broached fresh ideas which if then realized would have proven as radical as the Single Tax.

By the 1890's, the academic master of these techniques, especially in the theoretical and practical explanations of new ideas, was E. R. A. Seligman. A native New Yorker, the son of a banker, superbly trained at home and abroad, Seligman, who was for most of his adult life a Columbia University political economist, immersed himself in fiscal reform through his counsel to governments and through fertile studies from which came his *Progressive Taxation in Theory and Practice* (1894) and *Essays in Taxation* (1895), the earliest of several works, most of which became the standard scholarly explications of their subject.

Adopting a historical approach to institutional development and at the same time drawing upon strands of socialist theory, Seligman enlarged on the theme that modern governments were "no longer satisfied merely with raising adequate revenue." On the contrary, he explained, they were consciously employing political power "to interfere with the rights of private property in order to bring about a more equitable distribution of wealth." They had outgrown fiscal policies which looked "merely at the needs of administration" and had entered instead on a stage marked by "socio-political policy" in which, he observed, "all governments . . . allowed social considerations in the widest sense to influence their revenue policy." By framing his studies in this way, he was trying to accomplish two important shifts in informed thinking. Seligman was first trying to advance discussion beyond the search for *technical* substitutes for the old money machinery to an emphasis on social choices which could be realized through new fiscal policies, nearly all of which centered on forms of proportional taxation, toward policies which worked under the more flexible provisions of progressive taxation.[24] What segments of the great political parties had undertaken less rationally and more corruptly, but with considerable effectiveness, the experts were at last formalizing—and without the slightest evident awareness of it.

Almost instantly moving to the fore as the country's chief authority on progressive taxation, Seligman, the better to define his own middle-class position in the midst of Populist tumults, reviewed the historical arguments advanced for progressive taxation. It seemed to him that there were three motives for it: one was socialist, one compensatory, and one economic. With socialist motivations, he dealt swiftly and unsympathetically. "From the principle that the state may modify its strict fiscal policy by considerations of general national utility, to the principle that it is the duty of the state to redress all inequalities of fortune among its private citizens is a long and dangerous step," he wrote. Equalization of fortunes, he argued would preclude "any science of finance;" there would be just one economic guideline for the socialist —"Confiscate the property of the rich and give it to the poor." Consequently, while admitting that socialist motives often lay at the heart of demands for progressive taxation, he depicted them as so fallacious that they had to be "unconditionally rejected."[25]

How unfortunate it was, he felt, that among the middle classes the notion was current that because socialists favored the progressive principle, progressive taxation implied "socialism and confiscation." As he was at pains to demonstrate, a man could be "an arch-individualist and . . . logically advocate progression," as anyone caring to examine fiscal experience in many other countries should be able, he thought, to see.

Seligman likewise impugned the compensatory theory (a viewpoint ably expounded by Francis A. Walker, one of the best-known American economists) as a justification for progressive taxation. Seligman dismissed his opinions as "interesting but . . . not convincing." Walker's defense of progressive taxation had rested on two assumptions: first, he believed that disparities between men's properties and income were due "in no small part to the failure of the state in its duty of protecting men against violence and fraud." Contrary to the precepts of Social Darwinism, he presumed that a man's wealth or poverty was the consequence of the political actions of the state. Therefore, whenever it could be shown that inequalities in wealth prevailed because of "acts of the state itself for a political purpose," compensatory taxation was required to redress the imbalances created. On this score Seligman was sharply critical, arguing that it could never be entertained seriously because it offered neither practical standards nor general principles against which the state's role in creating inequalities of wealth could be measured.[26]

Having exposed to his own satisfaction the blatant inadequacies of reforms embodied in socialist and compensatory schemes, Seligman turned to examinations of the ubiquitous and venerable "benefit theory" and the closely related proportional theory of taxation, each of which lay in the ruins of general property taxation. And he took a somewhat novel approach to them. However false their premises were, however badly they had failed in their implementation, they struck him, nonetheless, as leading inexorably to the acceptance of progressive principles. "The situation is a curious one," Seligman wrote, "the benefit theory is usually regarded by its opponents as a narrow, extreme-individualist, almost atomistic doctrine;" yet under it, individualists who normally denounced progressive taxation as socialist came full circle. As understood in America, the benefit theory posited that taxes bore a direct relationship to the advantages which individuals derived from government; the greater a man's property, according to common explanations, the "greater . . . the benefits that accrue to him from the protection of the state." Taxes, in this context, were ostensibly computable like insurance premiums. The fallacies of this thesis, explained Seligman, were easily refutable, but refutations were rarely forthcoming and it was generally concluded that taxes had to be levied proportionately. "Writers who firmly believe in the benefit theory are forced, logically, as they think," declared Seligman, "to demand progressive taxation." Thus, "arch-individualists" ended up advocating what many men regarded as socialism. "It is a remarkable outcome of individualism," he observed. Ironies aside, he judged it unsatisfactory. The advantage which men derived from the actions of governments, he insisted were largely psychological; that is, they were not quantifiable. The benefit theory was simply too nebulous to premise any taxation upon for very long and it afforded no viable basis for what he called the "scientific treatment of taxation."[27]

Through elimination, Seligman's writings moved systematically to amass evidence in support of the faculty theory of taxation, that is, the notion that taxes ought to be levied according to a man's ability to pay. Faculty, in crude form, was an ancient concept and in Germanic fashion, as was his habit, Seligman traced its evolution from classical times to his own day in hopes of highlighting the attractive changes which had occurred in the earliest versions of the idea. Older versions, he noted, had simply linked a man's ability to pay to his general property holdings and, in turn, "both property and income as tests of faculty," explained Seligman, "had regard to conditions of production." This was the rule until demands arose for the exemption of a man's minimum of subsistence. When this shift happened, the determinants of faculty were no longer tied to production but to consumption instead. Since consumption itself was a dynamic conception, a man's faculty soon consisted of his productive power plus his capacity to use it in the satisfaction of his wants. "In other words," explained Seligman, "the idea of burden, or sacrifice, was introduced." Ability to pay taxes thereafter tended to be measured by the portion of a man's product or income "the loss of which would impose upon the individual an equal burden or sacrifice with his neighbor." Such theories, he indicated by way of putting his readers at ease, had already been evolved by French and English writers by the eighteenth century.[28]

Seligman, in sum, provided historical depth to theories of faculty and equality of sacrifice at a time (during the 1890's) when debates about these ideas were novel issues engaging critical minorities. As he interpreted the evidence, however, the discussion had attained scientific sophistication a century earlier. "Equal taxation," "equal" or "proportional sacrifice," rates of progression, degressive progressivity, had each been explored elsewhere while state and local money machines were breaking down in America. By the seventies, theories of progressive taxation even bore the imprimatur of Stanley Jevons' concept of marginal utility, the notion that the value of all commodities depended upon the contribution of the last usable portion to the satisfaction of some human wants and, as a result, final utility buttressed demands for progressive taxation resting on a gradual diminution in the rate of progression.

But Seligman was too shrewd to throw his informed audience off by making his case seem airtight or by claiming too much. "According as we choose our figures," he acknowledged, "we can prove the possibility of progressive, of proportional or of regressive taxation." Even the idea of sacrifice was not reducible to mathematical formulae; it, too, was a psychological proposition, hence unpredictable and inexact. Achieving equality of public burdens, he realized, meant broaching social and ethical problems; in fact, ethics and economics were to him inseparable. He therefore approached historical theorizing about progressive taxation with respect for the intellectual ingenuity invested in it, but skeptically as concerning the validity of its practical results. The principle, after all, was scarcely more perfect than other principles of taxation; it could never render what John Stuart Mill had called that "degree of certainty" on which legislators could proceed to act without risk of doing injustice to many of the population. "All governmental actions which have to do with the money relations of classes," Seligman wrote, "are necessarily more or less arbitrary;" as a consequence, he confessed that he could only draw "very vague conclusions as to the general legitimacy of the principle of progressive taxation."[29]

It is impossible to fathom the extent to which Seligman was being politic behind the deployment of his scholarship; in any event, his doubts did not stop him from rebutting arguments against the proposal of progressive taxation to the thinking public. He readily disposed of allegations that it would prove confiscatory, that it would prove to be a discouraging imposition upon the initiative of industry, or that it would fail to yield adequate revenues. He also examined social objections that graduated taxes would pose "the supreme danger to democracy" by saddling one class with the obligations of another, in the process, impelling the state "into vast schemes of extravagance" with impunity. As Seligman observed, this was a theme handled brilliantly in 1896 by England's William Lecky in his *Democracy and Liberty* and swiftly imported into the United States to support similar arguments then in progress. The point had been driven home in Seligman's own bailiwick before the New York State Legislature in 1897. Opposing the so-called Dudley Bill which the solons had enacted to arm the state with a progressive inheritance tax, W. D. Guthrie, who had argued the Pollock Case before the United States Supreme Court three years earlier, warned in language almost identical to Lecky's that "the great danger of all democracies is that one class votes the taxes for another class to pay. Heretofore," continued Guthrie, "our bulwark has been that, as all taxes were equally and uniformly imposed, classes could not be discriminated against, and this protected all." Once establish graduated taxes, he warned, and the "whole burden of taxation can be thrown on a few rich."[30] But Seligman, conscious of how little of the onus of public obligation had been borne by the American rich, was unimpressed by such threats. Ignoring the glaring unreality of Guthrie's description of the existing fiscal system, he denigrated it as a political rather than an economic argument; if permitted to run its logical course such wild speculation, he remarked, could only result in the complete distrust of democratic government.

Still, if Seligman believed the theoretical objections to progressive taxation were largely "destitute of foundation," he also believed that it was "a matter of considerable difficulty to decide how far or in what manner the principle ought to be actually carried out in practice." Theory, for example, could not provide a definite scale of progression; moreover, there were "considerations of expediency" that had to be heeded because of uncertainties about effects which the principle would have on the "interrelationships between the various parts of the entire tax system."

Just how far the progressive idea could be pressed, then, remained an empirical matter for Seligman. Experience demonstrated that while "progression of some sort" was required "from the standpoint of ideal justice," the practical barriers to its widespread application were, he thought, "well-nigh insuperable." In default of a single tax contrived to hit everyone on his *real* income, even an income tax seemed incapable of working except in "an exceedingly rough and round about way." The only significant tax, he ventured, to which the principle of progression could readily be applied was an inheritance tax. But he was prepared prudently to watch for opportunities; "in the last resort," he declared, "the crucial point is the state of the social consciousness and the development of the feeling of civil obligations."

In practice he was a little less philosophical and proceeded behind the scenes in company with New York politicians and with state and national reform associations to press for specific changes: the end of personalty taxation, the separation of revenues, the creation of permanent tax commissions, clearer definition of tax jurisdictions, the centralization of fiscal administration, closer correspondence between legal facts and economic facts, better assessment procedures and more expert assessors, a state income tax, and precisely drafted, hence uniform and effective corporate taxes. Throughout, the problems confronting local governments were conceived as of remediable rather than as soluble. The collapse of state and local fiscal machinery posed "one of the most difficult [situations] to solve equitably that the legislator meets," he observed, adding by way of emphasis that "you have got to attack the problem piecemeal . . . you cannot reform the thing all at once."[31]

In the sixties and seventies state and local fiscal reform was conducted chiefly by official commissions, by public officers, by experts and intellectuals, and by other reform groups as a minor adjunct to their major programs. Except briefly and sporadically, as was the case with a taxpayers' association in New York City in the mid-sixties, or with Henry Lea's Municipal Association in Philadelphia in the seventies, or, with similar bodies in the Iowa river cities, in Boston, or in Baltimore, the movement could not be characterized accurately as highly organized on a broad scale. This was especially true if most lobbies are excluded from consideration. By the eighties and nineties, however, nearly every major city in the iron rectangle nourished private fiscal reform organizations and by the early twentieth century many of these had become stronger and proliferated, while in the leading industrial states, New York, Pennsylvania, Massachusets, Ohio, and Illinois, for example, statewide organizations had appeared as well. Thus, when the National Tax Association was established in 1907, it was the logical, if not inevitable, culmination of a generation of private organizational effort.

Despite its "national" designation, the association, as intended, gave the overwhelming proportion of its energies to state and local fiscal problems. Indeed, the immediate "source of inspiration which developed and guided" its work was the New York (City) Tax Reform Association, created in 1891 to defeat Albany's attempt to enact a "listing bill" requiring citizens to render sworn statements specifying the extent of their possessions. Distinctly Northern, urban, and solidly middle class, the NTA represented a convergence of such state and local organizations, inclusive of many of their leaders, personnel, and programs.[32]

The organization's style was reflected by its leadership which in every particular epitomized the kind of men and ideas that had distinguished fiscal reform over the previous half century. Its chief organizer and first president, Allen Ripley Foote, was a staunch Republican from New York's "Niagara Frontier." Behind him, by 1907, lay nearly forty years of reform activity in New York, Michigan, Ohio, Illinois, Maryland, and Washington, D.C. A devotee of the cult of efficiency, he ardently opposed any threats to legitimate private enterprise and had few kind words for the expansion of government authority. Yet if Foote was in many ways a man of commonplace opinions, he was also fully aware of why the money machinery had broken down and what the consequences were of that breakdown, at least officially. On a practical level, he was likewise familiar with a number of vital urban problems. During the nineties, for example, he had written three books on the technical and moral questions facing municipalities in respect to electric-power companies, municipal-service industries, and the regulation of corporate activity; in addition, between 1899 and 1905, he wrote for and edited a leading Chicago reform publication.[33] In short, his rather common views had been broadened as well as refined by deep conviction, by attention to detail, and by years of more-or-less professional reformism. Lawson Purdy, who had almost become the NTA's first president and who did serve as its first vice-president, had a similar background and record. A one-time disciple of Henry George, by training a lawyer, he sported a long career in municipal reform, including service with the New York Tax Reform Association and with the Municipal League during the nineties. Subsequently, between 1907 and 1917, he was to sit as President of the New York City Board of Taxes and Assessments and as a member of the city's Advisory Commission on Taxation and Finance. Much the same type of career characterized Arthur Pleydell, E. L. Heydecker, and William Ryan who were among the NTA's early officials.[34]

Not surprisingly, the organization manifested a ponderous sobriety coupled with a very positive sense of direction. No doubt these qualities stemmed from the fact that unlike labor, socialist, populist, or even feminist reform groups which functioned beyond the pale of respectable values, the NTA was always considered eminently reputable. Its leaders were obliged to cope with public ignorance and indifference, but its activities were never damped down by charges that it was radical, extremist, or subversive. Its emphasis on the threat of big government, its accent on the virtues of local self-government, its enthusiasm for converting all government into a business (its insistence, that is, on careful public accounting, on technical and administrative efficiency, on the limitation of government debts and expenditures, and on removing the politics from politics) all clothed it with the best middle-class trappings. The association's first national conference thus attracted not only the country's chief tax and fiscal experts, such as Seligman, but also leading representatives of the business world, two governors, delegations appointed by a number of state governments, premiers of Canadian provinces, and several university presidents.

The NTA's statement of purpose was sufficiently restrained and academic to disenchant all but the well-trained, the dogged, and the scholarly. It sought first to secure "an authoritative and exhaustive discussion" of the subject of taxation in all of its ramifications. Having once solicited the "best thought" of fiscal experts it further sought to publish their information for the benefit of public officers, other experts, and particularly legislators. To the solons, the NTA hoped to offer a "concrete, up-to-date statement of the economic and business principles" applicable to state and local administration. As the fruits of this lobbying, the association intended to develop "a high degree of uniformity" in state tax laws and by doing so "to eliminate the evil" of changes in legal residence by businesses seeking to evade public obligation and the attendant evil of enterprises being induced to relocate because of persuasive differences in state tax laws. Not only would such steps curtail policies born of local mercantilism, but they would also hopefully create conditions favorable to the "effective and economical management of all state and local financial affairs."

Originally intending to confine itself to local problems, the NTA was driven, nevertheless, to grapple with certain national problems as well. As might have been assumed from the association's general style, these arose from alleged interference by Washington in the fiscal operations of local governments. Among the leadership, in fact, fears about the integrity of their local political establishments long predated the founding of the association. "The rapid extension of governmental functions," wrote Carl Plehn, one of the NTA's professorial authorities on public finance in 1896, "the invasion by government of fields of activity" lying close to "the welfare of the people" had encouraged Washington to encroach upon sources of revenue upon which the states themselves depended.[35] During the first part of this century, Ripley Foote and his staff continued to react unfavorably to "a growing disposition on the part of Congress" to appropriate sources of state revenue for federal purposes. Republican proposals in 1907, for example, that Washington commence tapping inheritances evoked heated protest from the NTA. Shortly afterward, the organization further denounced federal laws taxing corporations "organized under state laws and operating for profit" and federal acts laying taxes on the net income of certain corporations. A federal statute "creating a special privileged class of Federal beneficiaries" through the exemption from taxation of "certain instruments of credit executed, not for a governmental purpose" but rather in order to subsidize private business for private gain was also assailed. The business in this case, ironically, were federal land banks and national farm-loan associations. The sole purpose of the law, claimed Foote, was to enable "a certain class of farmers" to borrow money with which to underwrite their private operations; it was a brash vote-catching scheme, "obnoxious and dangerous" because blatantly contrary to the "fundamental principle of democracy—'Equal opportunity for all, special privilege for none' " and because, charged Foote, it arrogated to the federal government power to restrict sources of revenue which had been available to local governments since "the day of their creation."

Although its opposition to privilege (as it chose to construe it), politics, and paternalism at the national level became a theme of NTA activity, the organization still moved reluctantly, awkwardly, and defensively against Washington; it was far more positive and specific about local programs and proposals. At that level, its annual conferences, its steady production of papers and other publications, its ceaseless instruction of public authorities (particularly members of state and local tax commissions and assessors), its pooling of expertise, and similar activities made it the greatest educational force of its day in fiscal reform. In no sense did it alter the direction or change the content of reforms advocated during the nineteenth century; its functions were basically those of synthesis and the dissemination of middle-class viewpoints about the manner in which the money machines of the country should be reconstructed.[36]

With a sincere belief in its objectivity, in default of "scientific" objections from elsewhere in the community, the NTA proceeded on several assumptions. The first was that the middle classes, the most productive and responsible elements in the society, were bearing the heavy financial burdens of working people, of corporations, and of the rich. The second was that under pressures from other social interests the role of government could no longer be diminished significantly and would, in reality, perhaps even desirably, be increased continuously. The third assumption was that, short of disaster for the respectable classes, the burdens of paying for growing budgets would have to be spread, while its fourth assumption was that increased government fiscal activity accompanying the spread of burdens to other groups would be tolerable only if there were a tacit acceptance of the principle that governing was primarily a matter of utilizing efficient techniques and that, accordingly, government should operate much as any other business. Of hypocrisy in these assumptions there is no trace; nor was there evident doubt among reformers that the realization of the proposals advocated by the NTA would benefit every segment of the population. Even so, considering what such assumptions ignored, the needs of party, for example, and the expectations of other and more numerous minorities, there was a quiet unwitting audacity about the whole movement.

While social forces accentuate the conditions under which profits may be made, they tend to reduce the risks that attend business ventures. . . . While the liability is being reduced, the possibility of profits is being increased owing to the acceleration of social change and technological improvement . . . and the entrepreneur, because of his position at the financial center of things, is able to appropriate much of the increasing social productivity. . . . In this way, profitakers are enabled to secure a lead over the lagging wage earner, smaller salary earner, and recipient of agricultural income, and to appropriate wealth which is socially earned and which is not a necessary incentive to his own economic productivity.

HARVEY W. PECK
Taxation and Welfare [1925].

I therefore conclude . . . that the question of taxes is rather a question of quantity than quality. The governments in order to pay for their madnesses and in order to grease the paws of the politicians, subject the countries up to the limit that the resistance of the taxpayers prevents them from passing.

MAFFEO PANTALEONI TO E. R. A. SELIGMAN
March 1, 1896, *The Seligman Correspondence.*

8

The Main Lines of Reform

At the close of the nineteenth century, four of six major proposals for fiscal reform advanced during the preceding generation for the reconstruction of the Northern money machines remained viable. Two of the century's more sensational proposals, tariff reform and the Single Tax, which if implemented would have altered drastically the structure of state and local systems, appeared to have failed. Later it was apparent how misleading appearances were, for the tariff question was just momentarily dormant, while advocacy of the Single Tax literally never disappeared. Through moral indirection, in fact, it exercised a deep influence, fiscal and otherwise, on many leaders of the Progressive movement. Both of these schemes, it is worth noting, would have changed existing systems from the top down, while the four hardiest and most popular programs, all designed for state and local purposes, on the contrary, sought to rebuild public financial establishments from the ground up.

Closely related, these major reforms involved a separation of the sources of revenue relied upon by state and local fiscal authorities, an extension and ramification of corporate taxation, the taxation of incomes and inheritances according to progressive principles, and the structuring of fiscal laws and administration along scientific and nonpolitical lines.

Broadly, the objective of such reform was to secure what the business and professionally oriented middle classes considered a just distribution of communal burdens. Since, by definition, political processes were an uncertain means of securing this, justice seemed attainable only through governments devoted to the efficiencies of cost accounting. Systems built around the general property tax, moreover, provided neither the incentives nor the information which revenue reformers required for sound auditing or accurate bookkeeping, so that fair and sound remedies were believed to lie not so much in modifications of the theories and practices subsumed under general property taxation as in the discovery of substitutes for the tax itself.

One key to developing such substitutes was the taxation of privilege. This promised the established middle classes, particularly those elements which were heavily invested in realty and certain types of intangible personalty, relief from the incubus of unmodified general property taxation. As businessmen's support of the National Tax Association indicated, many business groups were prepared to abet such notions in hopes of establishing a semblance of badly needed uniformity in taxation. Better yet from their perspectives, both the anticipated relief and the uniformity implicit in the effort to shift burdens to special privilege comported with their interpretations of democracy.

Of the four principal paths chosen by reformers to lead them toward an efficient middle-class democracy through the achievement of fiscal security, the separation of revenues was usually considered the main route along which all such progress would have to begin. Some authorities, in fact, treated it as a well-trodden path; "segregation of the sources of revenue is by no means a novel idea," wrote Henry Carter Adams in 1894,[1] and while another expert attributed the idea to Adams, Adams attributed it to arguments that had arisen over the adoption of the Federal Constitution. Legislative bodies subsequently had given the idea frequent, though seldom favorable, consideration, but the concept fared much better among political economists. David Wells, in his Reports of 1871–72, was clearly moving in that direction when, for the sake of efficiency, uniformity, and equality of assessments, he urged that railroads and other corporations be taxed by New York State rather than by its local units of government, that the raising of state revenues be by specific taxes, and that the "extent of the jurisdiction of a state" over "various negotiable instruments" be explored with an eye to the division of fiscal activities.[2] Others found the idea attractive, too, because it seemed a logical and harmonious counterpart of the functional subdivision of American government and because at the federal level particularly it promised to insure greater financial flexibility than the country had enjoyed during the century's wartime crises.

But at the heart of the discussions about segregation of revenues was the goal on which reformers were in unanimous agreement, the abandonment of the general property tax implied by the application of the principles of segregated revenues locally. How this would be managed was explained publicly many times. Since the state itself created corporations, ran the argument, corporate taxation was in the natural purview of the state; other sources were reserved for the minor subdivisions in what was tantamount in most instances to a functional allocation of the sources of revenue. Barring a handful of counties in each state, explained the experts, the bulk of the population living in the minor polities were either farmers or men engaged in occupations related to agriculture, so that under the circumstances the remnants of the general property tax, really a tax on land stripped of its personalty provisions by the state, could be assigned exclusively to these units. Local governments would thus have been free to set their own valuations on landed property through the congenial medium of their local assessors while adjustments in valuation would have been a county responsibility. "Such a step," declared a respected political economist in the mid-nineties, ". . . would tend to decentralize political power and, consequently may be regarded as in harmony with the development of local self-government."[3] In addition, from an urban perspective, segregation would have brought the disentanglement of municipal fiscal systems from those which served the rural communities surrounding them.

All this accomplished, however, "the most difficult task remained:" the decision about which revenues were to be granted to the municipalities. To the experts, of course, urban taxation was especially tricky because of "the rapid state of development in which most municipalities" were to be found, making adjustments between the inhabitants themselves as well as with the people in adjacent polities a constant problem. Whatever the hazards, plenty of suggestions were offered to overcome them. Natural monopolies were the most obvious target, one about which there was no disagreement, but since they alone were incapable of supplying urban needs, a second source, consisting of the taxation of real estate on the basis of rental values, was suggested in addition. Adams' proposition of "securing direct contributions from professional men and merchants" went farther than any other on record and yet its audacity advertised the importance of all other proposals relevant to segregation.[4]

Before 1908 a substantial number of legislators had embraced the idea of segregating revenues, so fervently in fact, that nine states—New York, Pennsylvania, Connecticut, Ohio, New Jersey, Wisconsin, Massachusetts, Minnesota, and Missouri—incorporated the concept into their fiscal systems. Praised by a number of state tax commissioners, by the United States Industrial Commission of 1901, and by such reputable authorities on public finance as E. R. A. Seligman, the separation of revenues among governments won wide acceptance before 1910 as "the first and most important step" toward overall fiscal reform.[5] In a literal sense it was not the first step, but it was unquestionably an essential one.

Inevitably in some quarters the segregation of revenues assumed the character of a panacea. This was the case, to be specific, in California which had served as a weather gauge in tax legislation for observers in many Northern states. With obvious enthusiasm, the California Tax Commission of 1906 declared that "complete separation will abolish at once the expense, friction, and annoyance of the vain attempt to equalize between the different counties. Partial separation," continued the commissioners, "will lessen this evil." The commissioners hoped that as the proportion of state taxation borne by each citizen was reduced, incentives to engage in wholesale evasion would be reduced also. The commissioners were likewise counting on the divorce of state and local revenues to diminish the local political temptations from which it was believed vicious competition for control of the fiscal systems arose.[6] In circles outside of California there were equally high but slightly different hopes for the prospects of separation. Among some of these groups, for example, it was not conceived of primarily as a way of securing particular sources of revenue for certain levels of government, rather separation promised these men "more centralization in the revenue systems of the American Commonwealths." John Brindley, an expert on Iowa fiscal history, took this position after witnessing the interminable and grubby scramblings of Iowa counties for shares of railway taxation, precisely as did many other authorities whose experiences demonstrated to them that local control over money machinery militated against any real fiscal reform.[7]

However wise the drive toward separation was, and *that* by the turn of the century was not seriously in question, the early practical results of policies combining centralization and segregation were unimpressive. Delaware, to take one case, abandoned the general property tax for state purposes in 1877, thereafter placing exclusive reliance on licenses and special taxes on railroads for state revenues. But special taxation of this kind unfortunately tended to make the state's tax base inelastic and, or so it was seriously alleged, by removing them from direct obligation deprived most citizens of a strong sense of responsibility about how government handled their moneys.

Its flaws notwithstanding, the idea of separating revenues had gained statutory acceptability as an instrument of change, change toward more localism for some, toward greater centralization for others, depending upon whether the principle was construed as a means or as an end, in every Northern state before 1915.[8]

The segregation of revenues was inseparable from the question of *which* revenues were to be assigned to each level of government. Had each of the sources of revenue been equally accessible, expansive, or valuable, debate might have geared down to the disposition of administrative details, but revenues were of very disparate value. By the end of the last century, land was believed much less valuable than formerly and despite the possibilities of raised assessments, it appeared to be a shrinking reservoir from which to siphon taxes. On the other hand, corporate wealth was taken to be prodigiously valuable, more than anyone had ever dreamed. The world of securities, in truth, was so expansive and therefore so productive of fiscal imbalances that E. R. A. Seligman told congressmen in 1899 that the problem of "just taxation" in America "and to a less extent in almost every modern community" was the problem of corporate taxation.[9]

By 1910 there was one distinctive characteristic of corporate taxation in the states of the iron rectangle; whereas private individuals were almost entirely exempt from state taxation, corporations of all sorts had been brought under the aegis of the states' fiscal systems. A generation earlier, state taxation of corporate properties had been virtually unexploited in the North. Where it had been tried, (outside of Pennsylvania, the most notable exception to the general picture in its reliance on corporate taxation) the results were chaotic; from all perspectives, existing corporate taxes were also conceded to be inequitable. As of 1890, a leading authority on corporate taxation, fully aware that "the first reform of our direct taxation" lay in this direction, concluded typically that "perhaps no question in the whole domain of financial science" had been answered "in a more unsatisfactory or confused way."[10] Yet the chaos reflected vastly altered attitudes though more modestly altered practices. What then had been happening during the twenty years before and after 1890?

Legislation by the states to exploit corporate wealth as a major source of public revenue, though little publicized, represented one of the chief reform efforts of the last third of the nineteenth century. It was actually a series of reforms within reforms, for while general corporate taxation represented a significant innovation, there were many complicated alterations and amendments of it.

Many factors affected the wisdom and practicality of more justly harnessing the wealth of private corporations to the financial service of the North's public corporations, and most of these factors can best be understood by considering the development of corporate taxes before the end of the Civil War.

First of all, the early corporate environments were distinct from those in the latter half of the last century. The types of corporations were different. By 1830, for example, New York State had already chartered 766 corporations less than one-seventh of which were engaged in manufacturing or mining; turnpikes, bridges, insurance companies, and banks, in that order, were the commonest types. None of these was treated as a new institution and, even more important, legally and officially they were handled within the framework of waning "mercantilistic" or interventionist traditions. As a result, they were hard to charter and when chartered they were the legal creatures of the state, affected with a public interest and, accordingly, not regarded as fully private.[11] Moreover, they lacked advantages such as limited liability and, in general, they lacked the confidence of the public who viewed them with suspicion.

Thus, early corporations enjoyed only a modest position in the law, and early tax laws, as a rule, did not recognize them explicitly. Legislatures simply shuffled them into the corpus of existing statutes along with natural persons. "Our solons," wrote Seligman, "had neither the leisure nor the inclination to study the matter further."[12] It remained the custom thereafter of "the ordinary state legislator" to seize upon "the most obvious method" of raising revenue "without much regard to the general principles involved," explained a federal official at the turn of the century.[13] When, in 1823, New York became the first commonwealth to broach corporate taxation and when Connecticut and Massachusetts followed suit during the next decade, they each approached corporate wealth under the rules of general property taxation. Local authorities tried to assess all corporate realty and personalty, thus in practice treating them exactly as other citizens were treated. Before long this was nearly universal.

Pennsylvania was the lone significant exception to this pattern. After prior experience in the taxation of banks, the state government had by 1824 begun a policy of deriving its revenues from taxes on corporations rather than from levies on general property; and these corporate levies were controlled by the state rather than by local officials. Beginning in 1824, again in 1826 when the tax was extended from banks to iron companies, and in 1840 when the commonwealth enacted the first general corporation tax, the rule was to tax a percentage of the dividends of the corporations liable to public obligation. The trend toward financing the state by taxing corporate resources gained momentum, as Professor Louis Hartz indicated, from the movement in the 1830's toward free public education, an exceedingly expensive social experiment; and this juxtaposition of popular welfare and corporate properties, the one placing heavy strains on the fiscal capacity of government, the other seductively taxable with "greater regard to justice" than most other potential sources of revenue, characterized the subsequent history and rationale of corporate taxation.[14]

From 1865 until the nineties, reform of state taxation centered about converting the Pennsylvania system to the service of other state governments and abandoning general property taxes to local governments. "The State and its local governments must have revenue," warned the Wells Report of 1871, "their financial necessities are in no condition to warrant uncertain experiments," whereupon the commissioners advocated the taxation of "all corporations created by the State which are in the nature of a monopoly,"[15] a refrain soon echoing across the Northern tier of states thanks to the insatiable appetites of popular governments.

The City of Chicago revealed how enormous pressure for taxing corporations often arose from remorseless local problems which could only be appeased by fresh revenues. Having jacked itself out of the muck of Lake Michigan, and well underway to becoming the nation's second greatest city by 1885, Chicago discovered that its existence depended on supplies of fresh water. While the lake's capacities were assured, the city's intake of water was rapidly being polluted by its own drainage as well as that of satellite communities such as Calumet City, La Grange, and Des Plaines. The city was faced with building a master sewerage system or with drinking its own private and industrial wastes.

Unfortunately, neither economic nor political flexibility was one of the "givens" in the situation. Raising taxes would have been one approach but it was politically impossible, for local leaders had long been arguing that middle-class properties carried a disproportionate share of taxation. Conceivably, heavier taxes might have been arranged for surrounding farm areas, but these too were believed already overburdened with payments for Chicago's firefighting, police, and utilities services, all of dubious benefit to them. Theoretically an increase in valuations was possible, for Chicago's property was known to be grossly underassessed. Expertly (if unofficially) valued at a billion dollars as early as 1875, property in the city was *assessed* at less than one-third of that figure—and a decade later there had been no substantial improvement. But local mythology held that a rise in valuation would merely result in harassed Chicagoans paying a still larger share of state taxation. To be sure, the city might have appealed to the state legislature, but hardly with expectations of success. Controlled by rural interests whose hands stretched toward Chicago pocketbooks but whose ears were deaf to the city's problems, the legislature was worse than a court of last resort. Increasing local indebtedness or its ability to borrow, a sensible out, was also baffled by state legal and constitutional provisos which seemed impervious to swift change. As one Chicagoan summarized the city's plight, "general laws are quite sufficient to meet the wants of the entire agricultural portion of the State which overwhelmingly controls the legislature, but . . . are not all sufficient to meet the necessities of such a municipality as Chicago."[16]

With alternatives closed to them and with many corporations profiting from the *status quo,* Chicagoans probed expectantly at their properties locally. The railroads were especially tempting. Sixteen trunk lines entered the city in 1885 with local holdings privately valued at $40 million. Because Illinois had permited railroad officials in happier days to act as their own assessors, the $40 million passed onto the tax rolls as a mere $3,265,803 on which the roads paid $112,016 into the city treasury. Eager to scrounge heavier revenues out of such corporate holdings, critics and reformers brooked no opposition. Members of the city council believed suborned or otherwise persuaded by the corporations to defend them were heavily assailed, as were extant tax laws and the state constitution. Strenuous efforts were also made to centralize and make more uniform the disparate political structures embraced by Chicago. By the nineties, regardless of defeats and delays, the principle that corporations were under obligation to the city treasury was well established and the theoretical supremacy of the political corporation over the private corporation was acknowledged[17]—and supremacy of this kind always implied a greater responsiveness to the financial needs of government.

The State of Ohio's fiscal appetites in 1895 were as insatiable as those of Illinois or New York. "The state's revenues are inadequate to the needs of the state," declared Governor McKinley in a statement worn thin with overuse. Adequate income for the government had long been a matter of grave concern, McKinley reminded his public and "while full relief has not yet been found," he observed, he could point to some progress in increasing revenues without adding to the burdens resting upon "real or other property . . . bearing its full share of taxation." The drift was clear; subjects of taxation, which, according to the governor had previously "escaped their just share of the public burdens," that is, the corporations of Ohio, were "slowly, but with certainty, being placed upon the tax duplicate."[18] So it was everywhere.

Questions of the incidence of corporate taxation were, of course, vital to dialogues over corporate taxes, but, unfortunately, the incidence of taxes was a conundrum which finance had set for economic science only to secure in return a set of conflicting answers from the economists. "The path of a tax is so difficult to follow with the eye," wrote Edward Ross in 1892, "that it is doubtful if ever the actual shiftings will be observed, recorded, and, by the statistical or historical method, made to reveal the laws they obey."[19] A mystery even to experts, incidence was sufficiently discussed, however, by men such as Ross or Seligman so that the middle classes were convinced by the nineties that corporations were not paying their way.[20] And it was this conviction which increasingly had informed public policy.

The Secretary of the New York Tax Reform Association, Lawson Purdy, hammered specifically on this question in his *Burdens of Local Taxation and Who Bears Them* in 1901. Purdy cited two common errors, at least in his opinion, about the weight of taxation. The first error, he wrote, was "that all taxes are paid ultimately by the persons who make the actual payments to the tax collector." The second mistake lay in the notion that all taxes were "shifted from the persons who pay the tax collector to others" with the result that all taxes were "finally paid by consumers as such." Though taxes levied upon "things capable of reproduction," such as the manufactures of corporations, could be shifted to consumers, this was untrue, Purdy argued, of taxes levied on realty. The point made was clear. As one political economist observed, Purdy's major contribution was his analysis "showing how, even in a growing community, an increased tax upon real estate" brought such large quantities of land into the market that "the net results of increasing real estate taxes in the cities" was "not to increase the cost of living to the mass of the population however great the increase of burdens upon the owner of land and buildings."[21] Middle-class property holders were thus bearing the brunt of taxation, a thesis concerning incidence subscribed to by Henry Carter Adams, Edward Bemis, Frederick Clow, and Dana Durand, not to mention a number of influential ministers, editors, judges, public commissioners, and reformers. From this belief the movement toward greater and more discriminating corporate taxation gained great impetus.

The desire to have all property bear equal burdens created a dynamic of its own for the extension of corporate taxation; and the successful evasions under the general property tax simply diverted this desire into fresh channels. In his prize essay on "Equitable Taxation," the young Walter Weyl declared that the "complete failure" to reach banking, sleeping car, telephone, telegraph, and insurance companies under general property taxation had led directly to "the adoption of separate and distinct systems for their taxation." To be sure, he added in a critical comment on the ineffectuality of existing corporate taxes and their utter lack of uniformity from state to state, "taxes upon corporations have been the bugbears of state finance;"[22] nonetheless, they were, in his opinion, a great advance. He left no doubt why he and many others felt this to be the case, for the taxing power should have been employed in just this manner "to lessen economic inequalities" and to further "the socialization of wealth," a proposition which he later expounded vigorously in *The New Democracy*. "Attainment by the people of the largest possible industrial control and of the largest possible industrial dividend," he explained, required among other vital changes, a thorough reform of taxation so that "the community could divert to itself" the new wealth of natural monopolies and other great corporate enterprises. "A corporation tax law," he wrote, "marks the beginning of a wide investigation of all corporate actions." By thus dropping the state's siphon into the wellsprings of corporate properties, "the engine of taxation," he predicted, "like all other social engines, will be used to accomplish great social ends."[23]

Weyl's opinions were widespread among the middle classes. Corporate taxation was popular, wrote Bolton Hall, the founder of the New York Tax Reform Association, and was "generally recognized as specially adapted for state purposes," so much so, he noted, that the governor of New York expressed the hope in the early nineties that corporate taxation would someday pay all of the state's ordinary expenses. Hall himself supported the concentration of local taxes on real estate and a concentration of state taxes on franchises and the "special powers of corporations." To obviate "loss and confusion," he argued, taking the position which New York's respected revenue reformer, George H. Andrews had taken in 1877, he asked that assessment be placed in the hands of the state, so that corporations properly classed and uniformly taxed "would cease to be objects of jealousy and distrust."[24]

This distrust of corporations among farmers and workingmen and the independent critics within the urban middle classes was, admittedly, endemic; but among advocates of corporate taxation, there began to develop an appreciation of how much the successful taxation of corporate enterprises turned less on the vigor of reform spirit as on some sense of discrimination about the nature of that taxation as well as about the nature of the corporations to which it applied. Abstractly, it was obvious that just as the tariff had ceased being treated as a fiscal question alone and had become "a question of industrial legislation," so, too, state and local taxes ought to cease involving purely fiscal measures in order to assume "the character of industrial laws."[25] "Taxes on corporations" (corporations, that is, whose function was to amass "large aggregations of capital for more economic production or distribution of commodities") an official of the New York Tax Reform Association early in the nineties decried as "equally objectionable with all other taxes on capital." Among reformers hardly anyone wanted inadvertently to prevent the growth of enterprises "united for the purpose of carrying on business on a wider scale, at decreased cost to the consumer;" nor did anyone wish to drive them to other localities. But no such anxious considerations extended to corporations "owing their existence to a public franchise."[26] These attitudes were not analogues of the classic Progressive divisions between the New Freedom and the New Nationalism over the handling of the "trust" question; rather, they represented a sensitive estimation of the public price tag to be placed on publicly granted privilege.

Corporations, distrustful in their own fashion of the public and of popular governments, also grew less aggressively negative about their obligations and by initiating their own campaigns for centralized state taxation of their properties developed their own sense of discrimination. Under these circumstances, an array of authorities who were themselves privy to corporate problems, from Massachusetts' Charles Francis Adams, Jr., to Pennsylvania's Henry Charles Lea and Joseph Weeks, to Tennessee's Enoch Ensley and Iowa's Judge Nathaniel Hubbard, took the field in behalf of corporate rights to receive equal treatment and equal justice, as they described it, from fiscal authorities. Furthermore, they were assisted by various tax-reform groups, conscious of distinctions between varieties of capital and their "social behavior," as well as by chambers of commerce—Ohio's serving as a notable example toward the close of the century—and private tax conferences, the most famous of which was formed early in the nineties in Pennsylvania.

Fearful that the public was less discriminating about corporations and their fiscal relationships with the state than they were, men of pro-corporate persuasion manfully struggled to change reigning misconceptions. Like Philadelphia's John Wright who handled this problem in a special report appended to the larger Report of the Pennsylvania Revenue Commission of 1889, they were affronted by the idea which they believed was commonly held that "to levy heavy taxes" on corporations was "a righteous proceeding, by which the masses . . . [might] get back part of their property." They lamented the tendency to ignore "the human element" in discussions of corporate obligations, an oversight which purportedly led "the people to look upon capital as though it were a wild animal seeking whom it might devour." Wright concluded his remarks by calling for mutual toleration, a sense of fairness, and an appreciation of capital and its myriad problems, for Americans were, according to Wright, all capitalists.[27]

The corporate case against oppressive inequities in state taxation was carefully detailed by Theodore Sutro, Chairman of the Committee on Taxation of the American Bar Association and a former New York City Commissioner of Taxes. His remarks on the "Taxation of Competitive Industrial Corporations" would have been unnecessary a generation earlier and either indiscreet or in bad taste a generation later. But to him "competitive" and "industrial" were terms freighted with virtue, describing clean-cut corporations busily engaged in making things and following the healthy injunctions of the marketplace.

Taking as a wedge a principle of the National Tax Association that "property shall be so classified that every tax shall bear equally on all persons similarly situated," Sutro quickly moved to blur distinctions between natural persons and corporate persons. Granting that "if the government conferred upon [corporations] . . . such extraordinary privilege that . . . opportunities for the profitable transaction of their business were vastly superior to those of individuals" heavier taxes were undeniably due from them, Sutro argued that on the contrary their privileges were insufficient "to justify any such discrimination against them" as then existed "in contradistinction from individuals or firms in the same line of business."[28]

Denouncing the "hue and cry of demagogues" then inflaming the thoughtless masses against "everything that bears the name of corporation," Sutro, drawing on evidence from New York, New Jersey, and Pennsylvania, recited a long list of major tribulations. Industrial corporations were subject in nearly every state, he found, both to state taxation "of a continuous nature" as well as to local taxation, while individuals enjoyed complete exemption from state levies. Contrasting the tax obligations of two New York chemical manufacturers, the one incorporated, the other a firm, he calculated the differentials in the taxation borne by each, highlighting what he described as the inequalities suffered by the corporation. The assessments of corporate properties, too, from state to state and between corporations and individuals, he caustically observed, were grossly unfair; debt deduction provisions of corporate tax laws were utterly inadequate and the laws themselves were, he argued, "so technical and complicated," unlike those applicable to individuals, that they entailed serious losses of time and money. Even tax evasion proved far easier for ordinary citizens than for corporations, a handicap which Sutro made no suggestion to overcome.[29] As if this list of grievances were not long enough, Sutro further charged that state legislatures harassed corporations by trying to expose their assets to taxing authorities, an ignominious procedure in his judgment to which individuals who hid their intangibles were immune. But the most galling forms of discrimination, explained Sutro, was that corporations, in the language of a New York court decision, "simply because they . . . [were] corporations," were taxed more heavily than ordinary taxpayers for the same or very similar types of property.[30]

Like many pro-corporate spokesmen, Sutro had anticipated rebuttals. Why, after all, had corporations proven such successful vehicles in the accumulation of wealth "if the burdens of taxation imposed upon them are so disproportionately greater than those imposed upon individuals in the same pursuits?" His answer was adroit and legalistic; "the only question involved," he declared, "is whether there is any inequality in the measure imposing the burden," for if there were, the principle upon which the tax rested was a false one. Sutro could see "no reason in the world" why individuals conducting industrial enterprises should have been "unduly *favored* as against corporate bodies. The State," he argued, had no justification for "imposing exceptional burdens, through unequal tax laws, upon the very agencies . . . best adapted to further its prosperity." Instead of being crippled, corporations should have been rewarded as major instruments of national progress, through the profer-ring of special inducements,"[31] presumably by the state, although Sutro failed to clarify the point.

But his other suggestions for mitigating the embarrassments of corporations were both clear and bold. He called, first, for the exemption of corporations from annual state taxation, "the same as individuals," in lieu of which he proposed that they pay the state "a reasonable organization tax." Anticipating objections that states would be deprived of a real or potential source of revenues, he insisted that what governments had previously gained from enforcing the wrong fiscal principles they would somehow recoup indirectly through the liberation of private productive facilities. Few suggestions, however, could have cut more diametrically across the grain of the times; there was slight chance that such propositions would have found favor even in many parts of Northern business communities after the turn of the century. And, judging from other of his points, it seems unlikely that even Sutro intended to do more on this score than brazenly fly some tattered ensign for the interests which he represented.

Much more in the mainstream was Sutro's call for the abandonment of separate state laws on the taxation of industrial corporations and an end to legislative tinkering "with the laws of taxation individually without regard to the methods pursued by other states." He likewise urged the adoption of procedural uniformities: standardizing the data of assessments in order to prevent taxes falling on the same property twice for the same period of time, sounder and more scientific assessment techniques rather than the superficial and highly politicized methods generally in vogue, and the requirement of a "uniform system" of filing assessment information for people in identical occupations in order to end excuses for inquisitorial activities by tax collectors. Other reform legislation also appeared essential to him. The assessment of corporate properties should not have been driven above the assessments on competing individual properties; moneys on deposit, bills and accounts receivable, he wanted to be assessed "once and for all in the State of their incorporation;" shares of stock held by individuals, he believed, deserved exemption, while all "paper evidence" of interests in corporate property should have been directed against the corporation as a unit.[32]

In short, despite an addiction to stock pro-corporate jargon, Sutro is useful to us mainly because he is an index of the long step which corporate spokesmen had taken, in conjunction with other elements of the middle classes, toward grappling with the tedious realities of bringing their organizations into a more viable relation to government; in the context of his times his viewpoints were much less biased than one might allow at first glance. For example, Governor LaFollette's Wisconsin State Tax Commission of 1903 which, unlike Sutro, was unimpeachable in its dedication to reform, had previously given its blessings to several of the principles which Sutro and others like him later reiterated. It was recognized in Wisconsin, as it had been in New York, that the "highest authorities on economic[s] and public finance" were persuaded "that the problem of just taxation in this country [is] . . . very largely the problem of corporate taxation." The Wisconsin commissioners, therefore, considered it a "prime necessity" that the state proceed with the "adoption of a rational, harmonious, and efficient system." Since the wealth of the nation consisted largely of investments in corporate securities which, barring the "severest and most inquisitorial laws," could not have been reached for taxation, the commissioners felt that corporations deserved special treatment by the state. While appraising the corporations' ability to bear public burdens, they insisted that pertinent tax laws should also "satisfy the legal conception of uniformity and equality which is the fundamental idea of constitutional government." Fiscal authorities were urged, as a consequence, to inquire whether a particular statute was "just and equal between the corporations and the owners of real estate and personalty" and whether it was premised on sound principles.[33] Such was the drift of general sentiments.

A convergence of some of the views of the Wisconsin commissioners and Sutro suggest how and why it was feasible for many corporations or their spokesmen to participate in respectable fiscal reform movements. Areas of agreement were broad. There was agreement about the importance of corporations in the economy; there was agreement that they existed in rich and troublesome variety and that vis-à-vis individuals they were not automatically privileged or advantaged by government; there was agreement that taxes resting on them could and often did affect production; there was agreement, despite difference over details, that corporations deserved positive encouragement and assistance from government; there was agreement over the desirability of centralizing corporate taxing authority in the hands of the state rather than local governments, the better to insure uniformity and equality of burdens both within and between political units. Finally, there was a somewhat negative consensus about the advantages of federal intervention in the field of corporate taxation without it being agreed precisely how intervention was supposed to occur.

Thus, during the twenty years after 1890, the outcries against corporations, the countercries of corporations against discriminatory attacks on their properties, the needs of governments for fresh revenues and for greater exactness, security, uniformity, and certitude in the operation of money machinery, and the private and political desires to interdict the spread of anti-corporate campaigns among the voting public, promoted substantial change in the relationship of corporate enterprises to public fiscal systems. To be sure, even after the turn of the century, the general property tax remained the most common basis of corporate taxation in the North, but in order to achieve the traditional object of assessing and taxing corporate properties at their full value, a number of states provided for distinct methods of reaching them. Notwithstanding continuing debates over both their justice and efficacy, taxes were levied, for instance, on the capital stock of corporations, on their gross or net earnings, and on their franchises. Furthermore, for tax purposes corporations were differentiated from individual property holders as well as from other corporations, and the assessment of their most significant property was entrusted to state officials.

By 1903, to be specific, seventeen of the twenty states of the iron rectangle reached the capital stock of corporations under provisions of the general property tax as *specially* administered for certain classes of corporations. Under special definitions of personal property, moreover, eight of the twenty states, including New York, Michigan, Indiana, and Illinois, levied taxation on corporate franchises. But the most impressive shift away from the policies of the preceding generation could be traced in the fact that seventeen states of the Northern tier had inaugurated extensive systems of distinct corporate taxation, some general, some special.[34]

In one sense, these developments reflected the growing influence in government of fiscal experts and of the organizations which they often advised or directed: tax departments, state and local tax commissions, boards of equalization, and the like. Just as significantly, however, they registered a triumph of Mugwumpish political aspirations and the success of one strain of middle-class culture focused, as we have seen, on the virtues of standardization, uniformity, responsibility, and efficiency.

Paradoxically, the very groups whose business and industrial activities were making the North a more plural society, were striving busily at the same time to make it more conformist and commensurable.

The movement toward heavier and more discriminating corporate taxation deserves more detailed attention, however, for tremendous energies drawn from the most competent and articulate men of a vigorous generation were invested in the political and economic adjustments upon which the safety and prosperity of their properties publicly and privately depended.

A single example of the development of corporate taxation in Pennsylvania, the fight over the Tax Conference, or Riter Tax Bill (H.R. No. 239), in 1895, while incapable of representing adequately thousands of such events which transpired during a quarter of a century in twenty states, does suggest how complex and tedious the formulation of fiscal policy toward corporate wealth proved to be. The labyrinthine negotiations associated with it, moreover, occurred in a state which had more experience with the public taxation of corporate property than any other. By the opening of the twentieth century, in fact, Pennsylvania to outsiders seemed to possess model fiscal machinery, complete with an extensive system of general corporate taxation plus special taxes levied upon banks, railroads, insurance companies, sleeping car, telephone, telegraph, and express companies. During Theodore Roosevelt's administrations, indeed, the State of Pennsylvania was extracting over $17 million annually from its myriad corporations, roughly twice as much revenue of this type as was being secured by either of her closest financial and industrial rivals, Massachusetts and New York. But if taxation in Pennsylvania rested importantly on corporate properties, the problems and dissensions revealed by the Riter Bill indicate difficulties which dogged the commonwealth's movement in this direction every step of the way.[35]

The filing of H.R. 230 by Frank Riter, Chairman of the Pennsylvania House Ways and Means Committee on January 31, 1895 crystalized in the next six weeks "that bitter controversy," in the words of one commentator, "which has been waged for so many years between the corporate and agricultural interests of this Commonwealth." Yet on the face of it, despite the background of depression and Populism, the bill seemed routine and fairly innocuous; it sought "to provide revenue by taxation," to encourage greater uniformity of taxation, to divert certain taxes previously paid to the state to counties and lesser subdivisions of government instead, while seeking "more effectual means" for the collection of state, county, and local taxes.[36]

Yet the Ritter Bill was not what it seemed; its history placed it in quite a different light. First of all, if informed men in other states believed that Pennsylvanians had devised model money machinery, informed Pennsylvanians "universally admitted" by the early nineties "that a radical change in the tax laws was necessary." Discussions about the Revenue Act of 1891 had made this apparent; amid debate attending that bill, John Price, a state senator from Scranton urged the many interests which contributed significantly to the commonwealth's revenues to convene for the purpose of formulating some plan "on the basis of which the tax levies could be equitably adjusted." Late in January 1892, the gathering occurred in Harrisburg and resulted in the establishment of the Pennsylvania Tax Conference, a reform organization which began the collection of statistical information upon which any systematic reconstruction of the state's fiscal machinery necessarily relied.[37]

Filled with men prominent in the affairs of the state, the conference was distinctly corporative, embracing "representatives of Agriculture," "representatives of commerce and manufactures," "representatives of railroads," "representatives of labor," and "representatives of the county commissioners." Among these men were Joseph Weeks, the able and very well-known student of the state's major industries, later chairman of the tax conference; Joseph Harris, successor to the brilliant and histrionic Franklin Gowen as president of the Philadelphia and Reading Railroad, along with spokesmen for most of the other railroads of the commonwealth, including the Baltimore and Ohio; Leonard Rhone, Master of the State Grange and a National Grange official; and Terence Powderly, formerly leader of the Knights of Labor and William Weihe, President of the Amalgamated Iron and Steel Workers of Pittsburgh, both then employed by the U.S. Immigration Bureau. If the conference was stacked, as the governor indicated, in favor of "the leading industrial interests of the State," that did not diminish the value of its reports on wealth and property in the commonwealth, the first of which appeared in October 1892; nor did it blunt a vigorous approach to reforms which provoked hostilities among many of Pennsylvania's agricultural, commercial, transportation, and manufacturing enterprises.[38]

The tax conference was the sponsor of the Riter Bill as a piece of reform legislation in 1895, for despite the unmistakable mandates of the State Constitution of 1873, Pennsylvania manufacturing corporations were not paying state taxes. Since 2661 of the state's 7221 corporations were engaged in manufacturing in 1893 and since that number had increased in 1894 by an additional 410 concerns with additional capital of $21,000,000, their virtual exemption and consequent prosperity seemed intolerable to interests which already considered themselves heavily taxed. Equally insufferable was the exemption of new types of corporations from public obligation, particularly the exemption of building and loan associations. These organizations had become the state's most rapidly proliferating enterprises in the early nineties. Of the corporations chartered in 1894, for example, steam and street railways showed an authorized capital of $23,642,000 and manufacturing companies an authorized capital of $21,257,550. Both led all of the state's corporations in capitalization *except* building and loan associations whose authorized capital for that year, $120,184,920 was over four times greater than either of these latter new groups of corporations. But beside this situation, rural and urban underassessment was notorious throughout the commonwealth, evasion was widespread, and there were glaring inequalities, first, because of incongruous exemptions, and second, because of the inadequacies of railway taxation.[39]

These vexing considerations underlay the conference sponsorship of the Riter Bill, but the immediate excuse was the "plight of education," already a common ploy of reformers. "If at this time the condition of the finances of the State be such that it is necessary to diminish the appropriations to the counties for school purposes," warned one of the champions of the bill, "it will not be easy to justify to the intelligent public opinion of the State" the inequities of Pennsylvania's money machinery. For this reason, plus the fact that the bill earned the "support of the great majority of the representatives of the interests which bear the burden of taxation," the governor himself endorsed the bill.[40]

The brunt of argument in the house was borne by Joseph Weeks, who was chiefly responsible for bringing a mass of irrefutable statistical and technical data to buttress the bill, and by another conference member, C. Stuart Patterson, a Professor of Constitutional Law at the University of Pennsylvania, to whom as the formal author of the measure, the grand strategy was entrusted. Appearing "on behalf of certain corporate interests," notably the Erie Railroad, the Pullman Palace Car Company, Western Union Telegraph, and half a dozen smaller Pennsylvania railways, was a former tax conference member and Potter County lawyer of wide reputation, M. E. Olmsted.[41] Both presentations to the legislature were legalistic and technical; for example, in forty pages of argument Patterson alluded to nineteen statutes and sixty-nine judicial decisions, while his nineteen-page summation carried 268 sets of statistics, so the battle had little to commend it to the general public, although its outcome would inevitably affect all.

In behalf of the bill, Patterson brushed aside Olmsted's contentions that passage would mean much higher taxes and that it would likewise provoke endless litigation. "Indeed, gentlemen," declared Patterson, "if you wait to reform the present system of State taxation (which so sorely needs a thorough reformation) until someone shall draw a bill . . . so transparently clear in its expression, that Mr. Olmsted will concur with the construction which the Auditor-General and the State Treasurer shall put upon it, you will wait forever."[42] The field was thus cleared for the major contests.

These were the taxation of railroads and the taxation of manufacturing corporations. Precisely what the Riter Bill intended toward the railroads, Patterson tried to clarify by allusions to what it did *not* intend. It did not seek to alter railroad exemption from county taxation of such real estate as was indispensable to the exercise of their franchises; nor did the bill affect taxes on local railroad offices, depots, car houses, and other realty levied on under special laws in the cities of Pittsburgh and Philadelphia. But, as Patterson explained, the roads were taxed at the rate of five mills on their capital stock for state purposes under an act of 1891, at the rate of eight mills on their gross earnings, and at the rate of four mills on their bonds as the personal property of the holder. And, according to Patterson, "this system of State taxation" was "obviously unjust and unequal in its operation," besides which it permitted "a large amount of valuable property to escape State taxation."[43]

While everyone conceded that the existing machinery was ineffective and unjust, the controversy revolved around interpretations of *what* constituted taxable railway properties, and *how* and by *whom* it was to be valued. Backers of the bill flatly dissented from interpretations of the legislation of the preceding decade. Striking a theme that was repeated throughout the North, they noted that "under modern railroad construction and financeering, the real capital of a railroad is not only its share capital, but also its bonded or funded debt." Since new roads were built largely on proceeds from the sale of bonds, while shares were more or less "given away to the purchasers of bonds," Pennsylvania's tax on shares not only failed as a tax on the whole capital of these corporations, it was in actuality a tax upon the least valuable capital of the railroads. "The real capital," Patterson declared, "is not reached by a tax upon the shares."[44]

There were further serious objections, one of them relating to the tax on railroad bonds. Since Pennsylvania taxed these bonds in the hands of their holders, it could not reach bonds in the hands of non-residents; the courts had seen to that. Similarly, because foreign-held bonds were exempted from the state's taxation, Harrisburg derived no revenue from property which, as in the devastating rail strike of 1877, it sometimes protected at great cost. Another consequence of the exemption enjoyed by foreign-held bonds, as Patterson and Weeks explained to the legislators, recalling that the funded debt of a road often was its only real capital and that share capital was worthless, was a "great inequality in the burden . . . borne by different railroads."[45] Weeks had been at pains to document this earlier for the tax conference. Figures from the state auditor-general's office for 1894 showed, moreover, that although the bonded indebtedness of Pennsylvania's thirteen leading railroads was nearly $350 million, the amount owned in the state liable to taxation was less than one-fifth of that sum. Of the $90 million bonded debt of one company, for instance, only $20 million was subject to taxation; of $12 million in bonded debt of another line less than $90,000 was liable.[46] This situation, as Chairman Riter euphemistically remarked during hearings on the bill, was aggravated by the refusal of some roads to be "a little bit honest in their capitalization."[47] If it was true, as the Interstate Commerce Commission had insisted in 1893, that "no range of facts in railway accounting" were so "difficult of accurate statement as those which assume to present the capitalization and valuation of railway property,"[48] then neither the state nor the railroads had done much to clarify this state of affairs.

Patterson and other supporters of the bill acknowledged that a tax on gross receipts, theoretically, "would be the best form of railroad taxation," but here again the ideal approach in theory had grave practical disabilities. Revenues drawn from gross receipts were contingent upon the size of railway earnings, as Patterson indicated, and these fluctuated grandly. In 1894, by way of punctuating these uncertainties, gross earnings of the Pennsylvania Railroad's lines east of Pittsburgh and Erie dropped by $16 million. The meance to the state, should its major revenues become linked to such sources, was obvious. And gross receipts had other shortcomings, for the federal courts had decreed that Pennsylvania taxes could only be levied upon intra-state traffic; interstate traffic fell under the protective mantle of national authority and could not be reached by the commonwealth's collectors.[49]

Since the Pennsylvania Tax Conference closely monitored the views of the fledgling Interstate Commerce Commission, there is little doubt that Patterson and backers of the Riter Bill adhered to the judgment on railroad capitalization rendered in the first annual report of the commission's statistician in 1888. "So far as bonds" were concerned, observed the report, "it may be said that although in form they represent a mortgage, yet in reality their issue was one means of collecting the capital necessary to create the property against which the mortgage lies." Thus, noted the commission, "the stock . . . does not represent the entire investment, nor measure the full value of the property," to which it added "for the full value of that property one must take account of both stock and funded debt."[50] These studied official observations were of great interest to men hoping to reform local tax machinery.

Naturally, therefore, they were reiterated at Harrisburg. The value of Pennsylvania's railroad corporations, according to the Bill, were to be computed "by adding to the market value of the share capital, the market value of the funded debt capital,"[51] adjustments being made to comport with par values. Deductions likewise were permitted on corporation realty which was locally taxed in order to avoid double taxation.

Olmsted and opponents of the bill, guarding their interests skillfully, took the position that H.R. 239 combined the most pernicious features of local taxation and promised to contaminate the state's own money machinery. Because the bill called for the diversion of a million and a half dollars of revenue from the state treasury to local treasuries, Olmsted stressed the slim likelihood that the ensuing state deficit would be overcome by proposed increases in corporate taxation,[52] though Weeks had tried to persuade the legislature that on the basis of a projection of the state's income for the forthcoming year a surplus was quite possible. Anxious to impugn the motives of "our agricultural friends" with whom he identified the bill in order to weaken it, Olmsted struck hard also at the real-estate deductions allowed railroad corporations by one of its provisions. It was not a case of stepping out of character as a spokesman for these and other corporations, rather what distressed him were the inequalities which the bill would have produced to the detriment of corporations which he directly represented. Entitled to deduct the value of local realty from the value of properties subject to state levies, corporations invariably discovered, argued Olmsted, that local assessors had placed different valuations on the same types of railway property. Taking evidence on the disparities of local valuations amassed by Joseph Weeks himself when he had been chairman of the tax conference Committee on Valuation and Taxation, Olmsted cleverly indicated that county assessments in Pennsylvania ran from less than 15% to more than 138% of full value. Consequently, "in some counties, the real estate of such companies is assessed upon one basis and in another upon an entirely different one," he argued. Yet deductions contemplated under the Riter Bill would have been based on "those unequal and unjust assessments, so that a railroad company in one county," explained Olmsted, "may obtain five times the relative deduction which its rival in an adjoining county or . . . township would be entitled to receive under the bill,"[53] a point which in the short run of things was almost irrefutable. Like so many arguments against reform, it turned on the proposition that before there could be reform there had to be reform.

Resorting again to the tax conference's report of 1893 on the valuation and taxation of railroads, Olmsted tried hoisting the opposition on its own petard by demonstrating that railroads were already heavily burdened. "The average taxes paid on railroads in Pennsylvania," the conference report had observed, based on valuations similar to those of other property "were fully equal to the taxes paid on other property," an assertion literally repeated by Olmsted. Asked by Chairman Riter if the bill would not create "greater harmony and equalization of local taxation," Olmsted clung to his contention that amid the depression of the mid-nineties, discriminatory laws had been passed against corporate interests by spiteful farmers and their spokesmen. If the assessment on a particular piece of corporate property were raised, for instance, as a result of the passage of the bill, then to check such a tendency, he charged, rural assessors "would simply put up the assessment of this one property, and it would then pay five times as much local tax in the County of Potter to avoid paying three times as much State tax."[54]

Capable as he was, Olmsted marshalled a second-rate case for his clients, but that did not mean that for all of their positivism and ability his opposition, Patterson and the conference men, was in any final sense "right." There were too many complexities, motives aside, on both sides to warrant any judgment such as that.

Thus, the legislature postponed the fiscal millenium by refusing to enact the bill into law at that session. Needless to say, they were in favor of fair taxation, hence by joint resolution they authorized an expenditure of $10,000 to sustain interest in the subject at Harrisburg. But for practical purposes they were unflinching in the face of warm and learned disputations. Faced with deep divisions inside of the corporate world, faced with rapid changes, depressions, agricultural militancy, and uncertainty, they sat tight.

Praised in some quarters as wise, in others denounced as cowardly, legislative inaction had some merit. On a matter as complex as the reconstruction of the commonwealth's money machinery it was well not to move too fast without a keen sense of direction. This was essential since the Riter Bill promised to affect not only railroads but also the very important, wealthy, and rapidly growing, building and loan associations and manufacturing corporations. Even in the area of railroad taxation, where the legislative fight had centered, while Patterson furnished *more* direction than Olmsted, it was not necessarily *enough* considering the context into which his proposals were to have been fitted. Patterson, for instance, determined the taxable value of railway property by combining the market value of both capital stock and funded debt; but among experts there were a number of viable alternatives for discovering capitalization: cost of reproduction, the value of capital stock at market value, the value of capital stock at par, gross receipts, business transacted, and capital stock according to dividends, among them. It was all very tedious and technical especially to men whose first response was apt to have been a visceral, "is it going to cost me anything?"

Styles in railroad financing, moreover, had undergone sufficient change over the preceding generation to give pause to all but the most positivistic of men. The first railroads had been financed on stock; as late as 1855, according to federal estimates in 1901, the total amount of railway stock exceeded bonds by 42%. During subsequent decades, however, this situation had been reversed so that in years of rampant speculation most lines were financed by bonds. Although the tendency to finance by bonds persisted from the Civil War to the nineties, it was badly shaken by the Panic of 1873 and by the roads' defaulting on half a billion dollars of securities. Between 1893 and McKinley's entrance into the White House, another shift occurred and, in the process of extensive reorganization, railroads tried reducing their fixed charges by replacing stocks for bonds.

Thus, almost at the moment that Stuart Patterson and the tax conference were advocating one set of criteria for measuring the taxable value of the commonwealth's railroads, the roads were altering the foundations on which these criteria rested. To be more specific, the national picture was set in 1895 when the Atchison, Topeka, and Santa Fe, increasing its stock, cut its fixed charges by $4 million and the Northern Pacific cut its charges by nearly $5 million. In Pennsylvania, the Pennsylvania Railroad, as well as the Baltimore and Ohio, moved in the same direction. So pronounced was this trend, in fact, that in New England almost 61% of railroad capital was in stock; 76% of Boston and Albany capital, for instance, was in stock. As between individual roads and between sections, the picture remained varied, to be sure; the New York Central retained three-fourths of its capital in bonds, while the Reading had only 22% of its capital in stock. Nonetheless, the trend was set; during 1895 railway stock increased nationally by $127 million, the roads' funded debts by less than one-fourth that amount. During the years from 1896 to 1900 stocks overall exceeded funded debt in the capitalization of railroads. In what many estimable men thought of as the most tangible area of American life, the world of money and materials, nothing seemed to behave very stably,[55] and hard policy formulated in one moment became the illusion of the next.

Adapting the money machines to effectively locate, define, and tax corporate properties was everywhere distinctive; thus while discussion of the Riter Bill indicates the specifics of one time and place, it is useful to consider broader developments over a longer period elsewhere. Massachusetts supplied some of these broader perspectives. Like Pennsylvania, its tax system was also well thought of in many quarters. Political and legal experts frequently praised the state as a pioneer in the elaboration of corporate taxation during the late nineteenth century and by the opening of the present century the Federal Commissioner of Corporations still cited Massachusetts as "the best example of an efficiently administered corporate excess-tax"[56] a description many thought applicable to the state's corporate tax policies generally. Although these outlooks would have shocked many natives of the commonwealth, its system of corporate taxation was widely believed typical of the type of "intelligent taxation" to which theory could be much more readily applied than it could in the case of individuals. As one authority remarked, "there is no personal equation to be considered; corporate income and corporate property are much more matters of public knowledge;" corporate conditions were similarly depicted as "more permanent and easy of classification" than the conditions surrounding individual businesses.[57] To these statement and viewpoints there was at least this modicum of truth: the policies and motives behind Massachusetts' corporate taxation and the reforms in fiscal machinery accompanying it, had been better and more consistently articulated than elsewhere. That much granted, however, there remained ample reason, unfortunately, to continue describing the state's tax laws as a "system of confiscation tempered by favoritism."[58]

Prior to 1900, interactions of the state and corporate enterprise had produced three principal tax policies. One policy, an extension of the rural perspectives characterizing the general property tax, neither granted special financial favor to corporations organized for private profit nor required their special regulation. It was a policy premised on the assumption that all property, individual and corporate, ought to fall under the hand of the tax collector. Anything giving value to the corporation was treated as a legitimate subject of taxation. A second and concurrent policy assumed that those corporations which had received special but essential privileges from the state required regulation through the use of the taxing power. A third policy, paralleling the other two, rested on the supposition that very light taxes or exemption from such obligations was requisite to the success of quasi-public corporations whose chief object was not private profit but the advancement of public welfare. Among officials and informed citizens, it was appreciated, naturally, that the application of these three well-articulated policies left much to be desired.

Some of the influences shaping these fiscal policies were apparent. Inevitably, the spirit of the general property tax suffused Massachusetts' corporate taxation; the levy imposed on capital stock supplemental to taxation on tangible corporate property, for instance, was aimed at reaching all property likely to escape the eye of the assessor. This all-encompassing, unflagging pursuit of property, though thwarted by chicane and maladministration, characterized nearly all subsequent policy and not always in a positive way. It remained a strong policy while countrymen exercised appreciable power in the legislature and looked upon wealthy cities with jaundiced eyes. Since Massachusetts had a tradition of public suspicion towards all aggregates of power, it was almost inevitable that the state would try extracting substantial payment for the bestowal of corporate privileges. But again in conformity with a venerable tradition, the state stimulated certain types of enterprise presumed to be socially beneficial and vital to maintaining her competitive position against her neighbors.

Administrative factors also affected corporate taxation. Because of difficulties in reaching corporate shares in the hands of shareholders and in individual savings deposits, the state shifted away from the taxation of individuals. Since impersonal institutions were assessed rather than individuals, this meant in reality that there was "a further deviation from the principle of individual ability or faculty as the basis of the tax." State officials, in addition, stumbled onto the persuasive qualities of segregating revenues in order to make the state itself more opulent and independent than was practically possible under the general property tax, and before the end of the century the general corporation tax which they had carried through the legislature had demonstrated that their hopes were well-founded. The general corporation tax, however, did not extend to *more* property than older policies had and attempts to reach the intangible holdings of corporations were little more successful than they had been under the system prevalent before 1864.

Each of these influences structured Massachusetts' corporate tax policies during the half century following 1865. As was generally true, so too in the Bay State the exigencies of wartime finance precipitated both the breakdown of the old money machinery and serious campaigns to reorganize state and local fiscal operations. War had threatened depletion of the commonwealth's treasuries and had driven the government of the state to abandon exemptions on savings banks and insurance companies, while striking out simultaneously to tap the intangible wealth of other corporations. From these emergency measures state officials learned that without saddling enterprise with discouragingly onerous taxation the revenues of the state could be handsomely augmented.

During the twenty years after the war, it was a relatively simple matter for the commonwealth to reach certain insurance companies and savings banks by taxing the net values of premiums or average deposits, but it proved exceedingly difficult to touch the capital stock of most corporations organized for private profit. To make its machinery more efficient, therefore, two steps were taken by the central government: the state, first of all, elbowed aside the local assessor whose ingenuity had always outshone his honesty in order to substitute its own assessors. Subsequently, rather than quixotically attempt to tax shareholders, it derived the tax at its corporate source. Real estate and machinery, of course, were still taxable locally so that the prevention of double taxation required the state to tax only the market value of capital stock after the value of local property had been deducted. The state, in short, taxed the excess. It was a viable arrangement but not airtight. Since corporate debts were accounted equivalent to individual debts they remained taxable to individual bondholders with the result that Massachusetts through most of the late nineteenth century failed to tax the full value of its corporate properties.

Never having foresworn the supremacy of the political corporation over the private ones, Massachusetts developed one general approach toward its private corporations and toward its most significant type of foreign corporations, public service corporations. Some of the particulars of this approach were reminiscent of the way corporate properties were handled under the general property tax which, ironically, had once handicapped the public sector in its relations with private property. The rate imposed on corporations, for example, was intended to be equivalent to the general property tax rate on non-corporate property. Proceeds of this taxation were likewise distributed to localities on the basis of their resident stockholders. But the most similar and important objective of the tax was to deal with corporations as if they were private individuals. This was undeniably in keeping with the demands of many corporations, but it also had the support of farm and tax-reform groups, each of which for quite opposite reasons tended to see comprehensive virtues in this apparently fair and democratic method. This was true, in any event, until the turn of the century.

By the nineties, several new factors affected corporate taxation in Massachusetts. Large corporations, for one thing, had become vastly more complex than ever before while other corporations appeared on the scene almost overnight to lend fresh significance to the entire field of public service or utility organizations. At the same time, many smaller businesses were opting for the corporate form and increasing numbers of foreign corporations were choosing to operate alongside of them in the state. There was also a vigorous revival of municipal demands in the face of the state's centralizing authority over corporate taxes, that public service corporations compensate the communities which they served for the privileges extended to them through their franchises. And little by little the money machines were remodeled to meet these changing circumstances.

The incentives for the state to respond to these pressures came from its heavy stake in corporate enterprises generally. By the opening of the twentieth century, despite the much-decried stringency of its corporate regulations, Massachusetts boasted a larger number of active corporations in proportion to population than any other states—but two. Even as late as 1908, the state ranked fourth in the union in capital invested in manufacturing; the assessed corporate excess stood at $145 million, yielding the state almost $2½ million annually in revenue. As a result, the pleas of the cities, for example, were met by obliging street railways to pay the municipalities in which they operated for their special franchises and the existing tax on corporate-excess was allotted to these same cities as well. Foreign corporations also came in for new treatment since they could not be reached effectively under the state plan for tapping corporate excess, an admission, incidentally, that it was just as impossible to unearth corporate intangibles as it always had been to find and collect on individual personalty under the old general property tax system. By reducing the taxation levied on business corporations and by trying to discourage foreign corporations with a modest excise tax the state, therefore, sought to remove the temptation for Massachusetts enterprise to secure foreign charters.

By 1908, the unmodified general corporation tax in Massachusetts applied solely to financial corporations and public utilities. Directed toward the entire capital stock of these enterprises, the general corporation tax just forty years after its inception had become a special tax on favored and regulated corporations. But the total coverage of the commonwealth's array of corporate taxes was much broader, according to whether the corporation in question was technically serving the public or was merely in search of private profits. Public service, business and financial institutions such as banks, stock and insurance companies and trust companies, in fact, furnished at least 65% of the commonwealth's corporate tax revenues, an index of one price which the political process continued to exact for officially bestowing privilege. A common element, meantime, marked the taxation of every Massachusetts corporation; state and local assessors collaborated to tax corporations' capital stock, the proceeds from which were distributed to towns and cities to help sustain their political establishments.[59]

Although the Massachusetts Tax Commission of 1875 had pronounced the state's system of corporate taxation "a Massachusetts specialty" which the commissioners lauded as "a most valuable contribution to fiscal science"[60] and though the Commission of 1897 had similarly praised the system as "the simplest, most efficient, and most equitable in the taxation of corporate property," it nevertheless revealed many shortcomings. If it was claimed officially that "railways, banks, the larger manufacturing corporations, and others whose stocks are frequently quoted" were taxed "without a word of inquiry and without a possibility of escape," there were many corporations which managed to land "in a somewhat different position." There was ample indication that taxes on corporate excess were, as described in a masterpiece of Yankee understatement, "partially evaded."[61]

But the most telling complaint against the Massachusetts system was lodged against the very basis on which it rested; namely, on the taxation of the enterprises' capital stock. Despite their recognized importance this excluded corporate bonds from the picture. Originally bonds had been viewed in theory as debts instead of as preferred interest in corporations whose operations they helped finance. Legally, to be sure, they were taxable under the general property tax; practically speaking, of course, they were rarely located in this way. Corporate taxation, in consequence, remained inadequate in terms of two long-standing objectives of a democratic polity: first, a requirement that the full value of all the property protected and served by the state be included on the tax rolls and made to pay its own way and, second, an insistence that the same classes of property be taxed justly and equally. The Massachusetts approach, however, proved an unsatisfactory gauge of a corporation's net earnings and of its full property values. Furthermore, it led to serious inequalities between corporations, largely because those that were heavily bonded escaped their just burden of taxation. Among large enterprises, in fact, heavy bonding became an important means of avoiding public obligation without formally breaking the letter of the law. Consequently, wrote one expert on the state's fiscal affairs in 1907, the "Massachusetts system of taxing corporations for private profit is . . . unsatisfactory from the point of view of both theory and practice." What effectiveness it had attained—and that was considerable—was attributable to peculiarities of the commonwealth's general social, political, and economic conditions. That the system was transferable to other states seemed very dubious; "in its present form," warned an authority, "it can not be regarded as a model for other states."[62] It was one thing in the United States to have enjoyed forty-six potential laboratories of democracy, but it was discouraging to learn in how many ways each laboratory might just as well have been hermetically sealed.

By 1910 officials and experts were hazarding conclusions about the progress of corporate taxation during the previous generation. Reviewing the history of "the tendency of legislation and judicial interpretation in the most progressive states toward corporate taxation," E. R. A. Seligman summarized the abstract standards against which movement could be plotted. Corporations, he felt, should be taxed differently from individuals and separately from other properties. Locally, they ought to be taxed exclusively on their realty, while for state purposes he thought it desirable that taxation fall on their earnings or on their capital and loans. It was pointless trying to reach earnings or capital received or employed by corporations outside of the state and the sticky business of guessing how much taxable property actually lay within one state's jurisdiction, an acute problem with railway and transmission companies, he wanted to see determined on the basis of mileage of track, cable, or transmission lines. Distinctions between foreign and domestic corporations, he insisted, ought to be banished, each enterprise being taxed either for the business which it conducted or for the capital which it employed within the state; the old vexation of residence of shareholders and bondholders he suggested be treated as immaterial wherever capital and loans alike were taxed. Corporations liable on their local properties, on the basis of experience throughout the North, ought to have their out-of-state property exempted, while corporations which were paying on their capital stock, he continued, ought not be obliged to have to pay on their tangible property. Where property or stock were taxable, shareholders should be freed of taxes and, correspondingly, where corporate loans were taxed, bondholders, he felt, should be granted exemptions. Where shareholders and bondholders were residents of different states, taxation ought to be arranged, Seligman argued, as a part of interstate comity. As the last of his eleven rules, drafted on the basis of decades of experience, he advised that where circumstances had produced monopolistic enterprises, taxes supplementary to those normally imposed ought to be levied against these potentially anti-social aggregations of power and privilege.[63]

Where Seligman had summarized the abstract standards of corporate taxation as they were widely conceived among experts and had delineated a set of principles, realities were something else. The shortcomings of Illinois' corporate tax machinery furnished an additional measure, but this one between principles and practices as matter stood in 1910. It hardly mattered what portion of state machinery one viewed first, there were signs of weakness everywhere. Still degenerating, the State Board of Equalization, for instance, which was responsible for so many decisions in connection with corporate taxation was described expertly as a "clumsy and ineffective body, much too large for either the work of equalization or the valuation of railroad property or capital stock;"[64] much of this responsibility the board had simply abandoned leaving the whole question of the equity of local assessments of corporate properties up in the air. As a consequence, in proportion to railroad earnings and to the total of taxes levied in the state, taxes drawn from railways had been declining for several years. Similarly, under the ruling dispensation, only a handful of Cook County public utilities among the many public service corporations in the state were constrained to have their capital stock assessed; elsewhere they escaped assessment altogether.

Compared to large Eastern states, therefore, Illinois derived a significantly smaller share of state revenues from its corporations. Fitted into a broader picture of state fiscal operations this meant that the total revenue of Illinois was smaller than the revenue of other states with comparable population, wealth, and industrial growth. At the heart of this anomaly lay commonplace failures in assessment procedures. Assessment still tended to be both amateur and legally irresponsible and it was highly colored by local political influences. Administration and supervision of the money machinery, in short, were inadequate. Thus, the aggregate of the state's assessed corporate values was only a fraction of the true value even of the tangible properties belonging to such institutions in the state. The upshot was a high nominal tax rate and very sharp inequalities between different classes of persons and property. Differentials in taxation were most notorious, of course, in the field of intangibles: moneys, credits, stocks, bonds, and mortgages. Trying to reach such wealth in the same manner through which the law sought out tangibles instead of through special corporate taxes like those in some other states, Illinois vastly aggravated these injustices.

But if Illinois was a reminder of all that was not done, there and everywhere else in the North there had been real progress in corporate taxation. Because nearly every Northern state had suffered serious shortcomings in handling corporate taxes, despite the changes witnessed over the course of half a century, the conclusions of the U.S. Commissioner of Corporations in 1910 rose above parochial problems and provided a useful overview of developments. Each state of the Northern tier, reported the commissioner, had evolved what was substantially its own system of corporate taxation so that "as yet there is no marked tendency toward uniformity." No state handled all of its corporate properties exactly alike and, as between several types of corporations, he detected trends toward still greater differentiation. Changes in laws controlling corporate taxation, in fact, were so frequent that he interpreted this to mean that "as yet a satisfactory and ultimate method has not been discovered." Nonetheless, contrary to local problems like those of Illinois, the commissioner reckoned that throughout the iron rectangle governmental income from "corporate taxation is almost invariably increasing," partly, he felt, because of the growing size and number of corporations and partly because of more effective operations conducted through revamped money machinery. Although corporation lands were taxed like the lands of individuals, the drift was steadily toward segregating state sources of revenue from those of the localities, corporate taxation falling everywhere within the ambit of the state. The administration of corporation taxes had also become the main responsibility of state rather than of local officials. Having cast up these estimates, the commisioner had nothing to add except the observation that "it was safe to infer" from the results of his study "that each state would probably gain something by studying the system of other states."[65]

A bolder, less literal-minded, commissioner might have added more significantly that however lenient their tactics, however receptive or well-disposed their politicians were to corporations, the political establishments of the North had consolidated their authority over private corporations before the nineteenth century had closed. The law itself had been employed in reshaping the official side of the money machinery with a view to making privilege pay and by paying render obeisance to party government and evolving principles of communal responsibility. No longer was it seriously debated, as under earlier interpretations of capitalist theory it had been, whether the state possessed the right to tax and thereby to regulate corporations. This represented a long distance for so large a number of political units to travel over the course of a generation almost literally a statute at a time. In the most heavily industrialized states, the central issue, in truth, had been further refined by the opening of the present century. The "real problem in corporate taxation," announced one official less than a decade after the turn of the century, "is not, what shall be the subject matter of corporate taxation, nor how the tax once levied shall be collected, but rather, how shall the millions of dollars annually paid by corporations to the state be expended?"[66]

That the income tax is the best way of taxing both individuals engaged in business and general business corporations, was the opinion of practically every business man that appeared before our Committee. . . .

State of New York, Senate
Report of the Joint Legislative Committee on Taxation,
February, 14, 1916.

Business Men Ask State Income Tax

The New York Times, December 16, 1915

An income tax spares the business man in season of distress and helps him to weather the storm, but asks a return for the consideration shown in days of increasing prosperity.

RICHARD ELY
Supplementary Report on Taxation in Maryland, 1888.

9

The Breakthrough

Continuous struggles over corporate taxation, so central to reformation of the North's money machinery, slowly moved influential opinion away from its reliance on the old ideologies of public finance, lessening adherence to theories of benefit and increasing the acceptability of the theory of faculty. "We pay taxes," wrote Edwin Seligman in 1895, "not because we get benefits from the state, but because it is as much our duty to support the state as to support ourselves and our family; because, in short, the state is an integral part of us."[1] The creation of wealth was imputed more to society at large and less to the iron-willed virtues of individuals. This much, at least, even Henry George and his Single Taxers who conservatively rejected the theory of faculty in favor of traditional theories of natural rights and benefits shared with other revenue reformers, although the thrust of fiscal change soon knocked orthodox Georgites aside and left them in the dust. Thus it was after the early eighties that the theory of faculty coupled with governments search for new revenue centered attention on progressive taxation and began turning official machinery in directions already extralegally mapped out by administrative chicane and party machinery.[2]

The progressive principle, of course, was less new than newly emphasized in the last decade of the nineteenth century. Various fiscal expedients of the Civil War and early Reconstruction years, as informed men never forgot, had embodied the progressive idea in federal taxation both of corporations and of personal income; and aspects of this otherwise ill-starred federal taxation were incorporated in the Federal Income Tax of 1893. In addition, states such as Maine and Maryland had occasionally applied progressive devices to corporate taxation prior to the 1860's, though admittedly with no intention of furthering reformist theories of faculty. Thus the taxation of incomes and utilization of progressive rates had actually been a feature of the American scene for many years; the novelty introduced late in the last century lay in the integration of progressive corporate and personal income taxation under the theory of faculty the better to distribute wealth, to ease middle class burdens, as well as to raise fresh revenues.

On the face of things it might be wondered why income taxation, particularly on the state level was not an irresistible reform. Considering the potential opposition to corporate taxation, it might be supposed that, comparatively, income taxation would have carried the day with relative ease. Inheritance taxes, for instance, were accepted with little trouble in most Northern states and the grounds on which they rested were really very similar to those on which progressive income taxation was premised. Certainly the country's several thousand millionaires were an inviting target of tax collectors and, as Richard Ely explained in 1888, "one of the principles which controlled the action of Jefferson and other founders of this republic, was to abolish hereditary distinctions and privileges, and . . . give to all as nearly as practicable an equal start in the race of life," a proposition from which few would have dissented. Furthermore, even in conservative quarters, the fear of "big money" was general; a committee of the Illinois Bar Association struck this note bluntly in 1886 when it declared:

> There never was a time in the history of the world when the power of money in skillful hands was so great as the present; or when the use of that power was made so conspicuous. The new forces at its command are augmenting it with wonderful rapidity. Already the sceptre has passed from the sword to the countinghouse. The fact that one individual may monopolize hundreds of millions of the wealth of the nation . . . is a growing source of uneasiness among all classes of society.[3]

But quite beside these fears, the attraction of income taxation might have been heightened dramatically by concern over the failure of general property taxation and by the escape of professional and salaried men as well as those enjoying substantial incomes from intangible properties from public obligation. Yet, in fact, resistance *in principle* to corporate taxation, including the taxation of the corporation's ability to pay, was often surprisingly light, however hot the battles over the implementation of such taxes undeniably were, and in no Northern state was this form of taxation long delayed. On the other hand, until the first decade of this century, proposals for effective state or national income taxation remained unpopular and hence politically dangerous. If as E. A. Ross noted in 1892, "the predilection of modern democracies for direct taxes on property or income" signified "a revolution in State taxation" which would saddle the "special privilege classes" with heavier burdens, why was this so?[4]

The answer lay partly in the past. Before its merits were celebrated and its deformities were bared in the Congress in 1894 and before the Supreme Court the following year in the Pollock Case, the income tax in principle had been damned by the context in which it had originally been discussed and applied. Like a woman who had kept company only with the best people, its virtue was squandered after the civil war in the embrace of disreputable or highly suspicious elements; or so it seemed to many responsible men of the urban middle classes. It was judged by association, a guilt made all the more serious because of the impossible things which it advocates initially expected from it.

Many of the odious characteristics identified with the principles and practices of income taxation traced back to the Stevens-Morrill Act of 1861 and its amended versions which extended its longevity to 1873. If measured by the political backing it initially solicited, the act had a good start. As a wartime expedient, it was justified exclusively by its production of desperately needed federal revenues and congressional support for it from men like Thaddeus Stevens, Sumner, Conkling, and Fessenden was "bipartisan." Wartime patriotism rendered payments effective to a degree through fear and embarrassment, although neither the fear nor the embarrassment was insurmountable in many circles. Unhappily for its good repute, however, the tax lingered too long. The motives with which it was initially identified changed; its administrative weaknesses became manifest; and those upon whom it was levied ceased being pricked by conscience.

Even more specifically, "the agitation against the income tax, which led finally to its repeal, was perhaps far more owing to the excess of the rate charged," wrote David A. Wells, then serving as U.S. Special Commissioner, "than to any real objection to the tax itself." Furthermore, because of "the late time of its taking effect," it brought into the Treasury only a relatively modest $15 million in 1864. An amendment then hiked the rate from 3% to 5% on incomes up to $5000 and from 5% to 10% on incomes over $5000, but most of the tax for 1865 was collected under the old law. Ironically, therefore, the full impact of the tax registered after the war had ended. Collections of over $60 million in June 1866 carried returns to an historic highpoint and "this was but little diminished in the following year, 1866–67." Large postwar collection, irrespective of benefits to Washington, constituted a minor masterpiece of mistiming, for the refusal to grant relief to the classes paying the tax was frankly based on the hope of bringing "within reach of the . . . law great numbers who had hitherto avoided giving in their receipts at all, or had made imperfect or fraudulent returns in order to escape the excessive tax," a spirit precisely like that which underlay the general property tax. Arguing in behalf of lower rates, Wells, who at that time favored income taxation, accurately noted how the motives informing the tax had changed; "a tax of 5%," he wrote, "is evidently too high for revenue purposes"[5] and those who were asked to pay had not missed the point either.

Raising the rates under these circumstances exposed the debilitating administrative problems inherent in the American version of income taxation. Unlike the British income tax instituted by Peel in 1843 which reached income at its source, the Federal tax tried reaching into the individual pockets of those who were ready to proclaim publicly that their incomes were high enough to be taxable. The number disposed to do this stood at 460,000 in 1866, at roughly half that number during the next four years, and finally dropped to 74,000 in 1871 and to 72,000 in 1872, at which point Senator Morrill, a sponsor of the tax, flatly declared to Congress that it had become little more than the sum each man chose to pay on his own estimate of his income.

Other administrative disabilities stemmed from the fact that there never was a single statute designated as the Income Tax Act; in reality, there were eight separate acts plus many amendments passed and repealed over a span of years. As critics observed, most of these pieces of legislation were so crudely drawn that they left both officials and taxpayers confused. "The law of the last session," complained the *Commercial and Financial Chronicle* in 1871, "was drawn up so carelessly that it accidentally omitted to levy any tax at all on the profits of corporations and the interest on their bonds paid during the latter months of 1870." The slip was costly, as the editor observed, for a large part of the taxable corporate business seized its chance and distributed profits earlier to escape taxation entirely. To the *Chronicle* this emphasized "the injustice" of passing a new income tax law every year. For such reasons, noted this influential paper, "a great number who last session urged its retention have abandoned their opposition to the repeal of the Income Tax . . . out of Congress, very few voices are raised for its continuance."[6]

Finally, taken together, there is no doubt that the income tax laws were disappointing in that they touched less than one-tenth of the country's taxable values at the very best. Ohio's stolid John Sherman informed the Senate in February 1865 of steps which even under the spur of war were required to halt the "shameless and wholesale evasion" of the tax and of the efforts needed to curtail assessments and collections which he denounced as "a disreputable farce."[7] These were a few of the conditions marring what might otherwise have proven an enormously beneficial experiment.

Of these failures, unfortunately, there were memories lasting throughout the balance of the century. "The experience of the United States with the income tax levied in the Civil War and continued for a while after its close," declared the Massachusetts Tax Commission of 1897, "is fresh in the memories of many of our citizens, and does not encourage us to hope for certainty, equity, or honesty in the administration of a State income tax."[8] And the observation was typical.

Redemption for a reputation fallen on evil times conceivably might have come from the administrative experiences of the several states in the field of income taxation, for that experience was far from inconsequential. Massachusetts, for example, technically had retained an income tax from 1643 to 1871, as had a number of states like Maryland in the pre-war years. In all, before the twentieth century opened, sixteen states seeking a different distribution of tax burdens, increased revenues, or the regulation of certain businesses, resorted to taxing various incomes. By 1900 the development of state income taxes could be divided into three periods between 1840 and 1900. During the first two periods, from 1840 and 1850 and over the war decade, states were motivated chiefly by their need for revenues to pay off the enormous indebtedness arising principally from internal improvements but also from the demands of wartime financing. By the nineties, however, the chief motive had become the desire to insure a different—and ostensibly a more equitable—distribution of wealth and public burdens. The motive, in short, was as much social as economic.[9]

However, of the forty post-Civil War state tax commissions only two (barring the notable minority reports of Richard Ely in Maryland, John A. Wright in Pennsylvania, and George McNeill in Massachusetts) officially urged the employment of state income taxation. Both were Massachusetts commissions. To be sure, few experts denied that citizens ought to pay taxes in proportion to their capacities to pay or that a man's capacity was best measured by his income.[10] Furthermore, as one authority at the turn of the century correctly reported, "throughout the history of the tax in the several states the opposition . . . never seriously attacked it from a theoretical standpoint."[11] But that, of course, was precisely the point; theory aside, state income tax laws were regarded as a *practical* disaster. Administration and enforcement under law officials failed; evasion was encouraged by allowing taxpayers to assess their own incomes; certain types of income contemplated as taxable were not reached at all; and so on. "The experience of the states with the income tax warrants the conclusion that the tax, *as employed by them,* has been unquestionably a failure," wrote one commentator in 1900, to which he rightly added, "a careful review of the history of the tax leads one to a conclusion that the failure has been due to the administration of the laws."[12]

The *idea* of an income tax unquestionably suffered as well from the company it kept. Not only was it suspect because its justification rested with theoreticians, that is, with "intellectuals" and other impractical people, it was also commonly identified—one must say without much accuracy—with agitators, radicals, socialists, and other dissenters. Such associations branded the tax and the ideas underlying it as an instrument of class and sectional prejudice among responsible men of town and country, but especially among men of the Northern cities.

When efforts were made in the House of Representatives to revive an income tax law in 1878, for example, petitions against the bill from Baltimore, Philadelphia, Boston, and New York having first assailed it as impolitic and impractical proceeded to the heart of the matter—its character and its motives. Citing "the opinion of eminent lawyers," opponents of the bill argued that it violated a constitutional proviso (Art. I., Sec. 9) against "the fiscal oppression of one portion of the Union at the expense of another." The *Nation* praised arguments against the bill as unanswerable; they were, declared the liberal journal, "the kind of arguments . . . which ought to have the most weight with a civilized legislature," for into "nothing was it less proper to allow prejudice of any kind to enter [than] into the levying of taxes." Warned the editor, in no way could "the seeds of ineradicable social hates and dissensions be so readily sown as by making taxation the expression of hostility . . . or by imposing it in the interest of any class or section of the community." Startlingly naive and blinded by its own prejudices, this viewpoint, nonetheless, emanated from a center of Eastern urban intelligence, one which had even earlier raised the spectre of fiscal power placed in the wrong hands. "The present silver agitation," recorded the *Nation,* "has produced among the farmers and laborers of a large portion of the country hostile feelings toward bankers, merchants, and all that class of persons who do the business of exchange." Without promising a sound way of securing additional revenues, chided the editor, the bill merely provided a "good way of harassing an obnoxious class residing mainly in a particular region [the Northeast]," making it in effect a "bill of pains and penalties."[13]

Two months later, continuing its attacks, the *Nation* sharply contrasted the English income tax of which it approved with the income tax in the United States. Abroad, the "purely fiscal origins of the tax" had made it "efficient, decent, and inoffensive," a trinity of American middle class virtues in other words. Abroad, it had never been employed as a means of "gratifying social prejudices," while in America its revival was "part and parcel of an assault on that portion of the community which is supposed to be in possession of accumulated property, for the purpose of relieving another portion which is supposed to be in debt." Newspapers favoring the bill were charged with propitiating the growth of communistic ideas which had sprung up among "Western farmers," the mainstays of the Granger movement, and perpetrators of "pillage" and "arson." Income taxation, therefore, was portrayed in the house of its likeliest friends as the wild hope of the West and the South and, for their folly, these sections earned a sermon from New York. "The way of both the South and the West back to the old American peace and prosperity lies through industry and order," inveighed the editor in the classic idiom of the middle classes, ". . . and now that they have had their fling, and shown the Gold-Sharps that they do not care a snap for either the Ancient or Modern World, for Ancestors or Posterity, and can pass what bills they please, would it not be well to settle down to business and sober and rational life."[14] There is no evidence that the editor realized how widely he had missed the mark.

Cast against this background, disputes over income taxation during 1894 and 1895 in many ways were redundant; the relevant points had all been made before at many levels of American life from the Civil War onward. Throughout a full generation, the image of income taxation took on connotations of radicalism and sectionalism, in addition to associations of corruption and administrative failure and a reputation for being anti-democratic, anti-republican, and inquisitorial. But that was hardly an end to the matter, for the dialogues and debates over income taxation were far more complicated than has been suggested.

Since in the last decade of the nineteenth century income taxation seemed to have been defeated both at the state and the national levels, it is well to understand that while attacks on the tax were often narrowly legalistic, narrowly self-interested, and undoubtedly often disingenuous in the bargain, they were also in some regards well-founded. A considerable body of intelligence and experience both at home and abroad were ranged against it on *rational* as well as on emotional grounds; even friends of income taxation held very serious reservations about it and certainly none argued that it was a panacea. The Civil War tax had been administered inefficiently and was conducive to corruption; the experiences of the states bore out every suspicion of ineffectuality, inefficiency, and the escapes and evasions of the wealth being sought. Political economists and revenue reformers were divided about it; both conservative and liberal economists, that is to say, favored it; and both conservative and liberal economists opposed it. In these and other circles there was ready agreement that such a tax on faculty was theoretically wise and fair, but there was just as prompt disagreement whether this form of taxation would be any more effective than personal property taxation had been. That in fact was the stand of the Massachusetts and the Maine Tax Commissions of the nineties; if spokesmen for Southern and Western farmers favored income taxation, spokesmen for Northern farmers (who clung tenaciously to general property taxation on personalty) either flatly opposed it or found it no more promising than extensions of this traditional form of taxation on which they were already embarked. The divisions among business and other important interests do not appear any cleaner than those among economists and farmers.[15]

In large part it was the doubt and confusion surrounding the subject of income taxation that allowed the important national discussion, with all that its resolution implied for local polities, to run strongly along sectional and class lines, thereby encouraging sophistry and prejudice to weigh heavily in the public debates.

Argument centered largely on the motives imputed to proponents of the tax. Immediately after the Supreme Court annulled the federal tax in 1895, for instance, the *Commercial and Financial Chronicle* observed that the decision was properly conservative, favoring "the restoration of confidence;" yet, as the *Chronicle* explained, this was not true because "it relieved any number of people from an onerous tax." The editors were concerned solely because defeat of the tax promised "to help preserve the nation" and a regard for constitutional limitations on legislation "from the destructive character of Populistic ideas." It was really immaterial whether there was an income tax, continued the editors; *that* was "a minor question; but whether there shall be an inequitable one, is a vital principle."[16]

To many of the urban middle classes the point had relevance, for the income tax seemed to be a farmers' tax. Its stoutest roots, barring two Northern states, appeared to be in the South; indeed, twelve of the sixteen states that had experimented with the tax during the nineteenth century were Southern. Only one of the states employing it at the turn of the century was Northern and while both industrial Massachusetts and Pennsylvania had modest success with income taxation prior to 1900 and Wisconsin was soon to adopt it, the tax was more feasible, successful, and, therefore, popular in backward agricultural states.[17] It promised to be a colonials' tax on the metropolis.

Informed men in Northern cities well understood rural reasons for support of this type of legislation. They were intimately linked with the farmer's traditional desire to chase the new wealth to ground, easing burdens which he felt rested squarely on him. But if in the North attacks on proposed income taxation were colored inevitably by self-interest and by a rough measure of cynicism, the same self-interest and cynicism underlay the efforts of farmers and their political representatives to enact such tax legislation. Idealism was everywhere in short supply. From a rural viewpoint, the beauty of an income tax was that it scarcely touched farmers at all. Few of them, to begin with, earned incomes exceeding the usual proposed exemption level and fewer still had incomes which were readily calculable. It was almost a complete switch; under the general property tax, the intangibles that bulked so large in urban and industrial wealth were practically uncalculable for tax purposes; under income taxation, there promised to be almost insuperable problems of figuring the valuation of rural incomes.[18]

Proof of this did not seem lacking. Georgia's wartime income tax had demonstrated that factory centers and large trading towns paid the bulk of the tax, while major sums paid within these centers derived from a handful of big traders and large factories. Farmers were all but immune; in some rural counties rural legislators flatly informed their constituents that the Income Tax Act touched only general traders and speculators in the countryside, not farmers or planters. Attitudes changed little over the ensuing generation. A prominent Georgian, whose candid views were subsequently invoked against income taxation in the North, declared early in the nineties that "we are all for an income tax down in our part of the country; and so is Senator Walsh who represents us, because none of us here have four-thousand dollar incomes, and somebody else will have to pay the tax."[19] Everyone understood who "somebody else" was. As tax authorities had known for years "the knottiest problem in connection with the income tax is presented by the farmer," very few of whom kept any accounts and most of whom received substantial portions of their incomes, or so it was alleged, in hard-to-value non-monetary items.[20] Northeastern urbanites, therefore, had no need to ask for whom the bell tolled.

Many of these men felt that the historical record bore out their fears; the agricultural provinces "had at them" before. Repeatedly even the most responsible men recalled the impact of the Civil War income tax; seven states, Massachusetts, New York, New Jersey, Pennsylvania, Ohio, Illinois, and one state outside of the iron rectangle, California, possessing nearly 40% of the country's assessed property and roughly 40% of its population had then paid three-fourths of the entire income tax levied by the federal government. Or, as David Wells, a staunch opponent of the tax by the nineties, explained it: "the States which had sixty per cent of the wealth and population of the country paid only about one-fourth of the income tax."[21] New York alone, Wells reckoned, had paid over 32% of the entire tax collected during the war years. Thus when Congressman Miller of Kansas declared in 1910 that Western Republicans were pledged to stand fast beside the South to vote through the income tax against the bitter opposition of New England, the rejoinder from one New York lawyer caught the spirit of the East on the subject, "Why not?" he exclaimed. "They won't pay for it."[22]

Discussion of income taxation—unfortunately, considering the other disabilities from which it suffered—rarely rose above class and sectional fist-shaking exercises. As a result, even after the income tax had been proposed by a Republican President and passed by a Republican Congress, anomalies like the one in New York State occurred, where an overwhelmingly Republican legislature first rejected the amendment. "The reason the amendment failed," declared an Elmira assemblyman, "was because a majority of the assemblymen were unwilling to have the great wealth of the State of New York taxed for the benefit of the South and West whose Congressmen are in the majority and whose people would bear but little of the burden."[23] To have pressed the tax as a great social panacea on the one hand, or to have opposed it as a class, sectional, and communistic assault on the other, was to have missed the most profitable line of discussion, namely the need of all governments for additional revenues to finance the administrative and party machinery essential to handling a revolution of rising expectations.

Therefore, while the federal income tax issue proved a boon to the movement toward state income taxes in several respects, the actual experiments and dialogues connected with its development were in many ways a distinct disadvantage and made the national scene unhappily relevant to state and local discussions. Put bluntly by one tax reformer, the revival of a federal income tax "under circumstances of acrimonious partisan debate caused this method of taxation to be regarded with new disfavor by a great mass of our citizens."[24]

One of the ironies of the extended controversy over income taxation was that the two broad groups who strongly desired both more government service *and* relief from public obligations, that is, certain farmers, particularly those of the South and the West, and the urban middle classes of the North, were long pitted against each other over a form of taxation which would have relieved *both* of them. Each was faced with an increase in the assessment of their real properties without a corresponding increment in its value or productiveness. Meantime, no significant new sources of revenue appeared to be opening up rapidly and there was a relative decline in returns from the taxation of the new wealth. In the twentieth century the irony grew much less keen; there was some coalescence of previously hostile forces; if there had not been, of course, the final establishment of state and federal income taxation on a broadening scale and as a permanent feature of the money machines of the country during the Progressive Era would have been highly improbable.

All this background duly noted, it is no surprise that in the states of the North between 1890 and 1925 income taxation was enacted with a whimper and not with a roar. What might have emerged as one of the more dramatic social reforms of the age actually emerged stigmatized by the support of its friends and by the impoverished reputation it had earned historically and administratively.

On these points historians can discover something of a consensus. Among Single Taxers, whose *social* visions were as broad as any, income taxation suffered from being unscientific and unnatural; it was judged unlikely to be applied uniformly or administered justly either locally or between the states; it threatened massive double taxation and threatened to drive capital from many states; and, not the least of its disabilities, it could be shifted, they felt, to the shoulders of those who ought not to be made to bear it. At the other extreme temperamentally, committees of experts were at best divided, with a majority normally voicing fatal doubts about its practical efficacy. "What, then, should be our attitude toward an income tax?" queried a committee of the National Tax Association in its conclusions on state and local substitutes for general property taxation. "As to this," it replied, "your Committee are unanimously of the opinion that an income tax, assessed as is the personal property tax, would constitute no improvement whatever. If the personal property tax, assessed by local officials is a failure," continued the committee, "an income tax assessed by local officials would be no less of a failure. There would indeed be nothing to choose between them."[25] State income taxation, long entertained in select, academic circles, as late as 1909 simply did not loom large in many other quarters as a viable substitute for personal property taxation, detested as that was. Among political economists, many of whom judged it admirable in the abstract, there were few who recommended it for state or municipal use before 1910.[26]

But among the middle classes where fiscal enthusiasms were apt to be suspect, negative accents and negative approaches sometimes succeeded where more positive moves failed. So it was, in any event, with state taxation of incomes. Its appearance was heralded by the cautious intelligence that however bad it might be, it was superior to the taxation of personalty under the general property tax. Long standing failures in this quarter were sufficient to drive some men toward reform, for these failures resulted in tangible burdens and among businessmen there was nothing abstract about burdens. After consultation with a dozen of the state's major business associations,[27] with over 500 of the state's corporations, with over a dozen leading experts on fiscal affairs, and with a number of public commissions in the state, New York's Mills Committee delineated these burdens with some precision. Strongly arguing that the state could no longer rely on general property taxation for additional revenue because it would "threaten to disturb important business conditions," the committee cited the fact that "the real estate situation in New York City and other localities is already such as to cause apprehension." Discounting the "exaggerated claims of real estate men, on the one hand, and of a group of radical social reformers, on the other," it was careful to qualify in the light of evidence; but, this done, it concluded that "there are large sections of the city of New York, as well as parts of the state at large, where an increase in the tax rate might constitute nothing short of confiscation. Indeed," continued the committee, "the present high rates upon real estate have already through the reduction of net income, actually destroyed capital value." Earlier state tax conferences at Utica in 1911 and at Buffalo in 1912, as well as all of New York's previous tax commission reports sustained this conclusion—and New York was typical.

This was surely the case in Wisconsin, popularly acknowledged as the pioneer in experiments with modern state income taxation after 1909. A Milwaukee attorney, later chief of the State Income Tax Bureau, Kossuth Kennan, along with Professor T. S. Adams, the leading expert on Wisconsin public finance, wrote in 1911 that "the advocates of the law seemed to be guided not so much by any wild enthusiasm for the income tax as by a desire to find some substitute for the iniquitous personal property tax."[28] In a sense, therefore, state income taxation was initially viewed as a blunt instrument with which to batter away the most objectionable features of the antiquated general property tax system.

Yet even to conceive of state income taxation *negatively* required a substantial shift in the attitudes and opinions of many informed men. To careful observers in 1905, for example, the future of state income taxes, however rational a case could be made for them, seemed negligible. How and why, then, did influential views change or begin changing between the first and second decades of this century?

"The surprising thing about this," wrote Kennan, trying to clarify what had transpired in Wisconsin, "was that the people of the state should view with complacency the repeal of the tax on personal intangible property" following amendment of the state constitution in 1908 making possible substitution of an income tax. This, in Kennan's estimate, was "a step which usually aroused a storm of indignant protest from those who look upon any such move as being in the interest of the wealthier classes,"[29] an opinion, as we have often noted, traditional among farmers. Continually frustrated by their efforts to apply personalty taxes to intangible wealth decade after decade, Northern farmers had simply had their resistance worn thin. If they had not begun *active* support of state income taxation, they at least had *ceased* to *oppose* the search for substitutes and this fortunately was enough change to help in reform. Men who had exhausted themselves over the years trying to convince rural interests and their legislators that personalty taxation was unwise accepted rural complacency as about the most valuable outlook they could reasonably expect from that quarter.

Undoubtedly, too, decades of public discussion, however distorted, had produced positive as well as negative results. In this sense, the United States Supreme Court as well as the Populists and Socialists who were identified with income taxation each made their contributions. Talk made the strange familiar; "we have passed the stage," wrote Frederick C. Howe in the *American Law Review* in 1899, on the possibilities of state and local income taxation, "when we are likely to be frightened by the bogy of a name." To old allegations that income taxes were a foreign innovation, that they were un-American, and inquisitorial, the sorry record of uninhibited "patriots" was all too clear a rebuttal to everyone; they had "flitted to suburban tax districts" to "escape the personal property tax altogether by false returns." After the ill-repute of inquisitorial ferret systems such as Ohio's gained currency, moreover, and was widely associated with personalty taxation, an income tax could hardly appear "more inquisitorial than the personal tax as administered or attempted to be administered in the majority of . . . States." Penalty after penalty, it was noted, "have been enacted into legislation to secure honest returns and to incompass the cupidity and frauds of those who evade taxation, but all have proven futile . . . our legislators, auditors, assessors, and tax commissions," continued the commentary, "have retired baffled in their attempts to legislate men honest and secure complete returns."[30] Rural America was no longer in much doubt about this.

The knowledge also spread through the countryside that income taxation "works better in manufacturing and commercial than in rural communities, because of the difficulty of computing farmers' incomes."[31] There were accompanying seductions in the realization that it "would relieve real estate of a part of its burdens" and strike directly at "the very general escape of professional and salaried men," of whom farmers were at once notoriously envious and contemptuous. Such knowledge was a balm to fears; even the voracious financial appetites of the cities, it appeared, could now be satisfied "without further recourse to the present overburdened classes,"[32] another point before which rural opposition subsided.

While chance no doubt played its part, much of this type of information was purposefully circulated through the electorate. Sustained efforts were made both by private and public organizations, the NTA and its affiliates, for example, and state tax commissions or aggressive governors, to propagandize and enlighten farming peoples. In 1912 Kossuth Kennan, apropos of Wisconsin, wrote that "it must be remembered . . . that for ten years the Permanent State Tax Commission had been carrying on a campaign of education by means of their public reports and otherwise, which was calculated to bring out in bold relief the gross inequities and general ineffectiveness of the tax on intangible personal property" for which state income taxation, or some variety of corporate income taxation, were the substitutes.[33] Such campaigns were general throughout the North. To be sure, they did not invariably succeed in persuading the rural citizenry of states like Indiana or Ohio to adopt state income taxes; but because they were usually linked to other specific discussions of reforms in state and local taxation they tended to have similar enlightening effects. They focused attention, that is, on what reformers regarded as vital repairs in local money machinery and on viable alternatives.

Despite the weakening of farmer intransigeance about personal property taxation during the early part of this century, it was still mainly urban experts, middle-class academicians, businessmen, along with politicians and administrators who shared or reflected their perspectives, who were the most active force in securing state income taxes, just as they had been foremost in securing most other changes in fiscal machinery. Notwithstanding divided ranks, the members of the National Tax Association threw their weight behind the principles of state income taxation with tremendous effect; indeed, the extent of it may be judged by the fact that every fiscal measure passed by the New York legislature in the banner year of 1911 had been proposed to Albany by the NTA, most recently through the medium of the State Conference on Taxation, many of whose members were disciples of the NTA.[34] The powerful support of business groups throughout New York State, and it was typical of situations elsewhere, has already been alluded to.[35]

Difficult as it is to assign them relative importance, there were many reasons state income taxes received support from urban business and political interests, just as earlier they were identified with the support of workingmen, populists, and socialists who were anxious to shift public burdens onto comfortable middle-class interests. For businessmen, to begin, personal property taxation had always been loaded with menace; there were blatant threats in its rural origins and in the fact that it was poorly suited to urban needs; there were dangers which it imposed on otherwise reputable businessmen by forcing them to operate deviously, often illegally, or, failing this, to suffer disadvantages in competition; there were dangers in its inability to raise fresh revenues, thereby tempting legislatures to invoke inquisitorial devices and severe penalties for nonpayment; and there was the great threat, too, that if it were honestly paid as an act of conscience or if it were somehow rendered generally effective, its rates would prove confiscatory. These inevitable accompaniments of the tax dangled like a sword over the counters and coffers of urban businessmen;[36] together, they heavily disposed these men to alternatives.

But businessmen's predispositions were a latent factor; it required a vast amount of education by experts, reformers, "demagogues," and special interest groups, solid evidence that income taxes could be made to work properly, and the prod of perennial fiscal crises to convert some of them into activists.

Between 1911 and 1919, a period during which state taxation of incomes, and the progressive principle embodied in it, took legislative form, "two facts," declared one of Indiana's professorial champions of the tax, "were revolutionizing opinion as to the practicality of a state income tax." The first was "the practical demonstration in Wisconsin" that such a tax could be made "efficient." The second was "the adoption of the federal income tax and the popular acceptance of it as a part of the national fiscal system." People everywhere, it was argued, had been educated by both of these developments to understand that an income tax was not "contrary to the spirit of republican institutions," that it was not inconsistent with the nation's "political traditions and . . . business habits," and that it did not involve "intolerable double taxation."[37]

But contemporary testimony, debate, and writing relative to the establishment of state income taxes in Wisconsin, New York, Massachusetts, and Missouri before the end of 1919, indicate that there were many other motives specifically informing the minds of legislators. These had been taking shape over the previous generation. Foremost was the urgent need for new revenue from expansive sources, the desire to check the flight of the intangible new wealth (if only for social reasons), the hope of equalizing burdens, the desire to reach properties afforded sanctuary by federal statutes, and the expectation of profiting from more accurate methods of determining taxpaying capacities throughout the community.[38]

Wisconsin's experience was very closely watched since reform there represented common reactions to the failure of the general property tax and to swiftly rising state expenditures. Once the constitutionality of the law was affirmed in a collection of cases heard by the state supreme court in 1912, those who hoped to move in similar directions had few inhibitions about doing so, for the tax quickly appeared a practical success. Its yields were high, an important point since it was a substitute tax not an additional one in the state's fiscal system; the net ran close to $2 million in its second year. Moreover, it proved remarkably cheap to administer, costing only a percent or two of the tax assessed and the tax collected. Without question it introduced "a larger element of justice" into Wisconsin fiscal operations, falling upon both persons and properties unreached before and it distributed burdens far more equitably than they had been in a generation. Statistics from the Wisconsin State Tax Commission in 1914 after three years of collection substantiated this. Of the persons assessed for income taxation in that year, 41,732 earned less than $1000; making up 68% of the total number of taxpayers, they paid less than 11% of the tax. By contrast, 315 taxpayers earning $15,000 or more and accounting for only .5% of those assessed paid 40% of the total, an average of $1794 apiece. Only 1% of Wisconsin's laborers and fewer than 5% of her farmers were subjected to the tax.

Insofar as Wisconsin Tax commissioners, as well as many outside observers, were concerned, these very significant virtues were nonetheless subordinate to another. "Its first and chief merit," we are told, was "an indirect one;" namely, its toning up "the entire fiscal administration in the state." The tax was a triumph for the cult of efficiency. Centralization and concentration of power in the hands of the state tax commissioners was unprecedented. The commissioners appointed the assessors; collections were made by local collectors but they were responsible to the commission and were empowered by it to demand from individuals and corporations any information required for the enforcement of the income tax act. After collection there was an added attraction which had helped sell the program to the localities once it was in effect: the commission distributed 10% of the money to the state, 20% to the revenue's county of origin, and 70% to the city, town, or village of origin.[39]

By its manner of distribution, therefore, the tax began appeasing the appetites of the growing population centers. Without scaring them with exorbitant rates it harnessed corporations and rich individuals to the fiscal needs of the state, thereby rendering wealth more amenable to the middle-class values which underlay the tax and, at the same time, forcing them to pay from 10% to 12% of state revenues. Finally, the tax quietly wrested control of taxation from local officials in rural districts and placed it under the aegis of urban interests, commercial, political, and academic.

Wisconsin earned the lion's share of attention for its breakthrough with a successful state income tax and all that it implied socially and economically; but New York's enactment of an income tax in 1919 brought to fruition a statutory process which had begun quite self-consciously and systematically many years earlier than Wisconsin's. Moreover, even though it was passed eight years later, many experts believed that the New York law went much farther. By no means a disinterested spectator, E. R. A. Seligman, then the nation's leading authority on taxation, cited it as "a real fiscal revolution . . . an important milestone in the economic and political development of the United States." It was the "first comprehensive attempt made . . . by a leading commonwealth to substitute for an outworn and makeshift policy a well-rounded system of state and local taxation."[40]

The evolution of the New York law furnished, among other things, an excellent example of the influence on government of reform-minded experts, the value of whose advice was constantly evident in the North during the last third of the nineteenth century. Indeed, the impact of the country's first generation of professional political economists was immediate and impressive and in the case of New York the expert was Seligman. Starting in the eighties, upon his return from postgraduate studies in Germany, Switzerland, and France, though he was still in his twenties and just "beginning to pay some attention to tax problems," he was consulted by New York's legislative leaders "as to the best methods of extricating the state from its growing fiscal difficulties." The nature and extent of these troubles had been amply described in the Wells Reports, his debt to which Seligman generously acknowledged.[41]

That the general property tax was fast failing as the chief source of revenue was obvious; equally obvious was the political impossibility of a successful frontal attack on personal property taxation and on the related problem of the unequal assessment of realty. To circumvent these obstacles, Seligman decided that the most promising reform lay first in a separation of revenues drawn upon by the state and its local divisions. Allowing local assessors to value properties in their own jurisdictions, he realized, had driven them into competitive underassessment, whereas reserving realty taxation to localities would in time, he felt, cure the difficulty. He also believed that little by little advantage could be taken of the more liberal aspects of the state constitution by levying separate taxes on the various types of personalty, gradually dissolving general taxation "even for local purposes." He was, in short, a confirmed gradualist and probably thought it impossible to be anything else where such complexities as those posed by fiscal issues were involved.

"Under the influence of these ideas," wrote Seligman, legislative leaders were persuaded to act in accordance with this strategy. Consequently, between the early 1880's and 1890 some progress was made in providing independent taxes for exclusive enjoyment by the state government; most notably, a collateral inheritance tax, an organization tax on corporations, racing tax laws, and a direct inheritance tax. These steps, quite inadequate in themselves, were just a beginning.[42]

Fresh attempts, Seligman tells us, seemed feasible to attain "the ends originally planned" during the mid-nineties. To this purpose, the liquor license law of 1896 divided the yield between state and local subdivisions after it had been centrally assessed. While this had distinct administrative advantages, it also represented a shrewd piece of political maneuvering on Seligman's part, for distribution of the yield throughout the various levels of local government was intended to ease local pressures on personal property "and thus to speed the day" when personalty taxation could be abolished.

During the next decade, Seligman and his political mentors continued augmenting their twin principles: the segregation of revenues and division of the yield. Between 1901 and 1911, a special tax rate was levied upon banks and other lending institutions; a stock-transfer tax passed the legislature along with a mortgage tax providing for a division of the proceeds between the state and the localities; a mortgage-recording tax soon followed and finally, in 1911, the same year as the enactment of the Wisconsin income tax, a secured-debt tax was passed. Some very positive consequences flowed from this twofold and persistently pursued course. The proceeds of indirect taxation grew so rapidly and inequalities in assessments diminished so dramatically that it permitted reduction of the general property tax for state purposes year by year; by 1907, in fact, New York State abandoned direct state taxation.

Undeniably, given Seligman's objectives, this was progress; but it had moved the state farther in one direction than in others and serious obstacles remained. For one thing, division of the yield proved too modest after a time to tempt local assessors out of their underassessment game or to provide what localities came to consider adequate financial aid for themselves. And there were further complications. Beginning in 1910 and continuing into the next decade, both state and local governments showed what were believed to be unprecedented increases in their costs and expenditures. With the state's outlays rising by "leaps and bounds," all of the old fears reminiscent of the late nineteenth century were revived. Looking back on this earlier period from the mid-twenties, through adjusted price indices computed for the state legislature, it was clearly true that if these increases were not unprecedented, they were very close to it. Operating expenses rose by 183%, total expenditures by 173%, creating a novel situation which did violence to the reforms being pursued gradually.[43]

Seligman interpreted soaring costs and expenditures as "the final fruits of a democracy which was determined to utilize government to achieve definite social ends." The welcome slack that had developed in the state system as a result of the previous shift from general taxation to indirect taxation was quickly taken up by the "rapid amortization" of the state's large debt and by its high current expenses and in 1912 a reimposition of direct taxation became necessary. Although separation of the sources of revenue had been a useful approach, Seligman and state leaders felt that the real crisis was at last at hand and that the "next stage of reform" had to be found elsewhere. Their anxieties, it should be noted, were not entirely intellectual. Just as the state's situation had become aggravated, so to had many local situations grown more acute, most notably, New York City's predicament. Personalty there performed its customary disappearing act; the tax base again narrowed when it should have expanded; real estate interests were demanding relief while the articulate public, realizing the effects this might be having on rents, roundly supported them. It was scarcely an environment in which anyone making decisions about the operation of money machinery could afford to sit still.[44]

The critical question was which alternatives would the state choose? Momentarily two in particular seemed appealing to many authorities: one was a variation of the Single Tax as it was understood to have functioned in Canada and the other was a scheme for the classification of properties. Both were given study and both were eventually rejected as unsuitable to the needs of New York. After that, aside from a flirtation with lowering the rates on intangibles as Maryland and Connecticut had done in hopes of luring forth greater quantities of personalty, there were few plans of merit left except the income tax.[45]

This is not to say, however, that the income tax came to the forefront by default. Although he was reserved about some aspects of it, Seligman, for instance, had been assuming since the early 1890's that "changing conditions of economic life were gradually making income rather than property the proper measure of wealth and taxable capacity." At a time when corporate taxation was gaining acceptance, he had repudiated the use of a corporation's capital or its gross receipts as a yardstick for taxation in favor of income, that is, net profits. He was also a supporter of the federal income tax in 1894 when few other economists were of the same conviction. Undoubtedly, the combination of the U.S. Supreme Court's opposition to the tax and the "unreadiness of administrative and political conditions in New York" prevented early achievements in this direction. But by 1906 Seligman and others like him had their chance. The New York State Tax Commission Report of that year had in large measure been drafted by him and its chief recommendation was "the nearest approach to an income tax which seemed feasible at the time," an indirect income tax in the form of a habitation tax. Even this, however, in an immediate and practical sense proved premature.[46]

Subsequent discussions and the legislative fights over the adoption of the Sixteenth Amendment might naturally have afforded proponents of income taxation in New York another chance to press their case, but the effect of the amendment in the short run was to produce a spirit of caution. Because the contest over ratification, in Seligman's words, was "heated and close," he felt it wiser to employ every ounce of reformist energy to secure backing for the federal amendment; to have championed an income tax within the state simultaneously, he believed, would have jeopardized the national issue and would have impaired the slow but healthy progress which he thought was being made not only in New York but also in a number of other states.

The inauguration of the federal tax in 1913 gave local interests the green light once more. Having assisted Connecticut authorities to set up a state income tax modelled after the federal tax and feeling the time ripe for another thrust along these lines in New York, Seligman pressed his case before a mayor's tax committee in New York City and shortly after that before the state committee on taxation headed by Senator Ogden Mills. Seligman was fully aware that the fiscal crisis which had been a constant prod to the political establishment had spread throughout the political divisions of the state, that "the former weighty objections to an income tax had now lost their force," that the adoption of the federal tax was bound to make the administration of a state tax simpler, and that the state's political units, assured of a division of yield, would cease cavilling at the centralized assessment of an income tax, especially if they could wring political advantage by relieving their long-suffering real estate interests. In all of these judgments Seligman proved correct. Neither of the committees disappointed him, for each of them reported in favor of a state income tax embodying a division of yield between the various levels of government.

"The movement," wrote Seligman, "was now launched." Even so, nothing precipitous was undertaken which might have disconcerted public opinion; a piecemeal approach was still considered the order of the day. New York State, thus, first applied the progressive income principle to the taxation of various corporations under the Emerson Law of 1917. Considering the fact that the repeal of the state liquor law had just deprived Albany of nearly a third of its income, making its fiscal plight desperate, the act was notable primarily for its political restraint. But crisis and the convocation of a special legislative committee under Senator Davenport in 1918 finally produced the income tax law which went into effect the following year. "Thus for the first time in American history," remarked Seligman, "a leading industrial state discarded the general property tax and substituted a general income tax on both individuals and corporations."[47]

It had certainly not been easy; the law of 1919 had emerged gradually in an atmosphere of recurrent crisis in state and local money machinery during a period of almost forty years, if we mark its inception in the early eighties where Seligman suggested the beginnings really had been. The approaches to the tax had periodically enlisted the aid or provoked the opposition of every major interest and many lesser ones in the state. Eventually, and almost always in public, all of New York's private and public leaders, individually or in association, joined by many interested parties from outside the state, expressed themselves on the subject. Whatever experience had been gained either at home or abroad on income taxation had been carefully observed; whatever expertise was available along the Eastern seaboard had been tapped directly time and again. Professional politicians, businessmen, reformers, and political economists, usually moving against the grain of middle-class prejudice and often against the best judgment of their comrades and colleagues, had displayed skill and tenacity both in reading the public temperament and in gingerly handling what in essence was a dubious experiment under American conditions. Driven in most instances by the cities' insatiable demands for greater revenues, these men, however callous and obtuse they sometimes were, had not neglected questions of welfare and social justice. They had inspired or instructed eight important tax conferences in which even rural officials had displayed their first willingness to be taught by the cities. They directed the activities of no less than six highly educational state and local committees on taxation and, by laying careful siege to the obstacles before them, they had moved step by step toward income taxation and the renovation of the state's entire fiscal system through fifteen major statutes, through seemingly endless legal tangles and constitutional lacunae.

Faced with the anarchy of conflicting political boundaries and with economic realities which ignored outmoded governmental jurisdictions, they substantially renovated the old official money machinery, indeed, it would be fair to say, they replaced it with a *new* system. In so doing, among other things, they made it possible for New York City to function as the nucleus of an unprecedented urban industrial complex, "the cradle of a new order in the organization of inhabited space," "the hinge of the Continent," or Megalopolis as Professor Jean Gottmann has called it.[48]

The centerpiece of this fiscal reform, the state income tax law, admittedly had its defects. The barest obeisance to the theory of personal property taxation lingered on unconscionably; distinctions between earned and unearned income had not been made sharply; the assignment of administrative control to the state comptroller, a highly politicized office, rather than to the state tax commission rankled a number of experts, Seligman among them; and the exclusion of public utilities as well as certain financial organizations from the coverage of the tax had little to commend it. Yet none of these deficiencies was sufficiently serious to detract from the demonstrable virtues of the law.

Because the state was more cosmopolitan, more heavily industrialized and commercialized, and less of a debtor than Wisconsin, New York's income tax was unique and pacesetting in its own right. Besides a number of advantages which it enjoyed over the Wisconsin law where the two laws were similar, it had half a dozen distinctive features. In order to minimize inconvenience to administrators and to taxpayers, its definitions, deductions, and exemptions were nearly identical with those of the federal income tax. At the same time, the New York law included all sources of income regardless of whether incomes were reached in other ways. It was also less steeply graduated than the Wisconsin law because, as Seligman explained to a state tax conference, a steep scale would have produced more revenue than was required and "conduce to extravagance." To raise assessments in the political subdivisions of the state, the principle of division of yield was used as an incentive. Shares turned back to the localities were apportioned on the basis of their assessments; the higher they were, the larger the share. Breaking away from cloying arguments over the *situs* of property which under the general property tax had determined the difference between resident and non-resident taxables, the income tax was addressed to the new question of where the income was earned. Of the several possible reactions to this vexing problem, Seligman had suggested the course actually adopted: the taxation of residents on all the income which they earned in New York and the taxation of non-residents on their New York earnings with appropriate deductions if they paid income taxes on these sums in their native states.

Nor was that all. Control of the tax was not entrusted to the tender mercies of local officials. Seeking to avoid the pitfall of the general property tax, its administration was centralized at the state level. The steady expansion of central administrative techniques already operative for corporations, excise, and inheritance taxes made this a relatively easy transition. The New York tax, finally, was the first to preëmpt the key position in the state's money machinery, so much so that Seligman, although deeply involved and somewhat too sanguine as a result, was correct in describing it as "a distinct stage in the progress of modern taxation."[49]

The New York income tax may be considered symbolic of the arrival of the North's new or reformed money machinery and of the attendant interests and values this machinery was fashioned to express. It would be another generation, of course, before income taxes eclipsed, even rivalled, other sources of revenue anywhere, and what transpired in New York, surely, was special. But it was still, in terms of the precedents it set, indicative of the drift of events elsewhere in the North. By 1920 half a dozen states had commenced to experiment afresh with some variety of income taxation and by the close of the decade twenty states had taken the same steps. In some states, the tax fell solely upon individual incomes, in others exclusively on the incomes of corporations, while in states such as New York it rested upon as many types of income as the authorities thought they could conveniently reach.

Even where income taxation was considered unsuitable and was not resorted to, all the mechanisms designed to accomplish the same objectives had slowly been placed in operation: separation of the sources of revenue, division of yield, correction of underassessment, the classification of taxes, taxation of corporations, taxation of the wealthy and those enjoying inheritances, the institution of special taxes, the downgrading or complete abandonment of personal property taxation, appointment of assessors or some other effort to divorce them from local politics, centralization of administration, tightened accounting procedures, development of the budget idea, movement toward limited local option and home rule, rearrangement of debt limitations particularly on municipalities, and acceptance of the principle of faculty as the philosophical basis of fiscal operations.

The principles of progressivity and the idea of state income taxation as one manifestation of them (as debated and acted upon in the states of the iron rectangle during the late nineteenth and early twentieth centuries) owed surprisingly little to the inspiration or practical consequences of working-class movements, populism, socialism, or radicalism despite some vocal champions in all of these camps. Indeed, in the light of previous historical explanations, it must be emphasized that none of the changes presupposed by income taxation derived from these movements. Prevalent political and social conditions simply would not have permitted it; the character and temperament of the chief interest groups, rural or urban, progressive or otherwise, would not have permitted it; and, with the wisdom of hindsight, we know that the great gap between the aspirations of such minorities and the practical capacities and opportunities required for coping with administrative, legal, political, and economic complexities over long periods of time would not have permitted it. Until any taint of political or social radicalism, until any intimation of wild-eyed insobriety was expunged from the minds of the reformers, no such machinery would have been created and no such law would have been passed. The suspicion that they might have been fashioned under any such aegis, or the supposition that they ought to have been, are a misreading of what had been happening to American life in the North with the emergence of a timorous but powerful urban middle class and a new urban democracy during the late nineteenth and early twentieth centuries.

While there were excesses in this period, this was not an age of excess. Quite the contrary. The thrust of the urban or urbanized middle classes lay toward certainty, order, discipline, organization, stability, routine, and efficiency, each of which the new fiscal machinery at the official level promised to augment. The triumph of a fiscal system, after all, is also the triumph of an ideology. Undoubtedly this was why state income taxes excited so little *active* interest among farmers. Far from being dangerous panaceas, such taxes often struck them as beneath contempt, at best a matter of indifference. They seemed just another slick scheme, if not an especially dangerous one, devised by the holders of the new wealth to escape from personal property taxation with its much heavier rates—and it could hardly be denied that personal property taxation potentially was the more dangerous tax. As the twentieth century proceeded, however, rural and urban distinctions blurred, which, along with education about the issues, helped alter opinions in this quarter, again with notable exceptions. If in part the federal income tax could be considered the "popular" measure of Southern and Western farm spokesmen, state income taxes in the North and the major fiscal changes which underlay them, were of solidly respectable metropolitan origins; more to the point, they were the experts' and the businessmen's tax.

The point deserves even heavier emphasis, for many reformers considered state income taxation and its accompaniments inadequate. Thomas Shearman, for instance, a disciple of Henry George, argued rather typically that "even as a temporary expedient . . . the income tax in any form" was "entirely unfitted for use in American states or municipalities."[50] He objected on constitutional grounds that the tax was not a direct one, that its incidence would be upon the rents of tenants, that it would be administered without uniformity either within or between states, and, above all, that it would breed still more perjury and evasion. An advocate of income taxation during the early years of his career, David A. Wells eventually spurned this position for many of the same reasons that Shearman voiced and for the additional one that the tax's discriminations and exemptions adversely affected "the foundation and continued existence of every free government, namely, the equality of all men before the law." To Wells "any exemption of any portion of the same class of property or incomes" was "an act of charity" which, he believed, every patriot ought to reject. "Equality and manhood" demanded uniformity of burden.[51] Walter Weyl, whose interest in fiscal reform was lifelong, declared in 1912, after the Wisconsin experiment had been launched, that state income taxes "were of practically no value." They achieved nothing by way of reducing inequalities in wealth, he argued, and because of the ease of acquiring citizenship in other states men of means could easily continue escaping obligation.[52] Finally, among many administrators and political experts, powerful persuasions were essential to win their sanction for the experiment in income taxation, so dubious a venture did it promise to be.

As the twentieth century advanced, state income taxation in principle unquestionably attracted growing numbers of supporters, but it made headway in the North for reasons quite different than those which had sustained the federal income tax or state income taxes in the South. The federal tax as well as those in the South were motivated largely by reactions against rural or provincial injustices and were hostilely aimed, as was natural, against the Northeast as a section and, in the second instance, against the rich and the comfortable "in town." In no general sense were these motives at work, so far as we can tell, across the Northern tier of states. To be sure, the progressive income tax had been urged by the People's Party, among others, in states like Wisconsin; but Populist advocacy was not responsible for subsequent legislation. They neither originated the reform nor finished it. Professor T. S. Adams, who had a role in Wisconsin analogous to Seligman's in New York, after specifically denying that Populists had anything significant to do with the measure, recorded in 1911 that "the present bill seems to be the direct result of a controversy over the exemption of credits," a fight which had commenced *inside* the Wisconsin State Tax Commission eight years earlier.[53] Among the politicians and political elites who took the tax seriously, the social justice it allegedly promised was a secondary consideration; in any event, it was not handled as a social measure among the minorities who backed it. It had no mass appeal and no mass support; it was an insiders' substitute for fiscal machinery that was not bringing in adequate revenues either for government or for party. Outside of Wisconsin this was also true; instead of overalls and a straw hat, the measure everywhere wore a tight buttoned-down worsted, a high starch collar, and an iron derby. Its hallmarks had been affixed by organizations such as the NTA and the solid middle classes who indeed would be obliged to pay the tax.

Why, then, did they accede to it, even actively fight for it? One answer is that against the costly inefficiencies of general property taxation and the chaos produced by the old money machinery built around it, income taxation promised to be safe, practical, and serviceable to the cult of efficiency. It promised to raise badly needed moneys to soothe rising civic anxieties about schools, streets, highways, superior public facilities, more extensive police and fire protection, health and welfare programs, and the like—and, of course, the profits that came from the development of such communal projects. Since the income tax was *their* law, not one thrust upon them by unchecked rural legislatures, the middle classes had far less to fear from it, especially considering the generous rates and tolerant exemptions, than they did from personalty taxation. Thus, while income taxation, corporate taxation, and other changes engineered in the money machines of the Northern states and their municipalities were real reforms, they also promised to be a real relief to that small number of property holders who had long been convinced they were financing both the revels of the new wealth and the bread and circuses of the new democracy.

Q. Do you not think a great party should prefer to stand upon its moral and political principles, rather than upon the spoils?
A. Both, I think.

Testimony by Richard Croker before
The Special Committee of the New York State Assembly Appointed to Investigate the Public Offices and Departments of the City of New York. . . . Vol. I., [1900].
[The Mazet Committee].

By comparing the budget since consolidation there has been an increase of twenty-two millions . . . in the annual expense of the city. This increase is not caused by public improvements, for they are payable by bonds. Such an increase in the budget in two years is startling. From the enormous and ever increasing number of city officials it would seem as if a consistent effort were being made to find out how two or more men could be made to do the work of one.

The Mazet Committee, Vol. I, 26 [1900].

We all realize that great injustice and inequality exist in these . . . burdens. We must make progress in these matters slowly. We must progress step by step, so that at the end . . . if we can have united upon some proposition, however simple, which will tend to better the conditions existing, and tend to more equitably distribute the burdens of taxation, we will have accomplished the purpose of this Conference.

E. E. WOODBURY
State Conference on Taxation, Addresses and Proceedings,
Utica, N.Y., January 12, 1911.

When we have examined all its parts without sentiment, and gauged all its functions by the standards of practical common sense, we shall have established anew our right to the claim of political sagacity; and it will remain only to act intelligently upon what our eyes have seen in order to prove again the justice of our claim to political genius.

WOODROW WILSON
Congressional Government [1885].

10

The Nature of the Achievement and the Anomaly of Party Finance

The remarkable range of changes which fiscal reformers set in train can be interpreted as a victory for the expansive values of one kind of democracy—the respectable and somewhat limited version of the dominant middle classes. But for the more plebian variety of democracy and the politicians serving it, the victory did not obviate the necessity of maintaining invisible governments and the dual money machinery which financed the responsibilities and rewards of political parties. A triumphant cult of efficiency (which might have dismissed politics with Pope's quip, "Over forms of government let fools contest; / That which is best administered is best," continued posing threats to the loyalty of political professionals and to the integrity of party supply lines. The flood of injunctions loosed through books, periodicals, learned journals, speeches, conferences, bulletins by organizations like the National Municipal League, tax and finance commission reports, special studies, state and local reform investigations, and muckraking exposés between the turn of the century and the early 1920's, bore innumerable administrative and technical refinements aimed at converting government into a "responsible" corporation. If the urbanized middle classes were going to sanction taxation and spending, they intended to strike even harder at what they regarded as extravagance, waste, inefficiency, graft, boodle, welfare, and other such accompaniments of party. They intended, just as the Mugwumps had, to take the *politics* out of governing.

They had every incentive to pursue this course, for a glaring anomaly confronted them. In the state and local dimensions, they assailed as chaotic the official side of their governments; yet in the extralegal and illegal dimensions, parties represented masterpieces of political organization, thoroughness, and efficiency. Early in the present century, Edgar Dawson, a close student of politics, sketched the point in detail for New Yorkers. The state's formal administration, spending forty millions a year and employing over fifteen thousand people, he found to be "a drifting, amorphous mass, as helpless as a field of seaweed in the ocean." Power was dispersed through nearly 170 units of administration, meaning that there was "no head, no manager, no directing will *legally constituted* to preside." But looking at "the extra-legal and unofficial side" of the same structure, Dawson was dazzled by the contrast presented by the two highly developed political parties. In their structure, in their state within the state, there were no "loose ends, no irresponsible agents, no scattered bureaus and commissions. From the head downward," wrote Dawson, "authority is clearly defined, obedience is punctiliously exacted; the hierarchy is closely interlinked, complete, effective."[1] Everything that the respectable man hoped for, barring the politics of it, had been created by disreputable men with other people's money.

For this reason, efforts were made to keep party in a straitjacket and if they ultimately proved abortive, they were nonetheless serious. Chester Lloyd Jones, an authority on political and economic problems at the University of Wisconsin during the LaFolette era, a man on the side of the angels against corruption and invisible government, rendered an equally accurate appraisal of this situation in 1916. Discoursing on the vital connections between spoils and party, Jones observed that whatever concessions were won by civil service reformers from opposing professional politicians would be determined in the last analysis by "the average voter" and "by the opinion of the political parties as to whether they can get along without the highly valuable perquisite—the power to distribute offices." To Jones the theoretical means of lessening demands for spoils lay through the creation of fresh party financial assets in three ways: the development of a class of "men of means, who being independently wealthy could devote themselves to public affairs" and bear the costs of their own candidacies; "dependence on the largesse of great economic interests;" and reliance upon the "rank and file" of the parties for small contributions. What experience the country had with the first two alternatives was highly unlikely to encourage much more. As to the third alternative, the most attractive of the lot to him, Jones could only remark that "not until we have a radical and at present at least unexpected change in the attitude of the average voter can we hope for a cutting down of the pressure for spoils through this means." To which he added:

> The increasing legitimate expense of campaigns coming at the same time as the popular demands for limitation of the sources, amount and purpose of political expenditures taken with the demand that the valuable asset of spoils be given up, puts the parties in a difficult position. In this situation corrupt practices acts and civil service reform come to stand in a peculiar relation to each other. The argument runs: if you limit too strictly the amount which may be spent in a campaign you must make it up by letting the candidate distribute offices—money value in another form.[2]

Reasoning among professional politicians, certainly, could hardly have run any other way, and indeed it did not. Their survival depended upon recognition of the dual purpose of state and local money machinery.

Despised, constantly under fire from some "reputable" quarter of the community, political machines early in the twentieth century continued resisting the reform of spoils and the restructuring of their tax base just as they had been doing since the 1870's while steadily adjusting their private fiscal system to wring advantages from the new money machines.

On occasion the professionals were forced to surrender their positions or watch them buckle under the economy and efficiency drives of middle-class amateurs, academic experts, and political defectors. What occurred in Boston early in this century was indicative of similar battles being fought elsewhere. From 1909 through 1912, the city's finance commission slashed away at waste and extravagance in municipal government. In 1911 alone, the reform-bent commission held 114 meetings, 155 hearings, and published 52 reports. A major objective of this industry was to flense the fat from city payrolls and destroy other varieties of graft which had developed over the preceding decades. It likewise sought to end "years of subordination of business [the business of government] to political considerations" and, accordingly, heavy attacks were launched against most of the major city departments, notably those handling paving, sewers, sanitary and street cleaning operations, as well as the water and fire departments and to a lesser extent, the school system.[3]

Various exposures were made. The president of the common council was convicted of approving a $200 bill for books which were never delivered; an alderman was caught, and later convicted, of having raised the stipulated amount of a bill, pocketing the surplus; the school system was found to be riddled with politics and the inferior quality of teachers was directly attributed to "political and personal influence in securing appointments." Several volumes of commission testimony revealed that "for political reasons large numbers of teamsters, watchmen, and other laborers, who were not actually needed" had been "employed and retained by the city" with the result that the reorganization and disciplining of these divisions on an "economic basis" had proven impossible which, as the commissioners specified, meant that costs to taxpayers ran into "millions of dollars."[4]

Since reform in Boston as elsewhere really implied that the middle classes were distressed about the way money was being spent, events following these exposures took their usual course. Civil service and merit devices were extended by the reformers; payroll acts were enacted requiring close and responsible accounting; and wasteful or inefficient laborers were dropped from public employment. Departmental hirings were frozen or made sticky; work loads among trained personnel, in the fire and police departments for example, were increased, and so on.

To these actions, political reactions were swift and ingenious. "Emergency men" and "students" appeared on the payrolls of departments under the nominal aegis of civil service. In the street department, for instance, from 220 to 360 "emergency laborers" were hired between April and August, a period during which the civil service commission noted that "there were no snowstorms." Pay for such labor exceeded $2500 a week and all told such hirings cost the city hundreds of thousands of dollars. Overtime payments also rose in several departments and toward Christmas, the mayor paid favored employees bonuses which thereafter appeared on the city's books as overtime. Efforts to achieve economies in the highly politicized fire department, even to stripping the fire commissioner of his authority to regulate the hours of service within the department, served only to produce a bid for the firemen's vote at the subsequent mayoralty election—a successful one from which sprang an ordinance granting the men one day off in five instead of one in eight. The upshot was a drastic reduction in the number of firemen available for duty, as few as one-seventh of the force required in some ladder companies, so that the finance commission itself was obliged to request the hiring of additional men. As to the reformation of unwholesome practices in the school system, the "new rules" imposed by reform were judged "good as far as they went" by the commission, yet the opportunities for favoritism continued to be used by school board members. "Secret influence and often ruthlessly exercised power of the small subcommittees in charge of individual schools," it was reported, "did much to destroy the value of reform."[5] The Augean stables could scarcely have been more difficult to cleanse.

Were spoils kept intact? The answer in Boston was reflected in the city's general record of hirings. In the water department, for example, between 1895 and 1900 although changes in water distribution resulted in a 15% reduction in departmental work, the labor force increased by 50% or by 350 men. During the thirteen years from 1895 to 1907, the street and water departments, which together accounted for the bulk of the city's laborers, increased from 2931 to 4209 employees, with an increment in payroll allotments of more than one million dollars. The trend evident here did not change; in 1911–12, for instance, city and county employees rose by 324 men. The nature of the appointments was fairly obvious in most cases since the rate of growth was four times greater in departments under the mayor's control than elsewhere.[6]

Singular as Boston liked to think it was, its brand of payroll or money graft was common everywhere, for it was everywhere considered essential to the financing of party. Harold Howland of *The Outlook's* editorial staff informed a Buffalo gathering of the National Municipal League in 1910 that investigations of Chicago's sewer department revealed a typical municipal situation; payments to gangs of laborers who cleaned catch-basins ran from two and a half to three and a half times more than they reasonably should have, all of which was manna for the faithful, their faith being demonstrated by a tax paid to party worthies and by their loyal votes. Downstate, in Springfield, Illinois, party assessments and votes had also remained a commodity. There, Howland noted, a sixty-year-old blacksmith padded the payroll as a $3-a-day stenographer; thirteen men drew salaries for raising and lowering windows in two legislative chambers; and one employee received $3 a day for winding a clock once a week. So it went Back East in New York City; nearly $20,000 a year was being paid to keep cleaning men on the job in the Bronx Borough Hall when the job could have been handled by the retention of only $1800 worth of labor. None of these random selections was remarkable for its rarity.[7]

Such activities were normal in many strata of American life; party was just a portion of a continuum. Chauffeurs took kickbacks from repairmen; cooks took petty rake-offs from local butchers and greengrocers; prospective buyers expected and accepted presents or entertainment from prospective sellers; building superintendents took tips or private retainers to perform services for which everyone assumed they had been hired; city inspectors and health officers were tipped for their winks or favors; doctors and lawyers exchanged graft with hospitals and police courts, with bailbondsmen, medical, and bar examiners, with insurance companies, and with each other.

In the early twentieth century, graft was defined by reformers as the use of public office for private gain; but in reality graft often defied such literal and simplistic definition. It was a deeply rooted style of life in a loose society wedded to success and to the acquisition of money and power. Because it underlay the financing of party which created the process which in turn rendered government possible, public and private gain remained, in default of viable alternatives, an inseparable part of politics. Explaining the "true source of corruption" in 1892, Henry Carter Adams roundly averred that he could pinpoint it in a sentence: "the final explanation of municipal corruption is found in the fact that the present organization of society does not properly correlate public and private activity." Adams made it clear in subsequent discussion that this canker infected all American society, and no doubt he was correct. A popular phenomenon, graft was part of the very fiber of political parties and, though private organizations, parties inevitably viewed their interests as synonymous with the public interest—or they did whenever they had to think about such matters at all. It was too much to expect that reformers would expunge such pervasive attitudes and practices swiftly—and while the level of public morality as it was narrowly defined undoubtedly rose with the expansion of democracy, graft was not expunged.[8]

Attacks on graft as a component of party fiscal activity throughout the progressive era were frequently well-informed and courageous; however, courage did not insure success. For by creating a new official tax base through the renovation of the old money machinery and by establishing the functional basis for the vastly expanded governmental operations which urban life demanded, the urban middle class paradoxically allowed the political machines they detested to salvage their fortunes. In actuality, they afforded parties expanded opportunities for old as well as for newer styles of graft by inadvertently permitting them to develop a broader tax base of their own.

Generally speaking, there were two sets of reasons for this. The first, obviously, was that state and municipal governments handled ever-growing sums of money and ever-larger debts. With the exception of some counties and townships, all levels of government taxed, bought, spent, and borrowed more each succeeding year shortly after the turn of the century.

Continuing the pattern of earlier years, public expenditures in New York State and in the City of Boston provide overall indications of what happened in the states and cities of the North. Examining New York's situation in 1916, the Mills Committee reported that between 1885 and 1914 state expenditures, exclusive of interest on debts, sinking funds, and trust funds, rose by 500% while population increased by 82%, a per capita increase of 235%. If this placed New York somewhat in advance of other governments, it was not by much; the costs of federal government over the same time span rose by 400% against an 84% increase in population, while the average cost of all state governments between 1903 and 1913 increased by nearly 106% with only a 20% growth in population. From the perspectives of Albany's Special Joint

Committee on Taxation and Retrenchment in 1926 matters looked much the same as they had a decade earlier to the Mills Committee, even after allowances were made for changes in the value of the dollar.[9]

But the tribulations of states such as New York were no more acute than those involved in the financing of municipal governments. Famed for its profligacy during the nineteenth century, Boston had done nothing to diminish that reputation during the early twentieth century. Man for man, Bostonians as late as 1918 were paying directly over $48 a year to maintain their city's official expenditures; in none of the other ten largest cities of the country were per capita burdens this high. Bostonians, in fact, were paying fully $14 more toward city expenditures per capita than figures indicated were being paid in the rest of the nation's cities with populations over 30,000. By 1906, city spending pressed close to the $20 million mark while indebtedness rose to 10% of the value of its realty—over $100 million. Appropriations during three typical mayoralty administrations between 1909 and 1912 which had led reformers to warn that Boston's great wealth encouraged assumptions that the city's "capacity for bearing financial burdens was practically unlimited" indicate the trend on which the illicit and extra-legal features of party money machinery were able to capitalize. Each year saw bigger appropriations from taxes and revenues by the mayor and city council. When Mayor Hibbard left office in 1910 appropriations hit nearly $20 million. The first year of Mayor Fitzgerald's administration showed an increase of more than $450,000 and the second year an increase of almost $2 million over that record figure, or more than $2,390,000 over Hibbard's record. In terms of opportunity, politicians who were out of pocket for election expenses discovered a veritable bonanza in situations of this kind; in a sense, it may be fairer to say that instead of discovering them they helped create them.[10]

Such opportunities were not peculiar to the politicians of New York State or of Boston. Nationally, the states increased their expenditures in real dollars by 100% between 1902 and 1913 and doubled them again in the following decade, and municipal increments were fully commensurate with those of the states.[11]

Opportunities for political machines to use the growing sums of money flowing through government channels were increased by changes in the types of expenditures being made and by the functions of state and municipal debts. Early in the 1920's, for example, when Al Smith was governor of New York, the state was spending money in substantially different ways than it had a generation earlier. Only one-fifth of its operating expenditures was officially for activities the state had undertaken prior to 1880; the remaining 79% was spent on responsibilities assumed afterward. Nearly $25 million dollars, or over one-fifth of the entire state expenditure, went for activities undertaken after 1900. Thus, public works, which alone had accounted for almost 45% of state spending in 1850, was largely displaced by various welfare activities that by 1900 accounted for over one-third of its spending. Education, highway construction and maintenance, institutional care for the criminal and the insane, regulatory activities, agricultural promotion, and health, (although individually quite variable proportions of expenditures) together gave state spending its main character: a blending of the ambitions of two political concepts of democracy, one insistent mainly on direct or indirect economic subvention, the other politically committed to resource development through welfare spending.[12]

All this expenditure was political; all passed through the hands of men whose outlooks were largely shaped by party viewpoints; it was spent chiefly with an eye to party requirements. Where highways were built or improved and who was hired to labor on them, were political decisions; where institutions were located, what their appropriations were, constituted political decisions affecting the local structure of political power, local employment and payrolls, and general economic activity; how large a grant-in-aid the state made to counties for education was a political decision, and so on. Money, payroll, and privilege graft, all important to party machinery, had ample play here.

Although familiar forms of graft remained important to party finance, critics of the political establishment, sustained by impressive evidence, noted the rising frequency of what the inimitable Plunkitt dubbed "investment and foresight," or graft involving inside information concerning the thousands of contracts governments entered into. Boston's infamous Fenway scandals of 1904–5, for example, resulted from Mayor Collins' superintendent of streets having raised a large sum for Collins' reëlection from municipal contractors who then benefited from their association with the administration. Changes in high office altered the situation little. Between 1910 and 1912, Boston's Mayor Fitzgerald awarded 818 contracts to private interests each valued at more than $1000 apiece, a total of more than $7 million. Ten percent of these contracts were never advertised and among the rest irregularities and favoritism were common whether the contract concerned equipment for the Paris Street Gymnasium or street lighting apparatus.[13]

Obviously, as a mountain of evidence attests, Boston was in no sense exceptional. New York City's Bureau of Municipal Research revealed scores of instances in which Tammany let contracts at exorbitant prices for kickbacks and campaign contributions. Tin dippers worth sixty cents to the dozen were sold to the city for more than three times as much by a favored firm; iron valves worth six cents apiece were sold to it for twenty-five times as much; and where it bought and paid for one hundred tons of coal, the city received only half that amount. Opportunities of this sort abounded everywhere as budgets grew and The City became an industry in itself. In Schenectady, otherwise one of the least scandal-ridden polities in the state, municipal leaders in 1909–10 paid an electrical contractor for labor and materials which were never employed subsequently. Chicago's political guardians let a $45,000 contract for removal of shale from a sewer excavation where there was no rock whatever and, according to a citizens' committee, further paid a foundry company $30,000 more for waterworks castings than they were worth. It was much the same everywhere; only the size of the operations varied. To win contracts for holding Pittsburgh's $9 million in city deposits and for other inside favors concerning the sale of municipal bonds, the community's six leading banks paid out $105,000 in graft to the local administration for defrayment of party expenses. None of these opportunities for party financiers could be checked in the short run of things, as the Mills Committee correctly noted, "unless . . . the people of the State desire a complete change of public policy, and are prepared to limit the activities of government." Barring this shift, of which there were no signs, "there is little likelihood," declared the committee, "with the growing population and with the increased complexities of modern life, of any material decrease, no matter what administrative economies may be effected."[14]

Party necessities, individual greed, the lack of businesslike procedures, large legislative bodies, absentee government of the cities, and the lax regulation of public service corporations were all blamed for their aggravation of this situation. But Simon Sterne, a noted reformer and economist of sorts, who had gained familiarity with urban finance in New York during service in 1877 on the commission to devise a system of government for the cities of the state, wrote in the nineties of a slightly broader setting to the fiscal opportunism connected with public contracts:

> Two mistaken roads seem to have been followed in all legislation in this country as to cities . . . which have resulted in disaster. Insufficient analysis which has prevented our people from seeing that a city is at one and the same time a decentralized portion of the general government of the State, and a co-operative organization of property owners for the administration of private property. The mayor, when he enforces an ordinance for the preservation of the public health . . . is a public officer deriving his authority from the suffrages of the citizens in whose midst he holds sway. The mayor, when he signs an ordinance for the grading and regulating of a street between certain avenues. . . . is a mere instrument to make and enforce a contract between property owners.

Since the people who owned property through which a street was to be cut could rarely be expected to come to quick agreement about it, explained Sterne, the law expediently made "contracts through the instrumentality of the mayor for them." Legalities aside, Sterne was attempting to avoid the fictions about what government *ought* to be, the better to define it functionally; and in these contractual functions, as in so many others, the line between public and private was very obscure to men in power.[15] In politics obscureness in financial matters and opportunity were the same thing.

Along with large public contracts, public debts also became important adjuncts to party money machinery by the early part of this century. Because of their size and expansiveness this proved especially true of municipal debts. To be sure, indebtedness was uncongenial to many and the taint of debt made it tricky to use openly for party service. The obligations incurred in New York City during the depredations of Tweed, for example, were widely considered an abomination among respectable men, while experts and reformers generally found indebtedness an appalling evidence of the cities' disregard "for every rule laid down by the science of finance." To these men, debts were unsavory political reactions to public outcries for more governmental involvement in a variety of "unnecessary purposes;" or they were political responses, equally unsavory and unwise, to public demands "in excess of the requirements of economical expenditure" for essential purposes. Worse yet, as a close look at reform arguments over the years before the common council of Buffalo indicates, the handling of debts by political authorities seemed to them unduly mysterious. The "entire business" reputedly was "so veiled behind municipal bonds and suppressed contracts" that the public was kept "in general ignorance." The upshot of this was all the more pernicious, reformers believed, because of the public's unawareness that rigid debt limits established for the cities by state legislatures were frequently being circumvented by special legislation.[16] This, of course, was a matter of practical as well as of "moral" concern. In Boston, for instance, by 1909 30% of the assessed taxes had to be funneled into the payment of interest on the city's debt requirements. Thus, Justice Brewer's remark that the worst of all "trusts" was "trust in the future" possessed a special significance for many staid and reputable Bostonians, but the dubiety and repugnance toward debt implicit in his comment were general attitudes.[17]

Nevertheless, in the cities particularly, by the close of the nineteenth century, these traditional attitudes were going out of style; they were shrinking to a rhetorical convenience which, like opposition to Sin, was more honored in the breach than in the observance. These urban groups stylistically foreshadowed mid-twentieth century America in fiscal outlook and habit. Time and again both politicians and businessmen discovered that public spending and public indebtedness were useful and rewarding—at least at a functional, if not always at an intellectual, level this was increasingly true. The self-conscious employment of indebtedness in urban finance was an accompaniment of a politicized commercial democracy straining, for the most part successfully, to wrench free of taboos inherited from the days of monarchs and aristocrats, of destructive city mobs, and the dominance of heavy country minds. Prevalent theories of public finance left little room for such deviations and when they occurred deplored them. According to "leading" economists, cities should rarely have required deficit financing of the type undertaken during eras of internal improvement or times of crisis by state or national governments; but if this was the higher economic wisdom it was pointedly ignored in practice. In the Northern cities, while denying and denouncing their own actions every step of the way, many Americans were pragmatically converting their public indebtedness into a public virtue under the interested and mutually profitable guidance of their urban political machines.

Thus, just as cities in all of their dimensions were exerting tremendous influence upon the strategy and structure of great economic enterprises, so too they were the scene of a reshaping of fiscal necessities and fiscal habits. "It is not, then, an accident that the expansion of local credit took place almost immediately after the states had been shoved off the stage of industrial action," wrote Henry Carter Adams perceptively in 1887. Less than twenty years later "credit-financiering as a part of local administration" ostensibly in "subservience" to what Adams deemed popular wishes was everywhere being conducted on the premise "that . . . enterprises . . . of a private nature might rightfully receive the assistance of the local treasury."[18]

Such developments were partially an outgrowth of the aggressive spirit associated with urban business and politics, but one of their main causes was the contribution which they made to the financing of party money machinery.

To politicians debt and spending became many splendored things. They allowed them, first of all, to draw support from the very segments of propertied society upon whom taxes bore with increasing weight and who consequently furnished the most vociferous crusaders for economy and efficiency. The seductions were transparent. In cities, fresh demands for spending were arising constantly and the creation of sinking funds, the issuance of bonds, the multiplication of floating debts to care for them, afforded an escape from immediate burdens and the promise of an immediate profit for many interested parties. Real estate interests, for instance, almost invariably in the van of fiscal reform movements, faced and succumbed to tempting speculations which public indebtedness could and did abet; the roads, sewers, utilities, schools, and other public improvements useful for increasing the value of existing realty and attracting ever larger populations to particular areas could thereby come more swiftly. As early as 1868, a Pennsylvania commission observed that "the undue accumulation of debt in most cities of the State . . . has been the result of a desire for speculation on the part of the owners of property themselves." To which the same commission added:

> Large tracts of land outside the built-up portion of cities have been purchased, combinations made by men of wealth . . . largely in advance of the real necessities of the city. In many of these cases, owners of property need more protection against themselves than against the non-property-holding class.[19]

Speculators, often wrongly to be sure, gambled that improvements undertaken by municipalities through "credit-financiering" would never overtake them because of the attendant rises in property values and in the expansion of business. Men of substance, realtors, bankers, construction men, contractors, manufacturers, and suppliers of the varied equipage essential to urban growth, in this way first acceded to municipal indebtedness and then encouraged it. Thus did politicians without resort to Hamilton's grand manner achieve Hamiltonian ends. At the most dynamic level of government, the municipal level, they established another link between rising public debts and deficit spending on the one hand and the prosperity of political parties and the interests helping to sustain them on the other. What the politicos had recognized and begun to control was the discovery by the middle classes of *public welfare* for themselves and the relegation of *free enterprise* to the lower orders.[20]

Turning the renovated money machines of city and state governments to party purposes, however novel and necessary it was, still failed of itself to solve the basic problem of how parties were to be financed adequately and legitimately in an environment which was either niggardly toward them or flatly hostile. This situation may actually have grown more acute in many areas of the North by the early twentieth century, thanks to signs of decline in party strength or enthusiasm. Factionalism, bi-partisanship or non-partisanship, indifference, decreased membership, decreasing expenditures for campaigns, and a general lack of élan, were all believed to be making serious inroads into organizational power. Of party distress in Michigan, for example, Arthur Millspaugh, then a young political scientist, wrote from Whitman College that party was "caught . . . between legislation which saps its vitality and cripples its action and an independent opinion which either ignores it or seeks openly to destroy it."[21] Political organizations whose excess zeal had been a subject of great concern only a few years before seemed unable any longer to generate much interest. Although officially much had changed in respect to fiscal attitudes and practices, nevertheless, it was reasonable for the English commentator, Sydney Brooks, to remind readers of the *North American Review* in 1911 that the more America changed, the more there remained a "sameness of the questions that engage American attention," party financial questions prominent among them.[22]

Evidence from state and municipal investigations, from reformist and muckraking exposures, scholarly studies. and the frank admission of politicians indicates that the extralegal supplies of party funds continued to be tied closely to the assessment of candidates and officeholders, the taxation of interested individuals and corporations, subscriptions at club or convention meetings among the faithful, and donations from party clubs. Even after President Theodore Roosevelt, for instance, tried making an example of Lincoln Avery, a prominent Michigan Republican boss, by firing him from a customs collectorship for allowing political taxation among his employees, little changed. Later the very year of Roosevelt's assault, state employees in Lansing were assessed 2% of their salaries by the party. "They came down here to get soft places," observed a Democratic politician in Detroit in 1912 of local officeholders, "and it's only reasonable . . . they should help out on campaign expenses."[23] Neither of Michigan's parties could dispense with this type of financing. Across the Northern tier of states, this aspect of party money machinery, despite the advantages vouchsafed political organizations by growing budgets, stayed substantially intact. Where officials and officeholders were not formally assessed, out of deference to legislation against it which became much commoner after 1912, papers were circulated by party leaders indicating that workers were expected to contribute—and there is ample evidence that in many places assessments were pressed right up to the limit of 10% of the officeholder's salary. What was true of assessments also held true in spirit and practice for party's other extralegal revenues—and as had been so often demonstrated in the past, the fountainhead of these taxes too was public money.

If circumstances dictated retention of most of the extralegal mechanisms of party finance elaborated in the nineteenth century, many of the same circumstances likewise dictated the heavy reliance by much of the party organization on illegal revenues: graft, bribes, and blackmail drawn from criminal enterprises. Just as larger governmental budgets afforded opportunities for extension of the parties' tax bases, so attempts by "Puritan" legislatures to govern "pagan" cities opened wide another set of opportunities that greatly stimulated the economic vitality of party fiscal operations.[24]

We can never expect to know, in most instances, the full extent of these revenues. Certainly they varied greatly between Ingham County, Michigan and Manhattan; and they doubtless varied as campaign styles changed. But since we have such voluminous testimony on the nature and methods of "the system," as New Yorkers called it, we cannot doubt that in the larger cities these revenues ran into millions of dollars a year. General Bingham, one of the less popular, hence in his official career more short-lived, chief police commissioners of New York City, estimated that in 1912 if he had collaborated with "the system," he might easily have raked off $1 million a year. Overall, he guessed that $100 million in "revenues" moved through the illicit conduits linking politicians with criminal entrepreneurs. No doubt these figures were exaggerated, however soberly they were stated; nonetheless, if only 25% correct the amounts involved were huge.[25]

The new money machinery of the North functioned in two worlds; careful administrative studies, tax conference, academic analyses, and the high politics of reputable interests designed to gear these machines to middle-class visions of prosperity, all mirrored one set of realities; the dual tax system of America's invisible government rooted in the Camorra-like wards where political mamelukes and janissaries bought and sold protection with few apparent delusions about abstractions such as the public interest, mirrored another set of realities. Yet however distant from one another, the Seligmans and the Wells, on the one hand, and the criminal ward bosses, on the other, were all parts of an endless chain of party finance.[26]

Even at a mundane level, the dramatization of this was sometimes violent, involving in the one instance the assassination of Herman Rosenthal, the proprietor of an uptown Manhattan gambling den, on July 16, 1912. Lured from the Hotel Metropole at two in the morning onto the most brilliantly lighted strip of Broadway, Rosenthal was slain by four men who emerged from a touring car and emptied their revolvers into him. The assassins escaped without difficulty although there were half a dozen policemen within a stone's throw. The killing was not senseless. Two days earlier, Rosenthal, a top man in his profession, shaken down and driven to the wall by his silent partners on the police force, had sought out the district attorney, promising detailed revelations of "the system," the ways in which enterprises requiring political protection were assessed by the police. Having threatened the power of the "state," Rosenthal had expected death at the hands of his tax collectors, an expectation in which neither he nor the New York newspapers were disappointed. In a sense his slaying simply marked the passing of another embittered taxpayer.

The handling of the Rosenthal murder by the board of aldermen, the grand jury, the criminal branch of the state's supreme court, and the district attorney, who labored, it was noted, with an "inspiriting efficiency [and] absolute fearlessness," was fully in keeping with American precedent; the house cleaning which ensued, as Mr. Dooley suggested, was not accomplished by sprinkling the walls with cologne. Masses of evidence gleaned from attenuated, diffuse, and detailed examinations bared what everyone who had lived an unsheltered life had long known or suspected about the structure and financing of the city's invisible government. Conditions which the Lexow Committee had unearthed eighteen years before and the Mazet Committee had rediscovered in 1901, along with the findings of Manhattan's famous Committees of Fourteen and Fifteen, despite communal purges and soul-searching, were found to be flourishing.

The Rosenthal affair with its hurricane of revelations was a reminder that just as professional politicians drew party revenues from "respectable" interests whose money entered the official money machinery of municipal government as taxes, so professionals also dominated and drew revenues from the community's handsomely supported demimonde and underworld, well-integrated communities in their own right. "Crime in New York," wrote Sydney Brooks in the autumn of 1912, was not "an individual aberration" but "a business, massed, brigaded . . . organized at every point" and "controlled by the politicians." The anxiety manifested publicly by Tammany's leadership during the Rosenthal investigation stressed what was at stake for those who had been farming underworld taxes.[27]

Despite striking similarities, the institutions being exposed in 1912 were even more labyrinthine than they had been several decades before, primarily because they were more extensive and better, or at least differently, organized. Levies were determined by politicians who purveyed protection, the basic service of all government. Assessment and collection, in the hands of one kind of politicized assessor at the legal level, were entrusted to the police as the legality of the community's enterprises tapered off into the raw climes of some Tammany districts. Threats which might have been posed to the security of this system by the honesty, zeal, or innocence of police commissioners were readily neutralized. As Manhattan Commissioner Bingham explained:

> I had scarcely moved into the office in Mulberry Street when political leaders began to call upon me, for the most part to secure a continual shifting of the police for plausible but mysterious ends of their own. . . . I found . . . that among the officers of the force there were very few I could trust to carry out my orders in good faith. The reason was very simple. I was head of the Department for an indeterminate period, which might end at any time. Back of me was the mayor,

> who chose me, and whose office would also end at an early date. Back of him was the permanent political machine which elected him. As the policeman is in office for life, he very logically looked past both the mayor and me, and made his alliances with, and took his orders from, the only permanent influence concerned—the politicians.[28]

But that was only one aspect of the matter.

Political control of the police alone could not insure the security of "the system;" it always remained possible that the laws of New York's urban and rural middle classes might be invoked against it successfully, partly out of partisan motives aimed at jeopardizing the fiscal sources upon which opposing political factions relied, and partly from principle. Reformers always seemed to believe that much of New York's organized crime could have been suppressed in short order had the magistrates performed their duties. Adherents of the system accordingly felt it essential to politicize the city's fourteen police magistracies; and these ends were brilliantly achieved. Duties, of course, the magistrates did perform, but not the ones critics of the system had in mind. It was correctly understood that magistrates were "bought and owned at the disposal of the local political machine." Most of them could be "seen;" those who were financially honest were "politically dishonest." Everything conspired to make their subservience feasible. They gained place through appointment by the mayor. The mayor, in turn, as testimony contemporary with the Rosenthal murder showed, owed his post "to the politicians, who in turn owe their power to their thorough control and organization of the criminal and alien classes." It was a fairly airtight arrangement which rendered many forms of crime "the safest and most lucrative professions open to the ambitious New Yorker" while helping to keep one of the world's most complex governments viable. Investigations of other local scandals, meantime, in Penrose's Philadelphia or in the Chicago of Bath House John were, except for nuances, repetitions of the tale told in Manhattan.

Thus by the eve of the country's first great crusade to make the world safe for democracy, with Progressivism everywhere victorious, if nowhere permanent, the financial systems on which the vital extralegal portions of state and local government depended were light years removed from the expectations of the Boston Adamses or the stolidly solvent folk of Mt. Desert Township. If nothing else, Rosenthal's slaying reminded a few of the men who survived him that "a recasting of some of the average American's most cherished theories in regard to the structure and practice of local government" was long overdue. The cherished theory, in truth, would remain intact in wide areas of the middle class for many years to come. In the meantime, throughout the polities of the North, ordinary citizens with their normal ambivalence about party had adjusted to their twentieth century catchpenny realities.

Epilogue

During the sixty years which followed the Civil War, renovation and modernization of the money machinery of the Northern states was achieved detail by detail; it was a laborious process and, for the greater part, unsensational. As *process,* whether reform was conducted by specialists, private associations, or public commissions, it fell far short of the objective ideal later stated by men like Felix Frankfurter; namely, "to deflate feeling, define issues, sift evidence, formulate remedies . . . ascertain facts, pose problems, and enlighten the public mind."[29] And yet, however short of the total ideal, it is perhaps more remarkable that none of these criteria composing the ideal was absent from the reform process. This was true despite the vast blind spots which even in advanced states such as New York made it impossible for reformers or critics to describe accurately or completely the distribution of burdens through the population, to amass sufficient data to divide the varied interests of the states into useful categories, or to determine with much accuracy or certainty if or how fiscal burdens were being shifted or what their incidence really was.

Insofar as the course of change was marked by any dynamic focus, it centered about the fears and aspirations of important elements of the urban middle class, around the experts and professional politicians of the great public corporations, the cities, and around their interactions with spokesmen for the highly differentiated world of private corporations. Their motives were not often clearly illuminated, but their actions were informed by a high degree of technical skill in matters political and economic, by generous measures of common sense, and by a reasonable adherence to principle as they and their peers understood it. To be sure, as reformers there was little about them that solicits our compassion, for they were not among the multitudes of disadvantaged or dispossessed Americans; they enjoyed both advantage and special privilege. Yet it is nonetheless true that sweeping change in their time made their positions uneasy and uncertain; events did not move as they hoped or expected and they had few clues about where they were heading. New to the kind of power that they were beginning to exercise, their enormous smugness in some regards dissolved into an enormous insecurity in others. The bold face put upon affairs by reformers and experts as well as by businessmen and politicians masked considerable timidity and caution. Their aggressions, although made no more tolerable by the fact, were sometimes panicky measures of self-defense. Moreover, they did demonstrate the ability to learn, even if they obscured it by insisting rhetorically upon things which they had previously jettisoned in practice. Their paths, indeed, were littered with abandoned preconceptions and, if reluctantly, they nevertheless accepted compromises to which they were never entirely adjusted.

Obviously, that was the better face of the matter, for the careers of men from these same circles were frequently marred by speciousness, cant, hypocrisy, narrow self-interest, and chicane. As men who lived beyond the pale of respectability quickly recognized, the behavior of middle-class and corporate representatives sometimes linked them functionally if not actually with certain of the criminal classes. The major difference lay in the middle class's general command over judicial and legislative machinery; to a notorious degree for some of these elements, interest and expediency dictated and power was expected thereafter to sanctify.

Yet regardless of the behavior of men who, honorably or otherwise, controlled the money machines, it is still the divisions among and between them and other interest groups that impresses us; for from these differences and the attendant disagreements came the considerable limitations placed on the potential power of each group involved. The reconstruction of state and local fiscal systems was a strikingly democratic process. This was not true because in a supposedly democratic society, anti-democratic forces failed and true democrats triumphed; nor was it the case because controversies over fiscal machinery or party finances evoked mass participation. It was democratic because of the pluralism of the total situation; over time, each of the many active minorities through argument and appeals which reached every significant element of the populace, urban and rural, managed to gain *something* but none by its avowed objectives managed to triumph *fully.*

The relative absence of certain groups from the vital centers of events or their relative passivity or negativism, under the circumstances, appears somewhat anomalous. With notable exceptions, neither the very rich nor the very poor played sustained, active roles in shaping most of these developments. The rich made their mark by their escape or attempted flight from public obligation, although perversely this had a significant effect on the growth and vigor of tax-haven communities and on the inter-regional distribution of wealth and industry. The poor, an absolute majority of the population throughout the period, when their opinions were detectable and when they were not obviously indifferent to fiscal issues, were reported cynically amused by what seemed to them a fight among the well-to-do over burdens which more ordinary men were not constrained to bear. Yet the opportunities created by their latent votes and the drain established by their demands for assistance and welfare required the unceasing attention of politicians and hence of party fiscal machinery; incapable of being an actively constructive force, they were witlessly both a corrupting *and* a reformist influence.

For their part, unlike the relatively passive majorities of rich and poor, the rural middle classes were essentially a negative, though very important factor in the breakdown and reformation of Northern money machines. The reasons for their influence were obvious. They had substantially fashioned the old arrangements—the old *reforms* of the forties and fifties—based on general property taxation, so that their traditional affection for it tended to dominate, as well as give their fiscal character, to rural-oriented and increasingly malapportioned legislatures. Through an honest intransigeance born of direct and unfortunate experience, through ignorance and righteous prejudice mixed with petty greed, they not only fastened evils of which they complained upon themselves but gratuitously performed the same disservice for the people of the spreading cities, many of whom were as anxious as countrymen to tap the intangible wealth of rich men and great corporations. At heavy cost to themselves and to others, therefore, farmers undoubtedly delayed fiscal reform, certainly in any modern sense, everywhere. Whether in some long view of things these debits and delays were offset by extended discussion, education, and experiment on fiscal questions is perhaps open to what must surely be an unresolvable debate.

Even after the roles of rural and urban middle classes, experts, politicians, and businessmen have been identified, it still remains true that the complexity of the money machinery in its dual aspects leaves the record of change a diffuse one. The vast alterations necessary to finance expansive and deeply ramified popular governments and political parties in urban-industrial communities and in an ever more businesslike countryside were not the handiwork of any single prophet, despite the involvement of a number of social and economic seers in the process. Perhaps because of the anarchic localizing effect of a federalism operative throughout thousands of political units, neither an outstanding individual nor institution emerged to guide the *entire* career of fiscal reform, irrespective of contributions by scores of outstanding individuals and institutions to the pioneering of specific innovations or the handling of particular aspects of reform. In this connection, it must be noted that the work of political economists and technical experts for various state and local governments prefigured their invaluable—and always controversial—roles in government since the First World War. Between the seventies and the turn of the century, where they have been least noticed, the activities of these men deserve especially close attention. However, despite them, there was still no grand strategy for anyone proposing change to follow; whatever it may have been *morally*, *practically* the Single Tax made no sense to most of the men of George's generation; American complexities were simply too great to accommodate it. While a rudimentary science of finance emerged from the reforming processes and interacted importantly with it, a comprehensive strategy did not precede it and thereby instruct it. Furthermore, reform remained somewhat lopsided, for no positive attention was devoted by these "scientific theories" either to the existence or the exigencies of party finance.

More than any others, political considerations determined nearly every step of reform at every level of government. The advice of experts and the importunings and calculations of businessmen alike when they threatened to interfere were usually subordinated to politics. Last words are rarely possible on such subjects, needless to say, but there is certainly as much evidence to persuade us to abandon the general conviction that businessmen bought out and subsequently dominated our political establishments at state and local levels as there is to hold us to this view. We cannot doubt, of course, that commencing in the last third of the nineteenth century, the concept and structure of professionalized political parties came under sharp and intelligent attack from several quarters within the middle classes of the cities. Attempts to purge government of "politics" and transform it into a business run according to a middle-class cult of efficiency, much of which revolved around the redesigning and control of the money machinery, were prosecuted with great energy. Some of these anti-political drives arose from deep anti-democratic biases, others from a very restricted interpretation of democracy, still others from varieties of economic or political self-interest. None of these outlooks left much room for the inclusion of the masses and all displayed an interest at one time or another in actually rolling back the suffrage, especially in municipalities. Together, these eminently "respectable" sentiments gave impetus to one of the most powerful assaults ever launched against the *party system.*

Events admittedly cannot be abstracted from their contexts, but had it been achieved, a total victory for reform might have proven as great a political disaster for Americans as a total victory for powerful elements of business. In retrospect, we can hardly contemplate either possibility with equanimity. As it was, the enemies of party displayed some wisdom. They accurately discerned that urban demography had rendered extreme forms of partisanship obsolete, if not dangerous; they correctly grasped that the fiscal systems of New York and Boston, as well as of London, Rome, Paris, and Berlin were best handled as if they had certain non-political economic and administrative dimensions. Their alarms about the urban masses wielding power, or having power wielded in their name, badly, ignorantly, and corruptly, their fears about the social barbarism strikingly characteristic of urban-industrialism were well-founded. Moreover, considering the political records and the administrative capacities of the governments of their day, their suspicions about and their resistance to government interventions in economic life were oftentimes wise. That much must be said for them. Yet in a visceral way, party professionals had developed their own collective wisdom too. The suffrage had spread throughout the land before the urban middle classes rose to power and demands from below for favors, boodle, assistance, and welfare were realities with which they lived cheek by jowl. These were demands which the fiscal machinery of government were unable to service adequately. This incapacity was more than the consequence of neglect or opposition on the part of the dominant elites; two more generations of administrative experience would have to be accumulated before grand official efforts could be undertaken here and then not always with significant success, as the New Deal revealed. Meanwhile, making what use they could of existing governmental machinery, professional politicos solicited power by partially performing these services privately and, for the most part, beyond the bounds of the law.

The task of governing Americans in their local polities and paying for it was, therefore, a dual operation *within* the dualities of federalism. Functionally, it lent a magnitude to the careers of many nineteenth and early twentieth century governments which the traditional economic and political viewpoints have ignored. In this light, complaints about unconscionable fiscal burdens coupled with distress about the intensive politicization of life were justifiable; so much was this the case, in fact, that when government and party are treated properly as interpenetrations of one another in terms of their financial activities, the growth of formal governmental establishments during the twentieth century appears less of a great leap than we have supposed. What we have witnessed has been the enlargement and ramification of the official side of government activities which in 1880 or 1910 were still extralegal or illegal enterprises of the parties. Thus, for example, the parties' assessment of jobholders and political candidates, the political levies against corporations and certain criminal businesses on the basis of their ability to pay, in effect, have been formally incorporated into state income taxes or into a variety of special taxes on their earnings during this century. Similarly, what the parties once spent to perpetuate themselves in office or spent in response to demands for the subsidization of private business interests or for private welfare are now sanctioned officially; in that *official* sanction and in the *formal* mating of two versions of democracy alone lies their novelty.

The political conjunction of these two strains of democracy, each of which manifested a functional suppleness, created by 1925 money machinery whose official dimensions at least were sufficient to the basic needs of modern government. However imperfectly, a great shift in *kind* had been accomplished in fiscal theories and practice; the great shift in *scale* had to wait for the Second World War. But the major financial tools of the New Deal had been foreshadowed in developments in the cities of the North where practical experience was being acquired in relatively large spending, much of it either officially or unofficially for welfare, and in learning to live with deficits and indebtedness, most of which proved profitable to many local interests which eschewed them ideologically. New bases of taxation had been created out of the North's new wealth and having won firm support in legislation they were blessed by the courts. The flow of money into local treasuries certainly failed to satisfy everyone, but the reservoirs upon which treasuries drew as well as the conduits leading to them were more substantial than they had been in three-quarters of a century and the scale of the flow was unprecedented by previous standards. Administration also had been more tightly centralized and by middle-class criteria had been made more businesslike and responsible. Revenues had been segregated and concepts of citizenship and public purpose were probably more widespread than ever before and were undoubtedly more realistic and better articulated than they had been in the years from the fifties through the turn of the present century.

Stripped of futile provisions for taxing personal property, general property taxation in altered form, to be sure, remained a mainstay of state income, excepting always the state governments of Pennsylvania and Delaware. But the Census Bureau's *Financial Statistics of States* indicated that by the twenties, 42% of state taxes came from incomes, from the wealth of corporations or other businesses, and from inheritances. In Pennsylvania, where the extreme prevailed, the taxation of corporations and other businesses accounted for nine-tenths of state revenues. Elsewhere, in the counties of the iron rectangle, more than eight-tenths of the revenues from taxation, and in the cities over nine-tenths, came from reformed general property taxation, the balance of governmental revenues being drawn from non-tax sources; that is, from the earnings of departments, business and non-business licenses, and special fees. On an official plane what remained to be done, therefore, was principally the work of refinement, elaboration, and extension. Practically speaking, this meant that critics of most state and local systems, New York serving as a case in point, could still argue justifiably that burdens were not reasonably distributed, that real estate was still bearing a disproportionate share of the public obligation, that reformed systems were still not "workable, practical, and equitable" in all their dimensions, that the financial needs of the states and of their cities in particular were not "adequately" provided for, and last, but by no means least, that taxation and indebtedness were everywhere still rising.[30]

All this granted, state and local systems had still come a very long way as experts and major interest groups were frank to admit by the mid-twenties. If most systems were not "models," they came closer than ever to the Model Plan of State and Local Taxation promulgated by the National Tax Association in 1919;[31] most by that time possessed all, the greater number, or the most important parts of the following: an "objective property tax levied where property [was] located, without deductions and without consideration of the residence or economic strength of the owner, the base being restricted to real estate and perhaps tangible personal property;" a personal tax on net income levied where the person resided, without reference to the physical location of the property, and graduated so as to increase the revenue from larger incomes; and a comprehensive system of business, especially corporate, taxes, preferably on net income, levied at a flat rate in the place where the business income arose.

The middle class biases which underlay most of this change inspired relatively few positive improvements in the unofficial money machinery, however, although benefits and opportunities accompanying official reform often accrued indirectly to politicos who controlled the extra-legal and illegal dimension of the money machinery. Perhaps a dilemma faced by the élites of the middle classes had something to do with this; its origins were probably more emotional or stylistic than intellectual and the difficulties it posed were of a type familiar even to nineteenth century Marxists. That is to say, as deeply as the middle classes realized what they stood to gain from fiscal machinery operating on large scale in their own interests, they were just as deeply fearful of the monster into which a politicized mass democracy regimented by party professionals could convert it. As a result, the more they appreciated, along with their European counterparts, that wherever "the eye rove[s] East or West, North or South . . . the center of political power is inexorably moving downward," the more they tried placing restraints upon fiscal power, the budget being the classic example, and the greater was their temptation when the tide seemed to be running strongly against them to starve party by starving the state. In this way they tried to paralyze fiscal machinery which might have been geared to welfare. Even when in reality the mass democracy they feared proved to be only another political faction flying under a democratic banner, the rule of starvation was invoked anyway.

Thus, the great problem of legitimate financing for political parties of enormous structural range and depth remained unresolved satisfactorily. Expanding governments which were busy plying subventions and services to meet the rising expectations of democrats of all persuasions were subjected to recurrent emotional, hence fiscal, feasts and famines. Public plans were built like great ships only to be slid down ways ungreased with public money, stripped of all but skeleton crews distinguished by the formal cheapness of their labor. To countenance, let alone encourage, such anomalies was to ignore the requirements of the vast, permanent organizations upon which the country's democratic polity depended and to prolong the nineteenth century's extralegal expedients and criminal alliances in order to feed and furbish political armies.

The costs of maintaining this duality, if not calculable, were undoubtedly very high, but to have destroyed or suppressed invisible government, had it proven possible to do so, might have raised the costs in every sense still higher. Under the circumstances, political parties would have been the first and most serious casualties. Fortunately, or so I believe, the country's prior democratization gave politicians a very broad base which they tenaciously retained and sometimes they expanded their commanding positions by expedient adaptation of their financial methods. Northern communities, meantime, reluctantly but tacitly recognized how unwise it was to presume that rural and urban middle classes could apply their standards not only to one another, which was difficult enough, but also to the richer and poorer elements of a disparate society without corruption becoming more profitable everywhere. The catharsis of periodic scandals followed by reform crusades, in fact, served to remind all concerned of how insidious, expensive, and unstable this tacit compromise really was—and has remained.

But this discussion, in a sense, is the parochial side of the picture, for the evolution of the money machines across the Northern tier of states between 1860 and the mid-twenties was part of a broader context within which their significance also must be viewed. Beginning in the early 1880's, European writers preoccupied themselves with what later proved to be the central questions of welfare economics. What have since become classic explorations of public finance appeared in the work of Germans such as Max Sax, Adolph Wagner, and Lorenz Von Stein, in the works of Knut Wicksell in Sweden, Maffeo Pantaleone, Ugo Mazzola, and Giovanni Montemartini in Italy, Arnold J. C Stuart in Holland, Paul Leroy-Beaulieu in France, and Henry Sidgwick, F. Y. Edgeworth, and A. C. Pigou in England. At the heart of their learned inquiries lay the probing of issues which were fully as much political as economic, that is, how best to allocate resources between public and private interests and how best to tax in order to secure these resources in the first instance.

Both the theoretical and practical ranges of these studies were extensive, embracing definitions, classifications, and philosophies of taxation, including its relations to sovereignty, to the police power, and to other regulative powers of the state. They examined the segregation of revenues, the efficacy of general property taxation, the taxation of businesses and inheritances, and the application of various types of progressive income taxes. Everywhere on the Continent, in other words, increasing measures of industrialization and democratization with their attendant pressures for greater social justice were italicizing the inadequacy of existing fiscal systems regardless of whether governments, as in England and France, were national or unitary or, as in Germany and Switzerland, were federal.

While the studies from England and the far more impressive flow from Italy and Germany, reflected differences in the diagnoses of their national fiscal systems, they anticipated or paralleled reforms actually undertaken in each Western European country between the late eighties and the turn of the century. The traditional, sometimes almost medieval, fiscal practices were assailed because of the disproportionate advantages which "ruling classes" derived from them; in England, for example, under the promptings of men like Sir William Harcourt, Gladstone's Chancellor of the Exchequer and father of the "death duties," and Viscount Goschen, who succeeded to the Exchequer under Salisbury, reforms were launched late in the eighties toward extensions of the inheritance tax, the introduction of the progressive principle in income taxation, a shifting of tax burdens from working classes of both the city and the countryside, and the alleviation of deep dissatisfaction with relationships between local and national revenues. Similarly, in Holland in the early nineties, beginning with the financial ministry of N. G. Pierson, one-time professor and president of the Bank of the Netherlands, analagous reforms were enacted to end inequitable taxes falling upon the lower classes, upon businesses through vexatious excises, and upon personalty. Business taxation was expanded into a general income tax; a progressive principle was introduced into personal taxation; and local taxation was reorganized—or at least a reorganization was attempted so that it better complemented general taxation. Over the same years, Germany likewise initiated a thorough revamping of her entire tax system under the direction of a Prussian legislator who sought a massive shift from reliance upon the taxation of products to the taxation of persons by means of an income tax. The reassignment of sources of revenues between local and general governments, indeed, a reform of the whole local revenue system was begun, a culmination of these efforts coming with the passage of three major laws in 1894 accomplishing the modernization of German fiscal operations. Much the same movements, taking somewhat different approaches toward similar ends, were undertaken almost simultaneously in France, Italy, and Switzerland with varying degrees of success.

A generic parallelism between certain trends in Europe and the United States is obvious without more being said; were it necessary to explore them we would find that European failures, the failure of direct income taxation to win approval in France, for example, the cheating and evasion inspired by both the German and English income taxes, the inadequacies of corporate taxes, were familiar enough to Americans.

Neither in theory nor in practice were Americans less creative in their overall responses to the most fundamental of all political and administrative activity than Europeans, although some Americans thought so at the time. This appears the more remarkable when we remember the complexity of the problems attending American fiscal revolutions. Across the Northern tier of states lived a population of 33 million which from the eighties onward was inferior in size to none in Western Europe and was substantially greater than most. Among these people change proceeded through the governments and parties of twenty-four states, twelve hundred and fifty-four counties, sixty major cities, and nearly one hundred thousand lesser subdivisions of government exercising fiscal power of their own. Yet effecting change in these official quarters was only a modicum of the task, for Americans were not simply dealing with legal fiscal systems, as Europeans were; they were dealing with extralegal and illegal money machines, with invisible as well as with visible government. The realities posed by financing vast, permanent, and continually active political organizations were unlike anything known to Europeans until well into the present century. French experts, thus, might protest that the blocking of fiscal reform in their country sprang from special "democratic conditions, political divisions, and administrative instability," and Englishmen might deplore the gradual professionalization of their politics as the nineteenth century passed. But in these, as in other European instances, parties seemed ephemeral, individualistic, and inexpensive by American standards. Dual governments like those in the North, complete with their own sophisticated taxing, spending, and borrowing mechanisms were not something that Europeans lived with and paid for as the price for their brands of democracy. In a general sense, therefore, it may be fair to suggest that the major financial investment of nineteenth and early twentieth century Northern society was in the operation of the party system and the unique, if somewhat inchoate, democracy that attended it. Through this system and within the span of one lifetime, Northerners had accomplished a basic reorganization of their political and administrative establishments without peaceful precedent or close parallel among modern states. In doing so they enshrined in the basic institutions of the land, for better and for worse, middle-class definitions of democracy, efficiency, and stability.

NOTES

LIST OF ABBREVIATIONS FREQUENTLY USED IN NOTES

AER (*American Economic Review*)

AHR (*American Historical Review*)

ALR (*American Law Review*)

ASAP (American Statistical Association Publication)

Comm. Chronicle (*Commercial and Financial Chronicle*)

Fassett Committee (New York. Senate. *Testimony Taken before the Senate Committee on Cities . . .*, January 20, 1890.)

Harpers (*Harper's New Monthly Magazine*)

Hunt's (*Hunt's Merchants Magazine*)

JEH (*Journal of Economic History*)

JOA (*Journal of Accountancy*)

JPE (*Journal of Political Economy*)

Lexow Committee (New York. Senate. *Report and Proceedings of the Senate Committee appointed to Investigate the Police Department of the City of New York.* 1895)

LMPA (Landlords Mutual Protective Association [of Baltimore])

Mass. Committee Report 1875 (Massachusetts. House of Representatives. *Report of the Commissioners appointed to Inquire into the Expediency of Revising and Amending the Laws Relating to Taxation . . .*, January 1875)

Mass. Committee Report 1897 (Massachusetts. General Assembly. *Report of the Commission . . . Expediency of Revising . . . the Laws . . . Relating to Taxation,* October 1897.)

Mastick Committee 1932 (New York State Legislature. *Report of the New York State Tax Commission. . . .* Feb. 1932)

Mazet Committee (New York State. Assembly. *Report of the Special Committee . . . to Investigate the Public Offices and Departments of the City of New York. . . .*, January 1900.)

Md. Comm. 1888 (Maryland. General Assembly. *Report of the Maryland Tax Commission. . . .*, January 1888.)

Mills Committee (New York State. Senate and House. *Report of the Joint Legislative Commitee on Taxation . . .*, February 1916.)

MPSA (Michigan Political Science Association)

MVHR (*Mississippi Valley Historical Review*)

NAR (*North American Review*)

NICB (*National Industrial Conference Board*)

Ohio Committee Report 1893 (Ohio. General Assembly. House. *Report of the Ohio Tax Commission of 1893.*)

Pa. Revenue Comm. 1889 (Pennsylvania. *Report of the Revenue Commission Appointed by the Legislature of Pennsylvania,* May, 1889.)

Proceedings of NTA (Procedings of the National Tax Association)

PSM (*Popular Science Monthly*)

PSQ (*Political Science Quarterly*)

QJE (*Quarterly Journal of Ecoonmics*)

Weeks Report Pa. Tax Conference 1892 (Pennsylvania Tax Conference. *Valuation, Taxation, and Exemptions in the Commonwealth of Pennsylvania* Harrisburg, 1892.)

Wells Report 1871 (New York State. Assembly. *Report of the Commissioners . . . to Revise the Laws for the Assessment and Collection of Taxes,* February 1871.)

Wells Report 1872 (New York State. Assembly. *Report of the Commissioners . . . to Revise the Laws . . . of Taxes,* 1872)

Wells Papers (David A. Wells Papers, Library of Congress, Washington, D.C.)

Notes

Introduction

1. *Public Debts: An Essay in the Science of Finance* (New York: D. Appleton & Company, 1892), p. 23. Hereafter cited as Adams, *Public Debts.*

2. Carl Plehn, *Introduction to Public Finance* (New York: The Macmillan Company, 1896), p. vii.

3. Robert Tucker, "Evils of Indirect Taxation," *Forum,* 2 (1887), 628.

4. From the profusion of literature defining and examining elites from Mosca, Pareto, and Michels to C. Wright Mills, I have found Suzanne Keller's definition of strategic elites the most satisfactory. "Strategic elites are composed of individuals selected on the basis of individual motivation and capacity. Since such capacities and motivations may be distributed throughout the social structure, the recruitment of strategic elites is not confined to any specific group or class," writes Keller in *Beyond the Ruling Class: Strategic Elites in Modern Society* (New York: Random House, 1963), p. 57, to which she adds that such elites are distinct from "ruling classes" by virtue of being several in number, small and concentrated in size, short-lived, composed of people with expert skills who were relieved from high status by incompetence, special and limited in scope of authority, marked by no special cultural bonds, and relatively open to access.

5. For instance, Thomas Cochran, "The Presidential Synthesis in American History," *American Historical Review,* 53 (1948), 748–50; Samuel P. Hays, "The Social Analysis of American Political History, 1880–1920," *Political Science Quarterly,* 80 (1965), 373–94; hereafter cited as *PSQ;* Sidney Fine, *Laissez-Faire and the General Welfare State* (Ann Arbor: University of Michigan Press, 1964); John Sproat, *The Best Men: Liberal Reformers in the Gilded Age* (New York: Oxford University Press, 1968); James Weinstein, "Organized Business and the City Commission and Manager Movements," *Journal of Southern History,* 28 (1962), 166–82; Lee Benson, "Research Problems in American Historiography," in Mirra Komarovsky, ed., *Common Frontiers of the Social Sciences* (Glencoe, Illinois: The Free Press, 1957), pp. 113–83; also see Benson's *Merchants, Farmers, and Railroads* (Cambridge, Mass.,

Harvard University Press, 1955); Robert Wiebe, *Businessmen and Reformers* (Cambridge, Mass.: Harvard University Press, 1962) and his *The Search for Order, 1877–1920* (New York: Hill and Wang, 1967); Gabriel Kolko. *The Triumph of Conservatism: A Reinterpretation of American History* (New York: The Free Press of Glencoe, 1963), and Edward Kirkland's review in the *American Historical Review,* 70 (October 1964), 203–204; see, too, Kirkland's "The Emergence of an Industrial Economy," *Mississippi Valley Historical Review,* 43 (June 1956), 3–17, as well as his *Industry Comes of Age* (New York: Holt, Rinehart, and Winston, 1961); John Tipple, "The Robber Barons in the Gilded Age," in H. Wayne Morgan, ed., *The Gilded Age: A Reappraisal* (Syracuse: Syracuse University Press, 1963), pp. 14–37.

6. See Richard A. Musgrave and Alan T. Peacock, eds., *Classics in the Theory of Public Finance* (London: The Macmillan Company, 1962); Richard Musgrave, *The Theory of Public Finance: A Study in Public Economy* (New York: McGraw-Hill Book Company, 1959); Richard Musgrave and Carl Shoup, eds., *Readings in the Economics of Taxation* (Homewood, Ill.: Richard D. Irwin, Inc., 1958), as well as in the same series by the American Economic Association, Arthur Smithies and Keith Butters, eds., *Readings in Fiscal Policy* (Homewood, Ill.: Richard D. Irwin, Inc., 1955); A. C. Pigou, *A Study in Public Finance* (London: Macmillan & Company, 1928), and his *The Economics of Welfare,* 4th ed., (London: Macmillan & Company, 1962).

7. *Hard Times* (Philadelphia: H. L. Kochersperger, 1875), p. 5.

Chapter 1 *The Menace of the New Democracy*

1. Charles Francis Adams, Jr., "Boston," *North American Review,* 105 (April 1868), 587–88. Hereafter cited as *NAR.* Also see "Debts and Taxation of Our Large Cities," *Hunt's Merchants Magazine,* 57 (August 1867), 107–110. Hereafter cited as *Hunt's.* Also see "Debts and Finances of San Francisco," *Hunt's,* 57 (1867), 31–34; and "Our Debts and Resources," *Hunt's,* 57 (1867), 416–18. Many similar analyses of local indebtedness appeared throughout the North; for more general comments see Amasa Walker, *The Science of Wealth* (Boston: Little, Brown and Company, 1867), pp. 369–373. Also note Walker's comment on p. 363 that "a national debt may be regarded under the existing war policy of the world, as a fixed institution, an inevitable appendage of government."

2. Nathan Matthews, *The City Government of Boston: Valedictory Address to Members of the Council* (Boston: Rockwell and Churchill, 1895), p. 28. Especially see Chapter 3, "Expenditures and Revenues."

3. *Ibid.,* pp. 182–85; remarks at Phillips Academy were reprinted from the mayor's address of February 27, 1892.

4. *Ibid.,* p. 174.

5. William Minot, Jr., *Taxation in Massachusetts* (Boston: Alfred Mudge & Son, 1877), p. 12. Also see, *Petition to the Mayor and City Council of the City of Boston: The Assessment of Real Estate, 1876* and Massachusetts, House of

Representatives, *Report of the Commissioners appointed to Inquire into the Expediency of Revising and Amending the Laws Relating to Taxation and Exemption Therefrom*, No. 15, January 1875 (Boston: Wright and Potter, 1875). Hereafter cited as *Mass. Committee Report 1875*.

6. For example, see Francis William Bird, *Retrenchment and Reform in State Expenditure* (Boston: Lee and Shepard, 1879) and Bird's, *The Hoosac Tunnel Contract* (Boston: Wright & Potter, 1869), which caused a furor over state expenditures after the *Auditor's Report of 1876*, p. 16. Also William H. Whitmore, *Taxation in Massachusetts* (Boston: T. R. Marvin & Son, 1876), p. 1. David A. Wells, "The Reform of Local Taxation," *NAR*, 122 (April 1876), 357–403. Such arguments involved many other local worthies such as Francis Abbot, president of Harvard, George Prendergast, assessor of Cambridge, Arthur Latham Perry of William College on related matters such as the taxation of church property, the taxation of savings, or bank deposits, taxation of incomes, and so on. See William H. Whitmore's *Unjust Taxes: A Criticism of the Massachusetts System of Local Taxation* (Boston: T. R. Marvin & Son, 1877) which sums up many of these arguments.

7. Brooks Adams, "The Abuse of Taxation," *Atlantic Monthly*, 42 (October 1878), 453–58.

8. "Oppressive Taxation of the Poor," *Atlantic*, 42 (November 1878), 632–36; also Adams's "Oppressive Taxation and Its Remedy," *Atlantic*, 42 (December 1878), 761–68.

9. Brooks Adams, "Abuse of Taxation," p. 453.

10. James Parton, "The Government of the City of New York,"*NAR*, 103 (October 1866), 422. See also *Analysis of the Proposed Tax Levy for the City and County of New York for the Year 1866* (New York: Citizens' Association, 1866); *Items of Abuse in the Government of the City of New York* (New York: Citizens' Association, 1866); *An Appeal by the Citizens' Association of New York against the Abuses of Local Government to the Legislature of New York and to the Public* (New York: Citizens' Association, 1866); *Wholesale Corruption, Sale of Situations in Fourth Ward Schools. Report of the Committee Appointed by the Board of Education* (New York: Citizens' Association, 1866).

11. James Parton, "Government of the City of New York," p. 444. The figures are contemporary and unadjusted. Also see *Hunt's*, 42 (August 1867), 120–22.

12. For instance, see *The Commercial and Financial Chronicle*, June 24, 1871, p. 776; April 13, 1872, pp. 479–80; May 11, 1872, p. 616; November 13, 1880, pp. 494–95; October 29, 1880, pp. 494–95; December 6, 1890, pp. 769–71. Cited hereafter as *Comm. Chronicle*.

13. New York State, Assembly, *Report of the Commissioners . . . To Revise the Laws for the Assessment and Collection of Taxes*, Assembly Document No. 39, February 16, 1871 (Albany: The Argus Company, 1871), pp. 6–16. Cited hereafter as *Wells Report* (1871). For background see the *David A. Wells Papers*, Volumes 4–6 in the Library of Congress. Cited hereafter as the *Wells Papers*. See, too, Wells' "Reform of Local Taxation," *NAR*, 122 (April 1876), 357–403.

14. Daniel Harris, *Municipal Extravagance* (Philadelphia: Penn Monthly, 1876), pp. 3–11. This is a reprint studded with statistics from Harris's talk to the American Social Science Association.

15. "Municipal Finance," *Harper's New Monthly Magazine,* 69 (1884), 779–84. Cited hereafter as *Harper's.*

16. *Comm. Chronicle,* December 6, 1890, p. 771.

17. *The Baltimore Sun,* November 18, 1884; also see the *Sun,* December 1, 1884. Assessors thought that A. S. Abell, owner of the *Sun,* owed Baltimore County at least $400,000 in taxes. Abell died wealthy.

18. "The Government of Cities," *An Address to the Landlords' Mutual Protective Association,* August 20, 1889. Cited hereafter as *Address(es) to LMPA.*

19. "The Productiveness of Property and the Inequalities of Taxation," *An Address to LMPA,* July 9, 1889.

20. "Some Facts About Taxation," *An Address to LMPA,* August 6, 1889.

21. William A. Hammond, "Some Inequalities in Taxation," *An Address to LMPA,* June 11, 1889.

22. Michael Frisch, "From Town to City: Springfield, Massachusetts and the Meaning of Community, 1840–1880 (Ph.D. dissertation, Department of History, Princeton University, 1967).

23. "Debts and Taxation of Our Large Cities," *Hunt's,* 57 (August 1867), 107–110.

24. See, *Mass. Committee Report 1875.* Also, Harris, *Municipal Extravagance,* pp. 8–10, for Table "showing increase per capita from 1865 to 1875 in the Assessors' Valuation in the Amount of Taxes, and in the Public Debt of the Several Cities of Massachusetts," as it was then calculated. Also see, James Bryce, *The American Commonwealth,* 2 vols., (London: Macmillan & Company, 1888), Part 2, pp. 280–89 and following.

25. *Mass. Committee Report 1875,* Appendix, Table 12, p. 551. Harris, *Municipal Extravagance,* pp. 8–10; also pp. 5–7, 11–12.

26. *Hunt's,* 57 (August 1867), 110.

27. Also see, Thomas Cooley, "The Evils of Municipal Indebtedness," Lecture in *Thomas M. Cooley Papers,* University of Michigan, Ann Arbor, pp. 1–53. Also see, "Investors' Supplement to the *Financial Chronicle,*" May 1889; *Comm. Chronicle,* May 11, 1872, p. 616; *Bankers' Magazine,* May 1871, pp. 840–47; *Mass. Committee Report 1875,* pp. 113–15; Michael Mullin, "Some Facts About Taxation," *An Address to LMPA,* August 6, 1889.

28. William Ivins, "Municipal Finance," p. 783; also p. 780.

29. "The Forgotten Millions: A Study of the Common American Mode of Life," *Century Magazine,* 40 (August 1890), 556–64.

30. Based on U.S. census data and statistical studies such as Robert Porter's compilation in U.S. House of Representatives, Department of the Interior, Census Office, *Report on Valuation, Taxation, and Public Indebtedness in the United States as Returned at the 10th Census, June 1, 1880.* These figures were widely reported. See, Ivins, "Municipal Finance," pp. 781–85, for example, and John Kasson, "Municipal Reform," *NAR,* 137 (1883), 218–20.

31. Cooley, "Lectures on Political Science," V, "The Evils of Municipal Indebtedness," May 15, 1876, in *Thomas M. Cooley Papers;* also see the

Baltimore Sun, May 15, 1879; *Burlington (Iowa) Free Press and Times,* June 4, 1879 for Cooley's message spread beyond Maryland.

32. *Comm. Chronicle,* 51 (December 6, 1890), 769–71.

33. *Ibid.,* pp. 769–70.

34. May 1871, p. 841.

35. Adjusted figures on per capita state expenditures, by region have recently been produced by Lance E. Davis and John Legler, "Government in the American Economy, 1815–1902," *Journal of Economic History,* 26 (December 1966), 514–52. Cited hereafter as *JEH.* The major source of contemporary figures was in state auditors' and treasurers' reports and in census data, e.g., previously cited *Report on Valuation, Taxation, and Public Indebtedness* in 10th Census. Also see, Massachusetts, *State Auditor's Report 1864,* p. 7; *Mass. Committee Report 1875,* pp. 11, 12, 115; Harris, *Municipal Extravagance,* pp. 7–11; Francis William Bird, *Retrenchment and Reform in State Taxation (*Boston: Lee and Shepard, 1879); Robert H. Whitten, *Public Administration in Massachusetts* (New York: Columbia University Press, 1898); Charles Bullock, *Historical Sketch of the Finances and Financial Policy of Massachusetts, from 1780–1905,* publication of the American Economic Association, 3rd series, 7 (May 1907), Chapters 5–7; cited hereafter as Bullock, *Finances of Massachusetts.* There are two good compilations from the period in Henry B. Gardner, "Statistics of American Municipal Finance," *American Statistical Association Publications,* new series, number 6, (June 1889), pp. 254–69; cited hereafter as *ASAP;* and Edwin R. A. Seligman, "Finance Statistics of the American Commonwealths," *ASAP,* new series, (December 1889), pp. 349–468. Per capital debt was $5.47 in 1860, $12.60 in 1890, and $31.06 in 1906.

36. E. E. Woodbury, "New York's Needs," *Proceedings of the National Tax Association,* 7 (1913), 139. Cited hereafter as *Proceedings of NTA.* Also New York State, Senate and House, *Report of the Joint Legislative Committee on Taxation of the State of New York, February 14, 1916* (Albany: J. B. Lyon Company, 1916), pp. 2–12. Cited hereafter as *Mills Committee.*

37. Alexander Dana Noyes, *Forty Years of American Finance* (New York: G. P. Putnam & Sons, 1909), p. 18; J. B. Hunt to David Wells, April 26, 1873, *Wells Papers.*

38. "Taxation No Burden," *Atlantic Monthly,* 10 (July–December 1862), 115–18.

39. Albert G. Keller and Maurice Davie, eds., *Essays of William Graham Sumner,* 2 vols., (New Haven: Yale Universtiy Press, 1934), 2, p. 5. Hereafter cited as Keller and Davie, *Sumner Essays.*

40. Amasa Walker, *The Science of Wealth,* 5th ed. rev., (Boston: Little, Brown and Company, 1869), pp. 353–62.

41. McCulloch's *Annual Report,* December 3, 1866 is quoted in John Sherman, *Recollections of Forty Years in the House, Senate, and Cabinet,* 2 vols., (Chicago: The Werner Company, 1895), 1, p. 386; also see pp. 377–94; and McCulloch's *Men and Measures of Half a Century (*New York: Charles Scribner's Sons, 1888), pp. 238–39. Scholarly works referred to earlier in the paragraph as those of Stanley Coben, "Northeastern Business and Radical Recon-

struction: A Re-examination," *Mississippi Valley Historical Review,* 46 (June 1959), 67–90; Richard Timberlake, Jr., "Ideological Factors in Specie Resumption and Treasury Policy," *JEH,* 24 (March 1964), 29–52; Walter T. K. Nugent, *The Money Question During Reconstruction* (New York: W. W. Norton & Co., 1967), Robert Poindexter Sharkey, *Money, Class, and Party* (Baltimore: Johns Hopkins Press, 1959); James Kindahl, "Economic Factors in Specie Resumption: The United States, 1865–79," *Journal of Political Economy,* 59 (February 1961), 30–48; hereafter cited as *JPE;* Irwin Unger, *The Greenback Era: A Social and Political History of American Finance, 1865–79* (Princeton: Princeton University Press, 1964).

42. Well's estimate is in *Comm. Chronicle,* August 26, 1873, p. 263; also see April 13, 1872, p. 480.

43. William Ivins' summation in "Municipal Finance," pp. 781–84.

44. Peter J. Lesley, Philadelphia, January 3, 1875, letter to Allen, Box 6, *Peter J. Lesley Papers,* also see Lesley's letter to Chauncey, Box 6, May 24, 1865; letter to Lyman, Box 4, November 27, 1865; letter to Lyman, Box 7, January 7, 1866; also see Mary C. L. Ames, *Life and Letters of Peter and Susan Lesley,* 2 vols., (New York: G. P. Putnam's Sons, 1909), 2, pp. 522–23.

45. Albert Stickney, *The Political Problem* (New York: Harper & Bros., 1890), p. 184.

46. Keller and Davie, *Sumner Essays,* 2, pp. 351–52.

47. *Ibid.,* 2, p. 356.

48. Adams, "Oppressive Taxation of the Poor," pp. 632, 636.

49. For instance, see *Mass. Committee Report 1875,* pp. 558–61; also pp. 14–18, and Appendix Tables 10 and 12 for statistics on the polls by towns from annual assessors' reports.

50. Walker, *Science of Wealth,* 7th ed., (1874), pp. 332, 333; also his "Economy in Taxation," *Hunt's,* 58 (1868), 329 and following.

51. Francis Parkman, "The Failure of Universal Suffrage," *NAR,* 127 (1878), 2, 3, 20; also Adams, *Public Debts,* p. 359; Minot, *Taxation in Massachusetts,* p. 61.

52. James Parton, "The Government of New York City," pp. 445, 460, 464; Edwin L. Godkin, *Problems of Modern Democracy: Political and Economic Essays,* 2nd ed., (New York: Charles Scribner's Sons, 1897), pp. 123, 153. Also see Godkin, *Unforeseen Tendencies of Democracy* (Boston: Houghton, Mifflin & Co., 1898) and earlier editorials in *The Nation* and essays such as "Commercial Immorality and Political Corruption," NAR, 107 (July 1868), 267–97.

53. "The Problems of Municipal Government," *The Annals,* 4 (May 1894), 865, 869; also Godkin's, "A Key to Municipal Reform," *NAR,* 151 (1890), 422–31, 576–81; his "Taxation of Personal Property," *The Nation,* 32 (1881), 86–87. For a pertinent estimate of Godkin by a friend see James Ford Rhodes, *Historical Essays* (New York: Macmillan Co., 1909), pp. 267–97.

54. J. Sloan Fassett, "Why Cities Are Badly Governed," *NAR,* 150 (1890), 634. Fassett was later implicated in the Ice Trust Scandal in New York. Also see Harold Gosnell, *Boss Platt and His New York Machine* (Chicago: University of Chicago Press, 1924), p. 66; Thomas Collier Platt, *The Autobiography of Thomas Collier Platt* (New York: B. W. Dodge, 1910); the discussions on

Platt were numerous, of course; see the writings of Theodore Roosevelt, Lemuel Quigg, Delos F. Wilcox, and Elihu Root among others.

55. Ivins, "Municipal Finance," p. 781; also pp. 780, 787.

56. Andrew White, "The Government of American Cities," *Forum,* 10 (December 1890), 357; Emile de Laveleye, "The Perils of Democracy," *Forum,* 7 (May 1889), 235–45; James M. Love, "The Trial of Popular Government," *Forum,* 5 (August 1888), 591–602; Charles E. Pickard, "Great Cities and Democratic Institutions," *American Journal of Politics,* 1 (1889), 22–25; R. E. Wright, "Some Problems in City Government," *An Address to LMPA,* November 26, 1889. George Merriam, *The Life and Times of Samuel Bowles,* 2 vols., (New York: The Century Company, 1885), 2, pp. 317–18, 344. Harriette Dilla, *The Politics of Michigan* (New York: Columbia University Press, 1912), pp. 57, 74, 94–96, 108–111, 121, 150, 168, 173, 249. Alexander Winchell, "The Experiment of Universal Suffrage," *NAR,* 136 (1883), 128, 130; Charles Reemelin, *Critical Review of American Politics* (Cincinnati: Robert Clarke & Co., 1881), pp. 301–302.

57. Thomas Cooley, "Lectures on Political Science," 1; "The Sentiment of Equality in American Politics," *ms,* p. 25½, also pp. 2, 28–40 in *Thomas M. Cooley Papers. Baltimore Sun,* May 6, 1879; Parkman, "Failure of Universal Suffrage," pp. 4, 7, 8. The myth of the village is summarized by Sumner; see Keller and Davie, *Sumner Essays,* 2, pp. 328–30; also pp. 313–16.

58. Parkman, "Failure of Universal Suffrage," pp. 2, 4, 8.

59. Frederick Stimson, *My United States* (New York: Charles Scribner & Sons, 1931), p. 19.

60. Parton, "The Government of the City of New York," pp. 417–19.

61. Charles Nordhoff, "The Misgovernment of New York: A Suggested Remedy," *NAR,* 113 (October 1871), 321.

62. E. L. Godkin, "Criminal Politics," in his *Problems of Modern Democracy,* pp. 128–31; also pp. 13–14.

63. John P. Bocock, "The Irish Conquest of Our Cities," *Forum,* 17 (1894), 186–93.

64. Letter from Mrs. John Scott to Hayes, July 24, 1877, in the *Rutherford P. Hayes Papers* in Hayes Memorial Library; also see a letter from A. M. Sherman to Hayes, July 27, 1877 in *Hayes Papers.*

65. A. Cleveland Coxe, "Government by Aliens," *Forum,* 7 (August 1889), 589.

66. Nathan Matthews, *The City Government of Boston,* p. 175; also pp. 180–81.

67. Charles Phillip Huse, *The Financial History of Boston* (Cambridge, Mass.: Harvard University Press, 1916), pp. 112–16; and Tables in the Appendix; Charles Bullock, *Finances of Massachusetts,* Chapter 7; Boston, City of Boston, *Reports of the City Auditor, 1892–3;* Matthews, *Government of Boston,* pp. 28–40; on New York see, New York State, Senate, *Testimony Taken before the Senate Committee on Cities,* Documents of the Senate, 114th Session, 1891, 9, Number 80, Part 5, January 20, 1890 (Albany: J. B. Lyon, 1891), 5, pp. 392–406; cited hereafter as *Fassett Committee.* Comparative table of annual expenditures for governmental purposes of the various cities of the state, classi-

fied under general titles and based upon the answers to questions posed by the committee. There were many popular recapitulations of some of these materials as well as of those found in New York City, *City Comptroller's Annual Reports.*

68. Matthews, *Government of Boston,* pp. 180–81.

69. U.S., Bureau of the Census, *Historical Statistics of the United States from Colonial Times to 1957,* Series E 148–86 and Series E 101–112, E 113–139.

70. William Graham Sumner, "What Makes the Rich Richer and the Poor Poorer," *Popular Science Monthly,* 30 (January 1887), 289–92. Cited hereafter as *PSM.* Also see Keller and Davie, *Sumner Essays,* 2, pp. 150–62; Albert Keller, ed., *The Forgotten Man and Other Essays* (New Haven: Yale University Press, 1913), pp. 285–333; William Graham Sumner, *Taxation: What it is, and What are the General Principles by which it must be Controlled, and What are its Relations to Other Departments of Political Economy,* in Ms, *Sumner Papers,* Sumner Estate, Yale University.

71. Crandon, "Misgovernment of Great Cities," *PSM,* 30 (1886–87), 301, 302; also see Gamaliel Bradford, "Municipal Government," *Scribner's Magazine,* 2 (July-December 1887), 485–92, and his "Congressional Reform," *NAR,* 129 (October 1870), 330–51.

72. For typical examples, see Godkin, *Problems of Modern Democracy,* pp. 14–45.

73. Herbert Croly, *The Promise of American Life* (New York: Capricorn Books, 1964), p. 146.

74. See, for example, Eaton's *Government of Municipalities* (New York: The Macmillan Co., 1889); "A New Phase of the Reform Movement," *NAR,* 132 (1881); "Two Years of Civil Service Reform," *NAR,* 141 (1885); "Parties and Independence," *NAR,* 144 (1887); William Dudley Foulke, *Fighting the Spoilsmen* (New York: G. P. Putnam's Sons, 1919); Charles E. Norton, ed., *Orations and Addresses of George William Curtis,* 3 vols., (New York: Harper and Brothers, 1898), 2, Chapters 4–6 especially; Mark DeWolfe Howe, *Portrait of An Independent: Moorfield Storey, 1845–1929* (Boston: Houghton, Mifflin and Co., 1932). The literature on the subject is extensive: see Alfred Hodder, *A Fight For The City* (New York: Macmillan Company, 1903); Charles Merriam, *The American Party System* (New York: Macmillan Company, 1922), Chapters 4, 5; James Bryce, *The American Commonwealth,* 2 vols., (New York: Macmillan Company, 1922), 2, Chapters 50, 51. Also see Ari Hoogenboom's *Outlawing the Spoils: A History of the Civil Service Reform Movement (*Urbana: University of Illinois Press, 1961) which updates previous discussions.

75. Sydney Brooks, "Tammany Again," *Fortnightly Review,* 80 (December 1903), 921, 924, 925. The literature on Tammany in the period under consideration as well as afterwards is voluminous.

76. Gamaliel Bradford, "Our Failures in Municipal Government," *The Annals,* 3 (1894), 701.

77. See my "The 'Country Party' and the Rise of the Megalopoli: London, Paris, and New York, 1850–1910," Paper delivered to the Faculty Seminar of Western New York Colleges and Universities, Spring 1969.

78. Wells, "Principles of Taxation," *PSM,* 48 (November 1895), 5, 13; also p. 7.

79. *Ibid.*

80. Alexander Gunn, *Letters* (New York: The Author, 1902), p. 144. Richard Ely, *The Ground Under Our Feet* (New York: Macmillan Company, 1938), p. 66, also the Introduction and Ely's "Political Economy in America," *NAR,* 144 (1887), 133–39.

81. See, Michael Wallace, "Changing Concepts of Party in the United States: New York, 1815–1828," *AHR,* 74 (December 1968), 453–91.

82. Henry Adams, "The Butler Canvas," *NAR,* 114 (January 1872), 162; Reemelin, *Critical Review of American Politics,* p. 441.

83. Thomas S. Adams, "Ideals and Idealism in Taxation," *American Economic Review,* 18 (1928), 12. Cited hereafter as *AER.* For a more modern discussion see Louis Eisenstein, *The Ideologies of Taxation* (New York: The Ronald Press, 1961).

84. White, "The Government of American Cities," pp. 358, 368.

85. R. E. Wright, "Some Problems in City Government," *An Address to LMPA,* November 26, 1889; William Marbury, "The Government of Cities," *An Address to LMPA,* August 20, 1889; *Southern Bivouac,* October, 1886. For sources of complaints see, "Comparative Statement of the Expenses of the Corporation, 1860–1880," *Report of the Comptroller of New York, August 1, 1881;* William Reynolds, "The Relation of Civil Service Reform to Municipal Taxation," *An Address to LMPA,* October 8, 1889; also see, Baltimore, City of, *Annual Register, Register's Statement of Expenditures, 1889;* Joseph Packard, Jr., "Suggestions Toward A Reduction of Taxation," *An Address to LMPA,* September 3, 1889. Packard's evidence came from Baltimore, City of Baltimore, *First Branch Journal, 1889,* p. 822; City of Baltimore, *Register's Report, 1889,* p. 69. William Whitmore, *Unjust Taxes,* pp. 8, 10, 11, 12–13; F. C. Latrobe, Mayor, "City Government of Baltimore," *An Address to LMPA,* September 17, 1889. Latrobe made interesting comparisons between Baltimore's street cleaning department, then only seven years old and Boston's. He added: "It cannot be denied that taxes are high," but "the cost of municipal government like individual living, increases with the constant desire for luxuries." The mayor noted that "cities must add to their revenue by sale of franchises or privileges. In Europe everything of this kind pays a revenue; here we give it all away." Charles Wingate, "An Episode in Municipal Government," *NAR,* 120 (October 1875), 360; also continuations of the same article in Volumes 121 (1875) and 123 (1876).

86. It is worth noting that modern black militants have gone no farther rhetorically than angry middle class whites who enjoyed many of society's greatest advantages during the last century.

87. The *Reemelin Papers* are in the Cincinnati Historical Society and include letters, scrapbooks, notebooks from 1844–1890, as well as Reemelin's own *Life of Charles Reemelin* (Cincinnati: Weier & Daiker, 1892); pp. 1–201 are pertinent here. For related views see his *Critical Review of American Politics,* pp. 252, 272, 278–90, 297–301, 496–501; also the *Autobiography,* pp. 155–93, 261–333, 441, 496–97, 508, 510.

88. Crandon, "Misgovernment of Great Cities," pp. 521, 523, 528–29; White, "The Government of American Cities," pp. 358, 368, 370.

89. Keller and Davie, *Sumner Essays,* 2, p. 229.

90. Stickney, *The Political Problem,* pp. 125, 137, 162, 184.

91. Reemelin, *Critical Review of American Politics,* pp. 278–90.

CHAPTER 2 *The Escape of the "New" and the Old Wealth*

1. New York State, *New York States Assessor's Report 1879,* p. 7.

2. *Wells Report* (1871), pp. 5, 6, 20, 22, 27, 33, 41; New York State, *New York State Assessor, First Annual Report, 1860,* p. 12; New York State, *New York State Comptroller's Report 1859;* New York State, *New York State Assessor's Report, 1889,* p. 34.

3. *Wells Report* (*1872*), p. 13; also see *Wells Report* (*1871*), p. 33. James Malcolm, "A Remarkable Statistical Report," *The Arena,* 16 (June-November 1896), 585–94; John Ames, *The Taxation of Personal Property* (Des Moines: Mills & Company, 1877), p. 15.

4. Maryland, General Assembly, *Report of the Maryland Tax Commission to the General Assembly, January 1888* (Baltimore: King Brothers, 1888), p. 149. Cited hereafter as *Md. Comm. 1888.* Details fill auditors' and assessors' reports at state and local levels of government. See, e.g., John Fairlie's summation, "Taxation in Illinois," *AER,* 1 (1911), 518–34; Edwin R. A. Seligman, *Essays in Taxation* (New York: The Macmillan Company, 1895), "The General Property Tax."

5. Pennsylvania, *Report of the Revenue Commission Appointed by the Legislature of Pennsylvania, May 25, 1889* (Philadelphia: Collins Printing House, 1890), p. 10; cited hereafter as *Pa. Revenue Comm. 1889.*

6. Joseph D. Weeks, *Address to the Manufacturers' Association of Cincinnati and Hamilton County, Ohio, Lecture Series, No. 1, March 6 1894,* p. 11.

7. For a brief review of the development of property taxation see Seligman, "The General Property Tax," *PSQ,* 5 (1890), 43–60 and Brindley, *History of Taxation in Iowa,* 2, pp. 172–89. On apportionment see George H. Haynes, "New England Legislative Representation," *The Annals,* 6 (July-December 1895), 254–67; for other states see Legislative handbooks such as John A. Smull, *Legislative Handbook, Rules and Decisions of the General Assembly of Pennsylvania, Legislative Directory* (Harrisburg: Lane S. Hart, 1878), or *Smull's Legislative Handbook . . . 1896,* edited by Thomas Cochran (Harrisburg: Clarence M. Burch, 1898), etc. It was generally believed throughout the Northern tier of states that farmers were the real legislators; see Chester Lloyd Jones, "New England's Rotten Boroughs," *NAR,* 97 (1913), 486–98; Robert D. Seltzer, "Rotten Boroughism in Indiana," (Ph.D. dissertation, Department of Government, Indiana University, 1952); Paul Reinsch, *American Legislatures and Legislative Methods* (New York: The Century Company, 1907), pp. 197–202; *Comm. Chronicle,* 64 (April 3, 1897), 645–47; Charles Buckalew, *An Examination of the Constitution of Pennsylvania Exhibiting the Derivation and History of Its Several Provisions* (Philadelphia: Kay and Brothers, 1883),

pp. 58–60; Joseph Brislawn, "Taxation and the Farmer," *Proceedings of NTA*, 10 (1917), 274.

8. *The Nation*, February 10, 1881, pp. 86–87; Lawson Purdy, *Local Option in Taxation* (New York: New York Tax Reform Association, 1901), p. 7.

9. On the laws of assessments see, D. W. Welty, *Treatise on the Law of Assessments* (New York & Albany: Banks and Brothers, 1886); Francis Hilliard, *The Law of Taxation* (Boston: Little, Brown and Company, 1875), Chapter 10. For the quotation above representing but a small number of such comments see *Wells Report (1871)*, pp. 31, 33–75; New York State, *Constitutional Convention, Debates, 1867–68*, 3, pp. 1905, 1932, 1937–1938, 1950; *Mass. Committee Report 1875*, pp. 19–48, 139–49; Ohio, General Assembly, *Report of the Ohio State Tax Commissioners, April 24, 1893* (Cleveland: J. B. Savage, Printers, 1893); Edwin R. A. Seligman, *Essays on Taxation*, pp. 30–32; *Md. Comm. 1888;* Thomas Shearman, *Natural Taxation* (New York: Doubleday & McClure, 1898), pp. 74–75; and again Francis Hilliard, *Law of Taxation*, pp. 311, 312, 313.

10. *Wells Report (1872)*, p. 55; also pp. 14–15 for comments on the committee's views.

11. *Wells Report (1871)*, p. 36.

12. *Fassett Committee*, 3, pp. 2256–2257, 2260–2261, 2263, 2264–2265; also p. 2352.

13. *Ibid.*, 3, pp. 2353–2355, 2361–2363.

14. *Ibid.*, 3, p. 2361. The Supreme Court of New York heard *The People ex. rel. Benjamin Babbitt v. The Commissioners of Taxes and Assessments for the City of New York*, January 3, 1871.

15. *Wells Report (1871)*, p. 43; also *Wells Report (1872)*, p. 11.

16. *Fassett Committee*, 3, p. 2379.

17. *Ibid.*, 3, pp. 2356–2357.

18. *Ibid.*, 3, pp. 2361, 2373.

19. *Ibid.*, 3, p. 2373; also for an extended discussion of evasion see pp. 2238–2529. On Boston experiences see, Thomas G. Shearman, *Home Rule in Taxation: Taxation of Personal Property: An Address Before A Committee of the New York Legislature, February 8, 1893* (Brooklyn Revenue Reform Club, 1893), pp. 10–18.

20. New York State, Assembly, Documents of the Assembly of the State of New York. *Report of the Special Committee of the Assembly Appointed to Investigate the Public Offices and Departments of the City of New York and the Counties Therein Included, 124th Session, 1901, January 15, 1900.* 6 vols., (Albany: J. B. Lyon Company, 1900), 2, pp. 1452, 1541–1542. Cited hereafter as *Mazet Committee.*

21. *Ibid.*, 2, p. 1449.

22. Aside from Hamilton County, there was Cuyahoga County with Cleveland, Franklin County with Columbus, and Lucas County with Toledo.

23. *Wells Report (1871)*, pp. 7, 8, 9, 36, 40; *Md. Comm. 1888*, pp. 109–116; Shearman, *Natural Taxation*, pp. 88–98; Ernest L. Bogart, *The Financial History of Ohio* (Champaign, Ill.: University of Illinois, 1912), pp. 202–43 for background. Also see, Ohio, *Ohio State Auditor's Report, 1888, 1890, 1897;*

Thomas N. Carver, "The Ohio Tax Inquisitor Law," *American Economic Association Studies,* 3 (1898), 190–93.

24. Carver, "The Ohio Tax Inquisitor Law;" Shearman, *Natural Taxation,* pp. 88–96; *Shearman, Home Rule in Taxation,* pp. 11–12; *Ohio Tax Commission 1893,* pp. 7–85; E. A. Angell, "The Tax Inquisitor System of Ohio," *Yale Review,* 5 (February 1897), 355–58.

25. Angell, "The Tax Inquisitor System of Ohio," pp. 352, 355, 369–72; *Comm. Chronicle,* October 5, 1895, pp. 592–93.

26. Angell, "The Tax Inquisitor System of Ohio," pp. 358–72; Carver, "Ohio Tax Inquisitor Law," pp. 182–86, 190–91, 194–210 (Tables 1-5). Bogart, *Financial History,* pp. 240–42.

27. Carver, "Ohio Tax Inquisitor Law," pp. 90, 191, 194, 195, 206–210; Bogart, *Financial History,* pp. 206, 236–37; Angell, "The Tax Inquisitor System of Ohio," p. 358. Growth estimates are those of Raymond Goldsmith in U.S., Congress, Joint Economic Committee, *Hearings on Employment, Growth, Price Levels, Part 2, Historical and Comparative Rates of Production, Productivity and Prices, 86th Congress, 1st Sess., 1959,* pp. 230–79. Also see Robert Gallman, "Commodity Output, 1839–1899," in *Trends in the American Economy in the Nineteenth Century* (Princeton: National Bureau of Economic Research, Studies in Income and Wealth, 1960), 24, pp. 13–67.

28. *Mass. Committee Report 1875,* pp. 9, 10.

29. *Ibid.,* pp. 101, 102. Also Shearman, *Taxation of Personal Property: An Address,* pp. 12, 13–15; Minot, *Taxation in Massachusetts,* pp. 10, 32, 33, 35–36.

30. *Mass. Committee Report 1875,* pp. 118–119, 120, 121; Sherman, *Taxation of Personal Property: An Address,* pp. 12, 13–15; Minot, *Taxation in Massachusetts,* pp. 10, 32, 33, 35–36.

31. *Mass. Committee Report 1875,* pp. 120–21.

32. *Ibid.,* pp. 118–119, 120, 121; Minot, *Taxation in Massachusetts,* pp. 32, 33, 34–36; Shearman, *Natural Taxation,* pp. 72, 80–82, and his *Taxation of Personal Property: An Address,* p. 13. Massachusetts, General Assembly, *Report of the Commission appointed to Inquire Into the Expediency of Revising and Amending the Laws of the Commonwealth Relating to Taxation, October 1897* (Boston: Wright & Potter Printing Co., 1897), pp. 64–65; also pp. 29–67. Cited hereafter as *Mass. Committee Report, 1897.*

33. Frederick J. Stimson, *My United States* (New York: Charles Scribner's Sons, 1931), p. 113; *Mass. Committee Report, 1897,* p. 50.

34. *Mass. Committee Report, 1897,* pp. 23–36; also *Mass. Committee Report, 1875,* pp. 99–100.

35. New York, *Constitutional Convention, Debates, 1867–1868,* 3, p. 1932; *Wells Report (1871),* pp. 62–64; *Mass. Committee Report 1875,* pp. 100–101.

36. *Mass. Committee Report 1875,* p. 61, also pp. 58–60; Massachusetts, *Bureau of the Statistics of Labor, 1872,* pp. 293–338.

37. *Mass. Committee Report 1875,* pp. 62–65.

38. *Ibid.,* pp. 62–63; Massachusetts, *Bureau of the Statistics of Labor, 1873,* pp. 129–228; Minot, *Taxation in Massachusetts,* p. 20; Brooks Adams, "Oppressive Taxation of the Poor," p. 634. Also the Minority Report in *Mass. Committee Report, 1897,* pp. 151–52.

39. Adams, "Oppressive Taxation and Its Remedy," pp. 764–65; *Mass. Committee Report 1875*, pp. 70–71; see rejoinders in Committee of Associated Savings Banks, *The Taxation of Deposits in Savings Banks,* (1875), 4 pages; *Comm. Chronicle,* 60, April 13, 1895, p. 636.

40. William Endicott, Jr., *The Taxation Only of Tangible Things* (1875), 8 pages; *Mass. Committee Report 1875*, p. 408; Minot, *Taxation in Massachusetts,* p. 28.

41. Minot, *Taxation in Massachusetts,* pp. 34–37. For a later view see, *Mass. Committee Report, 1897,* pp. 157–58, 162–64.

42. For views of those who did not believe that farmers were bearing disproportionate shares of the public burden see: F. H. Noble, *Taxation in Iowa: Historical Sketch, Present Status, and Suggested Reforms* (New York: Columbia University Press, 1897), pp. 6, 7, 16, 18–21, 99; Shearman, *Natural Taxation,* pp. 84–100, 196–97; Roswell McCrea, "Taxation of Personal Property in Pennsylvania," *Quarterly Journal of Economics,* 21 (November 1906), 71, also pp. 50–95. Cited hereafter as *QJE.* John Rogers Commons, "Taxation in Chicago and Philadelphia," *JPE,* 3 (1894–95), 460; C. S. Walker, "The Massachusetts Farmer and Taxation," *Yale Review,* 6 (May 1897), 63, 69, 70, 73; John A. Fairlie, "Taxation in Illinois," *AER,* 1 (September 1911), 524–25; *Wells Report (1871),* pp. 31, 63–64; *The Nation,* February 10, 1881, pp. 86–87; Daniel Shorey, *Problems of Municipal Government for Chicago,* p. 15; John Brindley, *History of Taxation in Iowa,* 2 vols. (Iowa City, Iowa: State Historical Society of Iowa, 1911), 2, pp. 131–33, 199–201, 210; *Comm. Chronicle,* 61 (November 2, 1895), 776–77.

43. *Wells Report (1871),* pp. 31, 36, 37–38, 43; *Fassett Committee,* 3, pp. 2256–2257.

44. *Wells Report (1871),* pp. 33, 36–38, 63; New York State, *Report of the Comptroller of the State of New York, 1871;* John Schwab, "History of the New York Property Tax," *AER,* 5 (September 1890), 79–95, 107, 108.

45. M. Slade Kendrick, *An Index Number of Farm Taxes in New York and Its Relation to Various Other Economic Factors* (Ithaca: Cornell University Agricultural Experiment Station) Bulletin 457 (December 1926), pp. 3–30; also see New York State, Legislature, "Depression Taxes and Economy Through Reform of Local Government," *Third Report of the New York State Commission for the Revision of the Tax Laws, Legislative Doc. (1933), No. 56, February 15, 1933* (Albany: J. B. Lyon, 1933), Parts 2 and 3; also New York State, Legislature, *Report of the New York State Tax Commission for the Revision of Tax Laws, Legislative Doc. (1932), No. 77, February 15, 1932* (Albany: J. B. Lyon, 1932), pp. 132–35, Part 2, Tables 23–31. Cited hereafter as *Mastick Committee 1932.* See also *Historical Statistics of the U.S.,* pp. 282–83, series K 116–121.

46. See, *Ohio Tax Commission 1893* for general background along with *Ohio State Auditor's Report, 1887.* Shearman, *Natural Taxation,* pp. 88–91; Ernest L. Bogart, "Recent Tax Reforms in Ohio," *AER,* 1 (1911), 506–507, 510.

47. Ames, *Taxation of Personal Property,* pp. 11–12, 51–52.

48. Brindley, *Taxation in Iowa,* 2, p. 210.

49. Iowa. *Report of the State Auditor, 1893,* pp. 82–85; *ibid.,* 1908, p. 194.

50. *Ibid.,* 1893, pp. 82–85; *ibid.,* 1885, p. 129.

51. *Ibid.,* 1893, pp. 82–85; Brindley, *Taxation in Iowa,* 1, p. 131.

52. Brindley, *Taxation in Iowa,* 1, pp. 310–55; also pp. 100, 101, 138, 139, 191–94.

53. Missouri. *Bureau of Labor Report, 1896,* pp. 83–129; Shearman, *Natural Taxation,* pp. 98–99. Ames, *Taxation of Personal Property,* pp. 13, 51.

54. See reports in *The Nation,* February 10, 1881, pp. 86–87; James H. Canfield, *Taxation—A Plain Talk for Plain People* (New York: The Society For Political Education, 1883), p. 30; members of the society included David A. Wells, William G. Sumner, Charles Francis Adams, Jr., and Franklin MacVeagh. Also see George Andrews, "Taxation," *An Address before the Assembly Committee on Ways and Means . . . 1874–75; Special Investigation on the Subject of Taxation* (Albany: 1875); New Jersey, *Special Tax Commission Report* (Newark: 1880), in *New Jersey Documents, 1880,* Vol. 1, No. 38, pp. 3–32; David A. Wells, "The Reform of Local Taxation," *NAR,* 122 (April 1876), 359, 360, 402; *Mass. Committee Report, 1897,* pp. 164–67.

55. *Mass. Committee Report, 1897,* pp. 167–70.

56. *The Nation,* February 10, 1881; Shearman, *Natural Taxation,* pp. 76–79; *California Bond and Stock Herald,* December 17, 1880.

57. *The Nation,* February 10, 1881.

58. C. T. Hopkins, "Taxation in California," *The Californian,* 3, p. 139.

59. Shearman, *Natural Taxation,* p. 78.

60. Robert Luce, "Second Prize Essay," in *Equitable Taxation: Six Essays in Answer to the Question What, If Any, Changes in the Existing Plans are Necessary to Secure an Equitable Distribution of the Burden of Taxation for the Support of National, State, and Municipal Governments?* (New York: Thomas Y. Crowell & Co., 1892), p. 42.

61. *Chicago Tribune,* April 21, 1877.

62. Henry James Ten Eyck, "Recent Experiments in State Taxation," *PSM,* 28 (1885), 461, 462.

63. Noble, *Taxation in Iowa,* p. 89.

64. Edward C. Moore, Jr., "Corporate Taxation," *The American Law Review,* 18 (Sept.–Oct. 1884), 750–51. For background materials see, Charles Gerstenberg, *Materials of Corporation Finance* (New York: Prentice-Hall, Inc., 1915), pp. 50–70 and following; Edward S. Meade, *Trust Finance* (New York: D. Appleton and Company, 1910).

65. *The Nation,* April 24, 1879.

66. *Comm. Chronicle,* 30 (March 27, 1880), 309–310.

67. *Mass. Commitee Report 1875,* p. 123.

68. *Wells Report (1871),* pp. 40, 41, 65, 67; also *Wells Report (1872),* pp. 25–30.

69. See, for instance, Jacob P. Dunn, *The New Tax Law of Indiana* (Indianapolis: Indianapolis Printing Company, 1892), pp. 14–19, 50–65; also see *48 New York Reports,* p. 78.

70. James H. Coleman, *Letters &c. on Corporations and Taxation* (New York: S. P. Pinckney, n.d.); also *New York Daily Graphic,* June 14, 1879, for instance.

71. Coleman, *Letters &c on Corporations,* pp. 1–5; *New York Daily Graphic,* December 23, 1878; January 6, 15, 1879; April 11, 1879.

72. See, for example, *People ex rel. Broadway and Seventh Avenue Railroad v. Commissioner of Taxes,* 1 New York Supreme Court Reports, 635; *People v. Baker,* 48 New York 77; *Bertholt v. O'Reilly,* 74 New York Reports 97; also in nearby New Jersey see, *Message v. Pennsylvania Railroad,* 36 New Jersey Report 407. Also New York State. *Engineer's Report,* September 30, 1868 for statistics.

73. Coleman, *Letters &c on Corporations,* pp. 7, 8, 21, 31–34, 35–39, e.g., for statistics.

74. *Ibid.,* pp. 14–17.

75. *Ibid.,* pp. 5–6; *New York Daily Graphic,* December 23, 1878.

76. *People ex rel. Broadway and Seventh Avenue Railroad v. Commissioner of Taxes,* 1 New York Supreme Court Report 635; *Smith v. Mayor and City of New York,* 23 Sickles 552.

77. Coleman, *Letters &c on Corporations,* pp. 10–12, 15–17, for statistics.

78. *Ibid.,* pp. 22–26; *New York Daily Graphic,* February 6, 1879.

79. *Mills Committee,* Part 5, Chapter 3, p. 85; also pp. 80–88, 133.

80. *Md. Comm, 1888,* p. 138.

81. *Ibid.,* pp. 23–27.

82. Dunn, *The New Tax Law of Indiana,* pp. 14–17.

83. *Pa. Revenue Comm. 1889,* pp. 5–15, 16–17, 88–91; also pp. 65–66.

84. Joseph D. Weeks, *Valuation, Taxation, and Exemptions in the Commonwealth of Pennsylvania: A Report to the Pennsylvania Tax Conference by the Commission on Valuation and Taxation* (Harrisburg: 1892), p. 23. Hereafter cited as *Weeks Report Pa. Tax Conference 1892.*

85. For Ely's quoted materials see *Md. Comm. 1888,* p. 125; Charles Bonaparte, "How to Obtain a Full and Fair Assessment for Taxation of Real and Personal Property," *An Address to LMPA,* December 3, 1889.

86. *Comm. Chronicle,* 33 (October 29, 1881); John C. Schwab, *History of the Property Tax in New York* (American Economic Association Studies) 5, No. 5, September 1890, pp. 87–89, 107–108; also Robert Murray Haig, Part 2, pp. 65–247 of the *Mastick Committee* 1932; Canfield, *Taxation,* p. 30; "The Tax Question," letter by Enoch Ensley to Governor Brown of Tennessee (Nashville: the author, 1873).

87. *Comm. Chronicle,* 28 (February 15, 1870).

88. New York. *Constitutional Convention, Debates,* 3, p. 2314; William H. Cowles, "Sixth Essays," in *Equitable Taxation,* p. 91; David Wells, "Principles of Taxation," *PSM,* 51, pp. 775–76.

89. *Fassett Committee,* 3, pp. 2252–2253, 2261, 2378.

90. Ibid., 3, pp. 2249, 2250, 2304, 2328–2329, 2393; also *Mazet Committee,* 2, pp. 1448–1541.

91. *Fassett Committee,* 3, pp. 2219–2229, 2247, 2263–2265, 2354, 2363–2365, 2393, 2417.

92. *Ibid.,* 3, pp. 2224, 2239–2340, 2318; also 2272–2280, 2284–2285 (Exhibits).

93. *Ibid.,* 3, pp. 2214, 2240, 2324–2325, 2335–2336, 2340–2346, 2407; also 2307–2318, 2325, 2329, 2445; and 2, pp. 981, 1152–1153, 1160–1170, 1174; also *Mazet Committee,* 2, pp. 1449, 1500–1505, 1506–1536, 1537–1541.

94. Shearman, *Natural Taxation,* pp. 113–114; R. H. Whitten, "The Assessment of Taxes in Chicago," *JPE,* 5, pp. 175–178.

95. Commons, "Taxation in Chicago and Philadelphia," pp. 437–38.

96. *Ibid.,* pp. 437, 445, 460; James Malcolm, "A Remarkable Statistical Report," *Arena,* 16, pp. 586–87; Whitten, "The Assessment of Taxes in Chicago," pp. 175–79, 181, 186, 190, 193–95; John Fairlie, "Taxation in Illinois," pp. 521–25; Illinois. *Bureau of Labor Statistics Report, 1888,* and Robert M. Haig, *A History of the General Property Tax in Illinois* (Champaign, Ill.: Flaigan-Pearson Company, 1914), Chapters 7, 8.

97. Commons, "Taxation in Chicago and Philadelphia," p. 445; J. Malcolm, "A Remarkable Statistical Report," pp. 586–87; Whitten, "The Assessment of Taxes in Chicago," pp. 175–79, 181, 190, 193–95; Fairlie, "Taxation in Illinois," pp. 521–25.

98. Forty-five thousand copies of the report were snapped up during the first three months of publication and Governor Altgeld ordered a second edition of 20,000 copies.

99. *Chicago Tribune,* April 21, 1877; Ames, *Taxation of Personal Property,* pp. 40–42; Illinois. *Bureau of Labor Statistics, 8th Biennial Report, 1895,* pp. 3–28; Malcolm, "A Remarkable Statistical Report," pp. 585, 586.

100. Illinois. *Bureau of Labor Statistics, 8th Biennial Report, 1895,* pp. 3–85; Malcolm, "A Remarkable Statistical Report," pp. 588–89; Haig, *History of Taxation in Illinois,* pp. 148–49.

101. Illinois. *Bureau of Labor Statistics, 8th Biennial Report, 1895,* pp. 60–87.

102. *Ibid.,* 1895, pp. 60–85; Whitten, "The Assessment of Taxes in Chicago," pp. 178–87; assessors could not satisfactorily explain "$50,000 property (valued) at $2430 . . . of $175,000 . . . at $7980, of $1,300,000 property at $71,960, and so on."

103. Illinois. *Bureau of Labor Statistics, 8th Biennial Report, 1895,* pp. 60–87; John A. Fairlie, *A Report on the Taxation and Revenue System of Illinois Prepared for The Special Tax Commission* (Danville, Ill.: 1910), pp. 20–27, 48–49.

104. New York. *Constitutional Convention, Debates,* 3, p. 2321.

105. *Ibid.,* 3, p. 1909; *Wells Report (1871),* pp. 30, 31, 37.

106. *Wells Report (1871),* pp. 31–32. For an overview see Schwab, *History of the New York Property Tax,* pp. 81–83; also Robert Haig, Part Two, *Mastick Committee,* 1932, pp. 65 ff.

107. *Wells Report* (1871), pp. 30–32.

108. Calhoun, JoDaviess, Gallatin, and Pope counties, for instance.

109. DuPage, Kane, and St. Clair counties were typical.

110. Fairlie, *A Report on the Taxation and Revenue System of Illinois,* pp, 21–23, 24–26; U.S. Census. Bureau of the Census, *Report on Wealth, Debt, and Taxation (1909),* pp. 52, 94; Haig, *History of Taxation in Illinois,* pp. 176–79; F. B. Garver, "Some Phases of Tax Reform in Illinois," *JPE,* 19 (Jan.–Dec. 1911), 574–90.

111. See Bogart, *Financial History of Ohio,* pp. 202–40; Shearman, *Natural Taxation,* pp. 88–92; T. N. Carver, "The Tax Inquisitor Law in Ohio," pp.

206–210; Bogart, "Recent Tax Reforms in Ohio," *AER*, 1 (1911), 505–507; *Ohio Tax Commission 1893*, pp. 21–47, 69–70.

112. "Taxation in the Counties," in *Md. Comm. 1888*, p. cxc; also p. clxxxviii.

113. March 14, 1894; Iowa. *Report of the State Auditor, 1885*, pp. 129–35; *Ibid.*, 1893, pp. 82–85; *Ibid.*, 1908, pp. 194–198; Brindley, *Taxation in Iowa*, 2, p. 210; also 1, pp. 171–212.

114. *Pa. Revenue Comm. 1889*, pp. 63–65, 66, 68–69, 71, 156–57; *Wells Report (1871)*, pp. 8, 17–23; *Weeks Report Pa. Tax Conf. 1892*, pp. 5, 7, 10; *Baltimore: Report of the Committee of the Establishment of Manufactures* (Baltimore: Evening Bulletin, J. B. Printing Office, 1877), p. 37 for Andrews' remarks.

115. *Weeks Report Pa. Tax Conf. 1892*, pp. 1–14, especially Table 1.

116. *Pa. Revenue Comm. 1889*, pp. 51, 64–65, 66–71.

Chapter 3 *Inequity and Inequality*

1. Charles B. Spahr, "The Taxation of Labor," *PSQ*, 1 (1886), 400.

2. These widespread views are exemplified in *Mass. Committee Report 1875*, pp. 7–10; also Thomas M. Cooley, *A Treatise on the Law of Taxation* (Chicago: Callaghan and Co., 1876), pp. 55–60 and following; Francis Hilliard, *The Law of Taxation* (Boston: Little, Brown and Co., 1875), Chapter 1, "The Nature and Principles of Taxation;" Whitmore, *Unjust Taxes*, pp. 5, 8, 10; *Allen v. Jay*, 58 Maine 590; for Justice Doe's comments see 60 New Hampshire 255.

3. Sharswood's remarks are in *Durach's Appeal*, 62 Pennsylvania State 491–95. This was almost literally the same view as Justice Marshall's; it reappeared in 1874 in Justice Miller's remarks in *Loan Association v. Topeka*, 20 Wallace 665–68; *Mass. Committee Report 1875*, pp. 152–53 for Pattison's comment.

4. *Mass. Committee Report 1875*, pp. 9–11.

5. *Ibid.*, 1875, p. 11.

6. Bogart, *Financial History of Ohio*, pp. 240–47; Ohio. *Comptroller's Report 1889*, p. 34. Also see J. H. T. McPherson, "The General Property Tax as a Source of Revenue," *Proceedings of NTA*, 1 (1907), 475–84.

7. For summary discussion see Edwin R. A. Seligman, *Essays on Taxation*, Chapter 2.

8. Seligman, "The General Property Tax," p. 25.

9. For Pennsylvania see, M. E. Olmsted, *The Riter Tax Bill (House Bill No. 239) Argument of M. E. Olmsted, Esq . . . on Behalf of Certain Corporate Interests Before the Ways and Means Committee of the House of Representatives of Pennsylvania, March 19, 1895*, pp. 4–7; *Weeks Report Pa. Tax Conf. 1892*, p. 9; Lawson Purdy, "Outline of a Model Tax System of State and Local Taxation," *Proceedings of NTA*, 1 (1907), 54–74; Purdy's estimates were based on Table 20 U.S. Bureau of the Census, *Wealth, Debt, and Taxation* (1900).

10. Thomas L. Thornell, J. S. Schultz, Isaac Sherman, *Report on the Inequality of State Taxation: To the Union League Club, March 9, 1876*, p. 2.

For other samples of this extensive literature see, *Fassett Committee,* 3, pp. 2250, 2257, 2377–2378, 2444–2445; Shearman, *Home Rule in Taxation: An Address,* pp. 10, 12, 23; *Comm. Chronicle,* 61 (October 5, 1895), 592–93.

11. *Comm. Chronicle,* 61 (October 5, 1895), 592–93; "Report of the Committee on the Causes of the Failure of the General Property Tax," *Proceedings of NTA,* 4 (1910), 302–304; *Md. Comm. 1888,* pp. 104–116, 134; Shearman, *Natural Taxation,* pp. 88–98. *Pa. Revenue Comm. 1889,* pp. 169–70; "Outline of A Model System of State and Local Taxation," *Proceedings of NTA,* 1 (1907), 112–114; Ohio, General Assembly, House, *Report of the Ohio Tax Commission of 1893* (Cleveland: J. B. Savage, 1893), pp. 24–25, 28–34; hereafter cited as *Ohio Committee Report 1893.*

12. *Mass. Committee Report 1875,* pp. 122–23; *Ibid.,* 1897, pp. 182–83.

13. Roswell McCrea, "Tax Discrimination in the Paper and Pulp Industry," *QJE,* 21 (August 1907), 636, 637, 643, 644.

14. *Wells Report (1871),* pp. 102–103; New York State. *Report of the State Assessors, 1879,* p. 19.

15. Charles Francis Adams, Jr., W. B. Williams, and J. H. Oberly, *Taxation of Railroads and Railroad Securities* (New York: Atkins Prout, The Railroad Gazette, 1880), pp. 4, 8.

16. "Valuation and Taxation of Railroads in Pennsylvania," in *Valuation, Taxation, and Exemptions in the Commonwealth of Pennsylvania. A Report to the Pennsylvania Tax Conference by the Committee on Valuation and Taxation* (Harrisburg: 1892), pp. 15, 17, 18. For the statistics on which these conclusions are based see, pp. 2, 4–11.

17. *Ibid.,* pp. 16, 17; also Dunn, *The New Tax Law of Indiana, 1892,* pp. 14–19.

18. Dunn, *The New Tax Law of Indiana,* pp. 8, 9; for related discussion see, *Md. Comm. 1888,* pp. 16–56, 188–90; Adams, Williams, and Oberly, *Taxation of Railroads, 1880,* pp. 3–8; Coleman, *Letters &c. on Corporations, 1878,* pp. 4–54; also see E. Moore's, *Law of Taxation,* Chapter 9, pp. 257–89. Major state tax commission all dealt with this issue separately as did the National Tax Conference.

19. *Comm. Chronicle,* 27 (August 10, 1878); 28 (February 15, 1879), 30 (March 20, 1880); also (March 27, 1880), (April 10, 1880), (May 1, 1880), (May 8, 1880), 33 (October 29, 1881), for examples. For general discussions see Thomas J. Hillhouse *Taxation of Banks by the State of New York* (New York: E. Wells Sachett & Bros., 1880), pp. 5–61; T. J. Spear, "Bank Taxation," *Albany Law Journal,* 21 (1880), 427–30; *Fassett Committee,* 3, pp. 2272–2283; *Report of the Committee of Bank Officers of the City of New York in Relation to Bank Taxation* (New York: 1875).

20. *Comm. Chronicle,* 33 (October 29, 1881); also 30 (March 27, 1880).

21. They made this judgment on the assumption that in tax matters, thanks to various "pulls," banks would not all be treated equally by government officials.

22. *Comm. Chronicle,* 30 (March 27, 1880), (May 8, 1880). Also see, *Ohio Committee Report 1893,* p. 65; Shearman, *Natural Taxation,* pp. 57–60; Seligman, *Essays in Taxation,* pp. 143–50, 177–79; *Md. Comm. 1888,* pp. 127–28; *Fassett Committee,* 3, p. 2376.

23. *Comm. Chronicle,* 27 (August 10, 1878); 30 (March 27, 1880); 32 (May 14, 1881); 33 (October 29, 1881).

24. For instance, Haig, *History of Taxation in Illinois,* pp. 176–79; *Mills Committee,* Part 7, p. 136; *Mass. Committee Report 1897,* pp. 156–83; *Fassett Committee,* 3, pp. 2392–2395; summary comments can be found in the Reports of Maryland, Pennsylvania, Ohio, and Massachusetts Tax Commissions.

25. Illinois. *Fourth Biennial Report of the Bureau of Labor Statistics, 1888;* Haig, *History of Taxation in Illinois,* pp. 147–50; Commons, "*Taxation* in Chicago and Philadelphia," pp. 435–36; New York State. *Report of the State Assessors, 1888,* p. 5.

26. New York State. *Report of the State Assessors, 1877,* p. 10; New Jersey. *Report of the Comptroller of the State of New Jersey, 1887,* pp. 57, 95.

27. Seligman, "The General Property Tax," p. 27.

28. Illinois. *Report of the Revenue Commission 1886* (Springfield: 1886), p. 8; Connecticut. *Report of the Special Commission on the Subject of Taxation, 1887* (New Haven: 1887), p. 27; New Hampshire. *Report to the Legislature of New Hampshire of the Honorable George Y. Sawyer, Chairman of the Board of Commissioners to Revise . . . the Tax Laws of the State, etc. 1876* (Concord: 1876), p. 16; West Virginia. *Preliminary Report of the West Virginia Tax Commission* (Wheeling), p. 10; Oscar Leser, E. R. A. Seligman, James Forman, Nils Haugen, Frederick Judson, "Report of the Committee on the Causes of the Failure of the General Property Tax," *Proceedings of NTA,* 3 (1910), pp. 299–310.

29. See, *The People ex rel. Babbitt v. Commissioner of Taxes . . . of New York,* 824; *Hoyt v. Commissioner of Taxes,* 23 New York; *Parker v. The Commissioner of Taxes,* 23 New York 242; *Austin v. Low,* 13 Wall 29; There were many similar cases.

30. *Mitchell v. The Board of Commissioners,* etc. 1 Otto 206.

31. *Stilwell's Adminsters v. Corwin's Adminsters,* 55 Indiana 433.

32. *Mass. Committee Report 1897,* pp. 82–83.

33. John Winslow Cabot, "Fifth Essay," in *Equitable Taxation,* pp. 69–71.

34. *Md. Comm. 1888,* pp. 145–47; also p. 142.

35. Seligman, "The General Property Tax," p. 30.

36. *Md. Comm. 1888,* p. 146.

37. Seligman, "The General Property Tax," p. 33; Connecticut. *Report of the Special Commission on the Subject of Taxation, 1887,* p. 26; William Endicott, Jr., *The Taxation Only of Tangible Things in Massachusetts. Report of Committee, 1875,* pp. 407–16; Josiah Quincy, *Double Taxation in Massachusetts, etc.* (Boston: The Author, 1889); George Crocker, *An Exposition of the Double Taxation of Personal Property in Massachusetts* (Boston: The Author, 1885); also see Crocker's *The Injustice and Inexpediency of Double Taxation* (Boston: H. G. Gollins, 1892). R. H. Dana, *Double Taxation in Massachusetts. Exposition of the Injustice and Inexpediency of Parts of the Taxation System in Massachusetts* (Boston: The Author, 1895); Francis Walker, *Double Taxation in the United States* (New York: Columbia University Press, 1895).

38. B. Adams, "Oppressive Taxation of the Poor," pp. 632–36. David Wells, "The Reform of Local Taxation," pp. 370–72.

39. Adams, "Oppressive Taxation of the Poor," pp. 634, 636.

40. Endicott, *The Taxation Only of Tangible Things,* pp. 407–16.

41. Minot, *Taxation in Massachusetts, 1877,* pp. 11, 18–28, 53–57.

42. New Jersey. *Report of the Honorable Charles S. Ogden . . . to the Legislature of New Jersey on Taxation* (Trenton: 1868), pp. 11–14; New Jersey. *Report of the Special Tax Commission of the State of New Jersey* (New Brunswick: 1886), p. 20; *Mass. Committee Report, 1875,* pp. 86–99.

43. Moore, "Corporate Taxation," *American Law Review,* 28 (Sept.–Oct. 1884), 754–57; hereafter cited as *ALR.* Noble, *Taxation in Iowa, 1897,* pp. 40–44; *Mass. Committee Report 1875,* pp. 88–89; *Ibid.,* 1897, pp. 64–68.

44. Illinois. *Constitution of the State of Illinois, 1870,* Article 9; Moore, "Corporate Taxation," p. 757; *Danville Banking . . . Company v. Parks,* 88 Illinois 170; *State v. Newark,* 1 Dutch 315; *Pittsburgh Railroad Company v. Commonwealth,* 66 Pennsylvania State 77; *Lackawanna Iron Company v. Luzerne County,* 42 Pennsylvania State 424.

45. Seligman, *Essays on Taxation,* Chapter 8, especially p. 213, for general discussion.

46. For instance, Seligman, "The Taxation of Corporations," pp. 269–308, 438–67, 636–76; Edward Atkinson, *Argument of Edward Atkinson for a Change in the Law in Regard to Taxing Foreign Corporations, etc. 1877,* pp. 3–24 and summary details later in George Clapperton, Part 7, *Taxation in Various States and in Canada with Special Reference to the Taxation of Corporations* in *Report of the United States Industrial Commission 1902,* 9, "Agriculture and Taxation," pp. 7–171; Hilliard, *Law of Taxation,* Chapter 4; also *Argument of Moses Williams, Jr., Before the Committee on Taxation of the Massachusetts Legislature, February 18, 1880* (Boston: T. R. Marvin & Son, 1880).

47. See, for example, beside the above, John Commons, *The Legal Foundations of Capitalism* (Madison: University of Wisconsin Press, 1959), pp. 172–82; Wells, "Reform of Local Taxation," pp. 365–76 for discussions of Supreme Court decisions relative to corporate taxation.

48. See, Seligman, *On the Shifting and Incidence of Taxation* (Baltimore: American Economic Association, 1892), 7, pp. 5–191; Edward A. Ross, "Seligman's Shifting and Incidence of Taxation," *The Annals,* 3 (July 1892–June 1893), 444–63; Harry G. Friedman, *Taxation of Corporations in Massachusetts* (New York: Columbia University Press, 1907), pp. 164–77; Roswell McCrea, "Notes and Memoranda: A Suggestion on the Taxation of Corporations," *QJE,* 19 (1904), 492–97; also for ancillary discussions not cited above see, Connecticut. *Report of the Special Commission on the Taxation of Corporations* (Hartford: 1913); "The Taxation of Public Service Corporations: Report of a Committee of the National Tax Association," *Proceedings of NTA,* 7 (1914), 372–83.

49. See, Seligman, *Essays on Taxation,* pp. 254–58.

50. *Ibid.,* pp. 34–35, for instance.

51. For a few insights into the development of public purpose doctrine see Cooley's decision in *People v. Salem,* 20 Michigan 487 (1870); *The East Saginaw Manufacturing Company v. The City of East Saginaw,* 19 Michigan 274

(1869); *Gale v. The Village of Kalamazoo,* 23 Michigan 354 (1871). Wrote Cooley in *People v. Salem:* "it is not in the power of the State, in my opinion, under the name of a bounty or under any other cover or subterfuge, to furnish the capital to set private parties up in any kind of business after they have entered upon it. A bounty law of which this is the real nature is void." But then Cooley added with some apparent ambivalence: "The right to hold out pecuniary inducements to the faithful performance of a public duty in dangerous or responsible positions, stands upon a different footing altogether." He later added further: "Where the State itself is to receive the benefits of taxation, in the increase of its public funds or the improvement of its public property, there can be no doubt of the public character of the purpose." Cooley, of course, drew upon the Sharpless decision in Pennsylvania and in the Salem Case referred to it as "the leading case upon the subject" in 1870. He had already noted it in *A Treatise on the Constitutional Limitations which Rest Upon the Legislative Powers of the States of the American Union* (1868), Chapter 14, and in his *A Treatise on the Law of Taxation* (Chicago: 1876), Chapter 4. For background see particularly Louis Hartz, *Economic Policy and Democratic Thought: Pennsylvania 1776–1860* (Cambridge: Harvard University Press, 1948), pp. 104–113; C. K. Yearley, *Enterprise and Anthracite: Economics and Democracy in Schuylkill County, 1820–1875* (Baltimore: Johns Hopkins Press, 1961), Chapters 1, 2. Also see Ellis Waldron, "Sharpless v. Philadelphia: Jeremiah Black and the Parent Case on the Public Purpose of Taxation," *Wisconsin Law Review,* 1953, pp. 48–75. Opening arguments were reconstructed from *Philadelphia Daily Pennsylvanian,* July 27, 1853; 21 Pennsylvania 151–53; Barton A. Konkle, *Life and Speeches of Thomas Williams, etc.* (Philadelphia: Campion and Company, 1905), 1, Chapters 12, 13; also pp. 225–27 by Waldron. See, too, *Philadelphia Daily Pennsylvanian,* July 29, 1853; 21 Pennsylvania 158, 159, 160–71; *Diamond v. Lawrence County,* 37 Pennsylvania State 353; *Lowell v. Boston,* 113 American Law Register 493; *State v. Osawkee,* 14 Kansas 488; *Weismer v. Douglas,* 64 New York 91; and related decision like those which began with *Goddin v. Crump,* 8 Hugh. Virginia 1887; *Cincinnati, W. Railroad v. Clinton County, 1 Ohio State* (1852); similar decisions were rendered in Virginia, Ohio, New York, Connecticut, Tennessee, Kentucky, and Illinois. For instance, see, *Vieley v. Thompson,* 44 Illinois 9; *Scudder v. State,* 33 New Jersey 424; *Truesdell's Case,* 58 Pennsylvania 148; *State v. Demarest,* 3 Vroom 528; *Jenkins v. Anderson,* 103 Massachusetts, 74; *Curtis v. Whipple,* 24 Wisconsin 350; *Thomas v. Leland,* 24 Wend. 65; *Merrick v. Amherst,* 12 Allen 504; *Allen v. Jay,* 60 Maine 124; Hilliard, *Law of Taxation,* pp. 10–14.

CHAPTER 4 *The Cult of Efficiency and Party Finance*

1. See, New York. *Report of the New York Special Tax Commission (1907),* p. 7; Minnesota. *Minnesota Tax Commission (1908),* pp. 39–43; *Report of the Wisconsin Tax Commission (1903),* p. 115; *Report of the Kansas Tax Commission (1909),* pp. 16–30, for summaries of such views.

2. Matthews, *The City Government of Boston,* pp. 179–81, 184; Whitmore, *Unjust Taxation,* p. 14; on the same point see John A. Kasson, "Municipal Reform," *NAR,* 137 (1883), 225.

3. Matthews, *The City Government of Boston,* p. 178.

4. Aside from the usual recapitulations of this interpretation in most texts, the successors to this Mugwump version of history were Charles Beard, Matthew Josephson, Louis Hacker, and more recently Richard Hofstadter, Eric Goldman, and Ray Ginger.

5. To cite only a few scholars: Leonard White, Ari Hoogenboom, Irwin Unger, Edward Kirkland, Samuel Hays, and James Weinstein.

6. See Bryce's chapter, "Corruption," in *The American Commonwealth* (1889), 2, pp. 161 and following.

7. One of the earliest professional academic arguments along this line was by the noted reform-minded political scientist, Andrew C. McLaughlin, "The Significance of Political Parties," *Atlantic Monthly,* 101 (1908), 145–56.

8. For some of the many defenses of spoils see, Albion Tourgee, "Reform versus Reformation," *NAR,* 132 (1881), 305–10; Daniel Greenleaf Thompson, *Politics in A Democracy* (New York: Longmans, Green and Co., 1893).

9. Arthur Richmond, "Letters to Prominent Persons," *NAR,* 43 (1886), 238.

10. Bryce, *American Commonwealth* (1889), 2, pp. 127–28; Chester Lloyd Jones, "Spoils and the Party," *Annals,* 64 (March 1916), 73.

11. *Harper's,* 43, p. 18, 19, 20, 26.

12. Matthew Breen, *Thirty Years of New York Politics* (New York: John Polhemus Printing Company, 1899), p. iii; also see, Stickney, *The Political Problem,* pp. 16, 20. 55.

13. Ivins, "Municipal Government," pp. 292–93.

14. Bryce, *American Commonwealth* (1889), 2, pp. 62–63, 65, 72, 156.

15. *Ibid.,* (1889), 2, p. 467.

16. For instance, Fred Riggs, *The Ecology of Public Administration* (New York: Asia Publishing House, 1961), Chapter 5; also see Riggs' "Prismatic Society and Financial Administration," *Administrative Science Quarterly,* 5 (June 1960), 1–46; and "An Ecological Approach: The Sala Model," a paper delivered at the Meeting of the American Political Science Association, September 6–9, 1961, pp. 1–15; also see the newer materials on the "politics of modernization," such as David Apter, *The Politics of Modernization* (Chicago: University of Chicago Press, 1965), Chapters 6–8; C. E. Black, *The Dynamics of Modernization* (New York: Harper & Row, 1966), Chapter 3. For European developments see Eugene N. Anderson and Pauline R. Anderson, *Political Institutions and Social Change In Continental Europe in The Nineteenth Century* (Berkeley and Los Angeles: University of California Press, 1967).

17. Richard H. Dana, "A Substitute for the Caucus," *Forum,* 2 (1886), 497.

18. *Report of the Committee of 100* (November 1884); State of New York. Assembly. *Report of the Select Committee appointed by the Assembly of 1875 to Investigate the Causes of Increase of Crime in the City of New York, February 11, 1876, Assembly Document 106;* Jesse Macy, *Party Organization and Machinery* (New York: The Century Company, 1912), pp. 120–24, 158–62.

19. Philemon Tecumseh Sherman, *Inside the Machine: Two Years in the*

Board of Aldermen, 1898–99: A Study of the Legislative Features of New York City Under the Greater New York Charter (New York: Cooke & Fry, 1901), pp. 78–80; William Ivins, *Machine Politics and Money in Elections in New York City* (New York: Harper & Bros., 1887), pp. 56–57, 62–63. For a contemporary bibliography on party finance see Orman P. Ray, *Political Parties and Practical Politics* (New York: Charles Scribner's Sons, 1913), Chapter 11 Bibliography.

20. Sherman, *Inside the Machine,* pp. 62–63; also see Moisei Ostrogorski, *Democracy and the Organization of Political Parties,* 2 vols, (New York: Macmillan, 1901), 2 Part 4, Chapter 4 and Index on Finances of Party Organizations; Ray, *Political Parties,* pp. 293–97, list of documents and articles on party finance.

21. Sherman, *Inside the Machine,* pp. 42, 43.

22. *Ibid.,* pp. 60–61, 62, 63.

23. *Ibid.,* pp. 47–49.

24. *Ibid.,* pp. 54–55, 56–57.

25. *Ibid.,* pp. 57–58; Theodore Roosevelt, *American Ideals and Other Essays* (New York: G. P. Putnam's Sons, 1899), pp. 112–113, 121; Charles Eliot Norton, ed., *Orations and Addresses of George William Curtis,* 3 vols. (New York: Harper & Bros., 1894), 2, p. 495. John Townshend, *New York in Bondage* (New York: By the Author, 1901), credited John Kelly with overlording city organization disposing of over $30 million a year in 1871 through 12,000 party regulars. The source of this estimate reputedly was Samuel Tilden.

26. See, for example, "Buying and Selling Votes," *Century,* 47 (1893–94), 144–45; J. B. Harrison, "The Sale of Votes in New Hampshire," *Century,* 47 (1893–94), 149–50; *The Nation,* July 22, 1886; L. B. Richardson, *William Chandler* (New York: Dodd Mead & Co., 1940), pp. 165–67.

27. Macy, *Party Organization,* p. 159.

28. Herbert Croly, *The Promise of American Life* (New York: Capricorn Books, 1964), p. 118.

29. Wells, "Principles of Taxation," *PSM,* 48 (1895), 6; *PSM,* 49 (1896), 583–84; *PSM,* 51 (1897), 613.

30. Ivins, *Machine Politics,* pp. 10–11.

31. For instance, Dorman Eaton, "Political Assessments," *NAR,* 135 (September 1882), 218. Literature from the period on assessments is extensive.

32. *Ibid.,* p. 202; on removals, p. 198 and Norton, *Orations and Addresses of Curtis,* pp. 128–32 for samplings.

33. Eaton, "Political Assessments," p. 202. Also such writings as Robert C. Brooks, *Corruption in American Politics and Life* (New York: Dodd Mead & Co., 1910), Chapter 6; also for contemporary comments see *Cyclopedia of Political Science,* 1, pp. 152 and following; *Cyclopedia of American Government,* 1, p. 480; 2, pp. 623, 624.

34. Eaton, "Political Assessments," p. 202.

35. *Ibid.,* pp. 214–15; Norton, *Orations and Addresses of Curtis,* 2, pp. 163–64; *The Nation,* November 18, 1886, for instance. Francis C. Lowell, "The American Boss," *Atlantic,* 86 (September 1900), 297–99.

36. Eaton, "Political Assessments," p. 208; on Kelly see, for instance, E. J.

Edwards, "Tammany Under John Kelly," *McClure's,* 5 (June-November 1895), 325–29.

37. Joseph B. Bishop, *Money in City Elections: Its Effects and Their Remedies: An Address before the Commonwealth Club of New York, March 21, 1887* (New York: Evening Post Publishing Company, 1887).

38. Ivins, *Machine Politics,* pp. 54–58.

39. Eaton, "Political Assessment," p. 108. Also Warner Miller, "Businessmen in Politics," *NAR,* 151 (1890), 576–81.

40. *Mazet Committee,* 3, pp. 3450–3453; also 2, p. 1414; 5, pp. 5464–5468.

41. *Ibid.,* 4, pp. 3656–3657.

42. *Ibid.,* 1, pp. 1139–1140; also 1, pp. 342–43, 380, 383, 432, 481; 2, pp. 1265, 1268, 1414; 4, pp. 3662–3663, 3930. Croker's explanation of wiskinskies is in 1, p. 481. See, too, *Fassett Committee,* 2, pp. 1756–1758, 1760–1761.

43. *Mazet Committee,* 3, p. 3541; also 1, p. 31; 4, pp. 3650–3656, 3942–3945; also 4, p. 3925.

44. *Ibid.,* 3, pp. 3581, 3611.

45. *Ibid.,* 4, pp. 3923–3929.

46. New York. *Report and Proceedings of the Senate Committee appointed to Investigate the Police Department of the City of New York,* 5 vols., (Albany: J. B. Lyon, 1895); this was the famous *Lexow Committee,* cited hereafter as such; Ivins, *Machine Politics,* p. 24.

47. *Lexow Committee,* 5, pp. 5378–5379.

48. For instance, *ibid.,* 2, pp. 1594–1595, 2280–2287; 4, pp. 3614–3616, 3637–3638; 5, pp. 5373–5374. Many of these practices were common in the sixties and seventies; see, Townshend, *New York in Bondage,* Chapters 25, 27; also John Leavitt, "Criminal Degradation of New York Citizenship," *Forum,* 17 (August 1894), 659–65.

49. *Fassett Committee,* 2, pp. 1083–1085; also pp. 981, 1110–1235; 1, pp. 645–50 for typical instances of these operations.

50. *Ibid.,* 2, pp. 1083–1235.

51. Leavitt, "Criminal Degradation of New York Citizenship," p. 661; *Lexow Committee,* 2, pp. 1580–2285; 4, pp. 3620–4178, for instance.

52. Schmittberger testified before the *Lexow Committee,* 5; Captain Devery testified before the *Mazet Committee,* 1, pp. 133–48, 155–63, 183, 260–301, 1022–1025; Croker's testimony to the Mazet Committee covered several hundred pages closing with interrogations on the Ramapo Water Deal; relevant testimony here is in Volume 1, pp. 323–37, 341, 530–36. For general background see Josiah Flynt, *The World of Graft* (New York: McClure, Phillips Co., 1901), Chapter 2. Other aspects are treated in Committee of Fifteen, *A Report on The Social Evil with Special Reference to Conditions Existing in the City of New York* (New York: G. P. Putnam's Sons, 1902), Chapter 10; Committee of Fourteen, *The Social Evil in New York City: A Study of Law Enforcement* (New York: Andrew Kellogg, 1910), Chapters 1–3, particularly.

53. For instance, *Mazet Committee,* 2, pp. 2659–70, etc.; 3, pp. 3819–3835, 3898–3899; 4, pp. 3905–3910; 5, pp. 5068–5075; also Townshend, *New York in Bondage,* pp. 226–43.

54. For some of the ample background literature on Philadelphia see Herbert Welsh, "The Degradation of Pennsylvania Politics," *Forum,* 12 (Novem-

ber 1891), 330–45; George Vickers, *The Fall of Bossism: A History of the Committee of One Hundred and The Reform Movement in Philadelphia* (Philadelphia: A. C. Bryan, 1883); Clinton R. Woodruff, "The Progress of Municipal Reform in Philadelphia," *Harper's Weekly,* October 27, 1894; *The Report of the Committee of One Hundred, November 1884;* Bryce, *The American Commonwealth* (1888), 3, Chapter 89, "The Philadelphia Gas Ring;" E. S. Bradley, *Henry Charles Lea: A Biography* (Philadelphia: University of Pennsylvania Press, 1931), Chapter 5; Henry C. Lea, "A Letter to the People of Philadelphia," Forum, 2 (1886), pp. 532–38; Wayne MacVeagh, "A Great Victory for Honest Politics," *NAR,* 182 (January 1906), 1-18.

55. MacVeagh, "Victory for Honest Politics," pp. 6–7.

56. Bishop, *Money in City Elections: Address to the Commonwealth Club, 1887,* p. 7.

57. Alvan Sanborn, "The Anatomy of a Tenement Street," *Forum,* 18 (1894), 572.

Chapter 5 *The Dominance of the Politician*

1. Keller, *Beyond the Ruling Class,* pp. 3–64 especially; also such articles as Michalina Clifford-Vaughan, "Some French Concepts of Elites," *British Journal of Sociology,* 11 (December 1960), 319–31.

2. E. g., Samuel E. Morison and Henry S. Commager, *The Growth of the American Republic* 6th ed. rev., 2 vols., (New York: Oxford University Press, 1962), 2, p. 313; Matthew Josephson, *The Politicos* (New York: Harcourt, Brace & World, 1963), p. v; George H. Mayer, *The Republican Party, 1854–1966* (New York: Oxford University Press, 1967), brands the period "The Age of the Condottiere."

3. George Yeaman, "The Study of Government," *NAR,* 132 (July 1871), 199, a review.

4. E.g., see the recent writings of Sharkey, Coben, Kirkland, Wiebe, Weinstein, Timberlake, and Hays, among others, cited in Note 5 of the Introduction and Note 40 of Chapter 1.

5. Edwin L. Godkin, "Commercial Immorality and Political Corruption," pp. 248–66.

6. William B. Munro, *Personality in Politics: Reformers, Bosses, and Leaders* (New York: Macmillan Company, 1925), p. 76; Bryce, *American Commonwealth* (1889), 2, p. 108; Ostrogorski, *Democracy and the Organization of Political Parties,* 2, p. 204; also see pp. 101–105, 183–86, 196–97, 200–206; T. Roosevelt, *American Ideals,* p. 129; Ray, *Political Parties,* pp. 474–81 for the then standardized references on bosses and bossism. Elihu Root, *Addresses on Government and Citizenship* (Cambridge: Harvard University Press, 1916), pp. 201–202; William B. Munro's summary in his *The American Party System* (New York: Macmillan, 1922), Chapter 7.

7. Ostrogorski, *Democracy and the Organization of Political Parties,* 2, p. 632.

8. Roosevelt, *American Ideals,* p. 117.

9. Simon Newcomb, "Our Political Dangers," *NAR,* 130 (1880), 274.

10. Karl Mannheim, *Ideology and Utopia* (New York: Harcourt, Brace & Co., n.d.), Chapter 3 touches on the point.

11. There is an extensive literature of traditional political science and journalism, of course, on bosses; on Platt see Lemuel Quigg, "Thomas Platt," *NAR,* 191 (1910), 674; Harold Gosnell, *Boss Platt and His New York Machine* (Chicago: University of Chicago Press, 1924).

12. Samuel Pennypacker, *The Autobiography of a Pennsylvanian* (Philadelphia: John C. Winston, 1918), p. 322; also on Quay see pp. 195, 265, 281, 316, 320, 385, 440, 483–85; John Wanamaker *The Speeches of the Honorable John Wanamaker* (Philadelphia: Businessmen's Republican Association of the State of Pennsylvania, 1898), pp. 123 and following; Edward S. Bradley, *Henry Charles Lea* (Philadelphia: University of Pennsylvania Press, 1931) Chapter 5; Matthew Quay, *Pennsylvania Politics: The Campaign of 1900 as set Forth in Speeches* (Philadelphia: J. Campbell, 1901), which gives no clue whatever to Quay's abilities and indeed suggests that either he or the electorate or both were subnormal.

13. Roosevelt, *American Ideals,* p. 118; Fremont Bennett, *Politics and Politicians of Chicago, Cook County, and Illinois, 1787–1887* (Chicago: Blakely Printing Co., 1887), pp. 363–75; Gosnell, *Platt;* Thompson, *Party Leaders of the Time* (New York: G. W. Dillingham, 1906); Eugene Thrasher, "The Major-Flinn Political Machine," (M. A. Thesis, University of Pittsburgh, 1951); Ostrogorski and Bryce both acknowledged such sentiments and motives among party workers. Henry George thought the machine was due directly to the costs of elections; see *NAR* (March 1883).

14. F. T. Greenhalge, "Practical Politics," *NAR,* 162 (1896), 156–57.

15. Macy, *Party Organization,* pp. 159–61.

16. Herbert Welsh, "The Degradation of Pennsylvania Politics," *Forum,* 12 (1892), 336–37.

17. "New York's New Ruler," *The Nation,* 60 (January 24, 1895).

18. *Ibid.*

19. E. S. Nadel, "The New York Aldermen," *Forum,* 2 (1886), 58; also see Frederick Shaw, *The History of the New York City Legislature* (New York: Columbia University Press, 1954), pp. 3–18.

20. "The Growing Impudence of the Bosses," *Century,* 52 (1896), 155.

21. *Ibid.;* also 52, pp. 632–33.

22. *The Nation, 55* (November 10, 1892). On Hill see Independent, "The Political Career and Character of David B. Hill," *Forum,* 42 (November 1894), 257–69; "The Machine versus the People," *Century,* 44 (1892), 154.

23. *Comm. Chronicle,* 30 (March 27, 1880), 309–310; also 30 (March 20, 1880), 286; *The Nation,* 55 (November 10, 1892), 347–48.

24. Thomas Cochran, *Railroad Leaders 1845–1890: The Business Mind in Action* (Cambridge: Harvard University Press, 1953), pp. 190, 192; also see *Comm. Chronicle,* 61 (October 5, 1895), 59–93; Chauncey Depew, "Railway Men in Politics," *NAR,* 151 (July 1890), 86–89; Testimony before the *U.S. Industrial Commission,* 4 (1901), 986–88, for instance.

25. *The Nation,* January 17, 1895. "Taxpayers' Associations."

26. Canfield, *Taxation,* p. 16.

27. *The Nation,* January 13, 1881, for instance, "Mayor Grace on the Need for Municipal Reform," p. 23.

28. See, Lance Davis and John Legler, "Government in the American Economy, 1815–1902: A Quantitative Study," *Journal of Economic History,* 26 (December 1966), 514–27; cited hereafter as *JEH.* Austin MacDonald, "The Trend in Recent State Expenditures," *The Annals,* 113 (May 1924), 8–20; Henry Carter Adams, *Public Debts,* Chapters 2, 3; U.S. Bureau of the Census. *Historical Statistics of the U.S. (1960),* 726–27, series Y–536–47, 547–74; National Industrial Conference Board, *Tax Burdens and Public Expenditures* (New York: National Industrial Conference Board, 1925), pp. 1–5; New York. *A Report by the Special Joint Committee on Taxation and Retrenchment, February 11, 1926,* "State Expenditures and Wealth;" *Mills Committee,* Chapter 3, on the rise of state expenditures since 1885; New York. *Report of the Special Tax Commission of the State of New York (1907),* pp. 4–70.

29. Dana Durand, *The Finances of New York City* (New York: Macmillan Co., 1898), 359.

30. Canfield, *Taxation,* pp. 9–10.

31. *The Nation,* January 17, 1895, for instance.

32. William Reynolds, "The Relation of Civil Service Reform to Municipal Taxation," *An Address to LMPA,* October 8, 1889.

CHAPTER 6 *Obstacles to Reform*

1. See, e.g., Wells, "Principles of Taxation," pp. 155–56, 310–27; especially pp. 313–14; Nelson Evans, *A History of Taxation in Ohio* (Cincinnati: The Robert Clarke Co., 1906), p. 138; Reemelin, *A Critical Review of American Politics,* p. 238.

2. Bullock, *Finances and Financial Policy of Massachusetts,* p. 59; also Chapter 5; see Bullock's, "Taxation of Property and Income in Massachusetts," *QJE,* 31 (November 1916), Parts 2, 4; also Massachusetts. *Report of the Treasurer of the Commonwealth* (1868), pp. 9–10; (1870), pp. 21–22.

3. See, for instance, John H. Grant, *State Supervision of Cities* (Ann Arbor: Michigan Political Science Association, 1896), 2; John Dillon, *Commentaries on the Law of Municipal Corporations,* 1, pp. 22–56, 58–77, 96–469; Frederick Clow, *A Comparative Study of the Administration of City Finances in the U.S.* (New York: American Economic Association Studies, Vol. 2, No. 4, November 1901), Chapter 1, pp. 7–20; Durand, *Finances of New York City,* Chapter 10.

4. Samuel Edward Sparling, *Municipal History and Present Organization of the City of Chicago,* Bulletin of the University of Wisconsin, No. 23, pp. 143–57. Clinton Woodruff, "The American Municipal Situation," *Proceedings of the Cincinnati Conference for Good Government and the 15th Annual Meeting of the National Municipal League (November 15–18, 1909),* pp. 93–95; Haig, *History of Taxation in Illinois,* pp. 226–27; Daniel Shorey, *Problems of the Municipal Government of Chicago,* (Chicago: 1885), pp. 1–16.

5. For examples see, *Fassett Committee,* 3, pp. 2206–2240, 2363–2371, 2379,

2425, 2428, 2342–2443, 2575–2576, etc.; *Mazet Committee,* 2, pp. 1412–1428, 1432–1542, etc.; J. Winslow Cabot, "Fifth Essay," in *Equitable Taxation,* pp. 69, 71, 76; Dunn, *Taxation in Indiana,* 1892, pp. 62–65; Brindley, *Taxation in Iowa,* 1, pp. 115–40; Commons, "Taxation in Chicago and Philadelphia" *JPE,* 3 (1894–95), 455; also pp. 435–38; Seligman, "The General Property Tax," pp. 26–27; Wells, "Reform of Local Taxation," pp. 370, 401; *Fassett Committee,* 3, pp. 2250–2252; *Comm. Chronicle,* 64 (April 3, 1897), 646–47.

6. For instance, Baltimore City. *Report to the Mayor and City Council of Baltimore. Report of the Committee on the Establishment of Manufactures, 1877,* pp. 3–34, 36–39; *Pa. Revenue Comm. 1889,* pp. 86–89; Atkinson, *Argument of Edward Atkinson for a Change in the Law in Regard to Taxing Foreign Corporations, etc. before a committee of the Massachusetts Legislature February 27, 1877* (Boston: Smith and Porter, 1877) pp. 4–18; Canfield, *Taxation,* pp. 42, 43, 44–45; *Mass. Committee Report 1897,* pp. 139–46; *Comm. Chronicle,* 30 (March 27, 1880), 309–310; 30 (May 1, 1880), 445; 61 (October 5, 1895), 592–93; also *Comm. Chronicle,* 46 (January 14, 1888), 60–61; 48, p. 276; 30, p. 445; 46, pp. 213–14; 66, p. 349; *Md. Comm. 1888,* pp. 186–87; Ames, *Taxation of Personal Property,* pp. 48–49.

7. Enoch Ensley, *The Tax Question, Letter to Governor Brown. Suggestion for the People of Tennessee to Consider* (Boston: 1893) pp. 2–26.

8. Sparling, *Municipal History of Chicago,* p. 103; also pp. 158–75.

9. *Ibid.,* pp. 105–108; Haig, *History of Taxation in Illinois,* Chapter 10; also pp. 177–223; Fairlie, *Reports on Taxation,* p. 66; Letter to *Chicago Record-Herald,* November 25, 1913.

10. Shorey, *Problems of the Municipal Government of Chicago,* pp. 1–16; Sparling, *Municipal History of Chicago,* pp. 106–109; Fairlie, "Taxation in Illinois," pp. 523–24.

11. Frederick Clow, *A Comparative Study of the Administration of City Finance in the United States* (New York: AEA, Macmillan Company, 1901) Chapter 1, pp. 7–20.

12. *Harper's,* 67 (September 1883); also *The Nation,* January 13, 1881; Durand, *Finances of New York City,* pp. 87, 127–30, 160.

13. Tennessee. *Tennessee Session Laws,* Chapter 11, p. 89 (1879); Clow, *Comparative Study of City Finances,* p. 13.

14. Clow, *Comparative Study of City Finances,* p. 13; John Dillon, *Commentaries on the Law of Municipal Corporations,* 5th ed. rev., 5 vols., (Boston: Little, Brown, 1911), 1, pp. 96–469; Cooley, *Law of Taxation,* 1886, pp. 685–703.

15. Clow, *Comparative Study of City Finances,* pp. 14, 26; also Appendix; and *Fassett Committee, 5,* pp. 864–66, 899–900; also pp. 861–71, 888–915; for a sample constitutional proviso see, Pennsylvania: *Constitution.* Article 14, Section 7 (1873), p. 219; also sections 4–6, p. 218; E. P. Allinson and Boise Penrose, *City Government of Philadelphia* (Baltimore: Johns Hopkins Press, 1887), pp. 28–29.

16. This definition was Clow's, *Comparative Study of City Finances,* p. 14.

17. "The Development of the Budget Idea in the United States," *The Annals,* 112 (March 1924), vii, 16, 35 and earlier studies which differed from

Buck; Eugene E. Agger, *The Budget in the American Commonwealth* (New York: Columbia University Press, 1907); Seldon Gale Lowie, *The Budget* Madison: Demuret Press, 1912); C. F. Bastable, *Public Finance*, 3rd ed. (London: Macmillan and Co., Ltd., 1922), p. 634 was also widely cited; also Bastable's "The New Budget and the Principles of Financial Policy." *Economic Journal*, 9 (1899), 204–11.

18. Buck, "Development of the Budget Idea in the U.S.," pp. vii, 22, 35.

19. J. H. Dillard, "Taxation and the Public Welfare," *Proceedings of NTA*, 3 (1909), 50.

20. For writings on the cult see, for instance, Martha Bruere, *Increasing Home Efficiency* (New York: 1916); George B. Child, *The Efficient Kitchen* (New York: 1914); also Bruere's, "The Utilization of Family Income," *The Annals*, 48 (July 1913), 117–20; Mildred Maddocks, "The Efficient Household," *Good Housekeeping*, 67 (September 1918), 57 and following; Edward Purington, "The Efficient Home," *Independent*, 86 (May 15, 1916), 246–48; Raymond Callahan has examined the impact on the schools in his *Education and the Cult of Efficiency* (Chicago: 1962); also see Samuel Haber, *Efficiency and Uplift* (Chicago: University of Chicago Press, 1964).

21. Boston. *The Finance Commission of the City of Boston*, 7 vols., (Boston: Municipal Printing Office, 1908), 1, pp. 153, 216–20, 264–67; 3, pp. 69–85; Part 2, pp. 317–901; 4, Chapter 52; 7, pp. 226–31.

22. *Ibid.*, 2, pp. 238, 239, 272; see Harvey Shepard, "The Boston Finance Commission," *Proceedings of the Cincinnati Conference for Good City Government and the 15th Annual Meeting of the National Municipal League, November 15–18, 1909*, pp. 205–16.

23. *Boston Finance Commission*, 3, pp. 278–84; also 1, pp. 488–91, and 1, pp. 56, 207, 393, 411; 3, pp. 201–204, 255–58; 2, p. 42; and Wells, "Principles of Taxation," *PSM*, 48, pp. 295–98, 305.

24. H. C. Latrobe, "The City Government of Baltimore," *An Address to LMPA*, September 17, 1889.

25. See, New York State. *Report of the Select Committee appointed to Investigate the Causes of the Increase of Crime in the City of New York, February 1876, Assembly Document 106;* and the Lexow, Fassett, and Mazet committees.

26. Charles S. Walker, "The Massachusetts Farmer and Taxation," *Yale Review*, 6 (May 1897), 63, 66–67; Bullock, *Finances of Massachusetts*, pp. 95–96; Shearman, *Natural Taxation*, p. 197, also p. 183.

27. Walker, "The Massachusetts Farmer and Taxation," pp. 73–74, also pp. 63–65.

28. *Ibid.*, pp. 73–74, also *Mass. Committee Report 1897*, pp. 30–31, 40–42, 50–51, 52, 122–23, 138–39, 144–45.

29. Lawson Purdy, *Local Option in Taxation* (New York: the author, n.d.), p. 7.

30. Walker, "The Massachusetts Farmer and Taxation," p. 73; *Comm. Chronicle*, 61 (November 2, 1895), 776; also 775–77.

31. Walker, "The Massachusetts Farmer and Taxation," pp. 70–74; Massachusetts. General Court. *Hearing Before the Joint Special Committee, Sep-*

tember-December 1893 (Boston: 1894); Massachusetts. General Court. *Full Report of the Joint Special Committee on Taxation with Recommendations and Codifications relating to the Laws on Taxation* (January 1894), pp. 7–66.

32. Wells, "Principles of Taxation," *PSM,* 48, pp. 155–56, 310–27; Evans, *History of Taxation in Ohio, 1906,* pp. 205–216.

33. Of course, we still know too little about the economics of prostitution, elasticity of demand, etc. For details on the early 20th century in New York City see, "The Business of Prostitution," in George Kneeland, *Commercialized Prostitution in New York City* (New York: The Century Company, 1913).

34. *U.S. Report of the Industrial Commission, 1902,* 9, pp. 3, 101, 295, 1006–1012; see, for instance, the argument of Cyrus Elder, "The Tax System of Pennsylvania," *Social Science Association of Philadelphia, Papers of 1873,* read January 23, 1873, pp. 4, 9, 20; also see additional materials in *U.S. Industrial Commission,* 9, pp. 600–602, 987, 1028, 1035–1039; Edward Moore, "Corporate Taxation," *ALR,* 18 (1884), 752–53; Seligman, "The Taxation of Corporations," *PSQ,* 5, pp. 442–48, 462–63, 645–57; *Comm. Chronicle,* 32 (May 28, 1881), 565; 30, p. 288; 48, p. 276; Hillhouse, *Taxation of Banks by the State of New York,* pp. 7–61; also Albert Stickney, *The Political Problems* (New York: Harper and Brothers, 1890), pp. 98, 108; Albert Sutro, "Taxation of Competitive Industrial Corporations," *Proceedings of NTA,* 1 (1907), 614–15, 617, 619; Lawson Purdy, "Outline of a Model State and Local Tax System," *Proceedings of NTA,* 1 (1907), 66.

35. Wells, "Principles of Taxation," *PSM,* 50 (December 1896), 160–61; William Rapsher, "Dangerous Trusts," *NAR,* 146 (1888), 511.

36. *Adams Express Company v. Ohio,* 165 U.S. 194, 166 U.S. 185; Commons, *Legal Foundations of Capitalism,* pp. 172–77; Evans, *Taxation in Ohio,* p. 82; Seligman, "The Taxation of Corporations," *PSQ,* 5, pp. 293–98.

37. Reemelin, *Critical Review of American Politics,* p. 249; Charles Dunbar, "Economic Science in America," *NAR,* 132 (1876), 152; also pp. 143–45; William G. Sumner, "Taxation," p. 1, ms. in *Sumner Estate Papers;* also Wells, "Principles of Taxation," *PSM,* 48, p. 6; pp. 577, 583; Arthur L. Perry, *Elements of Political Economy* (New York: Charles Scribner's Sons, 1873), 579.

38. Wells, "Principles of Taxation," *PSM,* 48, p. 5.

39. *Ibid.,* pp. 5–6; Noble, *Taxation in Iowa,* p. 14.

40. Seligman's testimony before the *U.S. Industrial Commission,* 9, p. 600; also pp. 607–612; Lawson Purdy, "Outline of a Model System of State and Local Taxation," p. 55.

41. Joseph Brislawn, "Taxation and the Farmer," *Proceedings of NTA,* 10 (1916), 264–65, 266–67, 269, 274–75, 277, 282, 284–86, for example.

42. *Ibid.,* 10, pp. 265, 267, 269.

43. *Taxation: Its Principles and Methods,* translated by Horace White (New York: G. P. Putnam's Sons, 1888); Wells, "Principles of Taxation," *PSM,* 48, p. 434; for more on Cossa's relations with Americans see, Lee Benson, *Turner and Beard: American Historical Writing Reconsidered* (New York: The Free Press, 1960), Part 1.

44. Canfield, *Taxation,* p. 4; Gustav Cohn, *The Science of Finance* (Chicago: University of Chicago Press, 1895), Introduction; Wells, "Principles of Taxa-

tion," *PSM,* 49, pp. 577, 583; also *PSM,* 48, p. 12. William G. Sumner, "Taxation," pp. 1–2, ms in *Sumner Estate Papers.* Seligman and most other authorities held the same view.

45. For background see, George Coleman, "Special Franchise Taxation in New York," *Proceedings of NTA,* 1 pp. 649–54; Seligman, "The Franchise Tax Law in New York," QJE, 13 (1899), 445 and following; Delos Wilcox, "Elements of a Constructive Franchise Policy," *Proceedings of the Buffalo Conference for Good Government and the 16th Annual Meeting of the National Municipal League (1910),* pp. 170–89; *U.S. Industrial Commission,* 19 (1902), 1061–1062.

46. Elting Morison, ed. *The Letters of Theodore Roosevelt,* 8 vols. (Cambridge: Harvard University Press, 1951–54), 2, p. 981; cited hereafter as *Roosevelt Letters.*

47. *Ibid.,* 2, p. 981n.

48. *Ibid.,* 3, p. 18.

49. *Ibid.,* 2, p. 996.

50. Charles Lincoln, ed., *Messages from the Governors, Comprising Executive Communications to the Legislature and Other Papers, 1683–1906,* 11 vols., (Albany: Lyon, 1909), 10, pp. 35–37 for Roosevelt on the Ford Bill.

51. For example, see, "Tax Reform in the Middle West," *The Outlook,* 70 (March 8, 1902), 595–96.

52. For background on the shifting fortunes of these communities see, George H. Miller, "Origins of the Iowa Granger Laws," *Mississippi Valley Historical Review,* 40 (March 1954), 657–80.

53. B. F. Keables, the Marion County Legislator quoted in *Des Moines Daily Bulletin,* May 11, 1870.

54. Backgrounds of Iowa railroad taxation are discussed in Brindley, *History of Taxation in Iowa,* 2, pp. 3–168 and Noble, *Taxation in Iowa,* pp. 5–27, 89–100; also see an anti-railroad view expressed by Senator Samuel McNutt in his letter file cited in Brindley, 2, pp. 393–94; Benjamin Stambaugh, *Messages and Proclamations of the Governors of Iowa, 1836–1901* (Iowa City: 1903–1905), 3, pp. 314, 334, 335; 4, pp. 24, 25; *Daily Iowa State Register,* February 27, 1870; March 16, 1870; February 17 1872; March 9, 10 1872; *Daily Burlington Hawk-Eye,* March 14, 16, 1872; *Daily Gate City,* March 14, April 7, 1872; *General Assembly of Iowa, House Journal, 1872,* pp. 146, 394–426; Iowa. *Senate Journal, 1870,* pp. 417, 419; *Des Moines Daily Bulletin,* May 11, 1870; William Larrabee, *The Railroad Question* (Chicago: Schulte Publishing Co., 1893), pp. 205–30.

CHAPTER 7 *The Experts and the Instruments of Reform*

1. The compilation is mine.

2. Charles Albro Barker's, *Henry George* (New York: Oxford University Press, 1955) is sufficiently definitive to make extended comment on Henry George unnecessary in the context of this study.

3. See, *The Education of Henry Adams* (Boston: Houghton, Mifflin Co., 1961).

4. Lea's views were published by the Municipal Reform Association; for instance, "To Tax-Payers and Rent-Payers of Philadelphia," October 11, 1872, or "Reform Tracts, No. 1. Municipal Taxation," December 1871; see, too, George Vickers, *Fall of Bossism;* Bradley, *Henry Charles Lea,* Chapter 5, on Municipal Politics. Also see Lea's "Letter to the People of Philadelphia," *Forum,* 2 (1886), 532–38; "The Bill for Local Taxation," letter to Senator Boise Penrose, April 6, 1891. Literature on New York in Tweed's day and on the politics of the Ring is extensive, including the recent studies of Professors Alexander Callow and Seymour Mandelbaum, running back through the older works of Werner or Lynch, and the still earlier writings of Breen, Edwards, or Felden. Much of the material in these studies begins with the New York, *Report of the Special Committee of the Board of Aldermen appointed to Investigate the 'Ring' Frauds Together with Testimony Elicited during the Investigation of the Board of Aldermen, January 4, 1878, Document No. 8, 1878.* Also Jacob Hollander, *Studies in State Taxation* (Baltimore: Johns Hopkins Press, 1900); Thaddeus Thomas, *City Government of Baltimore* (Baltimore: Johns Hopkins Press, 1896); James M. Bugbee, *City Government of Boston* (Baltimore: Johns Hopkins Press, 1887); L. O. Rea, *Financial History of Baltimore* (Baltimore: Johns Hopkins Press, 1929); C. M. Armstrong, "A Simple Way to Reduce Taxes," *An Address to LMPA,* April 16, 1889; Frank Morling, "Men Hate to Pay Taxes," *An Address to LMPA,* April 23, 1889; Stimson, *My United States,* p. 83; Geoffrey Blodgett and Arthur Mann have illuminated the story of Mugwumpery and reform in Boston and in Massachusetts during the late 19th century; Gamaliel Bradford, "Municipal Government," *Scribner's,* 2 (July–December 1887), 491–92, and his "Our Failures in Municipal Government," *Annals* (May 1898), 23–24; Whitmore, *Unjust Taxes,* pp. 11–12; C. S. Walker, "The Massachusetts Farmer and Taxation," p. 71; Allen Ripley Foote, "Birth, Work, and Future of the National Tax Conference," *Proceedings of NTA,* 10 (1917), 23–25; *New York Times,* June 6, 1891; A. C. Pleydell, "Evolution of the New York System," *Journal of Accountancy,* 10 (July 1910), 174–75; cited hereafter as *JOA.* E. L. Heydecker, "The New York Law and Its Evil Effects," *JOA,* 10 (1910), 163–65; Heydecker also read numerous papers to state tax conferences in New York as well as to the NTA.

5. The *Henry Carter Adams Papers* are in the Historical Collections of the University of Michigan, Ann Arbor; for published background material see *JPE,* 30 (April 1922), 201–11; *AER.* (September 1922); *Journal of Social Philosophy,* 3 (April 1938).

6. Twenty-three volumes of Wells' Correspondence are in the Library of Congress, with scattered items in the Ford Collection of the New York Public Library. Materials on his early career are in Vols. 1–5. Wells' major writings are cited throughout this study, but representative selections would have to include: U.S. Congress, House of Representatives. *Report of the United States Revenue Commission for 1866, Executive Documents Nos. 5–49, 39th Congress, 2d Sess., Doc. No. 2, 1867,* and subsequent *Reports* to the House in 1867, 1868,

1869. Also *Cobden Club Essays, Second Series,* 1871–72 (London, Paris, New York: Cassell, Petter and Galpin, 1872); *Why We Trade and How We Trade; or An Inquiry into the Extent to Which the Existing Commercial and Fiscal Policy of the United States Restricts the Material Prospects and Development of the Country* (New York: G. P. Putnam's Sons, 1878); *The Silver Question, or The Dollar of Our Fathers Versus the Dollar of the Sons* (New York: G. P. Putnam's Sons, 1878); *A Primer for Tariff Reform* (London: Cassell and Company, 1885); for views on Wells see McCulloch, *Men and Measures; Yale Review,* 7 (1898), 245–46; Seligman, "Recent Reports on State and Local Taxation," *AER,* 1 (1911), 294–95.

7. Wells borrowed widely and acknowledged his debt to Luigi Cossa, J. S. Mill, Leroy-Beaulieu, and Menier among others; but Henry Carey's *Treatise on Wealth* (1838) and *Past, Present, and Future* (1848) and Isaac Sherman were apparently the earliest and most enduring influences as Wells suggests in "Principles of Taxation," *PSM,* 48, p. 325.

8. *Wells Report (1871),* pp. 106–108.

9. Wells, "Principles of Taxation," *PSM,* 48, p. 325.

10. "Reform of Local Taxation," p. 362.

11. "The Personal Property Tax," *JOA,* 10 (1910), 176.

12. *Essays in Taxation,* p. 399.

13. *Md. Comm. 1888,* p. 91. The Ely Papers are located in the State Historical Society of Wisconsin in Madison; a smaller collection is in the Eisenhower Library, Johns Hopkins University. Useful in many other ways, the Ely Papers on the whole yielded little material for this study that was more valuable than Ely's published works.

14. *Md. Comm. 1888,* p. 103.

15. Franklin Smith, "A State Official on Excessive Taxation," *PSM,* 56, p. 645. For a more general picture see Delos Wilcox, *The American City: A Problem in Democracy* (New York: The Macmillan Co., 1904), pp. 341–401.

16. Smith, "A State Official on Excessive Taxation," p. 646; New York State. *Report of the Comptroller 1897;* also see *Comptroller's Report 1898.*

17. New York State. *Comptroller's Report 1899.*

18. Smith, "A State Official on Excessive Taxation," pp. 651, 659.

19. *Ibid.,* p. 658.

20. New York State. *Report of the Comptroller 1899;* Smith, "A State Official on Excessive Taxation," p. 659; also Oscar Leser, et. al., "Report of the Failure of the General Property Tax," *Proceedings of NTA,* 4 (1911), 299–310; Seligman, *Essays on Taxation,* p. 36.

21. Joseph Dorfman, "The Seligman Correspondence," *PSQ,* 56 (1941), 270, 271n; also Dorfman, *The Economic Mind in American Civilization, 1865–1918,* 5 vols., (New York: Viking Press, 1959), 3, pp. 164–74.

22. Henry C. Adams. "Suggestions for a System of Taxation," *Michigan Political Science Association,* 1 (1894), 68. Cited hereafter as *MPSA.*

23. *Ibid.,* 1, pp. 49, 53, 54–56, 58–60.

24. Seligman, "The Theory of Progressive Taxation," *PSQ,* 8 (1893), 220–21; *Essays in Taxation,* pp. 362–63.

25. Seligman, "The Theory of Progressive Taxation," pp. 22–23. For a contrary view see, Wells, "The Communism of a Discriminating Income Tax," *NAR,* 130 (March 1880), 236–38.

26. Seligman, "The Theory of Progressive Taxation," p. 222.

27. *Ibid.,* pp. 223–24.

28. *Ibid.,* p. 230.

29. *Ibid.,* pp. 232–38; for a parallel but later discussion see, Kossuth Kennan, *Income Taxation* (Milwaukee: Burdick and Allen, 1910), pp. 1–17; also see Seligman, *The Income Tax at Home and Abroad,* 2d rev. ed., 2 vols., (New York: Macmillan, 1914).

30. Guthrie, "No Taxation without Representation," *JOA,* 10 (1910), p. 23; Seligman, 'The Theory of Progressive Taxation," pp. 240–48.

31. Seligman's testimony before the *U.S. Industrial Commission,* 4, pp. 602, 608; *Essays in Taxation,* pp. 53–61; *Progressive Taxation in Theory and Practice* (American Economic Association Studies, Nos. 1 and 2, 1894), Pt. 2, Chapters 3, 5, and Part 3.

32. George Pomeroy, "The Organization of the Conference," *Proceedings of NTA,* 10 (1917), 22–23, 52–53.

33. The journal was *Chicago Policy;* see his *Municipal Public Service Industries* (Chicago: The Other Side Publishing Company, 1899); *Economic Value of Electric Light and Power* (Cincinnati: Robert Clarke & Co., 1889); also see his testimony to the *U.S. Industrial Commission,* 9, pp. 103–23; Foote, "Birth, Work, and Future of the National Tax Conference," *Proceedings of NTA,* 10 (1917), p. 35.

34. Foote, "Birth, Work, and Future of the National Tax Conference," pp. 23–25; the *National Encyclopedia,* 43, pp. 592–93.

35. Carl Plehn, *Introduction to Public Finance* (New York: Macmillan, 1896), p. v; also see Charles Bullock, *Principles of Economics,* new and rev. ed. (New York: Ginn and Company, 1900), p. 498. Foote, "Birth, Work, and Future of the National Tax Conference," pp. 42–45.

36. Foote, "Birth, Work, and Future of the National Tax Conference," pp. 42–45; see Roy and Gladys Blakey, *National Tax Association Digest and Index, 1907–1925* (New York: National Tax Association, 1927), for an idea of the range of its activities.

Chapter 8 *The Main Lines of Reform*

1. "Suggestions for a System of Taxation," *MPSA,* 1 (1894), 50.

2. *Wells Report (1871),* pp. 89, 101–105; *Wells Report (1872),* pp. 36–37; also see *Weeks Report Pa. Tax Conference, 1892; Report of the Revenue Commission of Illinois (1886);* for early arguments in Iowa see Stambaugh, *Messages and Proclamations of the Governors,* 2, p. 328; Ely in *Md. Comm. 1888,* pp. 162–65, 175–77; later discussions of separation are legion, see, for example, Seligman, *Essays in Taxation,* pp. 401–403, 410, 412, 414–20; Seligman, "Tax Reform in the United States," *Proceedings of NTA,* 8 (1914) 186–

206; Seligman, "Separation of the Sources of Revenue," *Proceedings of NTA,* 9 (1915), 243–53.

3. Adams, "Suggestions for a System of Taxation," pp. 50, 58, 59; Adams, *Public Finance,* p. 501; Lecture, "Taxation" in *Henry Carter Adams Papers,* Michigan Historical Collection.

4. "Suggestions for A System of Taxation," pp. 59–61.

5. *U.S. Industrial Commission,* 4, p. 608; also pp. 599, 602–603, 608; Seligman, *Essays in Taxation,* pp. 401–403, 410, 413, 418–20; Seligman, "Tax Reform in the United States," *Proceedings of NTA,* 8 (1915), 186–98.

6. Carl Plehn was a leading academic figure in California tax reform; he drafted the Commission Report; see, *Report of the Commission on Revenue and Taxation* (Sacramento: 1906), pp. 77–81; also *Commission on Revenue and Taxation* (Sacramento: 1910); Seligman, "Recent Reports on State and Local Taxation," pp. 284–85.

7. Brindley, *History of Taxation in Iowa,* 2, pp. 166, 167; also 1, pp. 45–69, 162–66, 208–212.

8. For Delaware's actions see, Delaware. *Report of the Delaware Tax Commission to the General Assembly,* 2 Parts, (Wilmington: 1893); also see George Sparks, "Taxation in Delaware," *Proceedings of NTA,* 6 (1912), 459–65; Harley Lutz, *The State Tax Commission: A Study of the Development and Results of State Control over the Assessment of Property for Taxation* (Cambridge: Harvard University Press, 1918), pp. 627–38.

9. *U.S. Industrial Commission,* 4, p. 599. Seligman's testimony was taken December 6, 1899.

10. Seligman's, "Taxation of Corporations," *PSQ,* 5, p. 269.

11. New York State. *Revised Statutes, 1st edition,* 3, Appendix.

12. "The Taxation of Corporations," *PSQ,* 5, p. 271.

13. Herbert Knox Smith, "State Systems of Corporate Taxation," *Proceedings of NTA,* 5 (1911), 139–48.

14. *Pa. Revenue Comm.* 1890, pp. 7–18; for background also see pp. 32–159; *Pennsylvania State Treasurer's Report 1889,* pp. 8–9; for an outside appraisal see, *Mass. Committee Report 1897,* pp. 88–90; earlier comments are in *Wells Report (1871),* pp. 17–29.

15. *Wells Report (1871),* pp. 101–102.

16. Shorey, *Problems of Municipal Government for Chicago,* p. 15; also pp. 3–12; Whitten, "The Assessment of Taxes in Chicago," pp. 175–80; Haig, *A History of General Property Taxation in Illinois,* pp. 126–212; E. Moore, *Taxation of Corporations in Illinois other Than Railroads since 1872,* 2 vols., (Champaign: University of Illinois Press, 1913), 2, pp. 20–49; Fairlie, "Taxation in Illinois," pp. 519–34.

17. Fairlie, *Report on Taxation,* p. 218; Haig, *History of the General Property Tax in Illinois,* pp. 209–12; Fairlie, "Taxation in Illinois," pp. 521, 524–27, 528; Shorey, *Problems of Municipal Government for Chicago,* p. 10.

18. Ohio. *Governor's Message, Executive Document, 1895,* 1, pp. 5–6; Bogart, *Financial History of Ohio,* pp. 221–46; *Report of the Tax Commission of Ohio, 1893,* pp. 1, 3, 47–51.

19. Ross, "Seligman's Shifting and Incidence of Taxation," p. 53.

20. Seligman, *On the Shifting and Incidence of Taxation,* pp. 191–95, and following.

21. Purdy, *The Burdens of Local Taxation and Who Bears Them* (Chicago: Public Policy Publishing Company, 1901), pp. 7–8, 42.

22. "First Prize Essay," in *Equitable Taxation,* pp. 21, 25.

23. Weyl, *The New Democracy* (New York: Harper & Row, 1964), pp. 163–295, 297.

24. "Third Prize Essay," in *Equitable Taxation,* pp. 57–59.

25. Schwab, *History of the New York Property Tax,* pp. 97–98.

26. J. Whidden Graham, "Fourth Prize Essay," in *Equitable Taxation,* p. 67; Bolton Hall, "Third Prize Essay," in *Equitable Taxation,* pp. 57–59.

27. *Pa. Revenue Comm. 1890,* pp. 88–90.

28. "Taxation of Competitive Industrial Corporations," *Proceedings of NTA,* 1 (1907), 605–606.

29. *Ibid.,* p. 607.

30. *Ibid.,* p. 614; State of New York. *People ex rel. Weber Piano Company v Wells,* 180 New York 68.

31. "Taxation of Competitive Industrial Corporations," pp. 618–21.

32. *Ibid.,* pp. 614–17, 618, 619.

33. Wisconsin. *Report of the Wisconsin State Tax Commission, 1903,* pp. 171–74; also see discussions in J. C. Stamp, "The Tax Experiment in Wisconsin," *Economic Journal,* 23, pp. 142–46 and following; T. S. Adams, "Separation of the Sources of State and Local Revenue as a Program of Tax Reform," *Proceedings of NTA,* 1 (1907), 516–27. Adams was one of the leading authorities behind the writing of the Wisconsin Report.

34. "Taxation of Corporations in the United States," in Moore, *Taxation of Corporations in Illinois after 1872,* Chapter 10, pp. 167–99, particularly p. 168; also Herbert Knox Smith, "State Systems of Corporate Taxation," *Proceedings of NTA,* 5 (1911), 140–46; Lutz, *The State Tax Commission,* pp. 627–32, 636–37; Ely, *Taxation in American States and Cities,* pp. 324–33; *U.S. Census Report 1902 on Wealth and Taxation* for statistics on the assessment of corporate properties by state officials. Also John Merrill, "State Tax on Business Corporations," *State Conference on Taxation Addresses and Proceedings, . . . Utica, January 1911,* pp. 192–97; Seligman, "Assessment and Taxation on Corporations," *State Conference on Taxation, Addresses and Proceedings, Utica Conference, January 1911,* pp. 198–200 and following.

35. *Valuation, Taxation, and Exemption in the Commonwealth of Pennsylvania. Pa. Tax Conference, 1892,* pp. 16–17, 23–28, 30–33.

36. *Speech of C. Stuart Patterson, Especially on the Taxation of Railroads Before the Committee on Ways and Means of the House of Representatives, Harrisburg, March 19, 1895* (Philadelphia: Lane & Scott, 1895), p. 24.

37. *Ibid.,* pp. 21–23; also for background see Cyrus Elder, "The Tax System of Pennsylvania," *Social Science Association of Philadelphia, January 23, 1873,* pp. 1–30.

38. *Speech of C. Stuart Patterson . . . on Taxation of Railroads, 1895,* pp. 21–23; Joseph Weeks, *Lecture Series No. 1, Manufacturers' Association of Cincinnati and Hamilton County, Ohio, March 6, 1894,* pp. 5–7.

39. Joseph Weeks, *Effect of the Proposed Revenue Bill (H.R. No. 239 Session of 1895) on the State Revenue* (Pittsburgh: 1895), pp. 12–14; C. Stuart Patterson, *An Analysis of the Revenue Bill (H.R. No. 239 Session of 1895)*, pp. 9–10; Weeks, *Lecture Series No. 1. Manufacturers' Association of Cincinnati . . . March 6, 1894*, pp. 8–10.

40. Patterson, *Speech on the Taxation of Railroads, 1895*, pp. 22–23.

41. *Riter Tax Bill (House Bill No. 239); Argument of M. E. Olmsted, Esq., of Harrisburg on Behalf of Certain Corporate Interests Before the Ways and Means Committee of the House of Representatives, March 19, 1895*, pp. 1–3.

42. Patterson, *Speech on the Taxation of Railroads*, 1895, pp. 3–4.

43. *Ibid.*, pp. 6–10; Patterson, *An Analysis of the Revenue Bills*, p. 3; for background see *Pa. Revenue Comm. Report 1890*, pp. 7–14, 74–85, 111–14, 154–57, 174–76; *Weeks Report. Pa. Tax Conference, 1892*, p. 1–18, "Valuation and Taxation of Railroads. Pennsylvania had 303 railroads as of 1890 with a total mileage in the state of 8925 and 14055 outside of the state.

44. Patterson, *Speech on the Taxation of Railroads, 1895*, pp. 6–7.

45. *Ibid.*, p. 7.

46. *Ibid.*, pp. 13–14, also pp. 8–9.

47. Olmsted, *Argument in Behalf of Certain Corporate Interests*, p. 32; also pp. 16–17.

48. *Statistical Report of the Interstate Commerce Commission 1893*, pp. 35–38 and following.

49. Patterson, *Speech on the Taxation of Railroads, 1895*, pp. 20–21.

50. Cited in *Final Report of the U.S. Industrial Commission, 1902*, 19, p. 397.

51. Patterson, *Speech on the Taxation of Railroads, 1895*, p. 14.

52. Olmsted, *Argument on Behalf of Corporate Interests*, pp. 3–4.

53. *Ibid.*, pp. 30–31, also pp. 4–7.

54. *Ibid.*, pp. 14–15, 30–31.

55. *Final Report of the U.S. Industrial Commission, 1902*, 19, pp. 402–403; also pp. 397–419.

56. Herbert Knox Smith, "State Systems of Corporate Taxation," p. 143.

57. *Ibid.*, p. 140; Richard Abrams, "A Paradox of Progressivism in Massachusetts on the Eve of Insurgency," *PSQ*, 75 (September 1960), pp. 379–99.

58. Charles Bullock, "The Taxation of Property and Income in Massachusetts," *QJE*, 31 (November 1916), 22.

59. The best descriptions and analyses of the Massachusetts system are: *Mass. Comm. Report 1897*, pp. 13–26, 68–72, 76–82; Bullock, "Taxation of Income and Property in Massachusetts," pp. 1–61; Bullock, *Financial Policy of Massachusetts*, pp. 93–137; Friedman, *Taxation of Corporations in Massachusetts*, pp. 163–77; Moore, *Taxation of Corporations*, pp. 175–80; *Comm. Chronicle*, 61 (October 26, 1895), 729–30 and (November 2, 1895), 775–77.

60. *Mass. Committee Report 1875*, p. 124.

61. *Ibid.*, 1895, pp. 68–69; also see *Report of the U.S. Commissioner of Corporations on the Taxation of Corporations*, Part 1, pp. 14, 69–70, 101.

62. Friedman, *Taxation of Corporations in Massachusetts*, p. 175.

63. Seligman, *Essays on Taxation*, p. 262.

64. Fairlie, *Report on the Taxation and Revenue System of Illinois, 1910,* p. 66; Haig, *History of Taxation in Illinois,* pp. 200–16, 222–24; Moore, *Taxation of Corporations,* pp. 200–201.

65. *Report of the Commissioner of Corporations on the Taxation of Corporations, 1910,* Part 2, p. 2.

66. R. J. LeBoeuf, "Public Service Corporation Taxation in New York State," *Proceedings of NTA,* 7 (1913), 168.

Chapter 9 *The Breakthrough*

1. Seligman, *Essays in Taxation,* p. 72.

2. Seligman, "Annual Address of the President, 1913," *Proceedings of NTA,* 7, (1913), 13–20 "Annual Address of the President, 1914, *Proceedings of NTA,* 8 (1914), 186–206; Samuel T. Howe, "Need For Popular Aid in Tax Reform," *Proceedings of NTA,* 9 (1915), 146–64.

3. Illinois Bar Association quoted in *Md. Comm. 1888,* p. 185.

4. Ross quoted from his "A New Canon of Taxation," *PSQ,* 7 (1892), 591–92. Works on the Civil War Income Tax were common in informed circles at the close of the nineteenth century; allusions to it were frequent in writings on public finance. See, Ellen Sawyer, *Bibliography of Works on Taxation, January 1898, Special Bulletin of the Massachusetts State Library* (Boston: Wright & Potter, 1898), pp. 20–21 on Civil War income tax. Also see Joseph Hill, "The Civil War Income Tax,"*QJE,* 8 (July 1894), 416–52; Kossuth Kennan, *Income Taxation, 1910,* Chapter 12; Official comments are in the *Reports of the Commissioner of Internal Revenue, 1864–72.*

5. *Report of the Special Commissioner of Revenue Upon Industry, Trade, and Commerce of the U.S. for 1869* (Washington: 1869), pp. lxix, lxx; *Bankers' Magazine,* 48, pp. 428–35; also Wells, "Principles of Taxation," *PSM,* 48, pp. 151–55; Wells, "An Income Tax, Is It Desirable?" *Forum* 17 (1894), 7–9; Wells, "Is the Existing Income Tax Unconstitutional?" *Forum,* 18 (1894), 537–42. For summary see, Joseph Hill, "The Civil War Income Tax," pp. 437–44.

6. January 7, 1871; also see "The British Income Tax," February 25, 1871.

7. Cited by William Borah in "Income Tax, Sound in Law and Economics," *JOA,* 10 (1910), 28–29. Sherman's remarks in support of the wartime tax are in *Congressional Globe,* p. 4714.

8. *Mass. Committee Report 1897,* pp. 85–88.

9. Delos Kinsman, *The Income Tax in Commonwealths of the United States* (Ithaca: American Economic Association Studies, 1903), p. 111. Kennan, *Income Taxation,* pp. 209–210; Seligman, *The Income Tax at Home and Abroad* is the most thorough analysis.

10. Just what "income" was, of course, was the subject of other discussions and debates.

11. Kennan, *Income Taxation,* p. 236; Kinsman, *The Income Tax,* pp. 115–16, 117.

12. *The Nation,* March 7, 1878.

13. *The Nation,* March 7, 1878.

14. May 2, 1878.

15. Seligman's, *The Income Tax at Home and Abroad,* Chapter 4, for example.

16. On these imputed motives see, for instance, William Guthrie, "No Taxation Without Representation," pp. 17, 23; also Austin G. Fox, "Insert No Ambiguity in the Constitution," *JOA,* 10 (1910), 4. For a traditional sampling of opinion in the public debate, see. Elmer Ellis, "Public Opinion and the Income Tax, 1860–1900," *Mississippi Valley Historical Review,* 27 (September 1940), 225–42.

17. Kinsman, *Income Taxation,* pp. 110–111; also pp. 16–28, 30–32; J. K. Worthington, *Historical Sketch of the Finances of Pennsylvania* (Baltimore: American Economic Association, 1887), pp. 90–92; *Mass. Committee Report 1875,* pp. 51–55 and Appendix on the Massachusetts Income Tax; arguments for and against repeal pp. 431–50.

18. Charles Bullock, "The State Income Tax and Classified Property Tax," *Proceedings of NTA,* 10 (1916), 378. Bullock declared after analysis of state income taxes: "the value of farms and livestock is much easier to determine than the income of farmers; indeed, before the latter problem income taxes usually break down . . ." The opinion was widely shared among experts.

19. William Shelton, "The Income Tax in Georgia," *JPE,* 18 (1910), 610–27.

20. T. S. Adams, "The Income Tax as a Substitute for the Property Tax . . . in Wisconsin," *Proceedings of NTA,* 4 (1910), 95; Bullock, "The State Income Tax and Classified Property Tax," pp. 362–68, 383–84.

21. Wells, "Is the Exemption in Income Taxation Unconstitutional?" p. 541; Wells, "The Communism of a Discriminating Income Tax," p. 243; the theme was common later; see for example George Edmunds, "Salutary Results of the Income Tax Decision," *Forum,* 19 (1895), 518.

22. Austin Fox, "Insert No Ambiguity in the Constitution," pp. 6–7; George Tunnell, "Legislative History of the Second Income Tax Law," *JPE,* 3 (June 1895), 311–35.

23. *Elmira Advertiser,* May 7, 1910, remarks of Assemblyman Seymour Lowman. For some of the background in New York see Dwight Morrow, "The Income Tax Amendment," *Columbia Law Review,* 10 (May 1910), 379–81, 407–15; Guthrie, "No Taxation without Representation," pp. 13–25; Seligman, "The Relations of State and Federal Finance," *NAR,* 190, pp. 615–27.

24. *Mass. Committee Report 1897,* p. 87; Kennan, "Comparative Results of Income Taxation," *Proceedings of NTA,* 4 (1910), 11–38; *Report of the Special Tax Commission of the State of New York, 1907,* pp. 46–50 and following.

25. William Rawles, "The Income Tax as A Measure of Relief for Indiana," *Proceedings of NTA,* 10 (1916), 72.

27. The Merchants' Association, the Association of Manufacturers and Merchants, Trust Company Association, Association of Insurance Presidents, Savings Bank Association, New York Development League, New York Tax Reform Association, etc.

28. Kennan, "The Wisconsin Income Tax," *QJE,* 26 (November 1912), 171; T. S. Adams, "The Significance of the Wisconsin Income Tax," *PSQ,* 28

(December 1913), 569; Wisconsin, *Tax Laws of Wisconsin. Income Tax Cases,* 148 Wisconsin 456; Kennan, "Wisconsin Income Tax Law," *Proceedings of NTA,* 5 (1911), 103–11; also see National Industrial Conference Board, *State Income Taxes, I, Historical Development* (New York: NICB, 1930), a series of brief, narrowly descriptive and technical discussions.

29. Kennan, "The Wisconsin Tax," *QJE,* 27, p. 171.

30. Frederick Howe, "Some Possible Reforms in State and Local Taxation," *ALR,* 33 (1899), 688.

31. Bullock, "The State Income Tax and Classified Property Tax," pp. 382–83.

32. Howe, "Some Possible Reforms in State and Local Taxation," pp. 688–89; also see Howe's *Taxation and Taxes in the United States* (New York: T. Y. Crowell, 1896), pp. 96–99.

33. Kennan, "The Wisconsin Tax," p. 171.

34. New York Tax Reform Association, *Twenty-First Annual Report, 1911,* pp. 1–11; Arthur Pleydell, "Taxation in New York," *State Conference on Taxation, Second Conference, Buffalo, N.Y., January 9–11, 1912* (Albany: J. B. Lyon Printers, 1912), pp. 291–97; also Pleydell, "The Tax Law of New York," *State Conference on Taxation, Addresses and Proceedings, Utica, January 1911,* pp. 42–47; Pleydell, "New York Conference on Taxation," *AER,* 2 (1912), 243–44.

35. *Mills Committee,* pp. 8, 12, 18, 67–70, 117; also William Rawles, "The Income Tax as a Measure of Relief for Indiana," *Proceedings of NTA,* 10 (1916), 85.

36. For views as crystalized by commissions see, *Ohio Committee Report 1893,* pp. 19–23.

37. Rawles, "The Income Tax as a Measure of Relief for Indiana," p. 72.

38. On these "motives," see *Mills Committee,* pp. 12, 18, 47, 67–70, 117; also New York State *Annual Report of the State Tax Commission, 1896,* pp. 8–15 and following; same report 1903, pp. 11 and following. Thomas Byrnes, Chairman of the New York State Tax Commission, *State and Local Taxation* (Madison: National Tax Association, 1913), p. 187. NICB, *State and Local Taxing of Property* (New York: National Industrial Conference Board, 1930), p. 8; *New York Times,* October 7, 14, 22, 1915; Harley Lutz, "Progress of State Income Taxation since 1911," *AER,* 10 (March 1920), 66–91; Robert Haig, "New Sources of City Revenue," *National Municipal Review,* 4 (1915), 594–603; Seligman, "Reports on State and Local Taxation," pp. 272–95.

39. National Industrial Conference Board, "Income Taxation in Wisconsin," in *State Income Taxes,* 1, pp. 30–36; also see Wisconsin. *Report of the Wisconsin State Tax Commission 1914,* pp. 34, 57, 126, 157; Nils Haugen, "The Wisconsin Income Tax," *Proceedings of NTA,* 6 (1912), 321–33; Frank Strader, "Suggestions on State Income Taxation," *Proceedings of NTA,* 13 (1920), 317–22; Charles Bullock, "Income and Property Taxes: A Round Table," *Proceedings of NTA,* 15 (1922), 285–328; also previously cited articles by Kennan, Seligman, and T. S. Adams.

40. Seligman, "The New York Income Tax," *PSQ,* 34 (December 1919), 545; also NICB, *State Income Taxes,* 1, pp. 66–78.

41. Seligman, "The New York Income Tax," p. 522.

42. *Ibid.*, p. 523. Also see Percy Bidwell, *Taxation in New York State* (Albany: J. B. Lyon, 1918), pp. 105–119.

43. For statistics compiled from New York State and City comptrollers' reports see, Schwab, *History of the New York Property Tax*, pp. 79–91; Seligman, "The New York Income Tax," pp. 525–27.

44. Seligman, "The New York Income Tax," pp. 524, 527–28; Seligman, "The Taxation of Corporations," *State Conference on Taxation, Addresses and Proceedings, Utica, January 1911*, pp. 1–15.

45. On the Single Tax Experiment in Canada see F. C. Wade, "Experiments with the Single Tax in Western Canada," *Proceedings of NTA*, 8 (1914), 416–31.

46. Seligman, "The New York Income Tax," p. 526; Thomas Byrnes, "Problems and Plans of the New York State Board," *Proceedings of NTA*, 7 (1913), 187–96; E. L. Heydecker, "New York's Tax Legislation, 1911," *Proceedings of NTA*, 5 (1911), 85–93; E. E. Woodbury, "New York's Needs," *Proceedings of NTA*, 7 (1913), 139–57.

47. Seligman, "The New York Income Tax," pp. 527–28.

48. *Megalopolis: The Urbanized Northeastern Seaboard of the United States* (Cambridge: MIT Press, 1961), pp. 9, 102–105 and following.

49. Seligman, "The New York Income Tax," p. 539; also on the defects of the law according to Seligman see pp. 538–44; Seligman, "Our Fiscal Difficulties and the Way Out," *An Address* in Albany, January 1919 cited in Seligman's "The New York Income Tax," *PSQ*, 34 (1919), 530; also see *E. R. A. Seligman Papers*, Box 140, Columbia University; *Proceedings of the 8th State Conference New York State Tax Bulletin*, 4, No. 4, pp. 22–27; also L. A. Tanzer, "State Income Taxation with Special Reference to the New York Income Tax Law," *Proceedings of NTA*, 12 (1919), 385–97.

50. Shearman, *Natural Taxation*, p. 44.

51. Wells, "The Communism of a Discriminating Income Tax," p. 246.

52. Weyl, *The New Democracy*, p. 296.

53. T. S. Adams, "The Wisconsin Income Tax," *AER*, 1, p. 906; "The Place of the Income Tax in the Reform of State Taxation," *Papers of AER*, (1911), pp. 302–21; "The Significance of the Wisconsin Income Tax," *PSQ*, 28, pp. 569–70; also Kennan, "The Wisconsin Income Tax," p. 171.

CHAPTER 10 *The Nature of the Achievement and the Anomaly of Party Finance*

1. "The Invisible Government and Administrative Efficiency," *The Annals*, 64 (March 1916), 12, 13, 15, 18; for background and support for these views see Municipal Bureau of New York City, *The Constitution and Government of the State of New York: An Appraisal* (New York: 1915), pp. 35–167.

2. Jones, "Spoils and the Party," *Annals*, 64 (March 1916), 72, 73.

3. See, e.g., *The Finance Commission of the City of Boston. Reports and Communications*, 7 (1912), 6–37; for a reformer's views see Harvey Shephard,

"The Boston Finance Commission," in *Proceedings of the Cincinnati Conference for Good Government and the 15th Annual Meeting of the National Municipal League, November 1909,* pp. 205–16. Shephard was the lecturer on municipal government at Boston University in 1912.

4. *The Finance Commission of the City of Boston,* 7 (1912), 226–27 and pp. 26–27, 197–98; *The Finance Commission of the City of Boston: Report on the Boston School System* (1911), p. 70. Robert Treat Paine called the commission "as fine a body of able and disinterested citizens as ever devoted themselves for nearly two years to the study of conditions affecting a great city." "The Elimination of National Party Designations from Municipal Ballots," in *Proceedings of the Cincinnati Conference for Good Government and the 15th Annual Meeting of the National Municipal League,* p. 291.

5. *The Finance Commission of . . . Boston: Reports and Communications,* 7 (1912), 228–29; also pp. 26–27, 226–27; *The Finance Commission of . . . Boston: Report on the Boston School System,* p. 71.

6. *The Finance Commission of . . . Boston: Reports and Communications,* 7 (1912), 227; also *Ibid.,* 1, pp. 131, 132, 258, 274; 2, pp. 36–38, 150, 202–204, 216, 217; 3, pp. 222, 304, 306, 702, 1063.

7. Howland, "The Grafter at Work in American Cities," *Proceedings of the Buffalo Conference for Good City Government and the 16th Annual Meeting of the National Municipal League, Buffalo, November 1910;* Clinton R. Woodruff, ed., (National Municipal League, 1910), pp. 192–95; also Josiah Flynt, *The World of Graft* (New York: McClure Phillips Co., 1901), Chapters 2, 4, for example.

8. *Public Debts,* pp. 367–68; also pp. 369–75.

9. *New York: A Report by the Special Joint Committee on Taxation and Retrenchment, February 11, 1926* (Albany: 1926), Chapter 3, pp. 55–89; also see NICB, *State Income Taxes,* 1, pp. 67, 76–78; Schwab, *History of New York Property Tax,* pp. 79–89; Austin MacDonald, "The Trend in Recent State Expenditures," *The Annals,* 113 (1924), 8–10.

10. *The Finance Commission of . . . Boston,* Parts 5 and 6 of Vol. 7 (1912), 19–32; also 1, pp. 62, 131, 146, 205; on debt statistics, pp. 25, 102–107, 119–120.

11. MacDonald, "The Trend in Recent State Expenditures," pp. 8–10.

12. New York. *Report by the Special Joint Committee on Taxation and Retrenchment, February 11, 1926,* pp. 55–70, 75, 76, 87–89. For the broader picture see *Historical Statistics of the U.S.,* Series Y 536–74, pp. 726–27.

13. *The Finance Commission of Boston,* 7 (1912), 31–32; Richard H. Dana, "Taking Municipal Contracts Out of Politics," *Proceedings of the Cincinnati Conference for Good City Government and the 15th Annual Meeting of the National Municipal League, November 1909,* pp. 189–93.

14. See, Rufus E. Miles, "Municipal Research: A New Instrument of Democracy," in *Proceedings of the Cincinnati Conference . . . and 15th Annual Meeting of the National Municipal League, Nov. 1909,* pp. 289–90 on New York's Bureau. Miles was director of the Cincinnati Bureau of Municipal Research. Howland, "The Grafter at Work in American Cities," pp. 192–99.

15. Sterne's article, "The Administration of American Cities," from the *Cyclopedia of Political Science* is cited by H. C. Adams, *Public Debts,* p. 361.

Also see Sterne's earlier article "Crude Methods of Legislation," *NAR,* 137 (1883), 158–71.

16. Adams, *Public Debts,* p. 24.

17. *The Finance Commission of . . . Boston,* 7 (1912), 19–26; Le Grand Powers, "Municipal Budgets and Expenditures," *Proceedings of the Cincinnati Conference for Good Government and the 15th Annual Meeting of the National Municipal League, Nov. 1909,* pp. 258–72; Shephard, "The Boston Finance Commission," pp. 205–209; James Bugbee, *The City Government of Boston* (Baltimore: Johns Hopkins Press, 1887).

18. *Public Debts,* p. 357.

19. Cited in *ibid.,* p. 354. Adams incorrectly cites the authority as the Pennsylvania Commission of 1878; it was, in fact, the Pennsylvania Tax Commission of 1868.

20. Debt was tightly centralized; census figures indicated that as of 1880 fewer than 81,000 people, the overwhelming bulk of them living in New England and the Middle Atlantic States, held 84% of the registered federal bonds. Citizens of New York State and Massachusetts alone accounted for nearly 44% of the total number of bondholders.

21. Arthur Millspaugh, *Party Organization and Machinery in Michigan Since 1890* (Baltimore: Johns Hopkins Press, 1917), p. 181.

22. "The Politics of American Business," *NAR,* 193 (January-June 1911), 708.

23. *Detroit News,* September 12, 1912; *Detroit Free Press,* August 27; October 3, 16, 1908; Herbert Welsh, "Campaign Committees, Publicity as a Cure for Corruption," *Forum,* 14 (1893), 26–38; Millspaugh, *Party Organization,* Chapter 6. Literature on campaign contributions was extensive by the early twentieth century. See, for instance, Orman Ray, *Political Parties and Practical Politics,* pp. 293–97; also by a leading student of "corruption," Robert C. Brooks, "Publicity and the Regulation of Campaign Contributions," *Proceedings of the Cincinnati Conference for Good City Government and the 15th Annual Meeting of the National Municipal League, Nov. 1909,* pp. 63, 439; these ideas were expanded in Brooks' *Corruption in American Politics and Life,* Chapter 6; Chester L. Jones, "Spoils and Party," *The Annals,* 64 (1916), 66–76; Leonard White, "The Politician as Personnel Manager, The Cost to the Taxpayer," *The Annals,* 113 (1924), 306–11.

24. This familiar theme was well-stated by Sydney Brooks' "Tammany Again," *Fortnightly Review,* 80 (December 1903), 921–25.

25. On Ingham County see Millspaugh, *Party Organization and Machinery in Michigan,* pp. 96–97, 105, 106, 135, 140; Sydney Brooks, "The Problem of the New York Police," *Nineteenth Century,* 80 (October 1912), 699; the *Lexow Committee* earlier had detailed the same operations.

26. Aside from the *Lexow Committee,* numerous similar state and municipal investigations bared the structure of such relationships. See, for instance, *Mazet Committee,* 5, pp. 5552–5554; *Fassett Committee,* 1, pp. 368–75, 655–75; 2, pp. 980 and following, for materials of the type common throughout all five volumes; also *Report of the New York Committee of Fourteen (1910); Report of the New York Committee of Fifteen (1902)*; elsewhere see *Report of*

the Chicago City Council on Crime (1915); C. R. Woodruff, "The American Municipal Situation," *Proceedings of the Cincinnati Conference on Good City Government and the 15th Annual Meeting of the National Municipal League, Nov. 1909,* pp. 130–32; Charles E. Merriam, *The American Party System,* pp. 138–63; T. Roosevelt, "Administering the New York Police Force," *American Ideals and Other Essays,* Part 2.

27. Brooks, "The New York Police," p. 699; *New York Times,* July 17–20, 1912.

28. Brooks, "The New York Police," pp. 695–96.

29. *Mastick Committee, 1932,* p. 85; Frankfurter, "Democracy and the Expert," *Atlantic,* November 1930.

30. *Mastick Committee, 1932,* pp. 88, this was explained annually by the *Annual Report of the New York State Tax Commission (1920–30)*, for example; also see *Report of the Special Joint Committee on Taxation and Retrenchment, Legislative Doc., No. 72 (1922)*, pp. 42–45 and following.

31. Preliminary Report of the Committee appointed by the National Tax Association to prepare a Plan, C. J. Bullock, "A Model System of State and Local Taxation," *Proceedings of NTA,* 12 (1919), 426–70. For continuation of some problems see, State of New York, "Depression Taxes and Economy through Reform of Local Government," *Third Report of the New York State Tax Commission for the Revision of the Tax Laws, February 15, 1933,* pp. 15–20, etc., 34–41, 69–73, etc., 142–45, etc., New York State, *Constitutional Convention Committee, Problems Relating to Taxation and Finance* (Albany: J. B. Lyon, 1938), pp. 1–30; Chapters 2, 3, 10, 11, 13, 16 for examples.

SELECTED BIBLIOGRAPHY

Selected Bibliography

Manuscripts & Collections

Henry Carter Adams Papers, Michigan Historical Collections, The University of Michigan, Ann Arbor.

Herbert Baxter Adams Papers, The Johns Hopkins University Library, Baltimore.

City Reform Club of New York, Minutes, New York Public Library.

William Bourke Cockran Papers, New York Public Library.

Thomas McIntyre Cooley Papers, Michigan Historical Collections, The University of Michigan, Ann Arbor.

Richard Ely Papers, State Historical Society of Wisconsin, Madison & The Johns Hopkins University Library.

J. Sloan Fassett Clippings, New York Public Library.

Daniel Coit Gilman Papers, The Johns Hopkins University Library, Baltimore.

Frank Goodnow Collection, The Johns Hopkins University Library, Baltimore.

Andrew H. Green Papers, New York Public Library.

Grosvenor Collection, Buffalo & Erie County Public Library, Buffalo.

Rutherford B. Hayes Papers, Hayes Memorial Library, Fremont, Ohio.

Jacob Hollander Collection, The Johns Hopkins University Library.

Alfred Hutzler Collection, The Johns Hopkins University Library.

M. E. Ingalls Materials, Cincinnati Historical Society, Cincinnati.

Pamphlet Collection, Pennsylvania State Library, Harrisburg.

Peter Lesley Papers, Library of the American Philosophical Society, Philadelphia.

Charles Reemelin Collection, Cincinnati Historical Society, Cincinnati.

Edwin R. A. Seligman Papers, Columbia University, New York City.

William Graham Sumner Papers, Sumner Estate, Yale University Library, New Haven.

John Martin Vincent Papers, The Johns Hopkins University Library.

Richard W. G. Welling Papers, New York Public Library.

David A. Wells Papers, Library of Congress, Washington, D.C. & Items in the Ford Collection in the New York Public Library.

Federal Documents

U.S. Department of Commerce. Bureau of the Census. *Historical Statistics of the United States from Colonial Times to 1957,* Washington: 1960.

U.S. Department of Commerce. Bureau of the Census. *Financial Statistics of Cities, 1902–13, 1915–1919, 1921–25* (Title varied slightly over these years.)

U.S. Department of the Interior. Census Office. *Report on Wealth, Debt, and Taxation at the Eleventh Census: 1890, Part II: Valuation and Taxation. J. Kendrick Upton.* Washington: 1895.

U.S. Congress. 53rd Cong., 3d Sess., *Congressional Record,* Volume 26 (1894).

U.S. Congress. 61st Cong., 1st Sess., *Congressional Record,* Volume 44 (1909).

U.S. Congress. 48th Cong., Senate, Committee on Education and Labor. *Testimony before the Committee. Report of the Committee of the Senate Upon the Relations between Capital and Labor.* 5 Volumes (1885).

U.S. Congress. 50th Cong., 1st Sess., Senate, *Senate Report 2372, Part II, April 6, 1888.*

U.S. Congress. 62nd Cong., 2d Sess., Senate. Committee on Privileges and Elections, *Testimony before the Subcommittee* (1909).

U.S. Congress. 57th Cong., 1st Sess., House. Industrial Commission. *Report of the Industrial Commission, House Document 186,* Volumes 5, 7, 9, 10, and 19 of 19 Volumes. Washington: 1902.

U.S. Treasury Department. *Report of the Secretary of the Treasury for 1893.*

State and Local Documents

California: *Preliminary Report of the Commission on Revenue and Taxation of the State of California, August 1906.* Sacramento: 1906.

———: *Report of the Commission on Revenue and Taxation of the State of California, 1906.* Sacramento: 1906.

Connecticut: *Preliminary Report of the Special Commission on Taxation.* New Haven: 1886.

———: *Report of the Special Commission on Taxation.* New Haven: 1868.

———: *Report of the Special Commission to Inquire into the Conditions and Workings of the Tax Laws.* New Haven: 1881.

———: *Report of the Special Commission on the Subject of Taxation.* New Haven: 1887.

———: *Report of the Special Commission on the Taxation of Corporations paying Taxes to the State.* New Haven: 1913.

———: *Report of the Special State Commission on the Subject of Taxation.* New Haven: 1917.

Delaware: *Report of the Undersigned Members of the Delaware Tax Commission to the General Assembly, 2 Parts.* Wilmington: 1893.

Indiana: *Report of the Commission on Taxation to the Governor.* Fort Wayne: 1916.

Illinois: *Compilation of Tax Laws and Judicial Decisions of the State of Illinois . . . Albert M. Kales and Elmer Liessmann, under the Direction of the Special Tax Commission.* Springfield: 1911.

———: *Bureau of Public Efficiency: On the Office of the Coroner; 1911; On the Clerk of the Superior Court, 1912; On the Clerk of the Circuit Court, 1912.* Springfield: 1912.

———: *Eighth Biennial Report of the Bureau of Labor Statistics.* Springfield: 1894.

———: *Ninth Biennial Report of the Bureau of Labor Statistics of Illinois, Subject: Franchises and Taxation.* Springfield: 1897.

———: *Report of the Chicago City Council Committee on Crime, 1915.* Chicago: 1915.

———: *Report of the Investigation of the Municipal Revenue of Chicago by Charles Edward Merriam.* Chicago: 1906.

———: *Report of the Revenue Commission.* Springfield: 1886.

———: *Report of the Taxation and Revenue System of Illinois, by John Fairlie, Chief Clerk of the Commission.* Danville: 1910.

Iowa: *Report of the Auditor of the State, 1870–75, 1877, 1882–83.* Des Moines: n.d.

———: *Report of the Revenue Commission of the State of Iowa.* Des Moines: 1893.

Kansas: *Report and Bill of the Kansas State Tax Commission.* Topeka: 1901.

Maine: *Report of the Special Tax Commission of Maine.* Augusta: 1890.

Maryland: *Report of the Commission for Revision of the Taxation System of the State of Maryland and the City of Baltimore.* Baltimore: 1913.

———: *Report of the Maryland Tax Commission to the General Assembly, January 1888.* Baltimore: 1888. (Md. Comm. 1888)

———: *Report of the Tax Commission of Baltimore.* Baltimore: 1886.

Massachusetts: *Argument in Favor of the Proposed Constitutional Amendment permitting the General Court to Classify Property for Purpose of Taxation, by Charles Bullock for the Taxation Committee, Boston Chamber of Commerce, October 26, 1909.* Boston: 1909.

———: *Boston: Boston Executive Business Association. Report of the Special Committee on Taxation.* Boston: 1889.

———: *Committee on Taxation. Report of the Committee appointed to Inquire into the Expediency of Revising and Amending the Laws of the Commonwealth Relating to Taxation, October 1897.* Boston: 1897. (Mass. Committee Report 1897)

———: *Commission on Taxation: Report of . . . to Inquire into the Expediency of Revising and Amending the Laws Relating to Taxation and Exemption Therefrom, January 1875.* Boston: 1875. (Mass. Committee Report 1875)

———: *Boston: The Finance Commission of the City of Boston: Reports and Communications.* 7 volumes. Boston: 1912.

———: *A Full Report of the Joint Special Committee on Taxation.* Boston: 1894.

———: *Report of the Commission of Taxation to Investigate the Subject of Taxation and to Codify, Revise, and Amend the Laws relating thereto.* Boston: 1908.
———: *Report of the Commission appointed under the Provisions of Chapter 142 of the Resolves of 1909, To Investigate the Laws relating to Taxation.* Boston: 1909.
———: *Report of the Joint Special Committee of the Massachusetts Legislature on Municipal Finance, Doc. No. 1803, January 1913.* Boston: 1913.
———: *Report of the Joint Special Committee on Taxation, appointed to Consider the Expediency of Legislation in Amendment or in addition to the General Laws relating to Taxation, June 1907.* Boston: 1907.
———: *Report of the Special Commission on Taxation.* Boston: 1891.
———: *Report on State Finances and the Budget, submitted to the General Court by the Joint Special Committee on Finance and Budget Procedure.* Boston: 1918.
Michigan: *Preliminary Report of the Commission of Inquiry into Taxation of the State of Michigan.* Lansing: 1911.
———: *Report of the Commission of Inquiry into Taxation in Michigan.* Lansing: 1911.
Minnesota: *Report of the Tax Commission of Minnesota created by Chapter 13, General Laws of 1901, for the Purpose of Framing a Tax Code.* St. Paul: 1902.
Missouri: *Report of the State Tax Commission of Missouri, 1903.* Jefferson City: 1904.
Nebraska: *Biennial Report of the Auditor of Public Accounts of Nebraska, 1886.*
New Hampshire: *Report of the Legislature of New Hampshire of the Hon. George Y. Sawyer, Chairman of the Board of Commissioners to Revise, Codify, or Amend the Tax Laws of the State and for the Establishment of an Equal System of Taxation.* Concord: 1876.
New Jersey: *Preliminary Report of the Commission on Taxation made to Governor Abbott.* Trenton: 1891.
———: *Report of the Commission to Investigate the Subject of Taxation.* Trenton: 1896.
———: *Report of the Honorable Charles S. Ogden (and others) to the Legislature of New Jersey on Taxation.* Trenton: 1868.
———: *Report of the Special Committee of the House of the Assembly as to the Taxation of Railways and other Corporations in this State.* Trenton: 1883.
———: *Report of the Special Tax Commission of the State of New Jersey.* New Brunswick: 1880.
New York: *Advisory Commission on Taxation and Finance, Committee on Taxation and Revenue: Reports submitted at Meeting of May 9, 1905.* New York: 1905.
———: *Advisory Commission on Taxation and Finance. Report on City Debt and Its Relation to the Constitutional Limits of Indebtedness, etc., April 1907.* New York: 1907.
———: *Tax Reform Association: Annual Reports. 1893–1927,* 1st to 37th.

———: *Annual Report of the State Board of Tax Commissioners.* Albany: 1897–99, 1901, 1903, 1905–10, 1913–19, 1923–30.

———: *Constitutional Convention Committee. Problems Relating to Taxation and Finances.* 10. Albany: 1938.

———: *Constitutional Convention. Debates. 1867–1868.* 3 Albany: 1868.

———: *Department of Taxes and Assessments of the City of New York, Taxation of Personal Property in the State of New York.* New York: 1912.

———: *Decisions, Opinions, and Statistics compiled by the Tax Commission with their Report, Presented to the Legislative Joint Tax Committee of New York.* Albany: 1881.

———: *Depression Taxes and Economy Through Reform of Local Government, 3rd Report of the New York State Tax Commission for Revision of the Tax Laws, February 15, 1932 Legislative Doc. No. 56 (1933).* Albany: 1933. (Mastick Committee 1932)

———: *Final Report of the Committee on Taxation of the City of New York, 1916.* New York: 1916.

———: *Indexes to Reports of the Special Tax Investigation Commissions, 1916–38.* Albany: 1938.

———: *Annual Reports of the State Assessors, 1860–1887.*

———: *Report of the Joint Committee of the Senate and Assembly . . . appointed to Investigate corrupt practices in connection with legislation, and the Affairs of Insurance Companies, other than those doing life insurance business, Assembly Documents, No. 30, I, 1911.* Albany: 1911.

———: *Report of the Commissioners to Devise A Plan for the Government of Cities in the State of New York, Assembly Document. No. 68, March 6, 1877.* Albany: 1877.

———: *Report of the Commissioners appointed to Revise the Laws for the Assessment and Collection of Taxes in the State of New York, 1871.* New York: 1871. (Wells Report 1871)

———: *Report of the Commissioners appointed to Revise the Laws for the Assessment and Collection of Taxes in the State of New York, 1872.* Albany: 1872. (Wells Report 1872)

———: *Report of the Committee of Inquiry to Governor William Sulzer,* New York: 1905.

———: *Report of the Committee on Taxation and Revenue, December 1905.* New York: 1905.

———: *Report of the State Comptroller, 1895–1899.*

———: *Report of Counsel to Revise the Tax Laws of the State of New York.* Albany: 1893.

———: *Report on the Examination of the Accounts and Methods of the Office of the Sheriff of New York County April, 1913.* New York: 1913.

———: *Report of the Joint Committee of the Senate and Assembly Relative to Taxation for State and Local Purposes.* New York: 1893.

———: *Report of the Joint Legislative Committee on Taxation.* Albany: 1916. (Mills Committee)

———: *Report and Proceedings of the Senate Committee appointed to Investigate the Police Department of the City of New York.* 5 volumes. Albany: 1895. (Lexow Committee)

———: *Report of the Special Committee of the Assembly appointed to Investigate the Public Offices and Departments of the City of New York and the Counties Therein Included . . . January 15, 1900*. 6 volumes Albany: 1900. (Mazet Committee)

———: *Report of the Special Committee of the New York State Legislature to Investigate the City and County of Albany . . . March 29, 1912*. Albany: 1912.

———: *Report of the Special Joint Committee on Taxation and Retrenchment*. Albany: 1925.

———: *Report of the Special Tax Commission of the State of New York . . . January 15, 1907*. Albany: 1907.

———: *Report on the State Assessment Laws by the Joint Select Committee appointed by the Legislature of 1862*. Albany: 1863.

———: *Senate of the State of New York. Senate Documents,* No. 28, 133rd *Session, Proceedings of the Senate in the Matter of the Investigation Demanded by Senator Jotham P. Allds, I, November 28, 1910*. Albany: 1910.

———: *Senate: Testimony Taken before the Senate Committee on Cities Pursuant to the Resolution adopted January 20, 1890*. 5 volumes. Albany: 1891. (Fassett Committee)

———: *State Conference on Taxation: Addresses and Proceedings, 1st Conference Utica, New York, January 1911*. Albany: 1911.

———: *State Conference on Taxation: Addresses and Proceedings, 2nd Conference Buffalo, New York, January 1912*. Albany: 1912.

———: *Taxes on Personal Property in New York State, from 1880–1913*. New York: Department of Taxes and Assessments, 1913.

Ohio: *Report of the Honorary Commission appointed by the Governor to Investigate the Tax System of Ohio and recommend Improvements therein*. Columbus: 1908.

———: *Report of the Special Tax Commission of the City of Cleveland* (1915).

———: *Report of the Tax Commission of Ohio of 1893 appointed under a Joint Resolution of the General Assembly, April 24, 1893* (*House Joint Resolution No. 53*) Cleveland: 1893. (Ohio Committee Report 1893)

———: *Second Annual Report of the Tax Commission of Ohio* (1912).

Pennsylvania: *M. E. Olmsted, Riter Tax Bill House Bill No. 239, Argument of M. E. Olmsted, Esq., of Harrisburg, Pa. on Behalf of Certain Corporate Interests before the Ways & Means Committee of the House of Representatives of Pa., March 19, 1895*.

———: *Patterson, C. Stuart, An Analysis of the Revenue Bill* (*H.R. No. 239, Session of 1895*). Philadelphia: 1895.

———: *Patterson, C. Stuart. Speech of . . . on the Taxation of Railroads to the Committee of Ways & Means of the House of Representatives*. Harrisburg: 19 March, 1895.

———: *Report of the Auditor General on the Finances of the Commonwealth of Pennsylvania, November 30, 1877. Auditor General's Office*. Harrisburg: 1878.

———: *State Constitution of 1872. Debates of the Convention to Amend the*

Constitution of Pennsylvania convened at Harrisburg, November 12, 1872, adjourned November 27 to meet at Philadelphia, January 7, 1873. 6 volumes. Harrisburg: 1873.

———: *Pennsylvania Tax Conference. Valuation, Taxation, and Exemptions in the Commonwealth of Pennsylvania. A Report to the Pennsylvania Tax Conference by the Commission on Valuation & Taxation.* Harrisburg, October 13, 1892. (Weeks Report Pa. Tax Conference 1892)

———: *Report of the Auditor General, Secretary of the Commonwealth, and State Treasurer, on the Tax Laws of the State of Pennsylvania.* Harrisburg: 1867.

———: *Report of the Commissioners appointed under an ordinance of the City of Philadelphia to revise the laws relating to Taxation.* Philadelphia: 1865.

———: *Report of the Committee appointed to Examine the Tax Laws of Other American States and Report an Opinion For or Against the Governing Principles embraced therein.* Harrisburg: 1892.

———: *Report of the Committee appointed by the Tax Conference of Pa. Interests to Examine the Tax Laws of other American States and Report an Opinion For or Against the governing Principles Embraced therein.*

———: *Report of the Committee on Taxation . . . to the Council, City of Pittsburgh, 1916.*

———: *Report. The Joint Committee of the Senate and House of Representatives of the Commonwealth of Pennsylvania to Consider and Report Upon a Revision of the Corporation and Revenue Laws of the Commonwealth to the Legislature.* Harrisburg: 1911.

———: *Report of the State Tax Commission, Pennsylvania Legislative Documents of 1868.* Harrisburg: 1869.

Rhode Island: *State of Rhode Island and Providence Plantations. Report of the Joint Special Committee on the Taxation Laws of Rhode Island.* Providence: 1910.

Vermont: *Double Taxation in Vermont. Report of the Special Committee appointed to report a Measure of Relief to the Legislature.* Burlington: 1900.

———: *Special Report of the General Assembly, 1902, relating to Taxation of Corporations and Individuals. By the Commissioner of Taxes.* Burlington: 1902.

West Virginia: *Tax Commission. Final Report.* Wheeling: 1884.

———: *Tax Commission. Preliminary Report.* Wheeling: 1884.

Wisconsin: *Report of the Wisconsin State Tax Commission.* Madison: 1898.

———: *Report of the Wisconsin State Tax Commission.* Madison: 1914.

———: *Tax Laws of Wisconsin, Income Tax Cases, 148 Wisconsin 456.*

Miscellaneous Reports and Proceedings

Cleveland Chamber of Commerce: *Taxation. Report of Special Committee.* Cleveland: 1896.

———: *Taxation. Report of Special Committee.* Cleveland: 1895.

Maryland: *Baltimore: Report of the Committee on the Establishment of Manufactures to the Mayor and City Council, 1877*. Baltimore: 1877.

———: *Report of the Advisory Committee on Taxation and Revenue submitted to the Mayor of Baltimore*. Baltimore: 1908.

New York: *Report on the Inequality of State Taxation submitted to the Union League Club, March 9, 1876 by Isaac Sherman, J. S. Schulz, Thos. Thornell.*

———: *Report of the Committee on Finance and Taxation of the Merchants' Association of the City of New York on the System of Personal Taxation, March 26, 1910*. in *Merchants' Association Bulletin*. Spring 1910.

———: *Report of Andrew H. Green, Comptroller in Response to Certain Resolutions of the Board of Aldermen, February 18, 1875, "A Three Years' Struggle with Municipal Misrule,"* n.p., n.d.

———: *Chamber of Commerce of the State of New York. Report of the Committee on State and Municipal Taxation, October 4, 1900; Report of December 20, 1900; Report of January 3, 1901; Report of May 2, 1901; Report of December 5, 1901.*

National Conference on Taxation under the Auspices of the National Civic Federation Held at Buffalo, New York, May 23 and 24, 1901.

Proceedings of the Annual Conferences of the National Tax Association, 1907–1925. 18 volumes. *Digest and Index* by Ray and Gladys Blakey. New York: National Tax Association, 1927.

Proceedings of the . . . Conferences for Good City Government and the . . . Annual Meetings of the National Municipal League edited by Clinton Rogers Woodruff. National Municipal League, 1904–13.

Works Cited: Books & Articles

Abbot, Lyman. *Reminiscences*. Boston: 1915.

Abbott, Grace. "Immigration and the Municipal Problem," *Proceedings of the Cincinnati Conference, 15th Annual Meeting, National Municipal League,* (1909), pp. 148–57.

Abrams, Richard. "A Paradox of Progressivism: Massachusetts on the Eve of Insurgency," *Political Science Quarterly,* 75 (Sept. 1960), 379–99.

Adams, Brooks. "Abuse of Taxation," *Atlantic Monthly,* 42 (Oct. 1878), 453–58.

———. "Oppressive Taxation of the Poor," *Atlantic Monthly,* 42 (Nov. 1878), 632–66.

———. "Oppressive Taxation and Its Remedy," *Atlantic Monthly,* 42 (Dec. 1878), 761–68.

———. "The Platform of the New Party," *North American Review,* 119 (Oct. 1874), 33–60.

Adams, Charles Francis, Jr. "Boston," *North American Review,* 105 (Apr. 1868), 557–91; 105 (Jan. 1868), 1–25.

———. "The Currency Debate of 1873–74," *North American Review,* 119 (July 1874), 111–65.

———. "The Government and the Railroad Corporations," *North American Review,* 112 (Jan. 1871), 31–61.

Adams, Henry. *The Education of Henry Adams.* Boston: Houghton, Mifflin Co. 1961.

Adams, Henry B. "Civil Service Reform," *North American Review,* 225 (Oct. 1869), 443–75.

———. "The Session," *North American Review,* 223 (Apr. 1869), 610–40.

Adams, Henry Carter. *Public Debts: An Essay in the Science of Finance.* New York: 1892.

Adams, Henry Carter. *Public Debts: An Essay in the Science of Finance.* New York: 1892.

———. *Relation of the State to Industrial Action and Economics and Jurisprudence,* edited by Joseph Dorfman. New York: 1954.

———. "Suggestions for a System of Taxation," *Michigan Political Science Association,* (1894), 49–74.

Adams, Thomas S. "Constitutionality of the Wisconsin Income Tax Affirmed," *American Economic Review,* 2 (March 1912), 194–96.

———. "The Income Tax as A Substitute for Personal Property Taxation in Wisconsin," *Proceedings of the National Tax Association,* (1910), pp. 87–110.

———. "Separation of Sources of State and Local Revenues as A Program of Tax Reform," *Proceedings of the National Tax Association* (1907), pp. 515–27.

Addresses Delivered at the Landlords' Mutual Protective Association of Baltimore City. Baltimore: 1889.

Alexander, Arthur Jay. "Federal Patronage in New York State: 1789–1805." Ph.D. Diss., University of Pennsylvania, 1945.

Allen, Frederick Lewis. *The Great Pierpont Morgan.* New York: 1949.

Allinson, E. P. and Penrose, Boise. *The City Government of Philadelphia.* Baltimore: 1887.

American Academy, "Modernizing State Government: The New York Constitutional Convention of 1967," *Proceedings of the American Academy of Political Science,* XXVIII (Jan. 1967).

American Academy of Political Science. "Governing the City: Challenges and Options for New York," *Proceedings of the American Academy of Political Science,* 29, No. 4 (1969), 1–228.

———. "Municipal Income Taxes: An Economic Evaluation, Problems of Administration, Alternative Sources of Revenue," *Proceedings of the American Academy of Political Science,* 28, No. 4 (1968), 1–163.

———. "Wealth and Taxation," *Proceedings of the American Academy of Political Science,* (1924), 1–110.

American Statesman. "Taxation in the United States," *Contemporary Review,* 39 (Jan. 1881), 15–30.

Ames, John H. *The Taxation of Personal Property.* Des Moines: 1877.

Ames, Mary Lesley. *Life and Letters of Peter and Susan Lesley.* 2 vols. New York: 1909.

Anderson, Eugene N. and Anderson, Pauline R. *Political Institution and Social Change in Continental Europe in the Nineteenth Century.* Berkeley and Los Angeles: 1967.

Angell, E. A. "Antiquated Personal Property Tax," *Journal of Accountancy,* 10 (1910), 209–210.

———. "The Tax Inquisitor System in Ohio," *The Yale Review,* 5 (Feb. 1897), 350–73.

Apter, David. *The Politics of Modernization.* Chicago: 1965.

Arent, Leonora. *Electric Franchises in New York City.* New York: 1919.

Atkins, Gordon M. *Health, Housing, and Poverty in New York City 1865–1898.* New York: 1947.

Atkinson, Edward. *Argument . . . for Changes in the Law Regarding Taxation of Foreign Corporations Before a Committee of the Massachusetts Legislature, February 27, 1877.* Boston: 1877.

———. *Revenue Reform.* Boston: 1871.

———. *Taxation and Work* (New York: 1892).

———. "Taxation in the United States," *Engineering Magazine,* 10 (1895–6), 192–202.

———. "Taxation: No Burden," *Atlantic Monthly,* 10 (July–Dec. 1862), 115–18.

Atkinson, J. W. ed. *Motives in Fantasy, Action, and Society.* Princeton: 1958.

Austin, F. A. "Easing Taxpayers' Burdens," *American Economic Review,* 3 (June 1913), 510.

Baldwin, Henry DeForest. "It Shows How Ignorance Results in Oppression," *Journal of Accountancy,* 10 (May–Oct., 1910), 165–69.

Baltzell, E. Digby. *An American Business Aristocracy.* New York: 1962.

Banfield, Edward. *Political Influences.* New York: 1961.

Barker, Charles Albro. *Henry George.* New York: 1955.

Barrett, Eugene A. "John Frederick Hartranft" Ph.D. Diss, Temple University, 1950.

Bastable, C. F. "The New Budget and the Principles of Financial Policy," *Economic Journal,* 9 (1899), 204, 210.

———. *Public Finance.* London: 1892; also 3rd ed. London: 1922.

Beach, John K. "The Income Tax Decision," *Yale Review,* 5 (1896–7), 58–75.

Beecher, Henry Ward. *Hard Times* (Philadelphia: 1875), Pennsylvania State Library Pamphlets, Vol. 214, No. 32.

Bellows, Henry W. "Civil Service Reform," *North American Review,* 132 (1880), 247–60.

Belmont, Perry. *American Democrat: Recollections of Perry Belmont.* New York: 1940.

———. "Taxation, Its Sum, Justification, and Methods," *Forum,* 23 (Mar. 1897), 1–12.

Bennett, Fremont O. *Politics and Politicians of Chicago, Cook County, and Illinois.* Chicago: 1886.

Benson, Lee. *Merchants, Farmers, and Railroads: Railroad Regulation and New York Politics, 1850–1887.* Cambridge: 1955.

———. *Turner and Beard: American Historical Writing Reconsidered.* New York: 1960.

Bentley, Arthur F. *The Condition of the Western Farmer: As Illustrated by the Economic History of A Nebraska Township.* Baltimore: 1893.

Benton, Thomas Hart. *An Artist in America: My Halcyon Days.* New York: 1939.

Bernheim, A. C. "Relations of New York City and the State," *Political Science Quarterly,* 9 (1894), 3, 12.

Bidwell, Percy. *Taxation in New York State.* Albany: 1918.

Bigelow, John. *The Life of Samuel J. Tilden.* 2 vols. New York: 1895.

Bird, Francis William. *The Hoosac Tunnel Contract.* Boston: 1869.

———. *Retrenchment and Reform in State Expenditure.* Boston: 1879.

Bishop, Joseph Bucklin. *Money in City Elections: Its Effects and the Remedies: An Address, Commonwealth Club, New York, March 21, 1887.* New York: 1887.

Bispham, G. T. "Law in America, 1776–1876," *North American Review,* 122 (Jan. 1876), 154–90.

Black, Cyrus E. *The Dynamics of Modernization: A Study in Comparative History.* New York: 1964.

Blair, Montgomery. "The Republican Party As It Was and Is," *North American Review,* 131 (1880), 422–30.

Blakey, Roy G. and Gladys C. *The Federal Income Tax.* New York: 1940.

———. *National Tax Association Digest and Index, 1907–25.* New York: 1927.

Blodgett, Geoffrey. "The Mind of the Boston Mugwump," *Mississippi Valley Historical Review,* 48, No. 4 (March 1962), 614–34.

Blunden, George H. "British Local Finance," *Political Science Quarterly,* 9 (1894), 78–118.

———. "Incidence of Urban Rates," *Economic Review,* 1 (1891), 486–96.

———. *Local Taxation and Finance.* London: 1895.

Bogart, Ernest L. *The Financial History of Ohio.* Champaign, Ill.: 1912.

Bonaparte, Charles J. *Civil Service Reform as a Moral Question.* New York: 1889.

Bond, Henry H. "Problems of A Modern State Income Tax," *Annals,* 91 (May 1921), 263–68.

Boothe, Viva Belle. "The Political Party As A Social Process" Ph.D. Diss., University of Pennsylvania, Philadelphia, 1923.

Borah, William E. "The Income Tax Amendment," *North American Review,* 191 (1910), 755–61.

Bouroff, Basil. *The Impending Crisis: Conditions Resulting from the Concentration of Wealth in the United States.* Chicago: 1900.

Boutwell, George S. "The Income Tax," *North American Review,* 160 (1895), 589–606.

———. *Reminiscences of Sixty Years of Public Affairs.* 2 vols. New York: 1902.

Bower, Ladman F. *The Economic Waste of Sin.* New York: 1924.

Boyd, Carl. "Growth of Cities in the United States During the Decade 1880–1890," *Publications of the American Statistical Association,* 3, 416–20.

Brace, Charles Loring. *The Dangerous Classes of New York and Twenty Years Work Among Them.* New York: 1872.

Bradford, Gamaliel. "Congressional Reform," *North American Review,* 229 (Oct. 1870), 330–51.

———. "Municipal Government," *Scribner's Magazine,* 2 (July–Dec. 1887), 485–92.

Bradley, Edward Sculley. *Henry Charles Lea: A Biography.* Philadelphia: 1931.

Bradley, Erwin S. "Post-Bellum Politics in Pennsylvania, 1866–72" Ph.D. Diss., Pennsylvania State College, 1952.

Breen, Matthew. *Thirty Years of New York Politics.* New York: 1899.

Brewster, Benjamin H. *Argument of the Hon. Benjamin Harris Brewster on the subject of the Ordinance of the Constitutional Convention.* Philadelphia: 1873, Pennsylvania State Library Pamphlet, Vol. 705, no. 13.

Brindley, John E. *History of Taxation in Iowa.* 2 vols. Iowa City: 1911.

———. "Iowa Tax Problems," *Proceedings of the National Tax Association,* (1922), 62–66.

———. "Problem of Tax Reform in Iowa," *Proceedings of the National Tax Association,* (1910), pp. 141–58.

———. "Tax Administration in Iowa," *Proceedings of the National Tax Association,* 1912, 385 ff.

Brinley, Charles. *A Handbook for Philadelphia Voters, etc.* Philadelphia: 1894.

Brislawn, Joseph. "Taxation and the Farmer," *Proceedings of the National Tax Association,* 10 (1916), 264–86.

Brooks, Robert C. "Bibliography of Municipal Administration and City Conditions," *Municipal Affairs,* 1, No. 1 (1897), 1–326.

———. "Bibliography of Municipal Problems," *Municipal Affairs,* 5 (1901), 1–346.

———. *Corruption in American Politics & Life.* New York: 1910.

———. "Publicity and Regulation of Campaign Contributions," *Proceedings of the Cincinnati Conference, 15th Annual Meeting, National Municipal League,* (1909), pp. 439–40.

Brooks, Sydney. "Aspects of the Income Tax," *North American Review,* 197 (1913), 542–55.

———. "The Politics of American Business," *North American Review,* 193 (1910–11), 708–20.

———. "The Problem of the New York Police," *Nineteenth Century,* 80 (Oct. 1912), 66–72.

———. "Tammany Again," *Fortnightly Review,* 80 (Dec. 1903), 921–28.

Brown, John. *Parasitic Wealth.* Chicago: 1898.

Browne, A. G. Jr. "Governor Andrew," *North American Review,* 105 (Jan. 1868), 249–76.

Brownlow, Louis. *A Passion for Politics.* Chicago: 1955.

Bruere, Martha. *Increasing Home Efficiency.* New York: 1916.

———. "Utilization of Family Income," *Annals,* 48 (July 1913), 117–22.

Bryce, James. *The American Commonwealth.* 2 vols. New York: 1888.

Buck, A. E. "The Development of the Budget Idea in the United States," *Annals,* 113 (1924), 31–40.

Buckalew, Charles R. *An Examination of the Constitution of Pennsylvania.* Philadelphia: 1883.

Buel, James W. *Mysteries and Miseries of America's Great Cities, Etc.* St. Louis: 1883.

Bugbee, James M. *The City Government of Boston.* Baltimore: 1887.

Bullock, Charles. "Federal Income Tax," *Proceedings of the National Tax Association,* (1914), 264–79.

———. *A Historical Sketch of the Finance and Financial Policy of Massachusetts, 1780–1905.* New York: 1907.

———. *Introduction to the Study of Economics.* New York: 1900.

———. "Local Option in Taxation," *Proceedings of the National Tax Association,* (1907), 589–90.

———. "A Model System of State and Local Taxation," *Proceedings of the National Tax Association,* (1919), 426–70.

———. *Principles of Economics.* new & rev. ed. New York: 1900.

———. *Selected Readings in Public Finance.* Boston: 1906.

———. "State Income Taxation and the Classified Property Tax," *Proceedings of the National Tax Association,* (1916), 362–84.

———. "Taxation of Intangible Property," *Proceedings of the National Tax Association,* (1908), 127–28.

———. "The Taxation of Property and Income in Massachusetts," *Quarterly Journal of Economics,* 31 (November 1916), 1–61.

———. "The Wisconsin Income Tax," *Proceedings of the National Tax Association,* (1913), 339–41.

Burton, Theodore E. *John Sherman.* Boston & New York: 1906.

Callahan, Raymond. *Education and the Cult of Efficiency.* Chicago: 1962.

Callow, Alexander Jr. ed. *American Urban History.* New York: 1969.

———. *The Tweed Ring.* New York: 1969.

Campbell, Robert. "History of Constitutional Provisions Relating to Taxation," *Proceedings of the National Tax Association,* (1908), 559–77.

Canfield, James H. *Taxation: A Plain Talk for Plain People.* New York: 1883.

Cannan, Edwin. "The Financial Relations of English Localities," *Economic Journal* 13 (March 1903).

———. *The History of Local Rates in England.* 2d ed. London: 1912.

Carnegie, Andrew. *The Autobiography of Andrew Carnegie.* New York: 1920.

———. *The Empire of Business.* New York: 1912.

———. "The President's Puzzle: The Surplus," *North American Review* 146 (1888), 273–79.

———. *Triumphant Democracy.* New York: 1886.

Carver, Thomas N. "The Ohio Tax Inquisitor Law," *American Economic Association,* 3, No. 3 (New York: 1898).

Cater, Harold Dean. *Henry Adams and His Friends: A Collection of His Unpublished Letters.* Boston: 1947.

Champernowne, Henry. *The Boss: An Essay Upon the Art of Governing American Cities.* New York: 1894.

Chidsey, O. B. *The Gentleman from New York: A Life of Roscoe Conkling.* New Haven: 1935.

Chittenden, L. E. "The Rapid Transit Problem in New York City," *Harper's Weekly*, 35. (1891), 134 ff.

A Citizen of Philadelphia. "An Inquiry into the Causes and Cost of Corrupt State Legislation," (Philadelphia: 1863), Pennsylvania State Library Pamphlet Collection, Vol. 214.

Clarke, Charlene. *Village Life in America, 1852–72*. New York: 1902.

Clarke, William H. *The Civil Service Law*. New York: 1897.

Clawson, Marion. *The Land System of the U.S. An Introduction to the History and Practice of Land Use and Land Tenure*. Lincoln: 1968.

Cleveland, Frederick. "Popular Control of Government: Three Schools of Opinion in the United States with Respect to Budget Machinery," (1919), 237–61.

Clews, Henry. *The Wall Street Point of View*. New York: 1900.

Clifford-Vaughan, Michalina. "Some French Concepts of Elites," *British Journal of Sociology*, 11 (Dec. 1960), 319–31.

Closson, Carlos C. Jr. "The Unemployed in American Cities, 2," *Quarterly Journal of Economics*, 8, No. 4 (July 1894), 453–60.

Clow, Frederick. *A Comparative Study of the Administration of City Finance in the United States*. New York: 1901.

———. "St. Paul Method of Assessing Real Estate," *Journal of Political Economy*, 5 (1894–95), 71–80.

Cobden Club Essays. 2nd series, 1871–72. London, Paris, & New York: 1872.

Cochran, Thomas. *The American Business System, 1900–1955*. New York: 1962.

———. "The Presidential Synthesis in American History," *American Historical Review*, 53 (1958), 748–59.

———. *Railroad Leaders, 1845–1890: The Business Mind in Action*. Cambridge, Mass.: 1953.

Cochran, Thomas and Miller, William. *The Age of Enterprise*. New York: 1943.

Cochran, Thomas. "Local Taxation," *Social Science Association of Philadelphia Papers of 1871* (Philadelphia: 1871).

———. "Methods of Valuation of Real Estate for Taxation," *Social Science Association of Philadelphia Papers of 1874*. (Philadelphia: 1874).

Cohn, Gustav. *The Science of Finance*. Chicago: 1895.

Coleman, George. "Special Franchise Taxation in New York," *Proceedings of the National Tax Association*, (1907), 649–54.

Coleman, James H. *Letters, etc. on Corporations and Taxation*. New York: n.d.

Coler, Bird S. *Municipal Government*. New York: 1901.

Committee of Fifteen. *A Report on the Social Evil*. New York: 1902.

Committee of Fourteen. *The Social Evil in New York*. New York: 1910.

Commons, John R. *The Distribution of Wealth*. New York: 1893.

———. *The Legal Foundations of Capitalism*. Madison: 1968.

———. *Myself: The Autobiography of John Rogers Commons*. Madison: 1963.

———. "State Supervision for Cities," *Annals*, 5 (1894–95), 434–40.

———. "Taxation in Chicago and Philadelphia," *Journal of Political Economy,* 3 (Sept. 1895), 433 ff.

"Competency and Economy in Public Expenditures," *Annals,* 113 (May 1924).

Compilation. *Of Constitutional Provisions, Statutes, and Cases Relating to the System of Taxes in the State of New York.* Albany: 1885.

Conant, C. A. "New Corporation Tax," *North American Review,* 190 (Aug. 1909).

Connell, William H. "Public Works and Engineering Services on a Public Service Basis," *Annals,* 64 (1916).

Conway, Moncure D. "Our King in Dress Coat," *North American Review,* 144 (1887), 120–28, 261–71.

Cooley, Thomas M. "Limits to State Control of Private Business," *Princeton Review,* n.s. (1878), 233–71.

———. "State Regulation of Corporate Profits," *North American Review,* 137 (1883), 207–17.

———. *A Treatise on the Constitutional Limitations Which Rest Upon the Legislative Power of the States . . .* Boston: 1868.

———. *A Treatise on the Law of Taxation.* Chicago: 1876.

Corbin, William H. "Work of the Special Tax Commission Investigating Corporate Taxation in Connecticut," *Proceedings of the National Tax Association,* (1912), 449–58.

Cossa, Luigi. *Taxation—Its Principles and Methods.* trans. Horace White. New York: 1888.

Cox, Jacob. "The Civil Service Reform," *North American Review,* 112 (Jan. 1871), 81–113.

Coxe, A. Cleveland. "Government by Aliens," *Forum,* 7 (August 1889).

Crawford, F. Marion. *An American Politician* (Boston: 1885).

Crocker, G. G. *Speech at the Hearing before the Committee on Taxation, etc.* Boston: 1893.

Croly, Herbert. *The Promise of American Life.* New York: 1918.

Crowell, Foster. "Railroad Facilities of Suburban New York, etc., "*Engineering Magazine,* 10 (1896), 20–45.

Cruden, Robert. *James Ford Rhodes, The Man, The Historian, and His Work.* Cleveland: 1961.

Curtis, George W. *Orations and Addresses of George William Curtis.* Edited by Charles E. Norton. 3 vols. New York: 1894.

———. *Party and Patronage.* New York: 1892.

Dahl, Robert A. and Lindblom, Charles E. *Politics, Economics, and Welfare.* New York, 1953.

Dalton, Edward B. "The Metropolitan Board of Health of New York," *North American Review,* 106 (April 1868), 351–75.

Dana, Richard H. Jr. "Points in American Politics," *North American Review,* 124 (January 1877), 1–30.

———. "Substitutes for the Caucus," *The Forum,* 2 (1887), 491–501.

———. "Taking Municipal Contracts Out of Politics," *Proceedings of the Cincinnati Conference, 15th Annual Meeting of the National Municipal League,* (1909), 179–96.

Davenport, John I. *The Election and Naturalization Frauds in New York City, 1860–70*. New York: 1894.

Davenport, Walter. *The Power and Glory: The Life of Boise Penrose*. New York: 1931.

Davis, Lance and Legler, John. "The Government in the American Economy, 1815–1902: A Quantitative Study," *Journal of Economic History*, 26 (December 1966), 514–52.

Davis, Rebecca Harding. *John Andross*. New York: 1874.

Dawson, Edgar. "The Invisible Government and Administrative Efficiency," *Annals*, 64 (March 1916), 11–21.

DeForest, J. W. *Honest John Vane*. 1875.

Denison, Thomas S. *An Iron Crown*. Chicago: 1885.

Denslow, Van Buren. "Board of Trade Morality," *North American Review*, 137 (1883), 372–87.

Depew, Chauncey. "Railroad Men in Politics," *North American Review*, 151 (July–Dec. 1890), 86–89.

———. *My Memoirs of Eighty Years*. New York: 1922.

Derthick, F. A. "Farmers and the General Property Tax," *Proceedings of the National Tax Association* (1908), 139–481.

DeSantis, Vincent. *Republicans Face the Southern Question: The New Departure Years, 1877–97*. Baltimore: 1959.

Desty, Robert. *The American Law of Taxation as Determined by the Court of Last Resort in the United States*. 2 vols. St. Paul: 1884.

Dickerson, W. R. "The Letters of Junius Exposing to the Public . . . the Malpractices in the Administration of the law and corruption in the offices in the State House Row in the County of Philadelphia," (Philadelphia: 1850), Pennsylvania State Library Pamphlet, Vol. 214.

Dilla, Harriette M. *The Politics of Michigan*. New York: 1912.

Dillard, J. H. "Taxation and Public Welfare," *Proceedings of National Tax Association*. 3 (1909), 45–53.

Dillon, John F. *Commentaries on the Law of Municipal Corporations*. 5th ed. rev. 5 vols. Boston: 1911.

Dorfman, Joseph. *The Economic Mind in American Civilization, 1865–1918*. New York: 1959, 3.

———. "The Seligman Correspondence," *Political Science Quarterly*, 56 (1941), 107 ff., 270 ff., 393 ff., 573 ff.

———. *Thorstein Veblen and His America*. 5th ed. New York: 1947.

Douglas, Charles. *The Financial History of Massachusetts*. New York: 1897.

Dunbar, Charles F. "Economic Science in America," *North American Review*, 122 (Jan. 1876), 124–53.

Dunn, Jacob P. *The New Tax Law of Indiana*. Indianapolis: 1892.

Durand, Dana. *The Finances of New York*. New York: 1898.

Eastman, Frank M. *Courts and Lawyers of Pennsylvania: A History, 1623–1923*. New York: 1922.

Eastudey, J. H. "The Taxation of Money and Credit," *Proceedings of the National Tax Association* (1908), 149–59.

Eaton, Amasa M. *Reports of the American Bar Association,* 25 (1902), 292–372.

Eaton, Dorman B. *Civil Service in Great Britain: A History of Abuses and Reforms and Their Bearing upon American Politics.* New York: 1880.

———. *The Government of Municipalities.* New York: 1899.

———. "Parties and Independents," *North American Review,* 144 (1887), 549–64.

Eckstein, Alexander. "Individualism and the Role of the State in Economic Growth," *Economic Development and Cultural Change,* 6 (Jan. 1958), 81–88.

Edmunds, George F. "Controlling Forces in American Politics," *North American Review,* 132 (1878), 18–31.

———. "Salutary Results of the Income Tax Decision," *The Forum,* 19 (March 1895), 513–20.

Edwards, E. J. "Richard Croker as 'Boss' of Tammany," *McClure's Magazine,* 5 (1895), 542–50.

———. "The Rise and Overthrow of the Tweed Ring," *McClure's Magazine,* 5 (1895), 132–43.

———. "Tammany under John Kelly," *McClure's Magazine,* 5 (1895), 325–29.

Elder, Cyrus. "The Tax System of Pennsylvania," *Social Science Association of Philadelphia, Papers of 1873,* pp. 1–29.

Eliot, Charles. *American Contributions to Civilization and Other Essays and Addresses.* New York: 1907.

———. "The Forgotten Millions," *Century Magazine,* 40 (August 1890), 556–64.

Ellis, Elmer. "Public Opinion and the Income Tax," *Mississippi Valley Historical Review,* 27 (Sept. 1940), 225–42.

Ely, Richard, *Ground Under Our Feet: An Autobiography.* New York: 1938.

———. *The Past and Present of American Political Economy.* Baltimore: 1884.

———. "Political Economy in America," *North American Review,* 144 (1887), 113–19.

———. *Problems of Today.* New York: 1888.

———. *Taxation in American States and Cities.* New York: 1888.

Endicott, William Jr. *The Taxation Only of Tangible Things.* Boston: n.d.

Ensley, Enoch. *The Tax Question.* Boston: 1893.

Evans, Nelson W. *A History of Taxation in Ohio.* Cincinnati: 1906.

Fackler, David P. "The Personal Property Tax: It is a Tax Upon Honesty," *Journal of Accountancy,* 10 (May-Oct. 1910), 162.

Fairlie, John A. "Comparative Municipal Statistics," *Quarterly Journal of Economics,* 13 (October 1898), 343–53.

———. *Local Government in Towns, Counties, and Villages.* New York: 1906.

———. *Municipal Administration.* London: 1901.

———. *A Report on the Taxation and Revenue System of Illinois.* Danville: 1910.

———. "Taxation in Illinois," *American Economic Review,* 1 (Sept. 1911), 519–34.

Fassett, J. Sloan. "Why Cities are Badly Governed," *North American Review,* 150 (June 1890), 631–37.

Faust, M. L. "Sources of Revenue of the States with a Special Study of the Revenue Sources of Pennsylvania," *Annals,* 95 (May 1921), 113–22.

Fels, Rendig. *American Business Cycles, 1865–97.* Chapel Hill: 1959.

Field, David Dudley. "Centralization in the Federal Government," *North American Review,* 132 (1881), 407–26.

———. "Open Nominations and Free Elections," *North American Review,* 144 (1887), 325–29.

Fine, Sidney. *Laissez-Faire and the General Welfare State.* Ann Arbor: 1964.

Fish, Carl. *Civil Service and Patronage.* Cambridge, Mass.: 1904.

Fisher, Edmund D. "Efficiency of the Fiscal Operations of Cities," *Annals,* 41 (May 1912), 71–77.

Fisher, Joshua. "The Degradation of Our Representative System," Philadelphia, n.d. Pennsylvania State Library Pamphlet.

Flannery, M. M. "Tax Legislation Enacted and Pending during 1914," *Proceedings of the National Tax Association* (1914), 44–54.

Flick, Alexander C. *History of the State of New York.* 10 vols. New York: 1933–37.

Flynt, Josiah. *The World of Graft.* New York: 1901.

Foote, Allen Ripley. "Birth, Work, and Future of the National Tax Association," *Proceedings of the National Tax Association* (1916), 23–52.

———. *Economic Value of Electric Light and Power.* Cincinnati: 1889.

———. *"Municipal Public Service Industries.* Chicago: 1899.

Ford, John. "Taxation of Public Franchises," *North American Review,* 168 (June 1899), 730–38.

Ford, Paul Leicester. *The Honorable Peter Stirling.* New York: 1894.

Forney, John W. *Anecdotes of Public Men.* 2 vols. New York: 1873.

———. "The Diary of A Public Man," *North American Review,* 129 (1879), 120–40, 259–73, 375–88, 484–96.

Foster, Roger and Abbot, Everett. *A Treatise on the Federal Income Tax Under the Act of 1894.* Boston: 1895.

Foulke, William Dudley. *Fighting the Spoilsmen.* New York: 1919.

Fox, Austen G. "Insert No Ambiguity into the Constitution," *Journal of Accountancy,* 10 (May-Oct. 1910), 2–7.

Friederich, Carl; Beyer, William C.; Spero, Sterling, etc. *Problems of the American Public Service.* New York: 1935.

Friedman, Harry G. *Taxation of Corporations in Massachusetts.* New York: 1907.

Frothingham, Oliver B. "Democracy and Moral Progress," *North American Review,* 137 (1887), 28–39.

Gardner, Henry B. "Statistics of American Municipal Finance," *American Statistical Association Publications,* n.s. 6 (June 1889), 254–69.

Garlanda, Federico. *Eletto ed Elettori negli Stati Uniti D'America.* Turin: 1885.

Gatell, Frank Otto. "Money and Party in Jacksonian America: A Quantitative

Look at New York City's Men of Quality," *Political Science Quarterly,* 82 (June 1967), 235–52.

George, Ralph E. "Increased Efficiency as a Result of Increased Governmental Functions," *Annals,* 64 (March 1916), 77–88.

Gephart, W. F. "The Growth of State and Local Expenditure," *Proceedings of the National Tax Association* (1908), 513–26.

Gilroy, Thomas F. "The Wealth of New York," *North American Review,* 157 (1893), 307 ff., 403 ff., 541 ff.

Glazier, Willard. *Peculiarities of American Cities.* Philadelphia: 1883.

Godkin, Edwin L. "Commercial Immorality and Political Corruption," *North American Review,* 107 (July 1868), 248–66.

———. "Criminal Politics," *North American Review,* 150 (1890), 706–23.

———. "A Key to Municipal Reform," *North American Review,* 151 (1890), 422–31, 576–81.

———. *Life and Letters of Edwin Lawrence Godkin.* Edited by Rollo Ogden. 2 vols. New York: 1907.

———. "Money Interests in Political Affairs," *The Forum,* 10 (Sept. 1890), 1–10.

———. *Problems of Modern Democracy.* New York: 1896.

———. *Reflections and Comments, 1865–1895.* New York: 1896.

———. "Taxation of Personal Property," *The Nation,* 32 (1881), 86–87.

———. *The Unforeseen Tendencies of Democracy.* Boston: 1898.

Goodstein, Anita. *Biography of a Businessman, Henry W. Sage, 1814–1897.* Ithaca: 1962.

Gosnell, Harold. *Boss Platt and His New York Machine.* New York: 1924.

Gottmann, Jean. Megalopolis: *The Urbanized Northeastern Seaboard of the United States.* Cambridge, Mass.: 1961.

"The Government of the City of New York," *North American Review.* 103 (October 1866), 413–65.

Graham, J. Whidden. "Just Taxation," *New England Magazine,* 6, new series (1892), 706–708.

Grant, John H. *State Supervision of Cities.* Ann Arbor: 1896.

"The Greatest Political Necessity," *The Nation,* 55 (Oct. 6, 1892), 252.

Green, Andrew Haskell. *The Municipal Debt of New York.* New York: 1874.

———. *Three Years' Struggle with Municipal Misrule: A Report of Andrew H. Green, Comptroller In Response to Certain Resolutions of the Board of Aldermen of New York, Feb. 18, 1875* (New York: 1875).

Green, George Walton. "Facts About the Caucus and the Primary," *North American Review,* 137 (1883), 257–69.

Green, Thomas. *The Man-Traps of the City.* Chicago: 1884.

Greene, Francis V. "The Government of the Greater New York," *Scribner's Magazine,* 20 (July-Dec. 1896), 418–28.

Greener, John. *History of the Office of the Corporation Counsel and Law Department of the City of New York.* New York: 1912.

Greenhalge, F. T. "Practical Politics," *North American Review,* 162 (1896), 154–59.

Grodinsky, Julius. *Jay Gould: His Business Career, 1867–92*. Philadelphia: 1957.

Gumbleton, Henry A. "The Lodging House Vote in New York," *North American Review,* 144 (1887), 631–36.

Gunn, Alexander. *Letters*. New York: 1902.

Guthrie, William D. "No Taxation Without Representation," *Journal of Accountancy,* 10 (1910), 13–25.

Haber, Samuel. *Efficiency and Uplift: Scientific Management in the Progressive Era, 1890–1920* Chicago: 1964.

Hadley, Arthur T. *Economics—An Account of the Relations Between Private Property and Public Welfare*. New York: 1896.

———. "The Railroad in Its Business Relations," *Scribner's Magazine,* 4 1888), 473–88.

———. "The Relation Between Economics and Politics," *American Economic Association Studies,* 4 (1899), 5–28.

———. *The Relation Between Freedom and Responsibility in the Evolution of Democratic Government*. New York: 1903.

Haig, Robert Murray. *A History of the General Property Tax in Illinois*. New York: 1914.

Haig, Robert Murray; Shoup, Carl; Fitch, Lyle. *Financial Problems of New York City 1922–52*. New York: 1952.

Hall, Bolton. "The New Charity," *The Arena,* 16 (1896), 970–73.

Hale, E. E. "Social Forces in the United States," *North American Review,* 137 (1883), 403–412.

Halloran, Matthew F. *The Romance of the Merit System*. 2d ed. Hyattsville, Md.: 1929.

Halsted, Murat. "Revival of Sectionalism," *North American Review,* 140 (1885), 237–50.

Hamilton, Gail. *James G. Blaine*. New York: 1895.

Hamilton, Walton. "Affectation with Public Interest," *Yale Law Review,* 39 (June 1930) 1089–1112.

Harlan, A. D. *Pennsylvania Constitutional Convention of 1872–3: Its Members and Officers and the Results of their Labors*. Philadelphia: 1873.

Harris, Daniel. *Municipal Extravagance*. Philadelphia: 1876.

Harris, Elisha. "The Public Health," *North American Review,* 127 (1878), 444–55.

Harris, Thomas. *Juvenile Depravity and Crime in Our City*. New York: 1850.

Harris, Wilmer C. *Public Life of Zachariah Chandler, 1851–75*. Lansing: 1917.

Harrison, Carter. *Stormy Years: The Autobiography of Carter H. Harrison, Five Times Mayor of Chicago*. Indianapolis and New York: 1935.

Hart, Albert Bushnell. "The Rise of American Cities," *Quarterly Journal of Economics,* 4 (Jan. 1890), 129–57.

Harvey, George. *Henry Clay Frick: The Man* (New York: 1928).

Hasse, Adelaide. *Index of Economic Materials in the Documents of the*

States: (New York 1789–1902, Massachusetts, New Jersey, Ohio, Pennsylvania) (Washington, D.C.: 1907–1922).

Haugen, Nils. "The Wisconsin Income Tax," *Proceedings of the National Tax Association,* (1912), 321–41.

Hause, N.E. "Taxation for State Purposes in Pennsylvania," *Proceedings of the National Tax Association* (1912), 129–64.

Hayes, Rutherford B. *Diary and Letters of Rutherford B. Hayes,* edited by Charles R. Williams. 5 vols. Columbus: 1922.

Haynes, George H. "Representation in New England Legislatures," *Annals,* 6 (1895), 254–67.

Hays, Samuel P. "The Social Analysis of American Political History, 1880–1920," *Political Science Quarterly,* 80 (1965), 373–94.

Hensel, William U. "Decadence of the Legislative Branch of State Government of Pennsylvania," *Pennsylvania Bar Association, Report,* 4 (1898).

Heydecker, Edward L. "Municipal Finance and Taxation," *American Economic Review,* 2 (1912), 9, 1909.

———. "The New York Law [Personal Property Taxation] and Its Evil Effects," *Journal of Accountancy,* 10 (1910), 163–65.

———. "State Conferences on Taxation," *Proceedings of the National Tax Association,* (1912), 95–108.

Hill, Adams Sherman. "The Chicago Convention," *North American Review,* 107 (1868), 167–86.

Hilliard, Francis. *The Law of Taxation.* Boston: 1875.

Hills, Thomas. *Modern Taxation and the Single Tax.* Boston: 1894.

Hoffman, Wright. "Budget Making in Philadelphia," *Annals,* 95 (May 1921), 237–41.

Hollander, Jacob. "Municipal Taxation of Intangible Wealth," *Proceedings of the National Tax Association,* (1907), 406–14.

———. ed. *Studies in State Taxation* (Baltimore: 1900).

Hoogenboom, Ari. *Outlawing the Spoils.* Urbana: 1961.

Howe, Frederick. *The Modern City and Its Problems.* New York: 1915.

———. "Some Possible Reforms in State and Local Taxation," *American Law Review,* 33, 685–701.

Howe, Marcus DeWolfe. *Barrett Wendell and His Letters.* Boston: 1924.

———. *Portrait of An Independent: Moorfield Storey, 1845–1929.* Boston: 1932.

Howe, Samuel T. "Administrative Problems in Kansas Taxation," *Proceedings of the National Tax Association,* (1914), 83–91.

———. "Need of Popular Aid in Tax Reformation," *Proceedings of the National Tax Association,* 9 (1916), 146–64.

———. "The Tax Commission of Kansas," *Proceedings of the National Tax Association,* (1908), 443–56.

Howland, Harold J. "The Grafter At Work in American Cities," *Proceedings of the Buffalo Conference, 16th Annual Meeting, National Municipal League* (1910), 190–202.

Hudson, James F. "Modern Feudalism," *North American Review,* 144 (1887), 277–90.

Hudson, William C. *Recollections of an Old Political Reporter*. New York: 1911.

Huebner, S. S. "The Taxation of Inheritances," *Proceedings of the National Tax Association*, (1908), 195–206.

Hughes, Sara Forbes. *Letters and Recollections of John Murray Forbes*. Boston: 1899.

Hunter, Robert. *Poverty*. Edited by Peter D. A. Jones. New York: 1965.

Hurd, Richard M. *Principles of City Land Values*. New York: 1907.

Huse, Charles Phillips. *The Financial History of Boston*. Cambridge, Mass.: 1916.

"Income Tax and the Silver Agitators," *The Nation*, (March 7, 1878).

"Income Tax Here and in England," *The Nation*, (May 2, 1878).

Independent. "Political Career and Character of David B. Hill," *The Forum*, 18 (1894), 257–69.

Ingalls, John J. "Fetichism in the Campaign," *North American Review*, 146 (1888), 651–53.

Ivins, William M. *Machine Politics and Money in Elections in New York City*. New York: 1887.

———. "Municipal Finance," *Harper's New Monthly Magazine*, 69 (1882), 779–87.

———. "Municipal Government," *Political Science Quarterly*, 2 (1887), 291–312.

Jacklin, Kathleen B. "Local Aid to Railroads in Illinois, 1848–1870". M. A. Thesis, Cornell University, 1959.

James, Edmund J. "The Growth of Great Cities," *Annals*, (Jan. 1899), xiii ff, 1–30.

James, Henry. *The American Scene*. Edited by H. Auden. New York: 1946.

———. *Richard Olney and His Public Service*. Boston: 1923.

Jameson, John A. "Speculation in Politics," *North American Review*, 140 (1885), 269–79.

Janeway, Herbert M. "Campaign Contributions and Presidential Appointments," *American Journal of Politics*, 4 (1894), 186–89.

Jarvis, Edward. "On the System of Taxation Prevailing in the United States and Especially in Massachusetts," *Journal of the Statistical Society of London*, (Sept. 1860), 370–78.

Jay, John. "Civil Service Reform," *North American Review*, 127 (1878), 273–87.

Johnston, John W. "Railway Land Grants," *North American Review*, 140 (1885), 280–89.

Jones, Chester Lloyd. "The Rotten Boroughs of New England," *North American Review* 197 (1913), 486–98.

———. "Spoils and Party," *Annals*, 64 (March 1916), 66–76.

Jones, Eliot. *The Trust Problem in the United States*. New York: 1921.

Jordan, Francis. "Constitutional Reform," *Social Science Association of Philadelphia, Paper* (Feb. 1872). Pennsylvania State Library Collection Pamphlets, Vol. 705.

Josephson, Matthew. *The Politicos, 1865–1896*. New York: 1938.

"The Judiciary of New York City," *North American Review,* 105 (1867), 148–76.

Julian, George W. "Is the Reformer Any Longer Needed?" *North American Review,* 127 (1878), 237–60.

———. *Political Recollections, 1840–72.* Chicago: 1884.

———. "Railway Influence in the Land Office," *North American Review,* 136 (1883), 237–56.

Kasson, John A. "Municipal Reform," *North American Review,* 137 (1883), 218–30.

Kaufman, Herbert. *Politics and Policies in States and Local Governments.* Englewood Cliffs: 1963.

Keller, Suzanne. *Beyond the Ruling Class: Strategic Elites in Modern Society.* New York: 1963.

Kendrick, M. Slade. "An Index Number of Farm Taxes in New York and Its Relation to Various Other Economic Factors," *Cornell Agricultural Experiment Station Bulletin 457* (Dec. 1926).

Kennan, Kossuth. "Comparative Results of Income Taxation in Various Countries," *Proceedings of the National Tax Association,* (1910), 111–18.

———. *Income Taxation: Methods and Results in Various Countries.* Milwaukee: 1910.

———. "The Wisconsin Income Tax Law," *American Economic Review,* 3 (March 1913), 236–44.

Kinsman, Delos O. *The Income Tax in the Commonwealths of the United States.* Ithaca: 1903.

Kirkland, Edward. *Business in the Gilded Age: The Conservatives' Balance Sheet.* Madison: 1952.

———. *Charles Francis Adams Jr., 1835–1915.* Cambridge, Mass.: 1965.

———. "The Emergence of An Industrial Society," *Mississippi Valley Historical Review,* 43 (June 1956), 3–17.

———. *Industry Comes of Age.* New York: 1961.

———. "The Robber Barons Re-Visited," *American Historical Review,* 66 (October 1960), 68–73.

Kolko, Gabriel. "The Premises of Business Revisionism," *Business History Review,* 33 (1959), 330–44.

———. *The Triumph of Conservatism.* New York: 1963.

Komarovsky, Mirra. ed. *Common Frontiers of the Social Sciences.* Glencoe: 1957.

Konkle, Bartin A. *The Life and Speeches of Thomas A. Williams.* Philadelphia: 1905.

Kyrle-Money, R. E. *Psychoanalysis and Politics.* New York: 1951.

Lamar, Howard R. *Dakota Territory, 1861–1889, A Study of Frontier Politics.* New Haven 1956.

Lancaster, Lane W. "Sources of Revenue in American Cities," *Annals,* 95 (May 1921), 123–31.

Lang, Louis J. ed. *The Autobiography of Thomas Collier Platt.* New York: 1910.

Lansing, Gerritt L. "The Railway and the State," *North American Review,* 138 (1884), 461–75.

Lasswell, Harold and Kaplan. A. *Power and Society*. New Haven: 1950.

Lawrence, W. B. "The Monarchical Principle in Our Constitution," *North American Review,* 131 (1880), 385–409.

Lea, Henry Charles. "Constitutional Reforms: A Letter to John Price Wetherill Esq.," (Philadelphia: 1872). Pennsylvania State Library Pamphlets Vol. 214.

———. "Legislative Discouragement of Business," *The Nation,* 55 (Nov. 10 1892), 347–48.

———. "A Letter to the People of Philadelphia," *The Forum,* 2 (1886), 532–38.

———. "Municipal Taxation," *Reform Tract No. 1, Citizens' Municipal Reform Association* (Philadelphia: Dec. 1871). Pamphlet. American Philosophical Society Library.

LeBoeuf, R. J. "Public Service Corporation Taxation in New York State," *Proceedings of National Tax Association,* 7 (1912) 158–71.

Lening, Gustav. *The Dark Side of New York Life and Its Criminal Classes.* New York: 1873.

Leroy-Beaulieu, P. *Traité de la Science des Finances.* Paris: 1877.

Leser, Oscar. "Problems of Local Administration," *Proceedings of the National Tax Association,* (1908), 527–46.

———. "Report of the Common Failure of the General Property Tax," *Proceedings of the National Tax Association,* (1910), 299–312.

Leslie, T. E. Cliffe. "The Incidence of Imperial and Local Taxation," *Fortnightly Review,* 21 (1874), 248–65.

Lincoln, Charles Z. *Messages from the Governors . . . 1683–1906.* 11 vols. Albany: 1909.

Lockhart, Oliver C. "Taxation in Ohio," *American Economic Review,* 2 (Sept. 1912), 729–30.

Long, John Davis. *America of Yesterday*. Edited by Laurence S. Mayo. Boston: 1923.

Loomis, S. L. *Modern Cities.* New York: 1887.

Loos, Isaac. "Division Between State and Local Taxation," *Proceedings of the National Tax Association,* (1908), 59–68.

Lord, George. "State Tax Association," *Proceedings of the National Tax Association,* (1914), 57–69.

Lowell, Francis C. "The American Boss," *Atlantic Monthly,* 86 (Sept. 1900), 289–99.

Lutz, Harley L. *The State Tax Commission: A Study of the Development and Results of State Control Over the Assessment of Property for Taxation.* Cambridge, Mass.: 1918.

Machen, Arthur W. Jr. *A Treatise on the Federal Corporation Tax Law of 1909.* Boston: 1910.

MacVeagh, Wayne. "The Graduated Taxation of Incomes and Inheritances," *North American Review,* 18 (1906), 824–28.

———. "A Great Victory for Honest Politics," *North American Review,* 82 (Jan. 1906), 1–18.

Macy, Jesse. *Party Organization and Machinery*. New York: 1912.

Mailen, William R. "Cities as Units in Our Polity," *North American Review*, 128 (1879), 21–34.

Malcolm, James. "A Remarkable Statistical Report," *The Arena*, 16 (1896), 585–94.

Maltbie, Milo R. "Municipal Functions," *Municipal Affairs*, 2 (Dec. 1898), 577–799.

———. "Taxation of Public Service Corporations," *Proceedings of The National Tax Association* (1908), 477–512.

Martiis, S. Cognetti de. *Gli Stati Uniti d'America nel 1876*. Milan: 1877.

Martin, William M. "The Financial Resources of New York," *North American Review*, 127 (1878), 427–433.

Marx, Leo. *The Machine in the Garden*. New York: 1967.

Masters, Edgar L. *Across Spoon River: An Autobiography*. New York: 1936.

Mathews, Byron C. *Our Irrational Distribution of Wealth*. New York: 1908.

Matthews, Nathan. *The City Government of Boston*. Boston: 1895.

Matthiessen, F. O. *American Renaissance*. New York: 1941.

———. *The James Family: A Group Biography*. New York: 1948.

Mayer, George H. *The Republican Party, 1854–1964*. New York: 1967.

"Mayor Grace and the Need for Municipal Reform," *The Nation*, Jan. 13 1881, p. 23.

McAllister, Breck P. "Lord Hale and Business Affected with A Public Interest," *Harvard Law Review*, (March 1930), 759–91.

McCall, Samuel W. *The Life of Thomas Brackett Reed*. Boston: 1914.

McClelland, David. *The Achieving Society*. Princeton: 1961.

McClure, Alexander. *Recollections of a Half Century*. New York: 1888.

McCrea, Roswell C. "A Suggestion on the Taxation of Corporations," *Quarterly Journal of Economics*, 19 (Nov. 1904) 492–97.

———. "Tax Discrimination in the Paper and Pulp Industry," *Quarterly Journal of Economics*, 21 (August 1907), 632–44.

———. "Taxation of Personal Property in Pennsylvania," *Quarterly Journal of Economics*, 21 (Nov. 1906), 50–95.

McCulloch, Hugh. *Men and Measures of Half A Century*. New York: 1888.

———. "Problems in American Politics, *Scribner's Magazine*, 4 (1888), 423–34.

McDonald, John. *Secrets of the Great Whiskey Ring, etc*. Chicago: 1880.

McGuire, James K. *The Democratic Party of the State of New York*. 3 vols. New York: 1905.

McKelvey, Blake. *The Urbanization of America, 1860–1915*. New Brunswick: 1963.

McPherson, J. H. "General Property Taxation as a Source of State Revenue," *Proceedings of the National Tax Association*, (1907), 475–84.

McSherry, Richard M. *Talks on Taxation in Maryland* (Baltimore: 1894). Pamphlet 38 pp.

Means, David MacGregor. *The Methods of Taxation Compared with the Established Principles of Justice*. New York: 1909.

Meeker, Royal. "The International Tax Association," *Journal of Political Economy*, 18 (1910), 634–35.

Merrill, John. "State Tax on Business Corporations," *State Conference on*

Taxation, Addresses and Proceedings, Utica Conference, Jan. 11, 1911, pp. 192–97.

Miller, George H. "Origins of the Iowa Granger Laws," *Mississippi Valley Historical Review,* 40 (March 1954), 657–80.

Millspaugh, Arthur. *Party Organization and Machinery in Michigan Since 1890.* Baltimore: 1917.

Merriam, Charles. "Reform in Municipal Taxation," *Proceedings of the National Tax Association,* (1907), 415–23.

Merriam, George S. *The Life and Times of Samuel Bowles.* 2 vols. New York: 1885.

Merton, Robert K. *Social Theory and Social Structure.* Glencoe: 1957.

Meyerson, Martin and Banfield, Edward. *Politics, Planning, and Public Interest.* Glencoe: 1955.

Michels, Roberto. *First Lecture in Political Sociology.* Minneapolis: 1949.

———. *Political Parties: A Sociological Study of the Oligarchical Tendencies of Modern Democracy.* Glencoe: 1958.

Miller, Adolphe C. "On the Incidence of Taxation," *Journal of Political Economy,* 1 (1892–3), 450–60.

Miller, Delbert. "Decision Making Cliques in Community Power Structures: A Comparative Study," *American Journal of Sociology,* (Nov. 1958), 299–310.

———. "Industry and Community," *American Sociological Review,* (Feb. 1958).

Miller, Warner. "Business Men in Politics," *North American Review,* 151 (1890).

Mills, Cuthbert. "The Permanence of Political Forces," *North American Review,* 129 (1879), 604–11.

———. "Recent Movements of the Stock Market," *North American Review,* 46 (1888), 46–54.

Mills, Mark C. and Starr, George W. eds. *Readings in Public Finance and Taxation.* New York: 1932.

Minot, William Jr. "Local Taxation and Public Extravagance:" A Paper, *American Social Science Association,* Saratoga Springs, Sept. 5, 1877. Boston: 1877.

———. *Taxation in Massachusetts.* Boston: 1877.

M'Killop, Margaret and Atkinson, Mabel. *Economics, Descriptive and Theoretical.* London: 1912.

Montague, F. C. *Local Administration in the United States and the United Kingdom.* London: 1888.

Moore, Edward. "Corporate Taxation," *American Law Review,* 18 (1884), 754–57.

Morison, Samuel and Commager, Henry. *The Growth of the American Republic* 6th ed. rev. 2 vols. New York: 1962.

Morgan, H. Wayne. *The Gilded Age: A Reappraisal.* Syracuse: 1963.

Morrow, Dwight W. "The Income Tax Amendment," *Columbia Law Review,* 10 (May 1910), 379–415.

Municipal Bureau of Research. *The Constitution and Government of the State of New York: An Appraisal.* New York: 1915.

Munro, William Bennett. *The American Party System.* New York: 1922.

———. *A Bibliography of Municipal Government in the U.S.* Cambridge, Mass.: 1915.

———. "The Civic Federation Report on Public Ownership," *Quarterly Journal of Economics,* 23 (1908–1909), 161–74.

———. *The Government of American Cities.* New York: 1913.

———. *The Invisible Government.* New York: 1928.

———. *Personality in Politics: Reformers, Bosses, and Leaders.* New York: 1924.

Musgrave, Richard. *The Theory of Public Finance.* New York: 1959.

Musgrave, Richard and Peacock, Alan, eds. *Classics in the Theory of Public Finance.* London: 1962.

Musgrave, Richard and Shoup, Carl eds. *Readings in the Economics of Taxation.* Homewood, Illinois: 1958.

Myers, Gustavus. "The History of Public Franchises in New York," *Municipal Affairs,* 4 (March 1900), 71–85.

Nadal, E. S. "The New York Aldermen," *The Forum,* 2 (1886), 49–59.

National Industrial Conference Board. *State Income Taxes, I, Historical Development* New York: 1930.

"The New Jersey Monopolies," *North American Review,* 104 (April 1867), 428–76.

The New Tax Law of Indiana and the Science of Taxation. Indianapolis: 1892.

Newcomb, Simon. "Our Political Dangers," *North American Review,* 130 (1880), 261–79.

Newman, John. "Conceptualization in American Local Community Studies, 1953–64" Ph.D. Diss. Gainesville, Florida: 1966.

New York Bureau of Municipal Research. *Making a Municipal Budget.* New York: 1907.

New York Public Library. *Bulletin of the New York Public Library on State Finance.* 1. New York: 1897.

———. "New York Check List of Works Relating to the Financial and Commercial History, etc. of the City of New York in the New York Public Library," *New York Public Library* Bulletin. 5.

New York Reform Club. *True or False Finance.* New York: 1888.

Nicoll, De Lancey, "An Unfinished Constitutional Crime," *North American Review,* 146 (1888), 21–30.

Noble, F. H. *Taxation in Iowa: Historical Sketch, Present Status, and Suggested Reforms.* New York: 1897.

Nordhoff, Charles. "The Misgovernment of New York—A Remedy Suggested," *North American Review,* 113 (Oct. 1871), 321–43.

Noyes, Alexander. *Forty Years of American Finance.* New York: 1909.

Olsen, Bernard M. "A Representative Study of Capital Origins," *Economic Development and Cultural Change,* 6 (Apr. 1958), 204–16.

Orth, Samuel P. *The Boss and the Machine.* New Haven: 1919.

Ostrogorski, Moisei. *Democracy and the Organization of Political Parties.* Edited and abridged by Seymour M. Lipset. New York: 1964, 2.

Parkman, Francis. "The Failure of Universal Suffrage," *North American Review,* 127 (1878), 1–20.

Parkhurst, Charles. *Our Fight With Tammany.* New York: 1895.

Parsons, Talcott and Smelser, Neil. *Economy and Society: A Study in the Integration of Economic and Social Theory.* New York: 1965.

Parton, James. "The Government of New York City," *North American Review,* 103 (1866), 413–64.

———. "The Power of Public Plunder," *North American Review,* 133 (1881), 43–64.

Patterson, Robert. *Federal Debt Management Policies, 1865–1879.* Durham: 1954.

Payson, Edward P. "Unequal Taxation," *American Law Review,* 19 (1885), 234–50.

Peck, Harry Thurston. *Twenty Years of the Republic, 1885–1905.* New York: 1906.

Peel, Roy V. *The Political Clubs of New York.* New York: 1935.

Pennypacker, Samuel Whitaker. *The Autobiography of a Pennsylvanian.* Philadelphia: 1918.

Perry, Arthur L. *Elements of Political Economy.* 13th ed. New York: 1875.

"Personal Property Tax: A Symposium," *Journal of Accountancy,* 10 (1910), 161–78.

Peterson, Arthur E. and Edwards, George. *New York as An Eighteenth Century Municipality* 2 vols. New York: 1917.

Phelan, Raymond. "Centralized Tax Administration in Minnesota and Wisconsin," *Proceedings of the National Tax Association,* (1907), 97–106.

Phillips, Clifton. *Indiana in Transition: The Emergence of An Industrial Commonwealth, 1880–1920.* Indianapolis: 1968.

Pickard, J. L. "Why Crime is Increasing," *North American Review,* 40 (1885), 456–63.

Pierce, Frank C. "Taxation of Money and Credits," *Proceedings of the National Tax Association,* (1907), 340–57.

Pigou, Arthur C. *The Economics of Welfare* 4th ed. London: 1962.

———. *A Study in Public Finance.* London: 1928.

Plehn, Carl. *Introduction to Public Finance.* 1st ed. New York: 1896 and 4th ed. New York: 1925.

———. Plehn, Carl. "Problems of Tax Administration for State Purposes in California," *Proceedings of the National Tax Association,* (1914), 104–109.

———. "Taxation of Public Service Corporations," *Proceedings of the National Tax Association,* (1907), 635–48.

Pleydell, A. C. "Evolution of the New York Tax System," *Journal of Accountancy,* 10 (1910), 174–78.

———. "The Incidence of Taxation," *Proceedings of the National Tax Association,* (1907), 424–33.

———. "New York State Conference on Taxation," *American Economic Review,* 2 (March 1912), 243–44.

"The Political Situation from a Financial Stand Point," *North American Review,* 131 (1880), 464–74.

Pollack, Norman. *The Populist Response to Industrial America: Mid-Western Populist Thought.* Cambridge, Mass.: 1962.

Polleys, Thomas A. "Railroads As Taxpayers," *Proceedings of the National Tax Association,* (1910), 245–60.

Powers, L. G. "Municipal Budgets and Expenditures," *Proceedings of the Cincinnati Conference, 15th Annual Meeting, National Municipal League* (1909), 258–72.

Pratt, E. E. *Industrial Causes of Congestion of Population in New York City.* New York: 1911.

Pratt, John W. "Boss Tweed's Public Welfare Program," *New York Historical Society Quarterly,* 45 (October 1961), 399–411.

Price, Eli K. "Principles of Taxation," *Bankers' Magazine,* 5 (May 1871), 848–40.

———. "Public Administration and Partisan Politics," *Annals,* 64 (1916).

———. *Some Objections to the Proposed Constitution* (Philadelphia: 1873), Pamphlet, Pennsylvania State Library Collection, Vol. 705, no. 2. 31 pp.

Purdy, Lawson. "The Income Tax Amendment Should Be Ratified," *Journal of Accountancy,* 10 (1910), 8–12.

———. *Local Option in Taxation.* New York: n.d.

———. "Outline of a Model System of State and Local Taxation," *Proceedings of The National Tax Association,* 1 (1907), 54–75.

Quay, Matthew Stanley. *Pennsylvania Politics: The Campaign of 1900 as set forth in Speeches.* Philadelphia: 1901.

Quigg, Lemuel. "Thomas Platt," *North American Review,* 191 (1910), 668–77.

Rapsher, Eli M. "Dangerous Trusts," *North American Review,* 146 (1888), 509–14.

Ratner, Sidney. *American Taxation.* New York: 1942.

Rawles, William A. "The Income Tax as a Measure of Relief for Indiana," *Proceedings of The National Tax Association,* (1916), 64–87.

Ray, Orman P. *Introduction to Political Parties and Practical Politics.* New York: 1922.

Rea, L. O. *The Financial History of Baltimore.* Baltimore: 1929.

Redlich, Fritz. "Business Leadership: Diverse Origins and Various Forms," *Economic Development and Cultural Change,* 3 (1958), 177–90.

Reemelin, Charles. *A Critical Review of American Politics.* Cincinnati: 1881.

———. *The Life of Charles Reemelin.* Cincinnati: 1892.

Reinsch, Paul S. *American Legislatures and Legislative Methods.* New York: 1907.

A Republican. "Two Messages," *North American Review,* 146 (1888), 1–13.

A Republican Member of the League. "The Union League and the Political Situation in Philadelphia, (March 1873), Pennsylvania State Library Pamphlets, Vol. 214.

Reynolds, James Bronson, ed., *Civic Bibliography for Greater New York.* New York: 1911.

Rhodes, James Ford. *Historical Essays.* New York: 1909.

———. *A History of the United States from Hayes to McKinley, 1877–96.* New York: 1919.

Riggs, Fred. *The Ecology of Public Administration.* Bombay and New York: 1961.

Robinson, Charles. "Campaign Contributions and Presidential Appointments," *The American Journal of Politics,* 4 (1894), 57–62.

Robinson, Clement. "Tax Legislation of 1910," *Proceedings of the National Tax Association,* (1910), 367–78.

Roosevelt, Theodore. *American Ideals and Other Essays.* New York: 1897.

———. *The Letters of Theodore Roosevelt.* Edited by Elting Morison and John Blum. 8 vols. Cambridge, Mass.: 1951–54.

———. "Machine Politics in New York City," *Century Magazine,* 33 (Nov. 1886), 74 ff.

———. "Municipal Administration: The New York Police Force," *Atlantic Monthly,* 80 (1897), 289 ff.

———. "Taking the New York Police Force Out of Politics," *Cosmopolitan Magazine,* (Nov. 1895), 40–52.

Root, Elihu. *Addresses on Government and Citizenship.* Cambridge, Mass.: 1916.

———. "The Invisible Government," *Annals,* 69 (March 1916), x–xiii.

Roper, Charles L. "The Taxation of Incomes," *Proceedings of the National Tax Association,* (1907), 24–49.

Rose, Richard and Heidenheimer, Arnold. "Comparative Studies in Political Finance. A Symposium," *Journal of Politics,* 25 (Nov. 1963), 790–811.

Ross, Edward A. " A New Canon of Taxation," *Political Science Quarterly,* 7 (Dec. 1892), 585–97.

———. "Seligman's Shifting and Incidence of Taxation," *Annals,* 3 (1893), 52–71.

Rupp, Leila Lee. "Matthew Stanley Quay in Pennsylvania State Politics." M.A. Thesis. University of Pittsburgh, 1928.

Samuelson, Paul. "The Pure Theory of Public Expenditures," *Review of Economics and Statistics,* 32 (1955).

Sanborn, Alvan. "Anatomy of A Tenement Street," *The Forum,* 18 (1894), 554–72.

Sanford, Charles L. *The Quest for Paradise: Europe and the American Moral Imagination.* Urbana: 1961.

Schriftgeisser, Karl. *The Gentleman from Massachusetts: Henry Cabot Lodge.* Boston: 1944.

Schurz, Carl. "Corporations, Their Employees, and the Public," *North American Review,* 138 (1884), 101–119.

Schwab, John Christopher. *History of the New York Property Tax.* New York: 1890.

Scott, Roy V. *The Agrarian Movement in Illinois, 1880–96.* Urbana, 1962.

Seligman, Edwin R. A. "Annual Address," *Proceedings of the National Tax Association,* (1914), 186–98, 199–206.

———. *Essays on Taxation.* New York: 1895.

———. "Finance Statistics of the American Commonwealths," *American Statistical Association Publications,* n.s. (Dec. 1889), 349–468.

———. "The General Property Tax," *Political Science Quarterly,* 5 (1890).

———. *The Income Tax.* 2d rev. ed. 2 vols. New York: 1914.

———. "On Incidence of Taxation," *Journal of Political Economy,* 1 (1892–3, 444–52.

———. *On The Shifting and Incidence of Taxation.* Baltimore: 1892.

———. "Recent Reforms in Taxation," *Yale Review,* 3 (1895), 352; 4 (1895), 40.

———. "Recent Reports on State and Local Taxation," *American Economic Review,* 1 (1911), 272–95.

———. "Relations of State and Federal Finance," *North American Review,* 190, 615–27.

———. "Separation of State and Local Revenues," *Proceedings of the National Tax Association,* (1907), 485–511.

———. "The Taxation of Corporations," *Political Science Quarterly,* 5 (1890), 269–308; 5 (1890), 438–67; 5 (1890), 636–76.

———. "Theory of Progressive Taxation," *Political Science Quarterly,* 8 (1893), 220–51.

Seymour, Horatio and Boutwell, George, "The Political Situation," *North American Review,* 136 (1883), 153–65.

Sharkey, Robert P. *Money, Class, and Party.* Baltimore: 1959.

Shaw, Albert. *Municipal Government in Continental Europe.* New York: 1895.

———. "Municipal Problems of New York and London, "*Review of Reviews,* 5 (April 1892), 282–92.

Shaw, Frederick, *The History of the New York City Legislature.* New York: 1954.

Shearman, Thomas G. "The Coming Billionaire," *The Forum,* 10 (1895), 546–57.

———. "Home Rule in Taxation: Taxation of Personal Property," *Address Before a Committee of the New York Legislature, Feb. 8, 1893.* Brooklyn: 1893.

———. *Natural Taxation.* New York: 1898.

Shelton, William A. "The Income Tax in Georgia," *Journal of Political Economy,* 18 (1910), 610–27.

Shepard, Harry N. "The Boston Finance Commission," *Proceedings of the Cincinnati Conference, 15th Annual Meeting, National Municipal League,* (1909), 205–16.

Sherman, Philemon Tecumseh. *Inside the Machine: Two Years In the Board of Aldermen 1898–99.* New York: 1901.

Shields, R. "Railway Taxation Problems," *Proceedings of the National Tax Association,* (1910), 231–44.

Shorey, Daniel. *Problems of the Municipal Government of Chicago.* Chicago: 1885.

Shriver, Edward J. "American Taxation and Politics," *Westminster Review,* 141 (1894), 60–67.

Sims, C. A. "Divorcing the Assessor from Politics," *Proceedings of the National Tax Association,* (1916), 88–93.

Sims, Newell L. *A Hoosier Village: A Sociological Study.* New York: 1912.

Smith, Franklin. "A State Official on Excessive Taxation," *Popular Science Monthly* 56 (1899–1900), 645–59.

Smith, Ray Burdick. ed. *History of the State of New York*. Syracuse: 1922. 3, 4.

Smithies, Arthur and Butters, J. Keith. eds. *Readings in Fiscal Policy*. Homewood; 1955.

Soltow, Lee C. "Evidence on Income Inequality in the U.S., 1866–1965," *Journal of Economic History*, XXIX (June 1969), 279–86.

Spahr, Charles B. *The Present Distribution of Wealth* (New York: 1896).

Sparling, Samuel E. *Municipal History and Present Organization of the City of Chicago*. Madison: Bulletin of the University of Wisconsin, No. 23, 1898.

"Spoilsman's Effrontery, The," *The Nation*, 60 (April 25, 1895), 323–24.

Sproat, John. *The Best Men*. New York: 1968.

Stanton, Theodore. "France and the Income Tax," *North American Review*, 158 (1894), 373–76.

Staub, Walter. "Personal Property Taxation in Pennsylvania," *Journal of Accountancy*, 10 (1910), 171–74.

———. "State and Federal Taxation," *The Nation*, 55 (Dec. 15, 1892), 444–45.

———. "State Taxation," *The Nation*, 28 (Apr. 24, 1871), 278–79.

Sterne, Simon. "Crude Methods of Legislation," *North American Review*, 137 (1883), 158–71.

———. "Why Tammany Won," *Municipal Affairs*, 2 (1898), 148–50.

Steward, Frank Mann. *A Half Century of Municipal Reform: The History of the National Municipal League*. Berkeley: 1950.

Stewart, Alexander H. *American Bad Boys in the Making*. New York: 1912.

Stickney, Albert. *The Political Problem*. New York: 1890.

Stimson, Frederick Jessup. "The Ethics of Democracy," *Scribner's Magazine*, 1 (1887), 661–67.

———. *My United States*. New York: 1931.

Stoddard, Lothrop. *Master of Manhattan: The Life of Richard Croker*. New York: 1931.

Storey, Moorefield. "The Government of Cities," *New England Magazine*, n.s. 6 (1892), 432–441.

Strong, George T. *The Diary of George Templeton Strong*. Edited by Allen Nevins and Milton Thomas. 4 vols. New York: 1952.

Strong, Josiah. *The Twentieth Century City*. New York: 1898.

Studenski, Paul and Kroos, Herman. *Financial History of the United States* 2d ed. New York: 1963.

Suffern, Edward. "The Personal Property Tax: Economically Unsound, Practically Unjust," *Journal of Accountancy*, 10 (1910), 169–71.

Sumner, William Graham. *Essays of William Graham Sumner*. Edited by Albert Keller and Maurice Davie. 2 vols. New Haven: 1940.

———. *The Forgotten Man and Other Essays of William Graham Sumner*. Edited by Albert Keller. New Haven: 1913.

———. "Politics in America, 1776–1876," *North American Review*, *122* (Jan. 1876), 47–87.

Sutro, T. "Double and Multiple Taxation," *Proceedings of the National Tax Association*, (1908), 547–58.

———. "Taxation of Competitive Industrial Corporations," *Proceedings of the National Tax Association*, (1907), 605–21.

Syrett, Harold C. *The City of Brooklyn, 1865–1898: A Political History*. New York: 1944.

Tanzer, Laurence A. "Legislative Interference in Municipal Affairs and the Home Rule Program in New York," *National Municipal Review*, (1913), 597–604.

———. "State Income Taxation with Special Reference to the New York Income Tax Law," *Proceedings of the National Tax Association*, (1919), 385–97.

Taussig, F. W. "Some Results of An Inquiry on Taxation," *American Economic Association Publication*, 3, 102–105.

"Taxpayers' Associations," *The Nation*, (Jan. 17, 1895), 49.

Taylor, Walter. *The Economic Novel in America*. Chapel Hill: 1942.

Thomas, Thaddeus. *City Government of Baltimore*. Baltimore: 1896.

Thompson, Charles Willis. *Party Leaders of the Time*. New York: 1906.

Thrasher, Eugene C. "The Magee-Flinn Political Machines, 1895–1903" M.A. Thesis, University of Pittsburgh, 1951.

Timberlake, Richard. "Ideological Factors in Specie Resumption and Treasury Policy," *Journal of Economic History*, 24 (Mar. 1964), 29–52.

Todd, Edward S. "Study of Taxation in American Colleges," *Proceedings of the National Tax Association*, (1912), 109–116.

Tolman, William H. "Municipal Reform," *The Arena*, 16 (1896), 728–35.

Tourgee, Albion W. "Reform Versus Reformation," *North American Review*, 132 (1881), 305–19.

———. "The Renaissance of Nationalism," *North American Review*, 44. (1887), 1–11.

Townsend, John D. *New York in Bondage*. New York: 1901.

Tuttle, Leonard. "Local Option in Taxation," *Municipal Affairs*, 2 (1899), 395–410.

Twain, Mark and Warner, Charles D. *The Gilded Age: A Tale of To-day* 2 vols. New York: 1873.

Union League Club. *Alleged Frauds in the City Government of New York*. New York: 1884.

U.S. Civil Service Commission. *Civil Service in Periodical Literature: A Bibliography to and Including 1898*. Washington: 1899.

Upton, Jack K. *Money in Politics*. Boston: 1884.

Valentine, D. T. *Financial History of the City of New York*. New York: 1859.

Vickers, George. *The Fall of Bossism: A History of the Committee of One Hundred and The Reform Movement in Philadelphia*. Philadelphia: 1883.

W. C. C. "Debt Restrictions in Massachusetts," *American Economic Review*, 3 (1913), 731–32.

Waldron, Ellis L. "Sharpless v. Philadelphia: Jeremiah Black and the Parent Case on the Public Purposes of Taxation," *Wisconsin Law Review*, Vol. 1953, January, 48–75.

Walker, Amasa. *The Science of Wealth.* Philadelphia: 1871.

Walker, Charles S. "The Massachusetts Farmer and Taxation," *The Yale Review,* 6 (May 1898), 63–74.

Wallace, Michael. "Changing Concepts of Party in the U.S.: New York, 1815–28," *American Historical Review,* 74 (Dec. 1968), 453–91.

Wallas, Graham. *The Great Society.* New York: 1919.

Watterson, Henry. "The Reunited Union," *North American Review,* 140 (1885), 22–29.

Weber, Adna Ferrin. *The Growth of Cities in the Nineteenth Century.* Ithaca: 1967.

Weber, Bernard and Handfield-Jones, S. J. "Variations in the Rate of Economic Growth in the U.S.A., 1869–1939," *Oxford Economic Papers,* 6, no. 2 (June 1954), 101–32.

Weber, Max. *The Theory of Social and Economic Organization.* Glencoe: 1947.

Weeks, Joseph D. "Address: Manufacturers' Association of Cincinnati and Hamilton County," *Lecture Series No. 1* (March 6, 1894).

———. *Effect of Proposed Revenue Bill on the State Revenues.* Pittsburgh: 1895.

Weinberg, Ian, "The Problem of Convergence of Industrial Societies," *Comparative Studies in Society and History,* 2, no. 1 (Jan. 1969), 1–15.

Weinstein, James. "Organized Business and the City Commission and Manager Movements," *Journal of Southern History,* 28 (1962), 166–82.

Weiss, Nancy Joan. *Charles Francis Murphy, 1858–1924.* Northampton, Mass.: 1968.

Wells, David A. "Is The Existing Income Tax Unconstitutional?" *The Forum,* 18 (1894), 537–42.

———. "A New Chapter of Absurdity in American Local Taxation," *The Nation,* (Feb. 6, 1873), 91–92.

———. "Principles of Taxation," *Popular Science Monthly,* 48, 49, 50, 51 (1895–1897).

———. *Recent Economic Changes.* New York: 1890.

———. "The Reform of Local Taxation," *North American Review,* 122 (1876), 357–403.

———. *The Theory and Practice of Taxation.* New York: 1900.

Welty, D. W. *Treatise on the Law of Assessments.* New York: 1886.

Werner, M. R. *Tammany Hall.* New York: 1928.

Weyl, Walter E. *The New Democracy* (New York: Harper Torchbook, 1964).

———. et alia: *Equitable Taxation: Six Essays.* New York: 1892.

Wheeler, Everett. *Sixty Years of American Life: Taylor to Roosevelt, 1850–1900.* New York: 1917.

White, Andrew. "The Government of American Cities," *The Forum,* 10 (1890), 357–72.

White, Leonard D. ed. *The Civil Service in the Modern State.* Chicago: 1930.

———. *Introduction to the Study of Public Administration.* New York: 1926.

———. *The Republican Era.* New York: 1958.

White, Morton and Lucia. *The Intellectual Versus the City*. Cambridge, Mass.: 1962.

White, Thomas. *Commentaries on the Constitution of Pennsylvania*. Philadelphia: 1907.

Whitmore, William H. *Unjust Taxes: A Criticism of the Massachusetts System of Taxation*. Boston: 1877.

Whitney, Edward B. "The Income Tax and The Constitution," *Harvard Law Review*, 20 (1906–07), 280–96.

———. Whitney, Edward B. "Political Dangers of the Income Tax Decision," *The Forum*, 19 (1895), 521–31.

Whitten, Robert H. "Assessment of Taxes in Chicago," *Journal of Political Economy*, 5 (1896–97), 175–200.

———. *Public Administration in Massachusetts*. New York: 1898.

Wiebe, Robert. *Businessmen and Reformers*. Cambridge, Mass.: 1962.

———. *The Search For Order, 1877–1920*. New York: 1967.

Wilcox, Clair. *Public Policies Toward Business*. Revised. Homewood: 1960.

Wilcox, Delos. "The First Municipal Campaign of Greater New York," *Municipal Affairs*, 2, 207–220.

———. *Municipal Franchises: A Description of the Terms and Conditions Upon Which Private Corporations Enjoy Special Privileges in the Streets of American Cities*. New York: 1910.

———. "Party Government in the Cities of New York State," *Political Science Quarterly*, 14 (Dec. 1899), 681–92.

———. *A Study of City Government*. New York: 1897.

Wilkenson, Norman B. *A Bibliography of Pennsylvania History 2d ed.* (Harrisburg: 1957).

Willard, D. W. "State Systems of Public Welfare," *Journal of Social Forces*, 2, 79–84.

Williams, James M. *An American Town*. New York: 1906.

Williamson, Harold F. *Edward Atkinson: The Biography of An American Liberal, 1827–1905*. Boston: 1934.

Willis, H. Parker. "Relation of Federal to State and Local Taxation," *Proceedings of the National Tax Association*, (1907), 201–10.

Wilson, William L. "The Income Tax on Corporations," *North American Review*, *158* (Jan. 1894), 1–7.

Winchell, Alexander. "The Experiment of Universal Suffrage," *North American Review*, 136 (1883), 119–34.

Wingate, Charles. "An Episode in Municipal Government," *North American Review*, 145 (Oct. 1874); 146 (Jan.–July 1875); 148 (Oct. 1876).

Wolfe, Martin, "French Views on Wealth and Taxes from The Middle Ages to the Old Regime," *Journal of Economic History*, 26 (Dec. 1966), 466–83.

Woodbury, E. E. "The Work and Problems of Tax Commissions," *Proceedings of the National Tax Association*, (1908), 457–76.

Wood, Henry. *The Political Economy of Natural Law* 4th ed. Boston: 1899.

Woods, George B. "The New York Convention," *North American Review*, 107 (1868), 445–65.

Wooldridge, Clifton R. *Twenty Years A Detective in the Wickedest City in the World*. Chicago: 1908.

Worthington, J. U. *Historical Sketch of Finances of Pennsylvania*. Baltimore: 1887.

Wyllie, Irvin G. "Social Darwinism and the Businessman," *Proceedings of the American Philosophical Society,* 103, no. 5, (Oct. 1959).

Yearley, Clifton K. *Enterprise and Anthracite: Economics and Democracy in Schuylkill County, 1820–75*. Baltimore: 1961.

Young, J. "Administrative Centralization and Decentralization," *Annals,* 11 (Jan. 1898), 24–32.

Zink, Harold. *City Bosses in the U.S.* Durham: 1930.

Zimmerman, F. W. "Premium on Tax Lying," *American Economic Review,* 3 (March 1913), 3 ff.

Index